The Silk Roads

THE SILK ROADS
Highways of Culture and Commerce

Edited by

Vadime Elisseeff

Berghahn Books
New York • Oxford

UNESCO Publishing

Published in 2000 by
Berghahn Books
www.berghahnbooks.com

© UNESCO 2000

Library of Congress Cataloging-in-Publication Data
The silk roads : highways of culture and commerce
/ edited by Vadime Elisseeff.
p. cm.
Originally published : Paris : UNESCO, 1998
Includes bibliographical references and index.
ISBN 1-57181-221-0 — ISBN 1-57181-222-9 (pbk.)
1. Asia—Civilization. 2. Asia—Commerce—History.
3. Silk Road—History. I. Elisseeff, Vadime.
II. Title: Highways of culture and commerce
DS12.S57   1999   99-33018
950—dc21   CIP

British Library Cataloguing in Publication Data
A catalogue record for this book is available from the British Library

CONTENTS

Foreword by *Doudou Diène*   viii

Contributors   x

List of Abbreviations   xiv

Introduction   Approaches Old and New to the Silk Roads
    Vadime Elisseeff   1

Chapter 1   Perspectives on Buddhism in Dunhuang during
    the Tang and Five Dynasties Period
    Henrik H. Sørensen   27

Chapter 2   The Expansion of Buddhism into Southeast Asia
    (Mainly before A.D. 1000)
    J.G. de Casparis   49

Chapter 3   The Travels of Marco Polo in the Land of Buddhism
    Ananda Abeydeera   69

Chapter 4   Indus-Gulf Relations: A Reassessment in the Light
    of New Evidence
    Nilofer Shaikh   81

Chapter 5   The Southern Silk Road: Archaeological Evidence
    of Early Trade between India and Southeast Asia
    Ian C. Glover   93

Chapter 6   An Inscription in Memory of Sayyid Bin Abu Ali:
    A Study of Relations between China and Oman from the
    Eleventh to the Fifteenth Century
    Liu Yingsheng   122

Chapter 7   The Mongol Empire in the Thirteenth and
            Fourteenth Centuries: East-West Relations
            Bira Shagdar   127

Chapter 8   A Brunei Sultan of the Early Fourteenth Century:
            A Study of an Arabic Gravestone
            Chen Da-sheng   145

Chapter 9   Caravanserais along the Grand Trunk Road in
            Pakistan: A Central Asian Legacy
            Saifur Rahman Dar   158

Chapter 10   Maritime Trade from the Fourteenth to the
            Seventeenth Century: Evidence from the Underwater
            Archaeological Sites in the Gulf of Siam
            Sayan Prishanchit   185

Chapter 11   The Ban on the Export of Certain Articles from
            the Levant to the Mediterranean Ports during the Fifteenth
            and Sixteenth Centuries
            Zeki Arikan   199

Chapter 12   The Impact of the Macao-Manila Silk Trade from
            the Beginnings to 1640
            Rui D'Ávila Lourido   209

Chapter 13   Inner Asian Muslim Merchants at the Closure of
            the Silk Routes in the Seventeenth Century
            Isenbike Togan   247

Chapter 14   The Exchange of Musical Influences between Korea
            and Central Asia in Ancient Times
            Song Bang-Song   264

Chapter 15   The Trade Routes and the Diffusion of Artistic
            Traditions in South and Southeast Asia
            Nandana Chutiwongs   272

Chapter 16   The Development of China's Navigation
            Technology and of the Maritime Silk Route
            Sun Guangqi   288

Chapter 17   Mongol Nomadic Pastoralism:
    A Tradition between Nature and History
        Jacques Legrand   304

Chapter 18   The Spiritual Identity of the
    Silk Roads: A Historical Overview of
    Buddhism and Islam
        Amir H. Zekrgoo   318

Appendix: International Seminars and
    Colloquiums Held during the UNESCO
    Silk Roads Expeditions   329

FOREWORD

Doudou Diène

Towards the middle of the twentieth century, scholarly research revealed that the fabled Silk Roads, far from being mere trade routes, were also cultural highways that had played a pivotal role in linking East and West, intermittently bringing together nomads and city dwellers, pastoral peoples and farmers, merchants and monks, and soldiers and pilgrims.

Over the past ten years it has been UNESCO's role to revive the memory of this historic pattern by weaving it anew both on land and sea by means of the "Integral Study of the Silk Roads: Roads of Dialogue" Project. Since 1988 scholars and specialists of all nationalities have gathered to travel the Silk Roads with the international scientific expeditions organized by UNESCO, not this time in search of rare spices, luxury goods, or military conquest, but in order to highlight—by adopting a many-sided approach to the physical and intangible heritage through epics, languages and scripts, arts and living traditions—the dialogue and meeting of cultures. Thus the innovative concept of the Silk Roads expresses the slow process of underlying forces, movement … encounter … interaction.

The Project has proved very fruitful, consisting as it does of publications, documentary films, exhibitions, research scholarships for young scholars, a network of academic institutions and research projects, and a joint World Tourist Organization/UNESCO program, the goal of which is to help us to understand ourselves better by recognizing ourselves in others. These practical results are accompanied by less tangible achievements such as the emergence of the concept of a common heritage and plural identity. Indeed, the studies carried out under the Project have shown that identity, seen in the long-term perspective of history, cannot be viewed as a ghetto or an enclosure, but should be seen as the result of a whole process of synthesis and encounter between peoples and cultures.

The present book contains a small selection of papers from amongst all those presented on the occasion of the international seminars organized during the UNESCO Silk Roads expeditions.[1] Each and every paper delivered during the seminars warrants publication, and many have appeared in the publications produced by the national academic authorities responsible for the seminars held in their country. In order to give wider coverage to the knowledge they contain, all the available papers are being indexed at present. Reference to them will appear in the form of a bibliography that, in time, will be accessible on the Internet, today's major highway of information. The papers in this work have been selected because they focus more particularly on the different types of cultural exchange that resulted from the intermingling of commerce and culture along the Silk Roads, and because they illustrate, above all, various forms of cultural interaction along these ancient routes.

UNESCO would like to express here its deep gratitude to H.M. Sultan Qaboos bin Said of Oman, TV Asahi and Asahi Shimbun (Japan), and the Munhwa Broadcasting Corporation (Republic of Korea) whose contributions made the expeditions possible. The Organization also expresses its sincere appreciation to all the Member States who so generously hosted international seminars and the international teams during the expeditions; and to Ikuo Hirayama (Japan) whose Foundation provides scholarships for young researchers working on Silk Roads studies. Special mention and sincere thanks should go to Professor Vadime Elisseeff, President of the International Consultative Committee of the Silk Roads Project, who kindly agreed to write the Introduction to this book, and whose vast knowledge and deep wisdom have guided us throughout the last ten years. Finally, UNESCO also addresses its gratitude to the Members of the International Scientific Committee of the Silk Roads and to the scholars, institutions, groups, and national and local authorities—in particular the National Coordinating Committees in over thirty countries—for their unfailing support indicating their firm commitment to the aims of this very first integral study of the Silk Roads, highways of culture and commerce yesterday, and focus of a culture of peace today.

Notes

1. These are listed in appendix.

Contributors

Ananda Abeydeera graduated from the University of Sri Lanka, where he held a teaching position for several years. He also taught for some time at the École des Hautes Études en Sciences Sociales (EHESS) and at the Institut National des Langues et Civilisations Orientales (INALCO) in Paris as a visiting lecturer. His publications include articles on Sri Lanka in medieval travel literature and in the history of cartography. He was a member of the international team of specialists of the UNESCO Maritime Route Expedition.

Zeki Arikan is Professor at the University of Aegen in Izmir, Turkey. His main fields of interest are the social, cultural, and economic history of Turkey. His publications include *Yüzyillarda Hamit Sancagi: 15th to 16th Century* (Izmir, 1988) and *Muhittin Birgen, Tarihimiz ve Cumhuriyet* (Istanbul, 1997). He contributes to numerous periodicals. He took part in the international colloquium on "The Influence of the Silk Roads on Turkish Culture and Art," held in Izmir in 1990 during the UNESCO Maritime Route Expedition.

Bira Shagdar is a Professor and Academician of the Mongolian Academy of Sciences. He is also General Secretary of the International Association for Mongol Studies. Author of several books and numerous articles on Mongolian history and culture, and relations between Mongolia and other Central Asian countries, he is also a Member of the International Scientific Committee for the Preparation of the History of Civilizations of Central Asia (UNESCO). He took part in the international colloquium on "Nomads of Central Asia and the Silk Roads" held in Ulaan Baatar in 1992 during the UNESCO Nomad's Route Expedition, and is actively involved in the establishment of the International Institute for the Study of Nomadic Civilizations, Ulaan Baatar.

J. G. de Casparis is Emeritus Professor of the History of South and Southeast Asia at the University of Leiden, Netherlands. His main research concerns the early history and epigraphy of the Indo-Pakistani subcontinent, Sri Lanka, and parts of Southeast Asia, in particular Indonesia. He took part in the international colloquium on the theme "Sri Lanka as the mid-point in the East-West Silk Route and the Centre of Convergence of the Cross Currents of Buddhist Philosophy" held in Colombo during the UNESCO Maritime Route Expedition.

Chen Da-sheng is Research Fellow and Director of the China Maritime Silk Route Studies Centre, Fuzhou, and Director of the Fuzhou Centre of the École Française d'Extrême-Orient. He was a Member of the International Team of Specialists of the UNESCO Silk Roads Maritime Route Expedition and has since collaborated actively in many Silk Roads activities in China. His main field of interest is Islamic history and he has written several publications on Arabic epigraphy in China, including *Quanzhou Islamic Stone Carvings* and *Corpus of Arabic and Persian Inscriptions in China*.

Nandana Chutiwongs has a long career of research in the field of Asian art and archaeology. She is currently Curator of the Department of South and Mainland Southeast Asia, National Museum of Ethnology, Leiden, and a regular guest-lecturer at the Faculty of Archaeology, Silpakorn University, Bangkok. She took part in the international colloquium on "Ancient Trade and Cultural Contacts in Southeast Asia" held in Bangkok in 1991 during the UNESCO Maritime Route Expedition.

Saifur Rahman Dar's main fields of interest are museology, archaeology, and folklore. He specializes in Pakistan's historical relations with the Western World, particularly during the early historic period. He is the founding Director-General of Archaeology, Punjab, Pakistan, and has been the Director of the Lahore Museum for the last twenty-four years. He participated as a member of the international team of specialists in several expeditions organized as part of the UNESCO Silk Roads Project.

Ian C. Glover, former archaeologist at the Institute of Archaeology, University College, London, and President of EURASEEA, has worked in Southeast Asia for many years. He is the author of numerous papers and articles following his excavations in Thailand and Southeast Asia. He took part in the international colloquium on the theme "Ancient Trades and Cultural Contacts in Southeast Asia" held in Bangkok in 1991 during the UNESCO Maritime Route Expedition.

Jacques Legrand is Professor of Mongolian at the Institut National des Langues et Civilisations Orientales (INALCO) in Paris and Lecturer in Anthropology of Mongolian nomadism at Paris-8 University. He works mainly in the fields of Mongolian linguistics and history, and anthropology of nomadic pastoralism. Among his numerous publications is *Parlons Mongol* (Paris, 1997). He was a member of the international team of specialists of the UNESCO Nomads' Route Expedition and is collaborating closely with UNESCO in the establishment of the International Institute for the Study of Nomadic Civilizations in Ulaan Bataar.

Liu Yingsheng, Professor and Director of the Institute of Asian Studies of Nanjing University, China, obtained his Ph.D. from the Academy of Social Sciences of China. He is a specialist in Sino-Iranic-Altaic and Inner Asian studies, as well as in cultural exchange between medieval China and neighboring regions, including the Islamic world. He participated as a member of the international team of specialists in several expeditions organized by UNESCO in the framework of the Silk Roads Project.

Rui D'Ávila de Fontes Alferes Lourido studied at the Universidad de Nova in Lisbon and the Universita Degli Studi in Pisa. His main field of interest concerns relations between Portugal and China. He has extensively visited Asia and Southeast Asia, and is at present researching into the relations between Europeans and Chinese in the sixteenth and seventeenth centuries at the European University Institute, Florence, Italy. He is the author of several publications including *Portuguese Discoveries in the Pacific* (1996). He was a member of the international team of specialists of the UNESCO Silk Roads Maritime Expedition.

Sayan Prishanchit is an archaeologist and present Head of Researchers at the Sixth Regional Office of Archaeology and National Museum, Chang Mai, Thailand. He has written several publications and articles on archaeological discoveries of ceramic wares, mostly in Thai. He took part in the international colloquium "Ancient Trades and Cultural Contacts in Southeast Asia" held in Bangkok in 1991 during the UNESCO Maritime Route Expedition.

Nilofer Shaikh is Professor of Archaeology and presently Chairperson in the Department of Archaeology, Shah Abdul Latif University, Khairpur, Sindh, Pakistan. Her field of interest is the Neolithic and Bronze Age of South Asia. She participated in the colloquium "Al-Sind and Arab Seafaring: Culture, Commerce and Urbanization" held in Karachi in 1990 during the UNESCO Maritime Route Expedition.

Song Bang-Song, former Dean of the College of Music, Yeungnam University, is Professor of Korean Musicology at the School of Korean Traditional Arts, Korean National University of Arts. His publications in English include *An Annotated Bibliography of Korean Music* (1971) and *The Sanjo Tradition of Korean Komun'go Music* (1986). He was a member of the international team of specialists of the UNESCO Silk Roads Maritime Route Expedition.

Henrik H. Sørensen, former Supervisor at the National Museum of Copenhagen, has also lectured at the University of Copenhagen. His fields of interest are Chinese culture and religions, in particular Buddhism. He participated as a member of the international team of specialists in the UNESCO Desert Route Expedition in China.

Sun Guangqi is Director of the Port and Shipping Institute, Dalian Maritime University, China, and overseas Professor of the Korean Maritime University. He is also a Member of the Royal Navigation Institute, United Kingdom, which awarded him its 1993 Bronze Medal. He has a long established research interest in maritime history and shipping policy. He is the author of many publications including *Ancient Navigation History of China* (1989) and *International Shipping Policy* (1998). He took part in the international colloquium entitled "China and the Maritime Silk Route" held in Quanzhou in 1991 during the UNESCO Maritime Route Expedition.

Isenbike Togan took her Ph. D. in East Asian Languages and Civilizations at Harvard University. At present she is Professor of History at the Middle East Technical University, Ankara, Turkey. She has published many articles dealing with Inner Asian tribes, their relation to trade and state formations, including a recent book entitled *Flexibility and Limitation in Steppe Formations: The Kerait Khanate and Chinghis Khan*. She was a member of the international team of specialists of the UNESCO Silk Roads Desert Route Expedition in China.

Amir H. Zekrgoo, Professor of Eastern Art at the Art University, Tehran (Iran), is an artist, art historian, and Indologist. He has published two books and over eighty articles in Persian, English, and Urdu including *Indian Art, Art and Religion, Indian Mythology and Iconography,* and *Islamic Art of Calligraphy*. In 1996 he was awarded an Ikuo Hirayama Silk Roads Scholarship by UNESCO. He is active as an artist and has exhibited paintings at some twenty exhibitions in Asia, Europe, and America. He was a member of the international team of specialists of the UNESCO Buddhist Route Expedition in Nepal.

List of Abbreviations

BEFEO	Bulletin de l'École Française d'Extrême-Orient.
Beijing	Numbering of the Dunhuang manuscripts in the National Library in Beijing according to Dunhuang yishu zongmu soyin, Beijing, 1962-1983.
CEA	Cahiers d'Extrême-Asie (Revue de l'École Française d'Extrême-Orient)—Section de Kyoto.
CETH-1	Contributions aux études sur Touen-houang edited by M. Soymié. Geneva: École Pratique des Hautes Études, 1979.
CETH-2	Nouvelles contributions aux études sur Touen-houang, edited by M. Soymié. Geneva: École Pratique des Hautes Études, 1981.
CETH-3	Contributions aux études sur Touen-houang, vol. 3, edited by M. Soymié. Paris: École Pratique des Hautes Études, publications de l'École Française d'Extrême-Orient (135), 1983.
CMCT	Catalogue des manuscrits de Touen-houang, vols. 1-3, edited by J. Gernet and Wu Chi-yü, vol. 1, M. Soymié, vols. 2-4, Paris, 1970-1990.
DX	Dunhuang xue jikan (Lanzhou).
DY	Dunhuang yanjiu (Dunhuang).
EHSS	École des Hautes Études en Sciences Sociales.
Giles	L. Giles, Descriptive Catalogue of the Chinese Manuscripts from Tunhuang in the British Museum. London, 1957.
Lalou	M. Lalou, Inventaire des manuscrits tibétains de Touen-houang conservés à la Bibliothèque nationale (fonds Pelliot-tibétain), vols. 1-3. Paris, 1939-1961.
P.	Pelliot Chinois (numbering according to CMCT).
PEFEO	Publications de l'École Française d'Extrême-Orient.
PT.	Pelliot Tibétain (numbering according to Lalou).

S.	Stein Collection of Chinese mss. in the British Library (numbering according to Giles).
SCEAR	Studies in Central and East Asian Religions, (Copenhagen).
SEAB	Studies in East Asian Buddhism published by the Kuroda Institute and Hawaii University Press.
ST.	Stein Collection of Tibetan mss. in the India Office Library (numbered according to Louis de la Vallée Poussin, Catalogue of the Tibetan Manuscripts from Tun-huang in the India Office Library. London: Oxford University Press, 1962).
T.	Taishô shinshū daizôkyô (Tokyo, 1924-1932).

Introduction

APPROACHES OLD AND NEW TO THE SILK ROADS

Vadime Elisseeff

Once upon a time, in the late nineteenth century, a traveler was winding his way along a road in China from Lanzhou to Dunhuang. As he progressed, he gazed at the jagged horizon of the foothills of Nanshan. Yellow dust was being blown around by a strong wind, sticking to the rupestrian walls, filling the hollows, and catching on the range of crests. He too was prey to the torments which many of his colleagues and predecessors had related down the centuries as they set out to cross Central Asia in order to reach the western territories beyond.

The traveler was none other than an explorer, a German geographer, who was seeking confirmation of his theories on the Aeolian origin of loessial alluvium deposits at high altitude. He was Baron Ferdinand von Richthofen, renowned for his work in the field of morphogeology which he had pursued from Ceylon to the Philippines and Java and from California as far as Japan. In 1870 to 1872, he traveled through China. He was the author of many valuable explanations regarding the dating of orogenic movements and on the central role of depressions in Tibet and Turkistan, as well as that of Sichuan which he called the "Red Basin." Scholars throughout the world praised the quality of his research and, as a supreme tribute, gave his name to the Nanshan foothills, the Richthofen Mountains (now Qilianshan) Range. Besides being a geographer, his great scholarship led him to take an interest in economics and, to a lesser extent, history. Yet it is to the latter, paradoxically enough, that he owes his undying renown. In 1877, he entitled one of his short historical studies "Über die Centralasiatischen

Seidenstrassen …"[1] (On the Silk Roads of Central Asia …), a term that
was to have a fine future and is still current today. The following year, the
Geographical Magazine devoted four pages to an article on "The
Ancient Silk-Traders' Route across Central Asia."[2]

The Silk Roads were a subject of fascination, and travelers' tales
captivated the readers of newspapers, magazines, and books like those of
Jules Verne. Silk attracted merchants including those of Shanghai. In
1850, the North China Herald published "Notes on the Silk Trade of
Shanghai."[3] In its turn, the Shanghai Chamber of Commerce published
ten or more letters by von Richthofen which he had sent from the four
corners of China between 1870 and 1872.[4] In 1874, the Geographical
Magazine published yet another article by the explorer on "Land Communication between Europe and China."[5] The article reflected von
Richthofen's principal idea that Central Asia was not only a link but,
above all, a third partner—virtually a subcontinent—receiving and giving the cultural wealth of all those who cross its bleak steppes and
deserts, waging war or bringing peace, encouraging trade, propagating
religions, or merely traveling about in quest of knowledge.

At the end of the nineteenth century, the Silk Roads had increased
in number, thereby opening up an immense field of research. "It is the
whole of Eurasia lying to the west of China, including India, Serindia,
and Iran, between which relations and trade can be envisaged quite apart
from China."[6]

These roads, regardless of how they were called, have been known to
humanity for many centuries and, as far as the major routes are concerned, for several millennia. Most of them are the descendants of natural roads following patterns of vegetation whose ecological qualities
enabled man and beast to thrive in the days when palaeolithic hunters
tracked their game. These historical routes are also terrestrial and maritime, running from east to west and corresponding to waterways that
run from north to south. They introduced sedentary and nomadic populations, and opened up a form of dialogue between the cultures of East
and West. Thanks to archaeological excavations conducted in recent
years, we now know that, ever since the Neolithic period, quite a number of objects were exchanged between Mesopotamia and the Indian[7]
and Chinese[8] territories. Trade was conducted in all directions, crossing
the Pamirs and stretching from one water hole to another. Artifacts in
lapis lazuli, jade, bronze, and iron provide ample testimony to how this
trade was carried on.

During the first millennium B.C., bundles of raw silk and rolls of
silk material often went hand in hand with other goods. In Altai, along
the ancient route through the steppes, silk carpets and garments were
quite common as early as the fourth century B.C. Regardless of the

extent of relations in ancient times, from the very beginning of the Christian era and for centuries afterwards, an increasing number of travelers, pilgrims and merchants, scholars and explorers—translating Indian texts into their mother tongue or taking notes—drafted accounts of their travels and reports on local customs and festivities. Other records include traveler's itineraries in the steppes and deserts, and the logbooks of coastal and ocean-going sailors. These describe all there was to be seen, temples or palaces; all that was to be heard, songs and instrumental music; all that could be collected, stones and plants; and all that provided solace, whether inns or stopping-places, markets or caravanserai, monasteries or sanctuaries.

Travelers in Ancient Times

The West's awareness of the East began with Alexander the Great who was among the first to wage conquest far to the East.[9] In the fourth century B.C., he reached the Pamirs at the confines of China. Two centuries later, Zhang Qian crossed them from the east and, in turn, discovered a new world, with all its variety of goods and populations.[10] He had been sent by Wudi of the Han Dynasty in 139 B.C. in quest of an alliance against the disruptive Xiongnu. His mission did not prove successful in either Sogdiana or Bactria. On his second voyage, in 106 B.C., he took with him a large quantity of gold and silk. It was no longer a diplomatic visit but a trading mission, involving horses in exchange for silk. This marked the beginning of trading links. It is thanks to his contemporary, the great historian Sima Qian, that we have indisputable information on the travels and adventures of this pioneer, providing precious data about the territories lying to the West and the "barbaric" lands beyond the borders.[11] The same can be said, following his example, of the authors of dynastic monographs such as those of the *History of the Later Han Dynasty.*[12]

In the West we have little data at our disposal by comparison with the enormous volume of Chinese documentation. This may be due to the difficulty that existed in communicating between centers. Ancient Rome, for example, was only familiar with those territories that its legions had conquered. For the rest, ideas remained confused and in many instances vague. The Roman conquest of Egypt suddenly broadened the field of investigation, thanks to Alexandrine, Arab, Indian, Malay, and Persian navigators who used to travel as far as China, a country that was known to be the source of silk and was called Serica.[13] With the disintegration of the empire and the decline of Byzantium, however, the awareness of Asia gradually faded into oblivion.

In the West, the Greeks and Romans were the first to mention it. Some scanty information was provided by Herodotus[14] who, in the fifth century B.C., discovered in his itinerary the outermost boundaries of the "Hyperboreans," which he mistook, rightly or wrongly, for the Seres.[15] In the first century B.C., the Greek Strabo[16] referred, in his *Geographica,* to the same populations. When writing about the elderly in the land of Musicanus "who lived to the age of 130," he added that "some of the Seres live even longer." At the same time Virgil, Horace, and Pliny the Elder[17] evoked these distant regions in verse or prose. At virtually the same time, Periplus of the Erythrean Sea[18] described the western part of the area that interests us, that is to say, from the Persian Gulf to the Indus.[19] Later, the historian Ammianus Marcellinus drew attention to Chinese goods on show in 360 at the fair at Batanea on the Euphrates.[20] The best source, after Strabo, is still Ptolemy's *Geography* written in the second century, and which prefigures the routes.[21] His source, Marinus of Tyre, had collected an immense stock of information on the subject during the previous century. He had been in contact with a Graeco-Syrian merchant named Maës Titianus who had sent his agents on reconnaissance along the Silk Road leading from Antioch to Hamadan and then to Bactra and the Pamirs where the Stone Tower (Tashkurgan) had been erected. There the Levantines conducted their trade, bearing with them precious bundles of silk. They also learnt that the trail continued via the oases from Tarim as far as Thinai, which was probably the Luoyang of today. We have there an example of the way information circulated in ancient times, in several stages and through various intermediaries. That is why there are still many unanswered questions as to the exact location of the stages.

Until recently, much of the work of specialists consisted in identifying and locating the various stages through transcriptions or loan words.[22] Their degree of phonetic interference between one language and another is such that at times whole texts remain incomprehensible. We should also bear in mind how inclined the storytellers were to embellish their tales, how some accounts were suspected of being somewhat too inspired or even of having been copied from earlier works, if not purely and simply made up.[23] In spite of that, few reports were rejected, in general because the itineraries were very valuable. The way these accounts had been established was not the result of rapid surveys but, on the contrary, the sum of all the information, rumors, and hearsay garnered by a considerable number of merchants. Furthermore, the task was no easy one as all indications regarding the itineraries were considered by the profession to be highly confidential.

Buddhist Missionaries and Pilgrims

With time, traffic along the routes increased and the body of information grew as Buddhist pilgrimages and missions became more numerous.[24] The roads were opened to Indians and to Chinese seeking to impart or to acquire knowledge. A more noble concept of relations and trade emerged, namely that of cultural values. With the passage of pilgrims, and at the initiative of tradesmen, the stages became more important as stopping places, real cities that marked out the route, creating a long series of oases for caravans in Serindia.

The first of the great illustrious Chinese pilgrims who had set out to seek the Truth from Buddhist sources and to pray at the Holy Places was Faxian. In 399, he covered in stages of differing lengths the southern oasis route via Khotan. Then he crossed the Pamirs and reached Gandhâra where he followed the Valley of the Ganges as far as the Holy Places, including Bodhgayâ where Shâkyamuni, about a thousand years earlier, had reached the Awakening. He then embarked for Ceylon, the center of the oldest Buddhist tradition. After two years of meditation, prayer, and reading, he returned via the sea route and arrived at Ch'ang-kuang (Changguang in Shandong) in 414, after an absence of some fourteen years. His account, *Record of the Buddhistic Kingdoms,* of the more than thirty countries that he visited,[25] is the only one of its time to have reached us. It makes enchanting reading; his observations are precise and judicious and embellished by his descriptions of all the feasts and processions. Furthermore, by making his long circular journey, he initiated the "Buddhist Road," which duplicated the Silk Road in Middle Asia, China, and India. After the process was set in motion, it began to develop more and more. *The Biographies of Eminent Monks* [26] quote 710 names before A.D. 644, and 633 names between A.D. 645 and 988.

The most illustrious pilgrim, known by his contemporaries as the Prince of Pilgrims or the "Shâkyamuni of our time," was Xuanzang.[27] He is also the best known of the translators: the Buddhist Canon[28] lists seventy-six titles. Over a period of eighteen years, the work of his team of translators represents a quarter of all Indian translations into Chinese over a period of six centuries. In 629, he left the capital for India via the North Oasis road, through Turfan, crossing the Pamirs and going down to Samarkand and Bactra. From there, like many others, he followed the Valley of the Ganges towards the Holy Places and stayed at the famous monastery of Nâlandâ. His arbitration of various doctrinal disputes was highly appreciated by the Indians. In 645, he returned home with a whole library and then proceeded to draft, among other works, his *Record of the Western Regions at the Time of the Tang Dynasty,*[29] a veritable encyclopaedia containing information on the climate, products, customs, places, and the state of Buddhism in the various regions of Asia. It is still, even today, one of the principal sources of knowledge of ancient India. The same can be said of many Chinese translations which are the only remaining documents that can be consulted as the Indian originals have often disappeared.

He who ranks second after Xuanzang as an illustrious figure is Yijing.[30] Having set out for India in 671, he first stayed in Sumatra at the major Buddhist center of Śrîvijaya (now Palembang). He then reached Tâmraliptî, near Calcutta. From there he went on to the Buddhist University of Nâlandâ where Xuanzang had also prayed thirty years earlier. He returned home in 695, once again via the maritime route. He was the author of one of the earliest studies on the territories in the South Seas, *Record of the Buddhist Religion as Practised in India and the Malay Archipelago,*[31] a series of fifty-six biographical studies of eminent religious figures and some sixty-three translations quoted by the Buddhist Canon.[32] His impeccable knowledge of the rules of Discipline earned him the nickname of "the Rectifier."

Through its doctrine, Buddhism conveyed the cultural elements and scientific knowledge of the Indian world. This was one of the ways whereby relations between astronomers, mathematicians, and geographers became relatively common. Cartography was one of the privileged fields where great minds were to meet. The Chinese, as heirs to a long tradition, dating back to the third century, with all the relevant comparisons, were pioneers in that field. Many of the studies and maps are quoted in a variety of documents; but unfortunately, only fragments or even just references, now remain. The earliest treatise of geography that we have been able to trace dates back to 642,[33] but there is little left of it. The work of the most famous cartographer, Jia Dan, the *Treatise of Ten Regions* [34] hardly fared better; but his *Map of Populations within the Seas,* established in 801, served as a model for a long time. One of his contemporaries, Li Jifu, who was also an accomplished geographer, wrote a *General Geography of Prefectures and Districts during the Yuanho Period* (i.e., 806-820).[35] At the same time, a map of the Sino-Tibetan world was brought back from China in 858 by the Japanese monk Enchin (Chishô Daishi). It has been very carefully preserved at Onjôji (Miidera) near Kyoto. Finally, in the *New History of the Tang,* drafted in the eleventh century, several extracts of these geographies[36] were reproduced with comments on the itineraries stretching from China to Korea, Central Asia, and westwards as far as Baghdad. The maps, alas, have been lost but, at least as far as the eleventh century is concerned, we have two maps engraved on stone in 1137: *Maps of China and the Barbarian Countries,* probably dated 1040, and the *Map of the Track of Yu,* probably 1100.[37] These treatises and maps were known in their day as guides and pilots. As early as the twelfth century, there are satisfactory reports such as that of Rabbi Benjamin of Tudela, who began his *Journey around the World* between 1160 and 1173, an account written in Hebrew, translated into Latin and thence into French.[38]

However, while the road was safe, the sky was still very threatening. The emperor of China gave in to pressure from the Tungusic Dynasty of Jin. This meant a retreat southwards, beyond the Yangzi River, with Hangzhou becoming the temporary capital in 1135. This retreat enabled them to become more familiar with the southern region which had hitherto been alien to them and was still populated in the southwest by numerous mountain communities which were somewhat fierce and sometimes threatening. This raised questions as to how these populations should be approached and on the freedom of communications. In 1178, an official from Guilin, Zhou Qufei, recorded *Answers to Questions on the Regions beyond the Passes*.[39] There was also a need to report on the South Seas; Zhao Rugua, the superintendent of customs, undertook this task which resulted in the Record of Foreign Peoples,[40] prefaced in 1225, dealing principally with Sino-Arab relations in the twelfth and thirteenth centuries. Those relations were at their apex at the time, after having developed rapidly from the beginning of the Hegira onwards.

Arab Navigators and Merchants

The Arab conquests in Central Asia and in North Africa pushed Christianity back towards Europe and the various Persian religions towards China. There, from the seventh century onwards, the Court of the Tang welcomed the Nestorians and Zoroastrians, the Mazdeans and the Manicheans.[41] What had been Sino-Iranian frontiers became, in the eighth century, Sino-Arab frontiers on which the Abbassid Caliphs of Baghdad kept a watchful eye. With such patronage, the sky was the limit. Arab navigators and merchants were even able to lay claim to a monopoly of traffic on the Asian seas.[42] Their ports were rich trading posts, which had many warehouses and attracted the trading routes of the Arabs and Persians who, from Baghdad and Basra or Sîrâf,[43] also set out to buy Chinese goods first in Canton and subsequently in Zayton (Quanzhou). At the time, that was at the other end of the world.

The earliest record is that of the *Journey of the Arab Merchant Suleyman to India and China*, written in 851 and followed, towards 916, by a commentary by Abû Zayd Hasan.[44] The authors had to gather their information in the inner recesses of the port of Sîrâf, a familiar place to all seafarers of the ancient world. It was a major port, prosperous, well-stocked and, therefore, a marvelous rival to Zayton. Until the end of the reign of the Abbassids, who fell in the thirteenth century under the onslaught of the Mongols, the masters of the maritime route were well and truly the Arabs and Persians. Their chroniclers testify to this as in the case of Ibn Khurdâdhbah, in the ninth century, with his *Book of the Routes and Provinces*;[45] in the tenth century, Ibn Fadlan and the account of his travels between Baghdad and the Volga;[46] in the eleventh century, Mas'ûdî with his *Golden Prairies*;[47] in the twelfth century, the cartographer Idrîsî with his *Récréation de celui qui désire parcourir les pays*;[48] in the thirteenth century, Abû'l-Fidâ,[49] a geographer and historian; and in the fourteenth century, Rachid al-Din with his *Description of China*.[50]

Perhaps the most famous of these authors was an illustrious traveler, Ibn Battuta, who provided an enthusiastic description of Zayton.[51] This terminus was also the subject of considerable historical research, particularly on the port superintendence, which was entrusted to a Muslim, Pu Shougeng.[52] Furthermore, over the centuries, collisions and wrecks had transformed the depths of the port into a veritable phantom museum.[53] Today, we can conjure up visions of impressive junks, sometimes boasting four masts and as many as four decks, which could carry several hundred people, their goods, and all the necessary supplies. In those days, Chinese vessels were the finest in the world.

Christian Embassies and Missions

On land, during the same period, the Mongol patrols hunted down any prowlers and the squadrons saw to the rest—it was the "Pax Mongolica." That may have all been very well but, in Europe, people's minds were still haunted by the terror of the recent invasions of 1241. Nevertheless, this threat was counterbalanced by a redistribution of political influences. In 1245, the new pope, Innocent IV—having to cope with the victory of the Muslims, the separatism of the Greeks, and the hostility of Frederick II, King of Sicily and German Emperor—took control of the situation thanks to the support of Louis IX, King of France, the future Saint Louis.[54] What mattered most was to communicate with the nomads of the Steppe empire and not lose contact with the Nestorian Christians whose troops had often lent their support to the Mongols. It was through them that vital information was obtained. This was the case of the mission of the Nestorian monk, Rabban Bar Sauma, born in Peking in 1225 and who accompanied the Patriarch on a pilgrimage to Jerusalem.[55] In the course of their journey, he was entrusted by the Mongol King of Persia with the task of maintaining good relations between his country and Christendom. For this modest monk, this proved to be a singular mission which enabled him to visit Byzantium and Rome, to meet the King of England in Gascony, and Philippe le Bel in Paris. For many he was a bringer of good news.

The Mongol route was well and truly open with its famous roadside inns, but that was not enough. To communicate, a reason or pretext had to be found and one also had to know whether the pretext was accepted by the other party. Pope Innocent IV decided to send an envoy to Guyuk, the Great Khan of Mongolia, and entrusted this task to the Franciscan John of Plano Carpini. He was given a warm welcome and returned home with a valuable report, *Historia Mongolorum*.[56] In 1253, another Franciscan, William of Rubrouk, was sent by King Louis of France to visit the Nestorian Christians of the Volga. He extended his mission by going on to Karakorum where he met the Great Khan Mongka in 1254.[57]

The third great figure of the thirteenth century and the best known is Marco Polo who, after having crossed Asia along the Steppe Route, remained for twenty years in the service of Khublai Khan. He returned by the sea route and then via Mesopotamia and Trabzon on the Black Sea to Venice in 1245. When in captivity he dictated his memoirs in French under the title *The Description of the World*,[58] and these became a mine of information on Asia in that century. Not a year goes by without his book being quoted or commented on in works written in almost every language of the world.[59] The appearance of this work was followed by a succession of missions, both religious and commercial. The records of some of these missions also serve as references.

In the fourteenth century Odoric de Pordenone of the Minorite Order wrote his memoirs in *De Rebus incognitis et itineris*.[60] There was also Sir John Mandeville whose travels were the subject of many publications.[61] In 1340, Francesco Balduccio Pegolotti, a Florentine trader, wrote *Prattica della mercatura*,[62] a veritable handbook for the perfect trader. Ruy Gonzales de Clavijo served as ambassador of King Henry III of Castile to Timour in Samarkand from 1403 to 1406. On his return he wrote a *History of Timour* and his itinerary was published in Seville in 1582.[63] In the sixteenth century, mention should be made of the unfortunate Jesuit, Benoit de Goës,[64] who was sent on yet another mission to obtain news of the Nestorian Christians. He went via Yarkand and Turfan but died from exhaustion at Jiuquan on the Chinese border. Two other Jesuits, Jean Grueber and Albert d'Orville, wishing to avoid Macao, chose to go through Tibet via Koukounor and enter India via Nepal in order to reach the Valley of the Ganges and Bengal. There again, the torments inflicted on them by the sandstorms and snowstorms got the better of d'Orville who died from exhaustion at Agra.[65] Other travels had a happier outcome. During the same century, for example, at the request of the English merchants of "Moscovy," Anthony Jenkinson set out to obtain information on the itinerary from Moscow to Bukhara and beyond. He returned in 1558 with a comprehensive report.[66]

All these travels had their share of joys and sorrows, but the numerous texts they nurtured have only retained the feeling of wonder inspired by the good times. As these tales and memoirs were growing in number at the dawn of the Renaissance, the creation of libraries became a luxury that was much appreciated by men in high places and a resource of inestimable value for those of a curious disposition. The best example of this is in France in the library of Jean, Duke of Berry (1340-1416) and brother of King Charles V. At the behest of the Duke of Burgundy, a collection of travel accounts was commissioned as a gift for his uncle.[67] The title alone, with its highly distinguished language, set the tone which became a yardstick for all publishers: *Ce Liure Est Des Merueilles Du Monde. Cest assavoir de la Terre Sainte. Du Grant Kaan. Empereur des tartares…* (This book tells of the wonders of the world …). Another work,[68] bearing the imprimatur of 15 February 1528, begins its long illuminated title, using the same ancient and somewhat chaotic spelling, with what might well pass for a clarion call: *L'Hystore merueilleuse. Plaisante et Récreative du grâd Empereur de Tartarie …* (The wonderful history …), and is followed by a list of the contents. It may seem a bit long but it is still more attractive than a mere *History of Tartary*. These texts are a moving reminder of the much sought-after curiosities to be found in bazaars and markets and which were the dream of all travelers whether their inspiration was a message or money.

The number of such accounts, notes, and memoirs is very great. Fortunately, almost all the texts and translations are recorded in the five volumes of the *Bibliotheca Sinica, Dictionnaire Bibliographique* by Henri Cordier.[69] There is also ample Chinese information on the roads, ports, and means of transport in various local gazetteers.[70] For bibliographical research into all these sources, recourse can still be had to the venerable *Notes on Chinese Literature* by Wylie,[71] the numerous Japanese bibliographies, all the catalogues of specialized libraries such as that of the Harvard Yenching Institute,[72] and periodicals such as the *Revue de Bibliographie Sinologique*.[73]

Major Twentieth-Century Projects:
Exploration of Central Asia and International Cooperation

The most famous travelers and explorers of the late nineteenth century such as Sven Hedin,[74] Bonvalot,[75] Henri d'Orléans,[76] Séménov,[77] Prjevalsky,[78] Roborovsky,[79] or Kozlov[80] were invariably entrusted by well-known national institutions with missions in various fields including geography, natural history, archaeology, or quite simply, surveys for general information. These scholars proceeded with their work in a somewhat egocentric manner, and competition between them might well have compromised their work. To circumvent this risk, in 1899 Wilhelm Radloff[81] proposed the creation of an International Association for the Exploration of Central Asia.[82] The association, through its national committees, was to supervise the organization of work and the coordination of expeditions. All the scholars were able to rely on its assistance in their work and their various ventures.

In the course of geographical explorations, such as those of Sven Hedin,[83] numerous ruins buried beneath the sands of Chinese Turkestan (Xinjiang) provided traces of monuments from bygone civilizations. "Thanks to archaeology," pointed out Emile Senart when welcoming Pelliot on his return, "we have seen come out of oblivion and return to life many hidden corners of our earth which seemed shrouded in some sort of half light. Chinese Turkestan is the latest of those to 'escape' from the realm of darkness and silence."[84]

The Russian missions rank among the earliest such as those of the Grumm-Grzhimajlo brothers from 1884 to 1890,[85] Klementz from 1894 to 1898 on the antiquities of Turfan,[86] the Berezovsky brothers, fascinated by Kucha (Kuga) from 1903 to 1907, and lastly that of Kozlov who, in 1908, rediscovered Khara-khoto (Ejin Gi—Inner Mongolia) and its walls wherein lay a treasure of books, manuscripts, and various coins.[87] The explorer Dutreuil de Rhins was the veteran member of the French team. With Khotan (Hotan) as his point of departure, he roamed the high plateaux of Tibet between 1890 and 1895 on several reconnaissance missions.[88]

Besides Sven Hedin, the explorer of greatest renown was the Briton, Sir Aurel Stein, who, in addition to his many accomplishments, possessed considerable scholarship in the field of geography and archaeology. He undertook three expeditions between 1900 and 1916 and it can be said that from Kashgar (Kaxgar, Kashi) to Dunhuang, he not only saw virtually everything there was to be seen but recorded and published it.[89]

From then on, the missions followed in close succession. There were the German missions of Grünwedel[90] and von Le Coq,[91] who directed four expeditions between 1902 and 1914, excavating many sites in the vicinity of Kucha, including Qyzyl. Between 1906 and 1909, Paul Pelliot embarked on the treasure route. Following Stein's indications, he went to Dunhuang and found there thousands of manuscripts and painted banners in a cave which had been walled up since 1035.[92] In his footsteps when roaming the sandy wastes of the desert from 1909 to 1910 and from 1914 to 1915,[93] the Russian scholar Oldenburg gathered various manuscripts and records in Dunhuang. Lastly, in that first part of the century, three missions were organized by Count Otani between 1902 and 1914[94] on every circuit in the territory. The last archaeological mission conducted in the "old individual style" was that of the American Langdon Warner, who left in 1923 to see what remained after all the previous missions. He was able to observe that there were only a few items that could still be removed. He was able to gather together a dozen objects but his second journey proved to be far less successful.[95]

From then on, priority was given to joint missions, the first exponents of which were Sven Hedin and the Chinese archaeologist Huang Wenbi.[96] In 1931 and 1932, a special expedition was organized by André Citroën who hoped that China would give him another opportunity of doing what he had done in Africa with the Croisière Noire, namely, to test new half-track vehicles. This turned out to be the Croisière Jaune headed by Georges-Marie Haardt with the scientific collaboration of the Reverend Teilhard de Chardin and Joseph Hackin.[97]

However, the sky was already clouding over almost everywhere on account of the Sino-Japanese war and, all too soon, the storm was to burst with the bitter experience of the Second World War.

The Orient-Occident Major Project (1957-1966)

In the wake of such upheavals, the United Nations entrusted UNESCO with the task of promoting the spirit of peace. The Organization founded its endeavors on the historical studies in order to promote a better understanding between peoples. This effort marked the birth, in New Delhi in 1956, of the ten-year-long Orient-Occident Major Project relating to the mutual appreciation of cultural values of the Orient and the Occident. At its second session, the International Consultative Committee for the project adopted, by a unanimous vote, a "Joint Declaration."[98]

The purpose of the project was to provide action aimed at reducing the psychological and political obstacles to and improving the conditions for processes of change, and to develop as part of "a vast exchange programme." In view of the emotional reactions inherent in human relationships, it was recommended that such exchanges be commented upon and explained in the light of historical facts restored to their full authenticity. It was agreed that these facts should be viewed in the context of broad perspectives: the chronological perspective in order to highlight their relative duration and their position in historical developments; the geographical perspective in order to situate the regional effect of cultural factors in the context of interregional relationships; and the socio-economic perspective so that differences in living standards and lifestyles should be adequately borne in mind. The insights that emerged from these explorations would comprise a corpus of knowledge likely to foster better mutual appreciation through the highlighting not only of similarities but also of differences which deserved similar respect. In each particular field, the action of the Orient-Occident Project proved very fruitful. The testimony of the project remains the open-mindedness, generosity, and solidarity that UNESCO continues successfully to extend throughout the world.

As regards the Silk Roads, a scientific appraisal had already been prepared by the Japanese National Commission on the occasion of the International Symposium on the History of Eastern and Western Cultural Contacts (October-November 1957). This served as a guide, while the presentation brochure[99] listed the very many examples of research work already undertaken. Some twenty Japanese specialists enumerated all their problems with the aid of a bibliography of over 750 titles, amounting to an appraisal of the situation in 1957. Out of these endeavors emerged the notion of three intercultural routes: the Steppe Route, the Oasis Route, and the Maritime Route. The three routes were the subject of studies organized according to the main disciplines involved. Among the priority fields, mention should be made of those which continue to be key problems.

For the Steppe Route, the identification of the ethnic types among the ancient nomads (Xiongnu, Wusun, Uighurs, and Oguz) has yet to be clarified, as have the organization of political confederations, the types of languages and scripts (ancient Turkish, Mongolian, the Runic texts of Orkhon, and the language of the Khitan people), the role of institutions under the Mongol Empire of the Yuan, and the Christians living in the steppes of Mongolia. In terms of general history, considerable importance was attached to the antagonism between the nomadic and sedentary populations focused on opposition between pastoral and agricultural economies, along the axis of the routes which extend through Mongolian territory and Kazakhstan, as far as the northern shores of the Black Sea.

The Oasis Route was the subject of a rational appraisal of manuscripts and objects found in the Tarim Basin and dating from the beginning of the Christian era. These include medieval texts from Dunhuang, manuscripts in various languages, and accounts of Chinese military colonies from the Han until the Tang dynasties. This route also involves a more extensive study of the Graeco-Buddhist masterpieces from Gandhara to the Chinese Buddhist grottoes via Turfan to the north and Khotan to the south. The Tarim Basin was studied in a new light in terms of its relationships with its neighbors: the north-south routes showed that, in addition to the lateral east-west flows, there were transverse currents which brought Turks and Tibetans into greater contact with others.

The Oasis Route and the Steppe Route came therefore to be seen as the edges of a vast grid and not merely axes between China and Europe.

By virtue of the uniformity of the shipping routes, the Maritime Route had for long provided an opportunity of observing the coastlines and hinterland, and of taking account of the areas surrounding ports of call. The role that each center played was more developed than the mechanisms of mutual influences. From the early links with Rome in the first century A.D. to the impressive voyages of Zhengho in the fifteenth century, the cargoes were of silk, but already accompanied by porcelain and lacquer, and more especially perfumes and spices which, since the earliest times, had earned this itinerary the name of "Spice Route."

The emphasis placed on these three routes should not make us overlook those that have also been studied for a very long time but which it has not been possible to explore fully. The expedition known as the "Buddhist Road," which partly followed the Valley of the Ganges across India, was completed without actually connecting with the Dîpankara Road. Atîsha Dîpankara (980-1054), who was the superior of the Vikramashîla Monastery, traveled widely; he was invited to Tibet and reached Lhasa via Nepal. His monastery, which had been founded by Dharmapâla in Bengal towards 800, was the point of departure for Buddhists on their way to Tibet.

The other related and much frequented route, in spite of the presence of hostile tribes, was the Burmese Route extending from Bhamo[100] to Yunnan or Sichuan. It was the road which Chang Qian had already been looking for in the second century B.C. and which he had heard about in Bactria when discovering the silks and bamboo of Sichuan. It was also the road that Marco Polo walked on his way to Yunnan and the path followed by many Indian monks who went that way to visit southern China and to set up Buddhist establishments there, first in the Canton region[101] and subsequently beyond, towards Nankin. This is also the road referred to by Rasîd' al-Dîn.[102]

The Silk Roads: A Dialogue between Cultures

In accordance with the aims of the Orient-Occident Project, the UNESCO Project for the Integral Study of the Silk Roads: Roads of Dialogue was adopted for a period of ten years from 1988 to 1997. The problem is no longer to investigate patterns of behavior but, in more practical terms, the intercultural activities and stakes, with a main theme, that of a road network. In order to facilitate the progress of the program of expeditions and their related seminars, and to avoid duplication with the programs of the *History of Civilizations of Central Asia,*[103] the contents of which had been outlined since 1978, the study group of the International Consultative Committee adopted in Venice in 1990 the Guidelines for a Framework involving levels clearly defined in terms of time and space, regardless of any possible overlapping.[104]

The aim was to shed light on interregional mechanisms by tackling the degrees of increasing complexity of problems of synthesis. Four levels of research emerged. The first level could include studies focused on a leading subject such as silk, cotton, precious stones, rare metals, horses and camels, and others; and studies bearing on a particular theme, such as language systems, religious and secular ideas, institutions, and political ideas. The second level could encompass themes that necessarily involve dual or multiple facets, such as socio-cultural impacts (fashions, customs, religious movements, and technological or artistic change); socio-political impacts (the role of intermediaries and brokers, interpreters and officials); and lastly, socio-economic impacts. Thirdly, it would be useful to illustrate local typologies whose wealth of references could help to define cultural identities and social homogeneity. The fourth level could include comparative studies of local typologies and the definition of structural components which make up ensembles specific to major regions, such as an overview of Buddhism and Islam as in the case of some of the papers published here.

In the four stages, and it goes without saying as regards the project for the *Silk Roads: A Dialogue between Cultures*, it would be highly desirable that emphasis be placed on the dynamic effects of transmission, impact, and transfer whereby a clearer understanding might be had of variations specific to the multifaceted development on each itinerary and a clearer distinction could also be made of the genuine endogenous and exogenous values. It was clearly understood, naturally, that this outline was no more than a reference framework and not a specific guideline.

The concept of the project also rests on the specific role of the Silk Roads in which the destiny of so many people and so many communities is involved. A dialogue between cultures means exchanges not only of goods but also of ideas. The very term commerce suggests the exchange of objects as much as that of ideas. In this instance, as elsewhere, the term comprises two meanings: trading, admittedly, but also points of view, discussions, or even deliberations. In these circumstances, "the silk trade serves as a reactive agent and provides topical illustrations in the light of which history can be viewed not merely in economic but also in political, cultural and religious terms."

While the Silk Roads are channels for trade and the transfer of technology, the latter do not always flow at the same pace and towards the same destination. The same can be said of the dissemination of languages and the influence of ideas. They make up an ensemble that is virtually driven by some sort of Brownian movement, the interplay of multiple ideas that can generate new concepts and enrich our perception of history. No study has ever yet been devoted to a network or a range of means of communication both in terms of time and space. Modulations in these various components enable distinct series to be established and allow judicious comparisons to be made.

Another conceptual aspect of these roads is the formation of cultural identities, even national identities, with the traditional opposition related to the interplay of endogenous and exogenous elements. In the last resort, as it is difficult to be truly familiar with the origin of a component and to ascertain whether it is unique in the world, it is wiser and more generous first to accept that the exogenous elements warrant priority and then to determine at what point an exogenous element becomes endogenous. The various trends which we have witnessed over the centuries and even millennia have not left a single person unaffected, whether nomad or sedentary. The intermingling of populations along these roads was constant and contacts were established as much through immediate neighbors as through those who lived far away.

Taking Stock of Research

Up to now anthropologists and sociologists have not succeeded in devising a unified taxonomy of the various cultural areas and their subdivisions. Inspired by the progress of technology and the development of the cognitive sciences, they are attempting today to correlate in a more accurate manner the classifications of linguistic and ethnic groups and to reinterpret the more or less coherent data of their statistics. In the words of Mandelbrot: "Quantitative science is in the process of being supplemented by a second facet. In fact, alongside the science of order which was still considered only recently to be the very symbol of science and the only possible science, we are now witnessing the (disorderly) development of a science of disorder."[105] After the fashion of mathematics, it is possible to think of our forms as divided objects—fractals—whose harmonization rests on a theory of chaos,[106] i.e., the disorder of nature as the true realm of asymmetry with curls of smoke, wisps of cloud, crooked branches or the curious fringes of a boreal sunrise.[107]

The network of Silk Roads follows natural forms; in this regard, it is comparable to nature: a set of lines and intersections that intermingle, a mass of disparate objects and forms and, between them, exchanges and an interplay of influences of all kinds and at all times.[108] Furthermore, the itineraries are not always linear, in one direction and at the same speed. An artistic or an intellectual influence is not confined to a single effect. Its cause has repercussions not only by passing from the seed to the fruit but also through countercurrents, from the effect to the cause. All this is achieved through movements in all directions which can be repeated infinitely, like those of images in a kaleidoscope. Both here and there, the laws have yet to be discovered. It is not impossible that with new knowledge of the itineraries, as it emerges from the studies in the Silk Roads Project, it may be easier to define the relative proximity and remoteness between what is initial and what is terminal.

Road networks, often assimilated to arterial systems, present images of crossroads, intersections, junctions, and branches where forms set their course. Studies on petroglyphs conducted by H.P. Francfort[109] show a relatively homogenous ensemble, irrigated by transfers of forms, whether direct or indirect, proximate or remote. If looked at more closely, it would seem that many of these forms are germinations of the extremities of certain branches of the network, at varying dates that suggest that it was not merely a question of successive transformations but also, in some instances, of transfers. Everything would suggest that change is no longer governed by circulatory currents but by influx currents whose influence is no longer linear or channeled, but diffuse and vague as if we were dealing with neuromimetic structures. Each work, each fact is complex and its origins multiple, whereby it is difficult to distinguish the endogenous from the exogenous as impacts are often deferred, from one to another, according to the itineraries adopted.

If the studies undertaken are further pursued, clarification of the mechanism underlying inter-influences could bring about a better understanding of the components of each culture and greater appreciation of the mutual gifts that result from a secular intermingling of resources. Each of us would be able to discover, at long last, how he or she is a child of multiple origins and a crossbreed of the past.

The number of papers presented at all the seminars held on the occasion of the successive expeditions is such that it was obviously impossible to publish everything all at once. In actual fact, some 429 papers were presented in nineteen countries: forty-two on the Desert Route in China, 1990 (Dunhuang and Urumqi); 297 on the Maritime Route, October 1990-March 1991 (from Venice to Nara); fifty-three on the Steppe Route in Central Asia, April-June 1991 (Alma-Ata and Khiva); and thirty-seven on the Route of the Nomads in Mongolia, 1992 (Ulan Bator). A comprehensive compilation of all these papers would require a volume of some 4,000 pages. Obviously publication has to be spread over a period of time. In spite of the diversity of the papers, there is a certain degree of unity. In fact, the central theme suggests a predilection for subjects dealing with prospects, relations, transport, journeys, distances, neighboring environments, and the speed of assimilation.

According to this new approach, the keys to be found are those in the succession of events, the mechanisms of phenomena, and the interplay of influences that the movement inherent in any major causeway naturally produces. Within the unity of the problem dominated by the "dialogue between cultures," with its notion of mutual influences, and beyond the variety of their methods and regardless of the roads referred to, the texts presented in this volume can be divided into four groups: the first concerns religious movements illustrated by Buddhism as a cultural vector, its ramifications and its interference with local traditions, in China, Sri Lanka, and Southeast Asia. The second centers on interregional relations, with merchants and haulers, grouping relations between India and the Arabs, India and the Indian Archipelago, and China and the Arabs. The third group, focusing on the intercontinental trade of merchants and ship-owners, retraces the long expeditions along the terrestrial axes and shipping routes. The fourth group, comprising major regional themes, raises questions of art, technology, and sociology. Last but not least, attention should be drawn to the comprehensive nature of the research, which may serve as a constant reminder of the infinite complexity of causes and effects. The very abundance of these new correlations should always make us weigh up our conclusions more cautiously and temper their implications. Authors' individual spellings have been adhered to in the main in these chapters.

Notes

1. Ferdinard Von Richthofen, *Verhandelingen der Gesellschaft für Erdkunde zu Berlin*, vol. 4 (1877), pp. 96-122.
2. *Geographical Magazine* (January 1878): pp. 10-14.
3. *North-China Herald* (Shanghai), vol. 1, no. 2 (10 August 1850).
4. *Baron Richthofen's Letters* (Shanghai, North-China Herald Office, 1900), p. 149.
5. *Geographical Magazine*, 1 (July 1874): pp. 144-46.
6. P. Demiéville, preface to L. Boulnois, *La Route de la Soie* (Paris: Arthaud, 1963).
7. See "Les Liaisons routières de l'Inde ancienne et médiévale," in J. Deloche, *Recherches sur les routes de l'Inde au temps des Mongols* (Critical study of the sources), vol. 67 (Paris: Ecole Française d'Extrême-Orient, 1968), pp. 9-31.
8. Chen Ge, "Prehistoric Culture in Xinjiang," and Lin Zhichun, "The Silk Roads before Zhang Qian Opened the Way" (both papers presented at Urumqi, 19-21 August 1990.
9. J.W. McGrindle, *The Invasion of India by Alexander the Great as Described by Arrian, Q. Curtius and Justin* (Westminster, 1896), p. 432.

10. F. Hirth, "The Story of Chang Chien, China's Pioneer in West Asia," *Journal of the American Oriental Society* 37 (Boston, 1917): p. 89.
11. E. Chavannes, *Les mémoires historiques de Sse-ma Ts'ien*, 5 vols. (Paris: Ernest Leroux, 1895-1900; reprint 1967); and B. Watson, *Records of the Grand Historian of China*, 2 vols. (New York: Columbia University Press, 1961).
12. E. Chavannes, *Les pays d'Occident d'après le Heou Han Chou, T'oung Pao*, vol. 8 (Leiden, 1907), pp. 149-234; and F. Hirth, *China and the Roman Orient* (Shanghai: Kelly and Walsh, 1885, photographically reproduced in China, 1939).
13. T.W. Kingsmill, "The Serica of Ptolemy and its inhabitants," *Journal of the China Branch of the Royal Asiatic Society* 19, part 2 (Shanghai, 1884): pp. 43- 60; and Sun Pei-liang, *The Trade Route of the Scythian and Stories of Ancient Central Asia, Collected Essays in the History of Relations between China and the Rest of the World*, vol. 1 (Beijing: Zhonghua Publications, 1984).
14. Herodotus, *Histories*, edited by H.H. Huxley (Letchworth: Bradda Books, 1979). The first explorer, quoted by Herodotus, was probably the Greek poet Aristeas of Proconnessus, 7th century B.C.
15. D. Sinor, "Autour d'une migration des peuples au Ve siècle," *Journal Asiatique* (Paris, 1947).
16. M. Dubois, *Examen de la géographie de Strabon (1st century A.D.)* (Paris: Imprimerie Nationale, 1891), vol. 15, chap. 1, sec 25.
17. J. Edkins, "Allusion to China in Pliny's Natural History," *Journal of the Peking Oriental Society* vol. 1, no. 1 (1885); and J. André and J. Filliozat, trans., *Pline l'Ancien, Histoire Naturelle* (Paris: Belles Lettres, 1980), bk. 6.
18. H. Frisk, "Le Périple de la Mer Erythrée," *Högskolas Auskrift* 33 (Göteborg, 1927): 146-VIII; and J.-F. Salles, *Periplus of the Erythrean Sea and the Arab-Persian Gulf* (paper presented at Madras, 20-21 December 1990).
19. J. Taylor, "Remarks on the Sequel to the Periplus of the Erythrean Sea and the Country of the Seres as described by Ammianus Marcellinus," *Journal of the Asiatic Society of Bengal* 16 (Dacca, 1847): pp. 1-78.
20. J.C. Rolfe, ed. and trans., *A. Marcellinus, Res Gestae* (Cambridge, Mass. and London: Loeb Classical Library, 1963-1964).
21. A. Berthelot, *L'Asie ancienne centrale et sud-orientale d'après Ptolémée*, "23 cartes en noir et blanc et une en couleur," (Paris: Payot, 1930).
22. See E. Tryjarski, "Statut géographique et linguistique des Routes de la Soie," *Diogène*, 171 (Paris, 1995): pp. 18-28. These problems are a major field of interest for specialists of oriental languages. See *International Seminar*, by S. Akiner (Languages and Scripts of Central Asia, SOAS, University of London, April 1990); and the International Seminar organized by D. Sinor entitled "Linguistic interactions between East and West as reflected in loanwords," noted in *Diogène*, 171 (Paris, 1995).
23. This was the case of the Greek, Pytheas, born in Marseilles in the fourth century A.D., who traveled widely in the northern seas, and also of Marco Polo, born in Venice in the thirteenth century, the renown traveler of the southern seas and lands.
24. A. Lévy, *Les pèlerins bouddhistes de la Chine aux Indes* (Paris: J.C. Lattès, 1995).
25. Fa Hian (Faxian) Foe Koue Ki (Foguoji), *Relation des Royaumes bouddhiques…*, translated with comments from Chinese by Abel Rémusat (Paris: Imprimerie Royale, 1836), pp. 68, 424; and Fa-hsien (Faxian), *The Travels of Fa-hsien (399-414 A.D.) or Record of the Buddhistic Kingdoms*, retranslated by H. A. Giles, (1923; 2nd impression, London: Routledge and Kegan Paul, 1956), pp. 16, 99, front.
26. R. Shih, *Biographies des Moines éminents* (Kao seng tchouan) de Houei Kiao (Huijiao), translated and annotated, vol. 54 (Louvain: Bibliothèque du Museon, 1968), p. 175. The first text dates back to the sixth century. An addendum (Xu) was added

by Tao-hsüan (Daoxuan) in the seventh century. The document was updated by Tsanning (Zanning) in 988, under the Song dynasty.

27. Huei-li, *The Life of Hsuang-tsang, compiled by the monk Hui-li* (Peking, 1959); R. Grousset, *Sur les traces du Bouddha* (Paris: Plon, 1929; reprint 1957); and R. Grousset, *In the footsteps of Bouddha*, translated by L. Mariette (London: G. Routledge, 1932).

28. P. C. Bagchi, *Le Canon bouddhique en Chine*, 2 vols. (Paris: Paul Genthner, 1927 and 1938), pp. 473-94.

29. S. Julien, trans., *Voyages des Pèlerins Bouddhistes*, 3 vols. (Paris: Imprimerie Impériale, 1853-1858). Vol. 1 contains Huei-li's life of Hsüan-Chuang; vols. 2 and 3, Hsüan-Chuang's Hsi yü Chi. Also S. Beal, Si-yu-ki, *Buddhist Records of the Western World*, translated from the Chinese of Hiuen Tsiang (629 A.D.), 2 vols., 2d ed. (Delhi, 1884; London: Trübner, 1906; reprint, London, 1919); and Hsüan-Tsang, *Record of the Western Regions*, edited and annotated by Ji Xianbin et al. (Peking, 1985).

30. E. Chavannes, *Voyages des Pèlerins Bouddhistes*, Records of the Eminent high monks who sought the books of the law in the great T'ang dynasty (Ta T'ang si yu kiou fa kouo kao seng tchouan), by I-tsing (I-Ching, Yijing) (Paris: Leroux, 1984).

31. J. Takakusu, *A Record of the Buddhist Religion as Practised in India and the Malay Archipelago Sent Home from the South Seas* (Nan hai ji guei nei fazhuan), A.D. 671-695, by I-Tsing (London: Oxford University Press, 1896).

32. Bagchi, *Canon bouddhique en Chine*, vol. 2, pp. 525-40 and pp. 632-33.

33. *Gua dizhe de Wei Wangtai*, published in 642, which contains fragments of the *Collection of the Pavillon of Hainan*, published by Sun Xingyan in 1797.

34. *Shi dao zhe* of which only a few quotations remain in the encyclopaedias of the tenth century.

35. E. Chavannes, "Illustrated Geography of Li Jifu" (*Yuan ho jun xian tuzhe*), *BEFEO* 3 (1902): pp. 716-18.

36. P. Pelliot, "Deux itinéraires de Chine en Inde à la fin du VIIIe siècle," *BEFEO* 4 (1904): pp. 121-403.

37. E. Chavannes, "Les deux plus anciens spécimens de la cartographie chinoise," *BEFEO* 3 (1902): p. 244.

38. *The Itinerary of Benjamin of Tudela*, critical text, translation and commentary by Marcus Nathan Adler (London: H. Frowde, 1907). The first edition was published in Constantinople in 1543 and the tenth edition in Jerusalem in 1904. Other editions appeared throughout Europe, including Ferrara in the sixteenth century, Amsterdam in the seventeenth century, Paris in the eighteenth century, and Warsaw in the nineteenth century.

39. *Lingwai daida* (Information on what is beyond the Passes) with many details concerning the geography of the Guangdong and Guangxi provinces, and the region beyond, extending even to the far west and many Asiatic Kingdoms.

40. *Zhufangzhi cf. Chau Ju-Kua, His Work on the Chinese and Arab Trade*, entitled *Chu-fan-chi*, translated from Chinese and annotated by F. Hirth and W.W. Rockhill (St. Petersburg: Imp. Acad. Sciences, 1912; reprint, Amsterdam: Oriental Press, 1966).

41. Zoroastrism was the official religion in Persia under the Sassanids. When they lost power, their princes sought refuge at the Chinese court of the Tang. For similar reasons, the other religions, such as Nestorianism, Mazdeism, and Manicheism, specific to the Persians, were gradually supplanted by the newcomers and their believers also went into exile in China. See Ph. Gignoux, B.A. Litvinsky, and M.I. Vorobyeva-Desatovskaya, "Religions and Religious Movements" (1 and 2) in *History*

of Civilization of Central Asia, vol. 3 of *The Crossroads of Civilization A.D. 250 to 750* (Paris: UNESCO, 1996), chaps. 17 and 18.

42. G. Ferrand, *Relations de voyages et textes géographiques arabes, persans et turcs relatifs à l'Extrême-Orient du VIIIe au XVIIIe siècles*, translated, reviewed, and annotated, 2 vols. (Paris: E. Leroux, 1913-1914); and G.F. Hourani, *Arab Seafaring in the Indian Ocean* (Beyrouth, 1963).

43. Basra, the outer harbor of Baghdad, founded in 637, declined in the eleventh century as it became silted up and was ruined by the Mongol invasion. Sîrâf, the Iranian port in the Persian Gulf, was one of the major trading posts with the Far East until the twelfth century. The Omani port of Sohar played a major role on account of its position below the straits of Ormuz, therefore facing eastwards towards the Indus.

44. Akbhar as-Sîn wa'l-Hind, *Relation de la Chine et de l'Inde*, written in 851, translated by J. Sauvaget (Paris: Belles Lettres, 1948). This text which inspired the tale of Sinbad the Sailor contains a wealth of information supplied by the merchant Sulayman. See R.P. Khawan, *Les aventures de Sinbad le Marin* (Paris: Ed. Phebus, 1985).

45. Kitâb al-Masâlik, *Le livre des Routes et des Provinces by Ibn Khordabeh*, published, translated, and annotated by C. Barbier de Meynard (Paris: Imprimerie Impériale, 1865).

46. Ibn Fadlan, *Relation du Voyage d'Ibn Fadlan chez les Bulgares de la Volga* (921), translated by M. Canard, in *Annales d'études orientales*, 16 (Algiers, 1958); and Ibn Fadlan, *Voyage chez les Bulgares de la Volga* (Paris: Sindbad, 1984).

47. al-Mas'ûdî (fl. 956), *Les Prairies d'or (Murûj al-Dhabab)*, translation by Barbier de Meynard and Pavet de Courteille, 9 vols. (Part 1, Paris: Imprimerie Impériale, 1861; part 9, Paris: Imprimerie Nationale, 1877; 2d ed. revised, amended, and translated by P. Pellat, Paris: 1962-1965).

48. al-Idrîsî (1099-1166), *Récréation de celui qui désire parcourir le monde* (1150), translated from the Arabic by P.A. Jaubert, 2 vols. (1836). For the maps, see photographs in J. Needham, *Science and Civilisation in China*, vol. 3 (Cambridge University Press, 1959), fig. 239, p. 564.

49. Abû'l-Fidâ (1275-1331), *Géographie d'Aboulfeda* (Taqwīm al-Buldân), translated from Arabic by M. Rainaud and S. Guyard, 2 vols. (Paris: Imprimerie Nationale, 1846 and 1883).

50. *Description de la Chine sous le règne de la dynastie mongole*, translated from the Persian of Rachid Eddin, with notes by J. Klaproth (Paris: Imprimerie Royale, 1833).

51. Ibn Batoutah (1304-1378), *Voyages*, translated by C. Defrémery and B.R. Sanguinetti, 5 vols. (Paris: Imprimerie Impériale, 1853-1859; reprint, 3 vols. Paris: F. Maspéro, 1982); and G. Philippe, *Marco Polo and Ibn Batuta in Fookien*, edited by J. Doolittle (1870-1871); *Travels of Ibn Battûta*, translated from the Arabic, selected and edited by H.A.R. Gibb (London: Routledge and Kegan Paul, 1929); and Ibn Batouta, *Voyages* (Paris: La Découverte, 1990).

52. J. Kuwabara, *On P'u Shou-keng*, Memories of the Research Department of the Tôyôbunko 2, 7 (Tokyo, 1928 and 1935); and Lo Hsiang-lin, *A New Study of P'u Shou-keng and his Time* (Hong Kong: Institute of Chinese Culture, 1959) is a fairly recent complementary to the study of Kuwabara.

53. In 1973, during underwater archaeological excavations, whole cargoes were brought to the surface, comprising of lacquer, sandalwood, spices, incense, and even Chinese medicines bound abroad. Thanks to the retrieval of wooden components, it was possible, with a hull and a stern-post rudder, to rebuild some trading and seagoing vessels with a profiled keel.

54. E. Bretschneider, *Mediaeval Researches from Eastern Asiatic Sources*, fragments
towards the knowledge of the geography and history of Central and Western Asia
from the thirteenth to the seventeenth century, 2 vols. (London: Trübner, 1888); P.
Pelliot, "Les Mongols et la Papauté," *Revue de l'Orient Chrétien*, vols. 3 and 4
(1922-1931), 3d ser.; vol. 3, nos. 1 and 2 (1922-1923); vol. 4, nos. 3 and 4 (1924);
and vol. 8, nos. 1 and 2 (1931-1932); and O. Halecki, "Diplomatie pontificale et
activité missionnaire en Asie aux XIII-XVe siècles," *Histoire des continents* (Report,
2, of 12th International Congress of Historical Sciences, Vienna, 29 August–
5 September 1965), International Committee of Historical Sciences with the assistance of UNESCO through International Council for Philosophy and Humanistic
Sciences (ICPHS) (Vienna: Ferdinand Berger und Söhne).

55. *The Monks of Kûbilâi Khân, Emperor of China*, or *The History of the life and travels
of Rabban Saumâ, envoy and plenipotentiary of the Mongol Khans to the Kings of
Europe, and Markos who, as Mâr Yahbh-Allâhâ III, became patriarch of the Nestorian
Church in Asia*, vol. 16, 16 plates (incl. front., portraits, facsimiles), translated from
the Syriac by Sir E.A. Wallis Budge (London: the Religious Tract Society, 1928);
and H. Bernard, *La découverte de Nestoriens Mongols aux Ordos et l'Histoire Ancienne
du Christianisme en Extrême-Orient* (Tientsin: Hautes Etudes, 1935; reprinted from
Dossiers of the Synodal Commission of Peking, June-July 1935).

56. C.R. Beazley, *The Dawn of Modern Geography*, vol 2 (London: Murray, 1901), p.
179; vol. 3 (Oxford, 1906); Jean de Plan Carpin, *Histoire des Mongols*, translated by
Père C. Schmitt (Paris: Editions Franciscaines, 1961); and Jean de Plan Carpin, *Historia Mongolorum*, Dom J. Becquet and L. Hambis (Paris: Sinica Franciscana, 1965).

57. Itinerarium fratris Willielmi de Rubruquis de ordine fratrum Minorum, Galli,
Anno grat. 1253 ad partes Orientales (London: Hakluyt 1, 1599), pp, 71-92; and
Beazley, *Dawn of Modern Geography*, vol. 2, p. 320; and Guillaume de Rubrouck,
Voyage dans l'empire mongol, translated by C. and R. Kappler (Paris: Payot, 1985).

58. Sir H. Yule, Cathay and the way thither; being a collection of medieval notions of
China Hakluyt Society publications, 1913-15 (1st. ed., 1866), revised by H.
Cordier, 4 vols: vol.1, no. 38, Introduction: Preliminary Essay on the Intercourse
between China and the Western Nations Previous to the Discovery of the Cape
Route; vol. 2, no. 33, Odoric of Porderone; vol. 3, no. 37, John of Monte Cassino
and Others; vol. 4, no. 41, Battuta and Benedict of Gors, (photographically repro-
duced, 1942); Sir H. Yule, *The Book of ser Marco Polo the Venetian concerning the
Kingdoms and marvels of the East*, translated and edited with notes (London: H.
Cordier, 1903; with notes and addenda, London, 1920); A.C. Moule and P. Pelliot,
Marco Polo (1254-1325): The Description of the World, translated and annotated
(London: Routledge, 1938); A.C. Moule, *Quinsay*, with notes by other authors on
Marco Polo (Cambridge: Cambridge University Press, 1957); P. Pelliot, *Notes on
Marco Polo*, 3 vols. (Paris: Imprimerie Nationale, Lib. Adrien-Maisonneuve,
1959-1973); L. Hambis, *Marco Polo, La Description du monde* (Paris: Klincksieck,
1955); J. Heers, *Marco Polo* (Paris: Fayard, 1983); and J.P. Drège, *Marco Polo et la
Route de la Soie* (Paris: Gallimard, 1989).

59. A hundred or more editions were published in Europe in the form of books, travel
accounts or tales. The earliest, including the *Book of Marco Polo* printed in Nurem-
berg in 1477, were German, followed by Latin editions, such as Pepino's translation
(c. 1320), printed in Antwerp in 1485. The first Italian edition *Maranliose cose del
Mondo* dates back to 1496. The French edition, *La Description géographique*, is from
1556, as well as that of the Bibliothèque Nationale. *Le divisement du monde de
Messer March Pol de Venice*, printed in Karlsruhe, dates back to 1902. The English
editions were first printed in 1579. The popularity of this work may account for the

quest for the Indies, via a westward route, undertaken by Christopher Columbus who had the 1485 Latin edition, which he had carefully annotated. His copy, annotated by his own hand, has been preserved at the Bibliotheca Colombina in Sevilla.

60. Odoric de Pordenone (d.-1331), *Odorichus de rebus incognitis* (for Girolamo Soncino) (Pesaro, 1513); and *Les voyages en Asie au XIVe siècle*, du bienheureux père Odoric de Pordenone, religieux de Saint-François, publié avec une introduction et des notes par H. Cordier (Paris: Ernest Leroux, 1891).

61. Sir. J. Mandville (or Maunduyl, Manndeville), *The Voiage and travayle of syr Mandeville Knight, which traiteth of the way toward Hierusalem, and of marayles of Inde with other Ilands and Countryes* (London, 1568); H. Cordier Henri, *Jean de Mandeville*, T'oung pao (Leiden: E.J. Brill, 1891), vol. 2, 4, pp. 288-323; and J. de Mandeville, *Mandeville's travels*, edited by Letts (London, 1959). Sir Henry Yule was able to count 78 manuscripts for Marco Polo, 76 for Odoric de Pordenone, and some 250 copies for de Mandeville.

62. Francesco di Balduccio Pegolotti, *La Prattica della Mercatura* (Cambridge, Mass.: Allan Evans, 1936).

63. *Narrative of the Embassy of Ruy Gonçalez de Clavijo to the Court of Timour at Samarcand, 1403-1406*, translated for the first time, with notes, a preface and an introductory life of Timour-Beg, by R.M. Clements, fellow of the Royal Geographical Society (London: Hackluyt Society, 1859); and Ruy Gonzalez de Clarijo, *La route de Samarcande au temps de Tamerlan (1403-1406)*, translated and with a commentary by L. Kehren in *Voyages et Découvertes* (Paris: Imprimerie Nationale, 1990).

64. "Ex India Cataium Lustraturus mittitur è Nostra Societate Benedictus Goësius Lusitanus," *De Christ. Exp. apud Sinas, August. Vend.* (1615), book 5, chap. 11, pp. 544ff; and H. Bernard, *Le Frère Bento de Goes chez les musulmans de la haute Asie (1603-1607)* (Tientsin, 1934).

65. J. Grueber (1623-1675), "Viaggio del P. Giovanni Grueber tornando per terra da China in Europa," *Recueil de Thévenot*, 2 (Paris: Thom. Moette, 1966); and C. Wessels, *Early Jesuit travellers in Central Asia (1603-1721)*, map (The Hague: Martinus Nijhoff, 1924).

66. *The Voyage and Travels of Mr Anthony Jenkinson, from Russia to Boghâr, or Bockhara, in 1557*, to which are added some informations of others concerning the Road thence to Katay, or China (London: Hakluyt, 1599).

67. The library of Jean, Duc de Berry, was published in full by Hiver de Beauvoir, Paris, Aubry, 1834; and manuscript in folio bearing the Arms of France, Fr. 2810 (ancien 8392), Bibliothèque Nationale, Paris, quoted by H. Cordier in *Bibliotheca Sinica* (see note 69) col. 1936-37.

68. Small in-folio of 82 leaves, copy of ms. Fr. 1380 (ancien 7500c), Bibliothèque Nationale, Paris quoted by H. Cordier in *Bibliotheca Sinica*, col. 1930 with illustration on left, p. 62.

69. H. Cordier, *Bibliotheca sinica, Dictionnaire bibliographique des ouvrages relatifs à l'empire chinois*, compiled and annotated, 5 vols. (Paris, 1878-1924) is a remarkable, reasoned bibliography of European research from Antiquity to the twentieth century. A substantial part is devoted to relations between China and foreigners, extending well beyond purely Chinese issues. A further volume deals with the period from 1924 to 1958: Tung-li Yuan, *China in Western Literature*, a continuation of Cordier's *Bibliotheca Sinica* (New Haven, Conn.: Yale University, 1958). Also bibliography of explorations in *L'Asie Centrale, histoire et civilisation*, joint publication, dir. by L. Hambis with the aid of the Centre de Recherches sur l'Asie Centrale et la Haute Asie (Paris: Imprimerie Nationale, 1977).

70. *Fangzhi*, official local history and topography.

71. A. Wylie, *Notes on Chinese Literature and a list of translations from the Chinese into various European languages* (Shanghae and London: American Presbyterian Mission Press and Trûbner and Co., 1867), p. 260.

72. A classified catalogue of Chinese books in the Chinese-Japanese Library of the Harvard Yenching Institute at Harvard University, Historical Sciences, compiled by A. K'ai-ming ch'u (Cambridge, Mass.: Harvard Yenching Institute, 1940).

73. *Revue Bibliographique de Sinologie.* Focusing on current topical work, publishes annual surveys of the latest books and articles in the field of Chinese human sciences written in Chinese, Japanese, and Western languages (Paris: EHESS, 1955).

74. S. Hedin (1865-1952), pupil of Baron von Richthofen. Three expeditions between 1894 and 1908, with a fourth (Sino-Swedish) in 1927-1955, see notes 83 and 96.

75. G. Bonvalot, *De Paris au Tonkin à travers le Tibet inconnu.* A work containing a map in color and 108 prints of photographs taken by the Prince of Orleans (Paris: Lib. Hachette et Cie, 1892). Ap. In 8; pp. 150 + 1 f.n.c.

76. Henri d'Orléans (1867-1901), the explorer took part in Bonvalot's second expedition from 1889 to 1890 (see note 75).

77. P. P. Semenov, known as Tienshanian (1827-1914), made numerous expeditions to Dzoungarie and in the Tienshan. See V. I. Tcherniasky, and P.P. Semenov *Le Tienshanien et ses travaux géographiques* (in Russian) (Moscow: Geografgiz, 1955).

78. N.M. Prjevalsky (1839-1910), zoologist and army colonel, a disciple of P.P. Semenov (see above 77), four expeditions between 1871 and 1885. Also W. Salensky, *Prjevalsky's Horse* (Equus Prjvalsky), translated by Captain M.H. Hayes and O.C. Bradley (London: Hurst and Blackett, 1907), chap. 16, 65, ill.; and P. Yetts, "The Horse, a Factor in Early Chinese History," *Eurasia Septentrionalis Antiqua* 9 (1934): p. 231.

79. V. I. Roborovsky (1856-1910), explorer of Central Asia and the Tibetan borders, who took part in Prjevalsky's expeditions.

80. P.K. Kozlov (1869-1935), explorer and archaeologist who accompanied Roborovsky. See "The Central Asian Expedition of Captain Roborovsky and Lieut. Kozloff," *Geographical Journal*, vol. 8 (August 1896): pp. 161-73, and also note 87; and P. Hopkirk, *Foreign Devils on the Silk Roads: The Search for the Lost Cities and Treasures of Chinese Central Asia* (London: John Murray, 1980; French translation, Paris: Arthaud, 1981).

81. W. Radloff (1837-1918), a German specialist of Turkey, Director of the Asian Museum of Saint Petersburg from 1884 onwards, and member of the Russian Imperial Academy of Science.

82. Submitted before the Congress of Orientalists in Rome. It was adopted by the same Congress in Hamburg in 1902 and confirmed by the Emperor of Russia on 2 February 1903.

83. S. Hedin, *Scientific Results of a Journey in Central Asia, 1899-1902*, vol. 1, *Tarim River* (Stockholm: Lithographic Institute of the General Staff of the Swedish Army, 1904), p. 553; vol. 2, *Lop-nor;* vol. 3, *North and East Tibet;* vol. 4, *Central and West Tibet;* vol. 5, *Meteorology, Astronomical Observations;* vol. 6, *Zoology, Botany, Geology, Archaeology;* and S. Hedin, *Central Asia and Tibet*, 2 vols. (London: Hurst and Blackett, 1903); and S. Hedin, *The Silk Road* 922 p., 91 pl, 1 map (London: Routledge and Sons, 1938).

84   E. Senart, Member of the Institut, "Un nouveau champ d'exploration archéologique: le Turkestan Chinois," lecture given at the session of the Five Academies on 25 October 1905, *BEFEO*, nos. 4-5 (1905): pp. 492-97.

85. G. and M. Grumm-Gržimailo, *Opisanie putešestviya v zapadnaya Kitaj* (Voyage en Chine occidentale) in 3 vols., with plates and maps (St. Petersbourg: Société Impériale Russe de Géographie, 1886-1907).

86 D. Klementz, *Turfan und seine Altertümer* (Antiquities from Turfan) (St. Petersbourg: Publications de l'Académie des Sciences, 1908).

87. P.K. Kozlov et al., *Comptes rendus des expéditions pour l'exploration du Nord de la Mongolie* (eningrad: Acad. des Sciences de l'URSS, 1925); and P.K. Kozlov, *Mongolija i Amdo i mertvyï gorod Khara-khoto* (Mongolia and Amdo and the dead city of Khara-khoto), 300 p. (Moscow, 1947); E.I. Ljubo-Lesničenko and T.K. Šafranovskaya, *Mertvyï gorod Khara-khoto* (The dead city of Khara-khoto), 64 p. incl. 15 p. of illustrations (Moscow: Nauka, 1968).

88. J.L. Dutreuil de Rhins, *Mission scientifique dans la Haute-Asie, 1890-1895*, 3 vols. (Paris: Ernest Leroux, 1897).

89. Sir A. Stein, *Ruins of Desert Cathay*. Personal Narrative of Explorations in Central Asia and Westernmost China. 2 vols. (London: MacMillan and Co., 1912); Sir A. Stein, *Serindia: Detailed report of Explorations in Central Asia and Westernmost China Carried Out and Described Under the Orders of H.M. Indian Government*, 5 vols.: 1 to 3, texts; 4, Plates; 5, maps (Oxford: The Clarendon Press, 1921); Sir A. Stein, *Innermost Asia: Detailed Report of Explorations in Central Asia, Kansu and Eastern Iran*, 4 vols.: vols. 1 and 2, texts 1, 159 p. and index; vol. 3, 87 pl., 59 plans; vol. 4, maps, 47 of 1:500.000 and 4 of Darel, the Lop Desert and Seistan (Oxford: The Clarendon Press, 1928); Sir A. Stein and F.H. Andrews, "Ancient Chinese Figured Silks Excavated by Sir Aurel Stein at Ruined Sites of Central Asia," *Burlington Magazine* (London), 20 p. and 17 figs (1920); R. Whitfield, *The Art of Central Asia: the Stein Collection in the British Museum* 3 vols. (Tokyo: Kodansha, 1982-1985).

90. A. Grünwedel, *Altbuddhistische Kulstätten im Chinesisch-Turkestan...von 1906 bis 1907 bei Kuca, Qarasahr und in der oase Turfan*, 370 p.; 678 figs.; index (Berlin: Druck und Verlag von G. Reiner, 1912). A. Grünwedel, *Alt Kutscha*, 2 vols. (Berlin: Otto Elsner, 1920); and H. Hartel et al., *Zentralasien Turfan sammlung Katalog* (Berlin: Museum für Indische Kunst, 1976), pp. 101-44.

91. A. von Le Coq, *Die buddhistische Spätantike im Mittelasien, Ergebnisse der Kgl. Preußischen, Turfan Expeditionen*, 7 vols. (Berlin: D. Reimer [1 to 7], 1922-1933; reprint, Graz, Akademische Druck-u, Verlagsanstalt, 1973-1975).

92. P. Pelliot, *Mission en Asie Centrale*, pp. 58-68, reports of sessions of the Académie des Inscriptions et Belles Lettres, (Paris, 1910); P. Pelliot, *Grottes de Touen-houang* (Buddhist paintings and sculptures of the Wei, T'ang and Song periods), 6 vols., 376 pl. (Paris: Geuthner, 1920-1924). Photographs from C. Nouettes. Also K. Riboud and G. Vial, with the assistance of M. Hallade, *Touen-houang fabrics preserved in the Musée Guimet and at the Bibliothèque Nationale* (Paris, 1970); J. Giès et al., "La collection Paul Pelliot du musée national des arts asiatiques-Guimet," in *Les arts de l'Asie centrale*, p. 372, col. pl. 99 (Paris: Réunion des Musées Natio-naux/Kodansha, 1994); *La Route de la Soie*, exhibition at the Musée Guimet of works from the French collections (Paris: Réunion des Musées Nationaux, 1976); and *Treasures from China and North Asia, First Centenary of Paul Pelliot*, catalogue of exhibition (Paris: Bibliothèque Nationale, 1979).

93. S. Oldenburg, *Russkaja Turkestanskaja Ekspedicija 1901-1910* (By order of the Tsar, expedition equipped by the Russian Committee for the study of Central and Eastern Asia, under the protection of His Imperial Majesty) (St. Petersburg: Imperial Academy of Science Press, 1914).

94. N. Kumagai, "Higashi Turkistan to Otani tankentai" (Eastern Turkistan and the Otani expeditions) in *Bukkyô geijutsu*, 19, pp. 3-23, with a summary in English and

many articles on Bezeklik and Miran in Bijutsu Kenkyû from 1942. Also *Fiftieth anniversary of the Otani Mission along the Silk Road (1904-1912)*, 58 figs., 2 col. pls., 6 maps. Exhibition catalogue of Kyôto (Kyôto: Yomiuri Shimbun, 1963).

95. L. Warner, *Buddhist Wall Paintings: A Study of a Ninth-Century Grotto at Wan-fo-hsia near Tun-huang* (Cambridge, Mass.: Harvard University Press, 1938).

96. S.A. Hedin (1865-1952), *History of the expedition in Asia in collaboration with Folke Bergman* (Stockholm: Göteborg, Elanders boktryckeri aktiebolag, 1943). Reports from the expedition to the north-western provinces of China under the leadership of Dr. S. Hedin, Sino-Swedish expedition, publications 23-26.

97. G. Le Fèvre, *Citroën Expedition in Central Asia; the yellow cruzade; third Haardt, Audouin-Dubreuil mission,* followed by *Haute Asie* by Paul Pelliot with 95 engravings, 3 full-page maps, 3 in-text maps (Paris: Plon, 1933; reprint, *La Croisière Jaune, Expédition Citroën Centre-Asie, routes de la soie,* Paris: l'Asiathèque, 1990).

98. *Orient-Occident, nouvelles du projet majeur relatif à l'appréciation des valeurs culturelles de l'Orient et de l'Occident,* vol. 1, no. 2 (Paris: UNESCO, April 1958): pp. 5-10; and *Evaluation du projet majeur relatif à l'appréciation mutuelle des valeurs culturelles de l'Orient et de l'Occident, 1957-1966* (Paris: UNESCO, 1968).

99. *Research in Japan in History of Eastern and Western cultural contacts,* (Tokyo: Japanese National Commission for UNESCO, 1957), p. 154.

100. E.C. Young, "A Journey from Yunnan to Assam," *Geographical Journal* (August 1907): pp. 152-80; see P. Pelliot, note 36.

101. Lo Hsiang-lin (Lo Xianglin), *Kwang-hsiao Monastery of Canton during the T'ang with reference to Sino-Indian relations* (Hong Kong: Institute of Chinese Culture, 1960); and P.C. Bagchi, *India and China: a thousand years of Sino-Indian cultural contact* (Calcutta: China Press Limited, 1944), p. 240.

102. See *Description de la Chine*, note 50.

103. *History of Civilizations of Central Asia* (Paris: UNESCO): vol. 1, 1992; vol. 2, 1994; vol. 3, 1996.

104. *Report of the Study Group for Programmes and Projects*, Venice, Italy, 22-25 June 1990, Appendix 1 (Paris: UNESCO, 1990).

105. B. Mandelbrot, *Objets fractals*, 3d ed. (Paris: Flammarion, 1989); and Préface by B. Mandelbrot in I. Steward, *Dieu joue-t-il aux dés? Les mathématiques du chaos* (Paris: Flammarion, Nouvelle Bibliothèque Scientifique, 1992). Note *Does God Play Dice? The New Mathematics of Chaos* (London, 1989).

106. J. Gleick, *La Théorie du Chaos vers une nouvelle science* (Paris: Flammarion, 1991; American ed., New York: Viking, 1987).

107. H.O. Peitgen and P.H. Richter, *The Beauty of Fractals Images of Complex Dynamical Systems* (Berlin, Heidelberg, New York, and Tokyo: Springer Verlag, 1986).

108. We need only look at the lines drawn by a precise itinerary; the notion of a wide path disappears in the face of the kaleidoscopic fragments. See Deloche, note 7, pl., VI maps of the Hiuan-tsang roads in India (see Cunningham).

109. H.P. Francfort, "Les pétroglyphes d'Asie Centrale et la Route de la Soie," in *Les Routes de la Soie: Patrimoine commun, identités plurielles* (Paris: UNESCO, 1994).

Chapter 1

Perspectives on Buddhism in Dunhuang during the Tang and Five Dynasties Period

Henrik H. Sørensen

Introduction

The Silk Roads served as the main artery for trade and communication between East and West for more than a millennium, and the main bulk of the extant material relating to the cultures that flourished there is indisputably of a religious nature. This material includes architecture exemplified by cave temples and stupas, sculptures, wall-paintings, votive paintings, and a sizeable literature in more than ten languages including Bactrian, Chinese, Khotanese, Parthian or middle-Persian, Sanskrit, Sogdian, Tibetan, Tocharian, and Uighur. Most of it, in one way or another, concerns the main religious traditions of Central Asia, including Buddhism, Manichaeism, and Nestorianism.[1] Hence, it is important to recognize the significance of religion, not only as a general component of human civilization in the societies that flourished along the Silk Roads, but as the single most important factor in the cultural dissemination and exchange that took place in Central Asia from the beginning of the Christian era up to approximately A.D. 1000.

The town of Dunhuang, known as Shazhou in the period under discussion, and located in the westernmost part of modern Gansu Province, was an important Buddhist center with a large monastic population. Here, at the Mogao Caves situated some twenty-five kilometers from the town of Shazhou, Buddhist pilgrims from China, India, and Tibet met and actively exchanged doctrines and practices. The precious cache of manuscripts found in a side chamber of Cave 17 around the turn of this century, and the impressive and still well-preserved wall-paintings found in many of the caves there have provided us with a large body of primary information about the Buddhist community in Shazhou. Such propitious circumstances make Dunhuang particularly important and suitable for research on the relationship between religious life and society in the Chinese borderlands during the period of roughly five hundred years from A.D. 500 to 1000.

This chapter deals with the practice of Buddhism in Dunhuang, the emphasis being on its special characteristics. It includes a discussion of the Buddhist sects represented there, the Buddhist communities during the Tibetan occupation of Dunhuang, Tibetan Buddhism and Tantric practices in particular, Buddhist and Daoist syncretism, and popular Buddhist cults. While it does not claim to offer novel or tantalizing insights, it may well go some way towards providing a more complete picture of the diversities of Buddhist life in Dunhuang, and thereby indicate directions for further research. Questions of art history have generally been left to one side, and the author here confines himself to the information contained in the written sources, in other words the hoard of manuscripts from Cave 17.

A Reappraisal of Dunhuang Buddhism

Although Dunhuang and the prefectural town of Shazhou were situated within the time-honored borders of the Chinese Tang Empire (618-906), it is important to distinguish between Buddhism as practised in this frontier prefecture in western Gansu, or Hexi as it was then called, and Buddhism in the central provinces of China. Scholars have already succeeded in tracing a viable historical development for the mainstream Buddhist doctrines and practices in the Chinese heartland during the Tang on the basis of the large amounts of primary source material available.[2] It goes without saying that this evaluation owes a lot to the Dunhuang manuscripts which have afforded us a rare insight into details of everyday life that are usually absent from traditional Chinese material, whether Buddhist or secular. However, while the Dunhuang material has been used to elucidate obscure areas of Tang Buddhism in general, relatively little attention has been given to the kind of Buddhism that flourished in Shazhou during its "golden era" from the early Tang up to the beginning of the eleventh century. This is especially the case with regard to religious practices and popular doctrines, and somewhat less so when viewed from an art historical perspective.[3]

Dunhuang Buddhism is unique in that it does not have an exact counterpart anywhere else in the world. This is primarily due to the fact that the Dunhuang oasis was a main trading post and meeting-point for the caravans entering and leaving China. It therefore became a virtual melting-pot in which a wide range of international cultural influences merged and coalesced. Practically all new developments and trends in Northern Indian Buddhism—whether relating to scriptures, scholasticism, or art—arrived in Dunhuang at some point on their way to China; while, towards the end of the eight century, Tibetan influences—primarily in the form of esoteric Buddhist scriptures of the typical Indo-Tibetan brand—became increasingly common as well. The latest developments in Chinese Buddhism in the twin capitals of Tang in particular, as well as in Shu (now the modern province of Sichuan), a highly active provincial Buddhist center, were felt soon afterwards in Shazhou where they immediately became the object of great interest and devotion to the local Chinese Buddhists. Here it is interesting to note that various Indian Buddhist imports, which had reached China via the sea route, would in many cases eventually end up in Dunhuang and Turfan as integrated elements of the Chinese Buddhist culture there.[4] In short Buddhism in Dunhuang was both extremely composite and thoroughly international; it deserves our attention not only because it provides highly important information on Chinese Buddhism during the Tang, but in its own right as well.

On the Schools of Chinese Buddhism in Dunhuang

One of the major unresolved questions relating to Buddhism in Dunhuang is that of the schools or sects (Ch. *zong*), which are otherwise well-documented in the Chinese historical sources. The manuscripts found in Cave 17 contain material related to virtually all the major denominations of Chinese Buddhism that flourished under the Tang. However, a number of questions remain: were all these schools also represented *in situ* in Dunhuang? Did they exist as separate institutions, or was their presence simply due to individual adherents living together in the same communities? Did they produce sectarian Buddhist literature of their own? It is known that at different periods certain beliefs and practices were more prevalent among the Buddhists of Shazhou than at other periods; however, the contexts in which they occur do not indicate any distinct sectarian background. Hence, with the exception of a few obvious cases, the sectarian division of the Buddhist community in Dunhuang has up to now remained largely oblique. This problem is compounded by the fact that many of the scriptures that have an otherwise clear address are often found in a doctrinal context that can best be described as syncretic, i.e., they form part of a compilation of texts or excerpts belonging to different schools of Buddhism. In the following pages I shall try to provide answers to some basic questions concerning sectarian developments in Dunhuang.[5]

In the general study of Chinese Buddhism, that pertaining to Chan is undoubtedly the most rapidly expanding field of all. Thus, the Dunhuang manuscripts relating to Chan Buddhism have long been the subject of intense research and debate among concerned scholars. However, most of the studies carried out on the material have aimed at elucidating doctrinal and sectarian developments in this important school of Chinese Buddhism in China itself and have generally neglected their links with Chan Buddhism as practiced in Dunhuang.[6] In a recent preliminary survey I tried to make up for this deficit by showing that these Chan manuscripts to some degree reflect developments in the central provinces of China during the Tang.[7] Yet that study also indicates that there were aspects of Chan Buddhism in Dunhuang which were unique to the place. The most prominent of these related to syncretism and the transmission of the associated literature.

The manuscripts contain an abundance of material on the northern and southern schools of Chan from the eighth century onwards; however, with the exception of the Hongzhou School of Mazu Daoyi (709-788), later Southern Chan developments are also represented. One such text, the hymn *Nanzong zan* (In praise of the southern school [of Chan]),[8] appears to have been composed by a local Chan practitioner in Dunhuang. Another work related to Chan Buddhism, although not from Dunhuang originally, is the *Quanzhou qianfo xinzhu zhu zushi song* (Verses newly composed at the Thousand Buddha [Caves] in Quanzhou),[9] by Mingjue (n.d.). Written in red at the end of the manuscript can be read: "Recorded by Daozhen, the Śrāmaṇera of the Sanjie Temple in Shazhou." Daozhen was the abbot of the Sanjie Temple and a very prominent master of the *vinaya* during the tenth century.[10] Other Chan works recorded by him include two Northern Chan texts found in manuscript P. 2270. A popular Chan text among the monks in the Dunhuang area was the *Heze si heshang Shenhui wugeng chuan* (Five Watches of the Night Transmitted by the Ven. Shenhui[11] of Heze Temple)[12] of which a relatively large number have been identified. Information has also come to light on meditation caves (*chanku*) in Dunhuang. The mere designation of *chanku* does not indicate sectarian affinity, but simply means that it was a cave meant for the practice of meditation in general.[13] However, the sectarian issue does not appear to have been very prominent among Chan followers in Dunhuang, since we find texts related to both Northern and Southern Chan in the same manuscript. Another interesting feature is that Northern Chan texts continued to be in use in Dunhuang long after they had ceased to be used in the central provinces of the Empire.

Study of the voluminous Chinese material related to esoteric Buddhism or Mizong has to a considerable degree been neglected. This is rather surprising since esoteric Buddhism (*mijiao* or *zhenyan*) permeates nearly all aspects of Dunhuang Buddhism including literature, liturgy, art, and so forth. As far as can be ascertained there was no independent temple belonging to esoteric Buddhism in Mogao as such, but manuscript S. 2685, entitled *Qianyuan si qiqing wen* (Texts of the Qianyuan Temple for Making Invocations), suggests that the monks in this temple practised esoteric Buddhist rituals. The manuscript in question contains the *Shi egui shi shui zhenyan yin fa* (Mantra and Mudrï Methods [used] for the Offering of Food and Water to the Hungry Ghosts),[14] a canonical ritual text attributed to Amoghavajra (705-774), the third patriarch of orthodox Zhenyan Buddhism.[15] Manuscript S. 4723, which contains a translation of the (*Sarvadurgatiparisodhana*) *usnīsavijaya-dhāranī*,[16] also belonged to the Qianyuan Temple, which is a further indication of this institution's affiliation with esoteric Buddhism. It is also known that the *saṅgha* in the Sanjie Temple cultivated esoteric Buddhism.[17] A copy of the *Subāhupariprcchā sūtra*[18] is known to have belonged to the library of the Kaiyuan Temple.[19] A typical feature of the Chinese esoteric material is the large number of dhāranī manuals, or simply unstructured collections of dhāranīs and mantras.[20] Other examples of local esoteric material are the *Dabei tanfa biexing* (Additional Practices and Methods for [Making] an Altar to the Great Compassion),[21] and the *Dabei mantuoluo fa* (Methods [for Making] A Great Compassion Mandala).[22] Both of these texts are devoted to the worship of the Thousand-armed, Thousand-eyed Avalokiteśvara.

Material related to the Faxiang School is relatively abundant in the manuscripts. The popularity of the translator and pilgrim monk Xuanzang (c. 596-664) and his Faxiang School is naturally felt in the early material, but the high period of yogācāra Buddhism in Dunhuang appears to have occurred during the Tibetan occupation (c. 780 to 848). The prevalence of several manuscripts of the *Yujieshi di lun fenmen ji* (The Record of Doctrinal Points of the Yogācārabhūmi Śāstra)[23] by the Chinese translator monk Facheng (fl. ninth century), known from his Tibetan translations as Chos grub,[24] is noteworthy since it is not a standard canonical text, and has only been found in Dunhuang. Other related yogācāra material includes the *Yujie lun shouji* (The Hand Record of the Yogācāra-[bhūmi] Śāstra),[25] and so forth.[26] During the Tibetan occupation, the head of the Chinese Buddhist community (Ch. *sengdu*) was the monk Hongbian (d.c. 868).[27] Although his exact sectarian filiation has not been established, it is clear from his extant writings and biographical account that he was mainly a follower of yogācāra Buddhism. Furthermore, we know from his surviving writings [28] that Hongbian's chief disciple Wuzhen (816-895)[29] was a master of yogācāra or Yujia teachings. It is thought that, due to his great influence as *sengdu*, the teachings and practices connected with this school would have been quite widespread in the Hexi during the latter half of the ninth century. We do have some evidence of a public debate on yogācāra topics which took place after the establishment of the local Chinese reign under the Guiyi Jun, "The Returning Righteous Army," in A.D. 848.[30]

The Tiantai School, another of the major schools of Chinese Buddhism, is represented by a number of texts found among the Dunhuang manuscripts. These works consist of a few scriptures related to the de facto founder of the school, Zhiyi or Zhizhe (537-594), and include works such as the *Guanxin lun* (Contemplation of the Mind),[31] the *Tiantai Zhizhe dashi fayuan wen* (Text of a Prayer Made by the Great Master Zhizhe of Tiantai),[32] the *Tiantai wujie fenmen* (Doctrinal Points of the Five Precepts in Tiantai)[33] and the *Yangzhou Yi chanshi yu nuren wenda shi* (Poetic Dialogue between the Dhyāna Master [Zhi]-yi from Yangzhou and a Girl).[34] The latter work is of course not by Zhiyi, but may have been compiled by his followers or perhaps by adherents of one of the schools of Chan Buddhism. Other works related to the Tiantai School include the *Tiantai fenmen tu* (Chart of the Doctrinal Points in Tiantai),[35] and the *Tiantai Xin chanshi ke* (The Song of the Tiantai Dhyāna Master Xin).[36] Since the practice of Dhyāna (Ch. *chan*) in the form of *zhiguan* (Skr. Śamath-vipaśyanā) occupies a prominent place in the Tiantai teachings, these teachings were probably understood as Chan Buddhism by the monks in Dunhuang. In any case, Tiantai texts often appear in manuscripts together with material related to the so-called Northern Chan (Ch. *Beichan zong*).[37] Both from historical and doctrinal points of view there are great similarities between the contemplative systems of these two schools of Chinese Buddhism.[38] An incomplete manuscript from the period of the Tibetan occupation recording the proceedings of a public discussion, in which Zhiyi and his teaching occurs, shows that Tiantai Buddhism was practiced in Dunhuang at that time.[39]

Examples of Pure Land (Ch. *Jingtu*) practices in Dunhuang abound, and we shall limit ourselves here to some of the more interesting cases. As can be expected, the *Sukhāvatīvyūhā sūtra*,[40] the *Foshuo guan wuliang shou jing* (Sūtra on the Visualization of Amitāyus),[41] and the *Amituo jing*[42] form the basis of Pure Land faith prevalent here as in the central provinces of China. The colophons of the *Sukhāvatīvyūhā sūtra* in S. 2424 from A.D. 710 and that of the *Buddhanāma sūtra*[43] in S. 4601 from A.D. 986 provide good insights into the status which Pure Land faith enjoyed among lay devotees in Dunhuang. In both colophons the faithful dedicate the merit of their pious work of having the sūtra copied to the benefit of the imperial house, their relatives, and the people of the land. In addition to beliefs directly related to the canonical scriptures, we also find the mantra entitled *Amituo fo suoshuo zhou* (The Mantra Spoken by Amitābha Buddha) which in most cases is placed as an appendix to the *Sukhāvatīvyūhā sūtra*.[44] From the colophon of S. 1910 we learn of the method of practice with this mantra, its effectiveness proportional to the number of recitations, and the fact that it was translated from the Sanskrit text.[45] Although we are obviously dealing here with Pure Land Buddhism, it is interesting to note the esoteric element afforded by the use of this mantra. Another passage showing the practice of Buddha invocation (Ch. *nianfo*) in combination with Chan esoteric Buddhism and Faxiang can be found in the manuscript entitled *Nantian zhuguo Putidamo chanshi guanmen* (The Methods of Contemplation of the South Indian Meditation Master Bodhidharma).[46] This manuscript is a typical example of a "cut and paste" text of which we find so many among the Dunhuang material.[47]

Due to the fairly extensive amount of material related to the Sanjie School found in Dunhuang, we must surmise that this controversial Buddhist sect enjoyed considerable popularity there during most of the Tang dynasty.[48] Among this material we find some text fragments dealing with rituals, such as manuals,[49] rules for monastic training,[50] the *Lifo chanhui wen* (Text of a Buddhist Ritual of Repentance),[51] and a text called *Lichan* (Ritual of Repentance).[52] The fact that the latter of these works was copied in Dunhuang as late as A.D. 980 indicates that Sanjie beliefs and practices continued to be in use in Buddhist communities in Shazhou long after the sect had been officially proscribed.[53]

Although it constituted a major doctrinal tradition in Tang Buddhism, relatively few manuscripts among the Dunhuang manuscripts relate to the Huayan School. Most of this material consists of canonical scriptures, and there is almost no concrete evidence that this school had any direct influence on the Buddhist community here. However, the popularity and importance of the *Avatamsaka sūtra* and related scriptures is unquestionable, as can be seen in the paintings illustrating the various famous scenarios, or "transformation-tableaux" (Ch. *bianxiang*), such as the Nine Assemblies in Seven Locations, from this scripture.[54]

Buddho-Daoist Syncretism

Yet another feature typical of Buddhism in Dunhuang is the peculiar Buddhist and Daoist syncretism evident in a large number of the Chinese manuscripts. Among the texts included in this material are works such as the *Benji jing* (Original Limit Sūtra),[55] the *Foshuo sanchu jing* (Buddha Discourses on the Three Kitchens Sūtra),[56] the *Foshuo zhoumei jing* (Buddha Discourses the Sutra on Mantra'ing the Mei [demon?]),[57] the … *jinfang Longshu pusa jiutian Xuan nu zhou* (… the Secret Mantras of Nagārjuna Bodhisattva on the Dark Lady of the Ninth Heaven),[58] the *Shouluo biqiu jing* (The Sūtra of the Bhikshu houluo),[59] the *Qiqian foshen fu jing*,[60] the painted talismanic sheet of S. 5666,[61] the *Guanshiyin pusa fuyin* (The Talismanic Seals of Avalokitesvara Bodhisattva),[62] and the untitled text of P. 2153.[63] In the case of the Benji jing we are obviously dealing with a mixture of prajnāpāramitā and other types of Buddhist doctrine in combination with Daoist Lingbao ideology.[64] The Buddhist texts containing Daoist material are quite evidently examples of a local interpretation of esoteric Buddhism. This tradition started at a relatively early stage to "borrow" a number of original Daoist practices such as the use of talismans (Ch. *fu*), including various kinds of healing devices, all concerned with the purification of the adept and the warding-off of evil influences. Related teachings have also been found elsewhere in Chinese esoteric Buddhist material.[65]

The texts just mentioned are not directly related and their use of borrowed material differs considerably, but common to all of them is their adoption and even integration of doctrinal and other elements, which originated outside their own religious sphere. Although material of this kind is not unique to Dunhuang, these texts still constitute some of the earliest surviving examples of attempts at combining and integrating the doctrines and practices of both creeds.

We still lack information on the historical and practical aspects of this Buddho-Daoist syncretism including questions as to whether it existed as a sectarian reality with proper institutions or was simply practiced by Buddhists and Daoists alike irrespective of faith, the extent of its literature both in Dunhuang and in the central provinces of China, when it arose and the extent of its influence, and so forth. On the Daoist side, an investigation of the Buddhist influence on the Lingbao School prominent during the Tang is likely to provide an additional perspective on the background of this development.[66]

Popular Buddhist Cults in Dunhuang

A brief look at material related to popular beliefs and practices among Buddhists in Dunhuang reveals that several cults were prevalent. Although it is obvious that most of these cults operated within the structures of an orthodox saṅgha, they were generally unrelated to any particular school of Buddhism. Rather they provide evidence of the popularity of various Buddhist deities transcending both sectarian and institutional barriers.[67]

As was the case in Khotan and other places along the Silk Road, the cult dedicated to the Heavenly King Vaiśravana also enjoyed considerable popularity in Dunhuang. Scattered among the manuscript collections we find an abundance of material dedicated to him of which mention can be made of manuscript S. 4622, entitled *Longxing si Pishamen tianwang lingyan ji* (The Longxing Temple[68] Record of the Divine Responses [to prayers] by the Heavenly King Vaiśravana),[69] an original composition dated to A.D. 873, which refers to both the *Pishamen shenmu jing* (The Vaiśravana Mother of Spirits Sūtra)[70] and the important *Suvarnaprabhāsa sūtra*;[71] manuscript S. 5598, which is a prayer from the tenth century; and the *Foshuo beifang dasheng Pishamen tianwang qiqing jing* (Buddha Speaks the Northern Direction Great Holy Vaiśravana Heavenly King Prayer Sūtra).[72] A colophon to a copy of the *Renwang jing* (The Sūtra of the Benevolent Kings)[73] said to date back to A.D. 531 is one of the earliest examples of Vaiśravana worship in Dunhuang.

Another prominent cult was that devoted to Avalokiteśvara Bodhisattva. Among the manuscripts we find material related to both the exoteric as well as the esoteric aspects of this cult including texts such as *Guanyin li* (Ritual for Avalokiteśvara) based on the *Saddharmapundarīka sūtra*,[74] the *Dabei qiqing* (Invoking the Great Compassion), and a ritual dedicated to the worship of the Thousand-armed Avalokiteśvara of esoteric Buddhism.[75]

The Pure Land cult was also very popular and there are numerous manuscripts which point to various aspects of its local practice. Among this material we find a booklet from A.D. 955,[76] the *Wuhui nianfo zan* (Hymns for Repeating the Buddha's Name at the Five Assemblies),[77] and *Sifang jingtu zanwen* (Hymn Texts of the Western Pure Land).[78] The colophon of S. 4553 is a good example of the popular practice of having a sūtra copied as a means of accruing good karma to be transferred to parents and ancestors, so that they may be reborn in the Amitābha's paradise.

Tibetan Buddhism in Dunhuang

After the Tibetan conquest of Turfan and Dunhuang closed off the Silk Road to the Chinese, Buddhism in the oasis became isolated from eastern influences and a considerable impact from Tibetan tantric Buddhism was felt there as evidenced by the large amount of esoteric material from the collections in the Bibliothèque Nationale in Paris and in the India Office Library, London. For some unknown reason much of this material remains largely unstudied and we have good reason to suppose that considerable information shedding light on early Tibetan tantric Buddhism as well as the practice of Tibetan Buddhism in Dunhuang in general could be obtained from these manuscripts.

Research on the Tibetan Dunhuang material related to Buddhism has to a large extent been conducted by Japanese scholars, who have generally tended to focus on aspects touching upon Chinese Buddhism, especially on Chan and the so-called "Debate of Samye,"[79] with little regard for the importance of early, and mainly original Tibetan esoteric material.[80]

One of the main figures in ongoing research on Tibetan esoteric material from Dunhuang is undoubtedly Samten Gyaltsen Karmey who, in his study of the early Dzogs-chen tradition, has unveiled an important doctrinal aspect of early Tibetan tantric Buddhism.[81] The teachings, as represented by this Dzogs-chen material with their absolutist approach to the attainment of enlightenment, are reminiscent of the later doctrines on non-duality of Atiyogā as practiced by the adherents of the Nyieng-ma School of Tibetan Buddhism. It is of course always dangerous to take the existence of a particular type of scriptures as being generally representative, but in any case the works studied by Karmey may be seen as indications of the type of tantric discourse that was prevalent among members of the Tibetan-reading saṅgha in the Shazhou area during the first half of the ninth century.

Although the tantric material is extensive, the Tibetan material from Dunhuang is clearly dominated by standard Buddhist canonical material. Especially the sūtras and śāstras belonging to the *prajñāpāramitā* class, as well as the countless copies of the Daśabhūmika sūtra, give a clear indication that the Tibetan canon of the early ninth century was very much grounded in the Indian mahāyāna tradition. Likewise, the popularity of the Amitābha cult among Tibetan Buddhists in Shazhou was also great as is apparent from the large number of extant manuscripts related to this cult including various esoteric works.[82]

Likewise, the cult of Avalokiteśvara was also popular among the Tibetans living in Dunhuang as reflected in the many scriptures devoted to the cult of this important bodhisattva. Thus we find several versions of the *Ārya Avalokiteśvarasya mamāstā śataka*,[83] the *Amoghapāśa-hrdaya dhāranī*,[84] and the *Avalokiteśvara-bodhi-cintāmani-cakra strotra*,[85] all of which are esoteric scriptures. This indicates that several forms of the bodhisattva in question were worshipped including the Four-armed Avalokiteśvara, Amoghapāśa, and Cintāmanicakra. This is perhaps not so surprising, since it matches well with the Chinese material, and can also be corroborated from the banner- and wall-paintings.[86] Likewise the Thousand-armed, Thousand-eyed Avalokiteśvara figure was also worshipped as indicated by the existence of the Tibetan version of the *Nīlakanthaka sūtra* translated by Facheng from a Chinese version.[87]

We also find the popularity of the *prajñāpāramitā* as reflected in the tantric material. Among these manuscripts there are several scriptures such as the *Prajñāpāramitā-hrdaya-vrtti* [88] and the *Prajñāpāramitā-hrdaya-vyākhyā*,[89] which contain lengthy and integrated sections of dhāraṇīs and mantras.

Here it is important to note that the early Tibetan Tripitaka, as evident from the manuscripts found in Dunhuang, was still in the process of attaining its full form and size, something which may account for the many excerpts and hybrid texts. This is especially the case with regards to the tantric texts, many of which consist of a series of excerpts and passages lifted from a variety of different—sometimes quite unrelated—scriptures to form a more or less coherent whole.

However, large amounts of the early Tibetan tantric Buddhist material is still untouched as mentioned previously, and further research is needed in order to obtain a more detailed and precise knowledge of the tantric literature available in Dunhuang and the particular rituals that were practiced.[90] A now classical study on the tantric material by Kenneth Eastman has revealed that by the early ninth century full-fledged Indo-Tibetan Vajrayāna texts were in vogue in Dunhuang.[91] Part of Eastman's unpublished research has also involved the restoring to its original format of an untitled eighty-five folia manuscript from two fragments in the India Office Library and in the Bibliothèque Nationale respectively.[92] This text, the title of which is missing, is a compilation of material from various tantric sources and includes practices such as exorcism, ritualized sexuality (Tib. *yabyum*), homa or fire rituals, and so forth.

Sino-Tibetan Buddhist Developments

Chinese and Tibetan Buddhism entered into a sort of synthesis in which their respective literature became mixed and the object of study by both parties. Among the manuscripts there are many Sino-Tibetan bilingual or partly bilingual works which include the following categories: traditional scriptures (sūtras, śāstras, vinaya, etc.); library inventories; names of temples and copyists; lists of doctrinal terminology; and dhāraṇīs and mantras.

Although it is unclear to what extent Chinese Buddhists in Dunhuang were influenced by Indo-Tibetan Vajrayāna, those members of the Chinese saṅgha who were able to read or understand Tibetan are likely to have been exposed to these doctrines and practices. However, in the central and eastern provinces of China, tantric Buddhist practices of the Annutara and Mahāyoga types never exerted any influence on Chi-

nese Buddhism to speak of.[93] Not until the advent of the Tanguts and
Mongols during the twelfth and thirteenth centuries, and with them the
Tibetan lamas, did Vajrayāna Buddhism gain a foothold in China
proper.[94] Even then, the practices propagated by the Tibetan lamas never
really caught on among the Chinese population, but were mainly
restricted to the Imperial courts during the Yuan and the following two
dynasties in varying degrees. Hence, the presence of early Indo-Tibetan
Vajrayāna Buddhism in Dunhuang during the late eighth century to the
early ninth century is yet another feature which is unique to the Buddhist community here, indicating its position as a central locus for the
exchange of religious ideas and practices. Finally, it is more than likely
that the influence of Tibetan Buddhism lingered on in Dunhuang several years after the area had been retaken by the Chinese in A.D. 848.

A number of questions remain concerning the Buddhist community in Dunhuang such as the number of temples in use during the
Tang, the relationship between temples and caves, the sectarian affiliation of the temples, the distribution of the sexes in the temples, popular
festivals, temple schools,[95] the Dunhuang temples and their sponsors,[96]
and so forth. In recent years there has been an increasing number of
Japanese and Chinese studies on some of these aspects; however, many
issues have yet to be clarified.

During the Tibetan occupation of Dunhuang, and possibly later,
there was a relatively large Tibetan Buddhist community in the Shazhou
area. Although we do not have much information on this as yet, there
are indications in both the Chinese and Tibetan material that Tibetan
monks and nuns lodged in the Chinese temples there.[97] Some of the best
indications on the cohabitation of the Sino-Tibetan saṅgha are provided
by the bilingual library catalogues, Sino-Tibetan Buddhist liturgy,[98] and
lists of terminology. In a manuscript from the library of the Dayun Temple dated to around A.D. 800, we have a relatively strong indication that
the inmates of the Dayun Temple consisted of monks of both Tibetan
and Chinese nationalities.[99] On the basis of information dating to the
first half of the ninth century, the important Longxing Temple, which
was one of the largest Buddhist institutions in Shazhou, is known to
have kept both Chinese and Tibetan scriptures in its library. This may be
taken as indirect evidence that the saṅgha in this temple consisted of
both Chinese and Tibetan monks.[100]

In this regard, PT. 994 provides interesting data, as it consists of a
list in Tibetan, transcribed from Chinese, of the great temples of
Shazhou.[101] The exact implications of this list can only be guessed at,
since it is only a fragment; however, it appears to have been an official
document—perhaps a census paper—used by the Tibetan bureaucracy
during the occupation. It should be compared with the Chinese manu-

script of S. 2729 (1) which consists of a list of nine monasteries and their inmates dated to A.D. 800. The PT. 994 list is given here together with the corresponding Chinese names:

(a) Lun-khun zi   = Longxing si
(b) De-yan zi   = Dayun si
(c) Pho-ko zi   = Puguang si (a nunnery)[102]
(d) Gyan-yan zi   = Yongan si
(e) Le-zu-ci zi   = Lingxiu si (?) (a nunnery)[103]
(f) Ze-ho zi   = ?
(g) Khye-yan zi   = Kaiyuan si
(h) ... yon zi   = Baoen si (?)
(i) An-kog zi   = Anguo si (a nunnery)[104]
(j) De-cin zi   = Dasheng si (a nunnery)[105]
(k) Kyim-ko-mye zi = Jin guangming si
(l) Le-tu zi   = Lingtu si
(m) Hyen-tig zi   = Xiande si
(n) Gyen-mye zi   = Qianming si
(o) Le-te zi   = Liantai si
(p) Je-tu zi   = Jingtu si
(q) Pam-kye zi   = Sanjie si

Other indications of Sino-Tibetan communities are provided by manuscript P. 2449RV containing prayers for the Tibetan military governor in Guazhou,[106] and the untitled manuscript P. 2358V (4) which consists of various addresses by local dignitaries on the occasion of the construction of a Buddhist temple. Among the participants mentioned in this document are several Tibetans.

It is known for certain that the local Chinese and Tibetan clans cooperated in various large-scale Buddhist rituals and pious works. In the two related manuscripts, PT. 1000 and PT. 1001,[107] we find evidence of such an intercultural Buddhist project.[108] Both manuscripts were composed to commemorate the occasion of the donations of a series of major Buddhist scriptures such as the *Prātimoksa*, the apocryphal *Fanwang jing* (Brahmajāla sūtra), the *Vajracchedikā*, the *Vimalakīrti sūtra*, the *Praj'nāpāramitā-hrdaya sūtra*, etc. by a group of prominent monks and nuns belonging to the Chinese families Yin, Li, Pei, Shi, Song, Zhang, Wang, Cao, among others, and the Tibetan families Sñiṅ-choms, Stoṅ-sar, and Rgod-sar. On the basis of this information, we are provided with a vivid picture of a common type of Sino-Tibetan joint venture carried out by the Buddhists of Dunhuang towards the end of the Tibetan dominion over the area.

An equally important Tibetan manuscript for an understanding of Sino-Tibetan relations in Shazhou during the Tibetan occupation is

PT. 999.[109] The manuscript is dated to the "year of the Rat," i.e., A.D. 844,[110] just four years prior to the collapse of Tibetan power in Hexi. The first part mentions how the local people of Shazhou formerly had copies of the *Sukhāvatīvyūha sūtra* in both Chinese and Tibetan made as an offering to King Khri gTsug-lde-brtsan, also known as Ral-pa-can (rl. 815-838), who is referred to in the text as "Divine Prince."[111] It is further stated that upon completion, the scriptures were housed in the library of the Longxing Temple. Later, in A.D. 844 some 2,700 members of the local population collected funds with which to hold a large communal celebration to commemorate either the birth or ascension to the Tibetan throne by Od-srungs (Kaśyapa), the son of the Lady of Phen, one of the wives of Ral-pa-can, who ruled the disintegrating kingdom as Queen Dowager.[112] The manuscript ends with the information that those in charge of the project were the Chinese monk, Hongben (Lhong Bel), the Saṅgha Overseer, whom we have already discussed above, and an important Tibetan monk, possibly a vajracāryā, by the name of Wangchok.[113] Although there are several unclear points in PT. 999, it would seem that the copying of the numerous volumes of the *Sukhāvatīvyūha sūtra* was done as part of a nationwide prayer for the longevity of or perhaps even rebirth in the Pure Land of Ral-pa-can. This first event mentioned in the manuscript probably took place around A.D. 838, that is to say the year he passed away, or perhaps slightly before. The second event mentioned in PT. 999 describes how the local Buddhist families of Shazhou were mobilized under the spiritual leadership of Hongben and a Tibetan Buddhist leader to celebrate the continuation of the Tibetan royal line. This information not only provides us with further evidence that the saṅgha in Shazhou was composed of both Tibetan and Chinese monks and nuns, but also that there was a shared leadership of the saṅgha.

Conclusion

The picture that emerges of the sectarian developments in Dunhuang—despite the rather abundant written material with obvious sectarian affiliations—is clearly one of Buddhist pluralism and harmonization, including adaptation and modification, of a wide range of diverse beliefs and practices; a spiritual situation as it were in which the practical implications of sectarian boundaries were negligible. In short, during the Tang and Five Dynasties Period, Buddhism in Shazhou—and by extension in most of Hexi—expressed itself as a common denomination which essentially accommodated all types of beliefs and practices in an ecumenical spirit across all sectarian divisions. Except for one example in which the teachings of the Three Stages School are repudiated, there is virtually no real evidence of sectarianism in the Buddhist manuscripts, quite the contrary.[114] Furthermore, a brief survey of information on the temples in Dunhuang shows—to the extent that information can be had—that the saṅgha members followed a combination of methods based on the teachings and practices of several schools including Chan, Tiantai, Faxiang Mizong, and Jingtu.[115]

Whether this observation also applies to the relationship between the Chinese and Tibetan Buddhist communities and their respective teachings is another matter, which, despite its obvious importance, has only been treated in passing. On the basis of what has been presented here, it is clear that there were Sino-Tibetan Buddhist communities in Dunhuang during the Tibetan occupation, but how they functioned in practice is still not clear. What is known, however, is that during the Tibetan occupation of Shazhou we find no signs of inter-religious strife between the members of the Chinese and the Tibetan saṅghas. As we have seen, on several occasions they participated in unison in major communal rituals and in various pious projects.

Syncretism in Dunhuang was not only limited to the Buddhist schools and their teachings, but also applied to Buddhism and Daoism. As we have seen, there is a fairly large number of texts which can only be explained as a mixture between these two major Chinese traditions. The historical side of this Buddho-Daoist syncretism needs to be further investigated, not only with regard to the religious literature from both traditions which was a product of mutual influence, but also as regards shared beliefs and even practices.

Popular Buddhist cults in Dunhuang mainly followed the same trend as evidenced in Tang China. Among the major cults were those devoted to Amitābha, Avalokiteśvara, and Vaiśravana, something which is both evident from the manuscripts as well as from the banner-paintings and frescos. Closely connected with the popular aspects of Buddhism in Shazhou was the use of written and printed talismans. Beliefs and practices involving these cryptographs and magical charts—a system originally developed within Daoism—were eventually taken over by the Buddhists for whom they became equally important. The extensive material featuring talismans reveals that they were both common and popular.

An issue which has not been discussed in this chapter relates to the way in which Buddhism was practiced by the different social classes in Dunhuang. Also a more thorough presentation of the major figures active in the Buddhist milieu, and their spiritual achievements, would add more substance to our knowledge of religious life in Dunhuang. This question would also involve an investigation of the relationship between the leading local clans and the establishment of various temples and cave-sanctuaries at Mogao. Research along these lines is therefore likely to yield further information on Buddhist practice and its importance in the social context, and will thus be a worthwhile topic for future research.

Notes

1. Both the Daoist and Confucian traditions are prominently represented in the Dunhuang manuscripts; however, as they flourished mainly within the Chinese cultural sphere, their importance for the intercultural dialogue along the Silk Roads remains negligible.
2. See for example Stanley Weinstein, *Buddhism under the T'ang* (London and New York: Cambridge University Press, 1987); Kenneth Ch'en, *Buddhism in China: A Historical Survey* (Princeton: Princeton University Press, 1964), pp. 213-86; and Edwin O. Reischauer, trans., *Ennin's Diary: The Record of a Pilgrimage to China in Search of the Law* (New York: The Ronald Press Co., 1955).
3. A discussion on Dunhuang Buddhism during the period of Xixia domination, i.e., A.D. 1038-1226, is not included in the present paper. Obviously, Buddhism was still a prominent tradition in the area, and it received imperial patronage as the national creed of the Tanguts.
4. Among the most important of these developments was the type of esoteric Buddhism expounded by Amoghavajra (705-774), one of the major patriarchs of Zhenyan Buddhism. Around A.D. 741 he left Tang to go to South India after new esoteric scriptures, and returned in A.D. 747 with new manuscripts. During the years A.D. 754-756, the master lived in Wuwei near Liangzhou in Gansu, and it was during his sojourn there that he translated a number of the texts we find among the Dunhuang manuscripts. See *Song gaoseng zhuan* (Song History of High Monks), ch. 1, T. 2061, 712c-713a. Among the Dunhuang manuscripts, there are several copies of the works translated or edited by Amoghavajra. See P. 2105V, 2197 (10.1), 2368, 3022R (1), S. 6897V (3), etc.
5. For a short note on the different schools of Buddhism, see S. 4459. Unfortunately, it does not give any indication of sectarian divisions in Dunhuang.
6. For a highly useful survey of Japanese research on Dunhuang material related to Chan Buddhism, see Tanaka Ryōshō, "A Historical Outline of Japanese Research on the Chinese Chan Writings from Dunhuang," *SCEAR* 2 (1989): pp. 141-69. See also his major work, *Tonkō zenshū no kenkyū* (A Study of the Dunhuang Chan School) (Tokyo: Daito shuppansha, 1983).
7. H.H. Sørensen, "Observations on the Characteristics of the Chinese Chan Manuscripts from Dunhuang," *SCEAR* 2 (1989): pp. 115-39.
8. S. 4173.
9. S. 1635.
10. See S. 330, 347, 532, 1183, 2448, 4115, 4844, 4915, 5313, etc.

11. The Seventh Patriarch in the transmission of Southern Chan. His dates are A.D. 684-758. For a recent study, see Li Xueqin, "Chanzong zaoqi wenwu de chongyao faxian" (Important Discovery of Early Artefacts Relating to the Chan School), *Wenwu* 3 (1992): pp. 71-75. See also, "Luoyang Tang Shenhui heshang shenta taji qingli" (Inventory of the Stūpa-base of the Burial Stūpa of Ven. Shenhui from Luoyang under the Tang), *Wenwu* 3 (1992): pp. 64-67, 75.
12. See S. 4634, 6103 (2), 6923V (3 & 6), etc.
13. See S. 1947. This manuscript is dated A.D. 863. See also the brief report by Ma De, "Wu heshang—Wu heshang ku—Wujia ku (Ven. Wu—The Cave of Ven. Wu— The Cave of the Wu Family)," *DY* 3 (1987): pp. 62-64.
14. This work is more or less identical to T. 1315. For a similar text from the Dunhuang hoard, see S. 6897V (3).
15. For a study of this scripture and its related ritual, see Charles D. Orzech, "Esoteric Buddhism and the Shishi in China," *The Esoteric Buddhist Tradition*, SBS Monographs 2, edited by Henrik H. Sørensen (Copenhagen, 1994), pp. 51-72.
16. This copy is based on the translation by the monk Buddhapāli of Kabul from A.D. 683.
17. See S. 2566. This manuscript appears to be dated A.D. 918.
18. T. 895.
19. P. 2351 (only pin 5 to 9 is extant).
20. Examples of this can be found in S. 165, S. 4493, S. 4494, S. 5589, S. 5621, etc.
21. S. 2498 (2).
22. S. 2716RV.
23. P. 2035, S. 2552. See T. 2801.
24. For a very comprehensive study on the life and work of this monk, see Ueyama Daishuin, *Tonkō bukkyō no kenkyū*, pp. 84-246. See also Paul Demiéville, *Récents Travaux sur Touen-houang* (Leiden: E.J. Brill, 1970), pp. 47-60.
25. P. 2036, 2037, 2061, etc. This scripture was also studied by Tibetan monks. See also, P. 2061 which contains annotation in Tibetan. An extensive discussion by Ueyama can be found in his *Tonkō bukkyō no kenkyū*, pp. 219-46.
26. Ueyama Daishuin, "Tonk» shinshutsu no yuishiki kei ronso" (A New Discovery of Related Yogācāra Treatises and Commentaries from Dunhuang), *Ryūkoku Daigaku ronsō* 428 (1986): pp. 110-34.
27. S. 779. See also PT. 999, 1079, 1198, 1200, 1201, 1202, Tibetan documents in which Hongbian occurs.
28. Ibid., *La Vie et les Oeuvres de Wou-tchen* (816-95). See P. 2236, which consists of a copy of the Yogācārābhūmi Şāstra, which belonged to Wuzhen. For a recent Chinese study of this monk and the Buddhist works he collated, see Qi Chenjun and Han Qin, "Hexi bu sengtong Tang Wuzhen zho pin he jianzai wenxian xinian" (On the Works Collated by Tang Wuzhen, the Sangha Overseer of Hexi together with a Chronology of the Documents), *DX* 2 (1993): pp. 5-15.
29. Chen Tsu-lung, "La Vie et les Oeuvres de Wou-tchen (816-895): Contribution à l'Histoire de Touen-houang," *PEFEO* 60 (1966). See also Paul Demiéville, *Récents Travaux sur Touen-houang* (Leiden: E.J. Brill, 1970), pp. 61-64.
30. P. 3097RV. For a study of Buddhism in Dunhuang under the Guiyi Jun, see Tohi Toshikazu, "Kigi Gun to Tonkō bukkyō kyōdan" (Guiyi Jun and the Religious Order of Buddhism in Dunhuang), *Tonkō no rekishi* (The History of Dunhuang), edited by Enoki Ichiyū. 2 (Tokyo: Kōza Tonkō, 1980): pp. 259-92.
31. T. 1920. Not to be confused with the work by Northern Chan Master Shenxiu (605-705) under the same name.

32. P. 3183. See Paul Magnin, "Une Copie Amidique du T'ien-t'ai Tche-tchö Ta-che Fa-yuan Wen: Une étude sur le manuscrit P. 3183," *CETH* 1, edited by M. Soymié (Geneva: École pratique des Hautes Études, 1979): pp. 99-114.

33. S. 1310. Giles only mentions the work as an untitled doctrinal work of Tiantai provenance, see p. 168a.

34. S. 646 (4), S. 2672, S. 3441 (2).

35. P. 2131. See T. 2824.

36. This work is not extant, but mentioned in P. 2250R.

37. See. S. 2165, S. 2669, S. 3558, S. 3559, P. 3434, P. 3777, etc. For a major study of this tradition, see John McRae, "The Northern School and the Formation of Early Ch'an Buddhism." *SEAB* 3 (Honolulu, 1986). See also Bernard Faure, *La volonté d'orthodoxie dans le bouddhisme chinois* (Paris: CNRS, 1988); and "Le bouddhisme Ch´an en mal d'histoire: Genèse d'une tradition religieuse dans la Chine des Tang," *PEFEO* 98 (Paris, 1989).

38. Sekiguchi Shindai, "Zenshū to Tendaishū to no kōshō (The Chan and Tiantai Schools and Their Relationship)," *Taishō Daigaku kenkyū kiyō* 44 (1959): pp. 39-75. This relationship is briefly discussed by John McRae in "The Northern School of Chinese Chan Buddhism" (Ph.D. diss., Yale University, 1984), pp. 73-76.

39. P. 3256.

40. T. 360, 361, 362.

41. T. 365.

42. T. 366.

43. T. 447.

44. S. 317, S. 2107, S. 4930, etc.

45. For a full translation of this colophon, see Giles, p. 103ab.

46. S. 6958. For a study of this manuscript, see Tanaka Ryōshō, *Tonkō zenshū bunkan no kenkyū*, pp. 213-36.

47. In my survey, "Observations on the Characteristics of the Chinese Chan Manuscripts from Dunhuang," *SCEAR* 2 (1989): pp. 115-39, I argue for the existence of a common practice in Dunhuang of employing text modules, i.e., passages or sections from standard writings, and combining them to form a "new" scripture. Although the paper deals primarily with this issue within the framework of Chan Buddhism, I believe that we can observe many examples of this "cut-and-paste literature" in other Chinese material related to both Buddhism and Daoism. See S. 2669, P. 3913, et seq.

48. For a fairly comprehensive overview of the doctrines of this sect, see *Sangai kyō zankan* (Fragmentary Scrolls of the Sanjie Teaching), edited by Yabuki Keiki (Reprint Taipei: Xinwen feng, 1983). See also the pioneering study by Yabuki Keiki, *Sangai kyō no kenkyū* (A Study of the Sanjie Teachings) (Tokyo: Iwanami, 1927). A recent study by Antonino Forte brings some of the obscure points in the older studies up to date, see his "La Secte des Trois Stades et l'Hérésie de Devadatta: Yabuki Keiki corrigé par Tang Yongtong," *BEFEO* 74 (1985): pp. 469-76. See also "The Relativity of the Concept of Orthodoxy in Chinese Buddhism: Chih-sheng's Indictment of Shih-li and the Proscription of the Dharma Mirror Sūtra," in *Chinese Buddhist Apocrypha*, edited by Robert E. Buswell (Honolulu: University of Hawaii Press, 1990), pp. 207-38.

49. S. 5633.

50. S. 190. Dated to the seventh century.

51. S. 2574.

52. S. 5562.

53. For a study of the persecution of the Sanjie School, see Mark Edward Lewis, "Suppression of the Three Stages Sect," in *Chinese Buddhist Apocrypha*, edited by Robert E. Buswell (Honolulu: University of Hawaii Press, 1990), pp. 207-38.

54. The Huanyan tableaux as wall-paintings can be found in caves no. 6, 9, 12, 25, 44, 45, 53, 55, 61, 76, etc. For a complete list, see *Dunhuang Mogao ku neirong zonglu* (Record of the Contents of the Mogao Caves in Dunhuang), compiled by Dunhuang wenwu yanjiu (Beijing: Wenwu chuban she, 1982), pp. 227-28. For a very fine, unique example of a Huayan *bianxiang* in the form of a large banner-painting, see Jacques Giès, "Un témoignage du bouddhisme impérial tang à Dunhuang," *Les Routes de la soie: Patrimoine commun, identités plurielles. Mémoire des peuples* (Paris: Éditions UNESCO, 1994), pp. 65-79 (see p. 71). Note, however, that the article for some unknown reason does not provide a systematic or comprehensive discussion of the painting in question.

55. Full title *Taixuan zhenyi benji miao jing* (Wonderful Scripture of the Highest Mystery and Original Limit), P. 2392, 2393, 2398, 2463, 2366, 2331, 2437, 2379R, etc., S. 3135, 3563, 3387, 3139, etc. See also the commentary, *Benji jing shu* (Commentary to the Benji jing), P. 2361.

56. P. 3032. This apocryphal sūtra is mentioned in the *Kaiyuan shijiao lu* (The Kaiyuan Buddhist Catalogue), T. 2154, p. 672a. Some similarity with S. 2673 (T. 2894).

57. S. 4524. This manuscript consists of a fragment of the apocryphal sūtra *Foshuo shoumei jing* (Buddha Discourses on How to Use Mantras Against the Mei-demons), which contains seven talismans at the end. See T. 2882, which is based on the near complete manuscript of S. 418. This version of the scripture does not have the talismans however.

58. S. 2615V. Even from the title we can ascertain the Buddho-Daoist content of this text as it refers both to Nagārjuna, the founder of the madhyāmika system of thought, and to the Dark Lady, the reputed consort of the Yellow Emperor (Huang Di). See also the fragment contained in P. 3835V° (4). Another related apocryphal scripture is the *Longshu wuming lun* (Nagārjuna's Treatise on the Five Realizations), T. 1420, attributed to Nagārjuna.

59. S. 6881. The manuscript is dated to the seventh century.

60. T. 2904.

61. According to Giles a "coloured picture of the star-god Rāhu, with a prayer by a woman aged 64 begging his favour and protection against misfortunes that come." See Giles, p. 197a. However, the lower part of this painted sheet of paper also contains a large talisman referred to as a "talismanic dhāranī" (Ch. *fu tuoluoni*) in the inscription. The spiritual power of this talismanic dhāranī is said to effect the assistance of all the Buddhas in the ten directions.

62. S. 2498 (1). This is basically an esoteric Buddhist text containing dhāranīs from different sources.

63. P. 2153. The editors of CMCT, vol. 1 (J. Gernet and Wu Chi-ya) treat this manuscript as one single apocryphal work under the title *Guanshiyin pusa ruyi lun tuoluoni ... bing biexing fa* (Methods of Further Practices of Avalokitésvara Bodhisattva Wish-fulfilling Wheel Dhāranī), see ibid., pp. 97-98. The main deity is the Vajra Youth (Ch. *Jingang tongzi*). A brief perusal of the manuscript reveals that we are dealing with a ritual text composed of several excerpts of various individual works including the talismans from the *Qiqian foshen fu jing*.

64. Wu Chi-yu, trans., *Pen-tsi king: Livre du terme originel. Mission Paul Pelliot*. Documents conservés à la Bibliothèque nationale, I (Paris, 1960).

65. T. 1219, T. 1238, T. 1265, T. 1420 etc.

66. For a study of the Buddhist influence on the Lingbao tradition, see Stephen R. Bokenkamp, "Stages of Transcendence: The Bhūmi Concept in Taoist Scripture," in *Chinese Buddhist Apocrypha*, edited by Robert E. Buswell, Jr, (Honolulu: University of Hawaii Press, 1990), pp. 119-48. See also the comparative edition of Buddhist texts and text passages contained in the Daozang (The Daoist Canon), see Kamata Shigeo, *Dōzō nai Buōkyōshisō shiryō shuūsei* (A Selection of Buddhist Material Contained in the Daozang) (Tokyo, 1986). See also the review by A. Seidel in *CEA* 3 (1987): pp. 226-27.

67. For a discussion of the relationship between certain dated manuscripts and religious practices in Dunhuang, see Paul Magnin, "Pratique Religieuse et Manuscrits Datés," *CEA* 3 (1987): pp. 131-41.

68. The Longxing Temple was one of the seventeen large temples in Shazhou.

69. S. 381 (3).

70. This is an apocryphal sūtra, which has not been identified so far.

71. T. 664.

72. S. 5576. This is a short apocryphal sūtra intended for liturgical purposes.

73. S. 4528.

74. S. 5559.

75. S. 663, see T. 2843. See also S. 5564 (1), S. 5650, and S. 6110.

76. S. 5572. See Giles, 191-92.

77. P. 2147V (2). For a related manuscript see P. 2130 (2).

78. Beijing guo no. 41.

79. For a brief survey of Japanese research on early Tibetan Chan, see Ueyama Daishuin, "The Study of Tibetan Ch'an Manuscripts Recovered from Tun-huang: A Review of the Field and its Prospects," in *Early Ch'an in China and Tibet*, edited by L. Lancaster and W. Lai. (Berkeley Buddhist Series 5) (Berkeley: University of California Press, 1983), pp. 327-49. See also the excellent studies on the issues of the Samye debate by Luis O. Gómez based on the Tibetan material from Dunhuang, viz. "The Direct and Gradual Approaches of Zen Master Mahāyāna: Fragments of the Teachings of Mo-ho-yen," in *Studies in Ch'an and Hua-yen*, edited by Robert M. Gimello and Peter N. Gregory, *SEAB* 1 (Honolulu: University of Hawaii Press, 1983): pp. 69-167, and "Purifying Gold: The Metaphor of Effort and Intuition in Buddhist Thought and Practice," in *Sudden and Gradual: Approaches to Enlightenment in Chinese Thought*, edited by Peter N. Gregory, *SEAB* 5, (Honolulu: University of Hawaii Press, 1987): pp. 67-165.

80. For one exception, see Ueyama Daishuin, "Peyan cho no daiyuga bunken: P. tib. 837 ni tsuite" (The Mahāyoga Literature Written by dPal-dbyans: Concerning PT. 837), *Bukkyō bunka kenkyūsho kiyo* 16 (1977): pp. 1-13. See also his *Tonkō bukkyō no kenkyū*. For a review in English of this important work, see *SCEAR* 3 (1990): pp. 136-39.

81. *The Great Perfection: A Philosophical and Meditative Teaching of Tibetan Buddhism* (Leiden, New York, Copenhagen, and Cologne, 1988). It contains a full discussion of the manuscripts ST. 594, ST. 647, and ST. 698 (2), together with annotated translations.

82. See ST. 308-10, 463 (2), etc. For examples of the esoteric works, see ST. 452 (3), and ST. 724.

83. ST. 315 (1) and ST. 316 (1).

84. ST. 311, ST. 312 (2) and ST. 372 (2). There is also a description of an Amoghapāśa manrala. See ST. 384 (2).

85. ST. 311 (3).

86. For a discussion on the iconography related to these forms of Avalokiteśvara, see Henrik H. Sørensen, "Typology and Iconography in the Esoteric Buddhist Art of Dunhuang," in *Silk Road Art and Archaeology* 2 (1991/92): pp. 285-349 (especially pp. 302-9).

87. ST. 214. See also the related Avalokiteśvara-mahā-kārunikāya namah, ST. 323 (2).

88. See ST. 122

89. See fx. ST 123.

90. See PT. 41, PT. 42, PT. 240, PT. 241, PT. 283, PT. 286, PT. 288, etc. In fact there are numerous Vajrayāna ritual texts among the Tibetan Dunhuang manuscripts, a study of which would prove of great value for our further understanding of the formation of early Tibetan Vajrayāna in general and of Tibetan tantric practices in Dunhuang in particular.

91. K. Eastman, "Tibetan Tantric Texts at Dunhuang," paper presented at the international symposium, "The Esoteric Buddhist Tradition" (Samso College, Denmark, 21-24 August 1989). See also his earlier study, "Mahāyoga Texts at Tun-huang," in *Ryukoku daigaku zō tibeto go bunken no kenhyū* (A Study of the Tibetan Literature in the Library of the Ryukoku University), edited by Ueyama Daishuin (Kyoto, 1983), pp. 42-60.

92. ST. 419 and PT. 42

93. In the case of the Tanguts, who controlled Dunhuang and the Gansu corridor from the early eleventh century up to A.D. 1228 when their rule was terminated by the Mongols, Tibetan tantric practices enjoyed a high status and appear to have been rather influential. See the list of Tangut Buddhist scriptures in Nishida Tatsuo, *Seika bun Kegon kyō* (The Avataṅsaka Sūtra in Xixia Script), 3 vols (Kyoto: Kyoto daigaku bungaku bu, 1977), vol. 3, pp. 13-59. See also *Xixia wenwu* (Cultural Material of the Xixia), edited by Shi Jinbo et al. (Beijing, 1988), pl. 81-7, 99, and pp. 295, 297. This book contains fine pictorial material, but the text as such is useless.

94. Here it is interesting to note that we find wall-paintings in Dunhuang (cave nos. 95 and 265), bespeaking the tantric Buddhist influence during the Yuan dynasty. See Su Bai, "Dunhuang Mogao ku mijiao yiji zhaji" (A Record of Historical Remains of Esoteric Buddhism in the Mogao Caves at Dunhuang), part 2, *Wenwu* 10 (1989): pp. 79-84. For a discussion of this material, see Henrik H. Sørensen, "Typology and Iconography in the Esoteric Buddhist Art of Dunhuang," in *Silk Road Art and Archaeology* 2 (1991/92): pp. 285-349 (especially pp. 319-22). See also *Art Treasures of Dunhuang*, edited by the Dunhuang Institute for Cultural Relics (Hong Kong, 1981), pl. 113, and p. 236.

95. Li Zhenyu, "Tang Song shidai de Dunhuang xuexiao," *DY* 1 (1986): pp. 39-47.

96. Jiang Boqin, "Lun Dunhuang siyuan de cangzhu baixing," *DY* 1 (1981): pp. 43-55. For a fine study of the sponsors of various caves based on stele inscriptions, see Yi Yongning, "Dunhuang Mogao ku beiwen lu ji you guan wenti," part 1, *DY* 1 (1981): pp. 56-79; part 2, *DY* 2 (1982): pp. 108-26. For a study of the economy and functioning of the Dunhuang temples during the ninth to tenth centuries, see Kitahara Kaoru, "Ban Tō Godai no Tonkō ji-in kyōsai" (Economy of the Temples and Cloisters in Dunhuang during the Late Tang and Five Dynasties Period), in *Tonkō no shakai* (Dunhuang Society), edited by Ikeda On (Tokyo: Kōza Tonkō 3, 1980), pp. 371-456. Unfortunately this otherwise excellent article only gives minimal information on the religious practices in the temples.

97. PT. 1001. At the very end of the northern caves in Mogao one can still see the remnants of a Tibetan inscription over a cave. It is also known that Tibetan monks lived in the Yulin Caves outside Anxi, east of Dunhuang during this period. See also PT. 997.

98. P. 3346.
99. PT. 1257. This manuscript also includes a bilingual list of Buddhist key terms.
100. See PT. 999. See also Wang Yao and Chen Jian, *Dunhuang tufan wen shulun wenji* (Tibetan Manuscripts from Dunhuang—Collected Works and Essays), Sichuan minzu chuban she (Chengdu, 1988), pp. 202, 413-15.
101. Lalou 2, p. 33.
102. S. 476, S. 2712.
103. Ibid.
104. Ibid.
105. Ibid.
106. Guazhou was the neighboring county to the east of Shazhou, situated between Dunhuang and present-day Anxi.
107. For an annotated and commented edition of this manuscript, see Wang Yao and Chen Jian, *Dunhuang tufan wen shulun wenji* (Tibetan Manuscripts from Dunhuang–Collected Works and Essays) (Chengdu: Sichuan minzu chuban she, 1988), pp. 203-5, 416-23.
108. These manuscripts are both fragments. See Lalou 2, p. 35.
109. Ibid., p. 34.
110. Since the name of Khri gTsug-lde-brtsan occurs in our text, it must necessarily refer to a date after his reign which ended in A.D. 838. There is only one "rat year" after his reign and before the Tibetans were thrown out of Dunhuang, namely A.D. 844, which must therefore be the year referred to in the manuscript.
111. Wang Yao and Chen Jian, *Dunhuang tufan wen shulun wenji*, pp. 202, 413-15.
112. For further information on her reign, see Luciano Petech, "The Disintegration of the Tibetan Kingdom," in *Tibetan Studies* (Fagernäs) 2 (1992): pp. 649-59 (esp. p. 651, note 16).
113. Wang Yao and Chen Jian, *Dunhuang tufan wen shulun wenji*, pp. 202, 413-15. For a brief note, see Lalou vol. 2, p. 34.
114. S. 6108.
115. Examples of manuscripts containing a combination of the teachings of several schools are numerous. See S. 2144, S. 2583, S. 2669, S. 2973, S. 3558, S. 3559, S. 4064, P. 2104V, P. 2791, P. 3777, etc.

Chapter 2

THE EXPANSION OF BUDDHISM INTO SOUTHEAST ASIA
(Mainly before A.D. 1000)

J. G. de Casparis

In contrast to the wealth of studies on the expansion of Islam and Christianity, it appears that the expansion of Buddhism, third of the world religions in terms of numbers, has hitherto aroused little interest. It is true that most general works on Buddhism devote a chapter or a section to its expansion beyond South Asia but, although such sections often contain interesting and important observations, they do not deal with all the problems in sufficient depth for such studies. The present chapter is intended to call attention to some of those problems.

The first question that springs to mind is a basic one: *why* did Buddhism expand at all? The two other world religions that I mentioned above both contain strong admonitions to their respective followers to do everything in their power to spread the faith to every corner of the earth. The manner of such proselytizing is well known. Muslims, for instance, had and still have a special tax (the *jizya*) imposed on all non-Muslims; and had recourse not infrequently to more violent methods to force infidels to convert to Islam. Christians, for their part, had missionary organizations besides employing different forms of pressure and persuasion to make others adopt their faith. However, no similar forms of pressure exist in Buddhism. There is, of course, a fundamental difference between Islam and Christianity on the one hand and Buddhism on the other, in that the latter is not, or not first and foremost, a religion of faith. Buddhist texts invariably emphasize or imply that Buddhism is above all a matter of understanding the nature of things, which have no existence of their own (*asvabhava*), since their apparent existence depends on a number of factors. The idea which is sometimes expressed but more often implied is that one is bound to become a Buddhist if one understands the relations between causes and effects, in particular the origin of evil and suffering.

Yet the first conversions are surrounded by an aura of mystery, although they are described in one of the most basic Buddhist texts: the *Mahavagga* of the *Vinayapitaka*. They concern Lord Buddha's first disciples and closest companions: Sariputta (Sariputra) and Moggallana (Maudgalyayana). It is told that one of the original five human auditors of the First Sermon at Sarnath, the Venerable (*ayasma*) Assaji, had an encounter with the wandering ascetic (*paribbajaka*) Sariputta, who posed him a question about the essence of the doctrine revealed by Lord Buddha. Assaji then proceeded to pronounce what is called the "terse expression" of the Law propounded by the Buddha (*dhammapariyaya*), namely, the famous verse inscribed thousands of times in Buddhist countries in Pali, Prakrit, and Sanskrit, although with minor variations:

> Ye dhamma hetuppabhava hetun tesam Tathagato avocat tesam ca yo nirodha—evamvadi mahasamana.

On hearing this verse, recounts the *Mahavagga*, "there arose to Sariputta a dhamma- vision, dustless, stainless …," and so forth. It was, in other words, a revelation which immediately changed Sariputta's life, for he now understood the origin of suffering and its cessation. A little later Sariputta met another wandering ascetic, Moggallana, and recited the verse that he had heard from Assaji. The effect was the same, for Moggallana too was converted to Buddhism. The same again happened to a certain Sanjaya who subsequently revealed the truth to his two hundred and fifty followers.

The story given here in what appears to be its oldest version is interesting for several reasons. In the first place it follows that this most famous of all Buddhist verses was not revealed in this form by Lord Buddha Himself; it is actually regarded as the essence of the doctrine preached by the Lord at Sarnath as summarized and interpreted by Assaji! In the second place, however, it should be noted that this so-called Buddhist Creed is actually a very difficult text. Much has been written on the meaning and implications of the use of *dhamma* here, while the meaning of the stanza as a whole is by no means clear. Actually, it gives no explanation of the causes (*hetu*), but merely states that these were revealed by Lord Buddha. How then could the "wandering ascetic" Sariputta, who did not attend the First Sermon, understand it? It is therefore clear that the whole story of the "conversion" of the two first disciples is placed on a superhuman level, as though Sariputta received a clear intuition of the Truth. This is, at least, what the text of the *Mahavagga* would have us believe. What actually happened must remain a secret in the absence of any near-contemporary account. In the third place, and this is the most significant point, it is clear that these first conversions took place at an intellectual level. The first disciples became Buddhists because they *understood* the Truth: in particular the origin of suffering and the manner in which this suffering can be brought to an end. This intellectual approach with its emphasis on correct understanding has always remained characteristic of Buddhism. It is no less evident in two other "conversions."

The story of the encounter between King Devanampiya Tissa and the Mahinda is rightly famous and does need to be summarized here. Once again its essence is intellectual: a learned dialogue between the king and the monk who had mysteriously appeared before him. The other "conversion" is that described in the *Milindapanho*—again a non-Indian king (Milinda, i.e., the Indo-Greek ruler Menander)—engaged in a philosophical dialogue with an Indian Buddhist monk, Nagasena. As a result of this dialogue the king not only honoured Nagasena, but even "handed over the kingdom to his son, and after going forth from home into homelessness and increasing his insight, he attained arahantship.[1]

The last example is particularly interesting because of the absence of any superhuman elements: the king was clearly convinced of the correctness of Nagasena's arguments and realized that Buddhism was the right way to complete liberation. Yet the question arises whether the text presents a true account of a conversion to Buddhism by a foreign king. Although the story itself seems plausible we should be careful before accepting it as evidence. It has been argued that there is no reliable data proving that Menander did become a Buddhist. It is true that Menander's coinage reflects no influence of Buddhism,[2] but is this clear evidence to refute the story as given in the Pali text? It seems more likely that Menander would have continued with the type of coinage to which his subjects had been accustomed irrespective of his religious persuasion. But it is often forgotten that the Buddhist relic casket with the Kharosthi inscription of the time of King Menander (*Minadra*)[3] is at least a clear indication that the king showed some kind of devotion to Lord Buddha. As to the negative evidence of his coinage it should not be forgotten that the *Milindapanho* clearly stipulates that Menander abdicated in favor of his son; so he would not have issued any coinage after his conversion.

It therefore seems likely that Menander was indeed converted to Buddhism, but this does not imply that the story of his conversion should be accepted as given in the text. For the *Milindapanho* is above all a doctrinal text in which a number of current problems within the Buddhist community are discussed and dealt with. This is achieved in the form of a dialogue in accordance with ancient Buddhist tradition. Most of the texts of the *Tipitaka* are in the form of dialogues in which Lord Buddha gives discourses on particular points of discipline or of doctrine in reply to questions put to Him by people of all classes. The usual term "dialogue" is perhaps misleading insofar as there is no real discussion (in contrast with Plato's dialogues, for example). It is rather a method by which, instead of giving an overall systematic view of doctrine and discipline, each discourse deals with one among hundreds or thousands of separate issues, just as parsons do in their Sunday sermons. In the *Milindapanho* we read of questions such as: "What is in the world that is not Born of Cause?"[4] The somewhat surprising reply is that the only two things not born of a cause are Space (*akasa*) and *Nibbana*. Normally *akasa* is considered one of the six elements (*mahadhatu*) subject to the laws of cause and effect in the same way as the other elements (earth, water, and so on). In the brief discussion that follows, however, the king accepts *akasa* as uncaused but *Nibbana* as caused—quite the opposite of what one would have expected! Whatever one may think of this argument, there is here, and at a few other places in the text, at least some real discussion.

Unfortunately such elaborate descriptions of conversions are rare.[5] What strikes us most, however, is the completely intellectual character of the discussions preceding the conversions. This aspect may to some extent reflect the didactic nature of our texts and does not necessarily describe the manner in which large numbers of people came to embrace Buddhism.

As to the conversion of King Asoka, who from a cruel fratricide (*Candasoka*) was tranformed into one of the foremost patrons of Buddhism, the account in the *Mahavamsa* (most of Chapter V) inspires little confidence. The account not only mentions philosophical dialogues of the type found in the *Milindapanho*, but also the most decisive episode, which removes all the king's doubts is the miracle wrought by the thera Tissa Moggaliputta who "caused the earth to tremble" (V-262). The idea that Asoka was converted to Buddhism after the massacres of the Kalinga campaign is a modern view.[6]

Although such examples tend to emphasize the intellectual approach in the process of conversion to Buddhism, it does not follow that this was the general rule. It must, however, have been an important aspect. The monks who went from door to door begging their daily food (at least, before this practice was "institutionalized") were expected to spread the good word in exchange, delivering a little sermon or, rather, replying to some of the questions posed by the householders. In their replies the monks would talk about the calamities of disease, old age, death and rebirth possibly in an undesirable state, as well as about the Path which may ultimately lead to the suppression (*nirodha*) of such forms of suffering. In this manner a subtle link between the Sangha and the population in general could be established, which in some cases must have led members of the population to "seek refuge" in the Buddha, the Dhamma, and the Sangha. It is, however, clear that such forms of conversion could only apply to areas where monasteries had already been established. In addition, they could only have success in regions such as South Asia where, centuries before the rise of Buddhism, there had been a long tradition sanctifying the practice of begging.

For Southeast Asia, where such conditions did not prevail, Buddhism was not likely to have spread in this manner, at least not in its initial stages. Probably, the examples of King Milinda and Devanampiya Tissa would be more appropriate. This remains, however, conjectural as long as little is known about the earliest Buddhist developments. A few early traditions may be discussed in some detail.

The story of the two merchants Tapassu (Taphussa) and Bhalluka (Bhallika), the first disciples of Lord Buddha, is well known from the Tipitaka itself. Thus, the *Anguttara* (I, 24) mentions these two as the first who took refuge, while other texts, enumerated in Malalasekara's *Dictionary of Pali Proper Names,* tell us that the two merchants, "urged by a deity, who had been their relation, ... offered the Buddha rice-cakes and honey provided by the Four Regent Gods. They became the first lay disciples of the Buddha ...." Here is therefore a clear superhuman element in the story, but no indication is given as to *why* they became disciples of the Buddha. This conversion would not be of any great interest were it not for the fact that it had important implications outside India.

The Sanskrit inscription of Tiriyay, palaeographically datable to the end of the seventh or the first half of the eighth century, deals with the foundation of the Girikanda-cetiya, dedicated to Avalokitesvara, by the *Trapussakair-Villikakair-Vanig-ganaih,* "the companies of merchants who were followers of Trapussa and Bhallika," according to Paranavitana, or by the guilds of merchants who "in their devotional ardour ... compared themselves to the two merchants, Trapussa and Bhallika" (as rendered by Chhabra).[7] Although Chhabra's version may be preferable, on account of the use of the suffix (*ka*) and the plural, the idea that there was a tradition tracing the *cetiya* back to the two first disciples of the Buddha is quite plausible. Whichever may be the correct interpretation, the inscription gives clear evidence for the early expansion of Buddhism outside India.

But the story of Taphussa and Bhallika has another implication for Southeast Asia since these names have been associated with the foundation of one of the earliest Buddhist *stupas* in Myanmar (formerly

Burma), namely, the great Shwe Dagon Pagoda at Pagan. The inscription of King Dhammaceti[8] relates a long story of Taphussa and Bhalluka as having originated in an Asitanjuna town and traveled to the Bodhi Tree where they received eight of Lord Buddha's hairs which they subsequently enshrined in a *stupa* on top of Mount Tamagutta in their home country (southern Myanmar). Yet, the inscription goes on to relate, although these were precious relics in the country, there was none who knew the *ceti* of hair-relics and none to worship and revere it, (vide the Mon part of the inscription, B-14 to 15). This only changed in the year 236 after the Nibbana (c. 250 B.C.), when the two *theras* Sona and Uttara came and established the Sasana in the city of Suvannabhumi.[9]

This is the tradition as laid down in the Shwe Dagon Pagoda inscription concerning the beginnings of Buddhism in (central) Myanmar. It is, of course, a mythical account that attempts to trace the beginnings of Buddhism back to the time of Lord Buddha or rather that of King Asoka. There is, however, no evidence to support such traditions because the earliest evidence for the presence of Buddhism in southern Burma dates from about six centuries later, in other words the end of the fourth century A.D. This does not necessarily mean that there were no Buddhists in the country before that time, but if there were they left no trace of their presence.

From about the end of the fourth century (a date established on the basis of the palaeography of some inscriptions, not that of actual references) there is evidence for the presence of Buddhism in the ancient Pyu kingdom of Sriksetra with its center at Hmaw-za, not far from present Prome. The capital city must have been large, as appears from the city walls which still surround much of the ancient site. The inscriptions are written in a script resembling that of the Pallavas of South India but also show some particular features.[10] One of the most interesting is that inscribed on twenty gold plates recovered from what is described as Khin Ba's Mound Relic Chamber. Each plate is inscribed with three lines of about 25 *aksaras* each (except for no. 19 with four lines and no. 20 with two).

As already stated, the type of script can be defined as Pallava, but of a type not found in this particular form in India where the earliest Pallava inscriptions found in present Andhra Pradesh are written in a cursive type of script. However, in Sri Lanka the Ruvanvalisaya Pillar Inscription of King Budadasa (Buddhadasa), son of Jetatisa (Jetthatissa),[11] who reigned between c. 341 and 370, would appear to provide the closest parallel, although there are differences. Thus the three vertical strokes of the *ha*, the third of which is very short in the Sri Lankan inscription, are of equal height in the Hmaw-za script, and a similar feature is apparent in the form of the *sa*. These and some other features may suggest a slightly later date for the Hmaw-za gold plates, which would therefore probably belong to about the beginning of the fifth century.

The texts inscribed on the gold plates all belong to the Pali *Tipitaka*. It is again striking that *Abhidhamma* and other "learned" texts are well represented, whereas more popular stories, such as *Jatakas* and *Avadanas*, episodes of the life of Lord Buddha, are absent. This clearly suggests the presence in Sriksetra of Buddhist scholars from the early fifth century A.D., if not earlier. Such scholars could not have existed in a vacuum but must have been supported by a significant Buddhist community, probably including the royal court. This would imply that this élite would have embraced Buddhism at a time well before these texts were written down, that is by the end of the fourth century A.D. at the latest, and well before the time of Buddaghosa. This again raises the problem as to how Buddhism expanded into southern Burma.

Apart from the tradition of Sona and Uttara, mentioned above, which would place the introduction of Buddhism half a millennium before the earliest inscriptions, there is, unfortunately, no written data about this important development. This is not surprising since the same applies to the "expansion of Indo-Aryan culture," to use Chhabra's terms, in general. The expansion of Buddhism is part of this early expansion, but with a major difference. The use of Pali in the texts of Sriksetra clearly shows that this Buddhist "current" must have come from Sri Lanka where the *Tipitaka* and many commentaries had been written or translated into "Magadhi." The same may apply to the script used in Sriksetra in this early period. Several scholars, such as Duroiselle,[12] have emphasized the likeness of this script to that of the Kadambas of Vanavasi and the Pallavas of Kanci but, as explained earlier, the closest similarity is with some of the Sri Lankan inscriptions. The script shows, however, a few special features not found elsewhere. In this connection I may mention the form of the initial *i*, that of the *ca* and the *ba*. The *jha*, not as rare in Pali as it is in Sanskrit, is expressed by a ligature of *ja* and *ha*, a method I have not met elsewhere. This shows an independent development already at this early stage. It is therefore likely that the script of South Indian origin (further precision does not appear possible at the present stage) had been introduced into Sriksetra at some stage, probably several generations before its earliest known appearance in inscriptions.

The fact that most such Buddhist idealists must have joined merchant ships to cross the oceans indicates that there was a close link between Buddhism and trade. This is hardly surprising since we know that Lord Buddha Himself received a good deal of aid and encouragement from rich traders. The best-known case is that of Anathapindika, the wealthy Sravasti (Savatthi) merchant who made a donation to the Sangha of the famous Jetavana, site of most of Lord Buddha's discourses. One may justifiably conclude, therefore, that the efforts of missionaries were particularly important during the periods of lively trade between South and Southeast Asia. The fifth century A.D. must have been such a period, the time of the "Expansion of Indo-Aryan Culture during Pallava Rule" (Chhabra's title),[13] when a number of Indian-style kingdoms emerged in several parts of Southeast Asia. A typical example of the links between Buddhism and trade is the case of *Mahanavika* Buddhagupta, inhabitant of Raktamrttika. The latter is considered to be the name of a monastery in Eastern Bengal (present Bangladesh) or that of the area in present Kedah, where he had settled. This Buddhagupta has left two inscribed stone slabs. The first of these, found at Gunung Meriah near the estuary of the Merbok river, Kedah, Malaysia, carries an interesting engraving of a stupa and several inscriptions, one of which mentions Buddhagupta's name and function.[14] The term *mahanavika* probably indicates the captain of a merchant ship.[15] The script is a kind of Pallava script, not unlike that found in several Sanskrit inscriptions of Sri Lanka such as that of Kucchaveli[16] and of Western Java (the stone inscriptions of King Purnavarman), which can be dated back to the fifth century A.D.

If Buddhagupta was not only a pious Buddhist but also endeavored to spread the Good Doctrine, he may have been successful, as we find several Buddhist inscriptions in the area which all appear to belong to the same period. Yet, Buddhism did not make a lasting impact in that part of the Malaysian Peninsula, for the later antiquities are all Saiva, as far as their religious basis can be determined.[17] At least, no clearly Buddhist statues of other symbols are found there.

The same, incidentally, is true of maritime Southeast Asia as a whole. Unlike mainland Southeast Asia, where Pali can be traced back to the fourth century A.D., not a single Pali text or inscription has been discovered in the maritime part. On the other hand, all known written evidence for Buddhism is in Sanskrit and belongs to Mahayana. This is a remarkable dichotomy, which is not limited to the early period. From the end of the thirteenth century Islam spread over the major part of maritime Southeast Asia, but made little impact on the mainland, with the exception of Campa which occupies a special place in other respects too.[18] It should be added that those parts of maritime Southeast Asia which were not Islamized by the sixteenth century were mostly converted to Christianity: these included southern Maluku and most of the Philippines except southern Mindanao and the Sulu archipelago. On the other hand, neither Islam nor Christianity made any real impact on mainland Southeast Asia. The possible causes of this dichotomy are no doubt quite complex and cannot be studied here. The main point to note is the fact that maritime Southeast Asia, namely, the present states of Malaysia, the Philippines and Indonesia also constitute a linguistic community in that (almost) all of the languages used in the region belong to the great Austronesian linguistic division.[19]

After this brief diversion it is proper that we should return to the period under discussion, in other words the fourth and fifth centuries A.D. It is to this period approximately that we should date the so-called "Amaravati" Buddha statues found in different parts of the region. These consist of a small group of some eight bronzes found in Celebes, Java, Sumatra, Thailand, and Viet Nam. They are always represented standing and are further recognizable by the many-folded *samghati,* which, except for one example, leaves the right shoulder uncovered. Such representations of Lord Buddha are well known in Amaravati and other sites in Andhra Pradesh from where they also spread to Sri Lanka.

In a short article that has deservedly become famous,[20] Dupont demonstrates that these statues, though closely related, can be further divided into several groups. The main point is that six of these "Amaravati-style" images show features which relate them to Sri Lankan Buddha images. Although the ultimate source of this style has to be sought in or around Amaravati, there seems to be little doubt that the direct prototypes were some Buddha images in Sri Lanka of the Anuradhapura period. This conclusion carries important implications for the chronology. It is generally thought that the direct influence of Amaravati did not extend far beyond the fourth century A.D. If the Southeast Asian Buddha images originated in Amaravati, they would probably belong to the first few centuries of the Christian era. If, on the other hand, they were made in or were directly influenced by Sri Lanka, they could well be dated to several centuries later. Actually, Dupont distinguishes several groups among these so-called Amaravati-Buddhas, some of which do not predate the fifth or sixth century.

Dupont also emphasized that these Buddha statues were found either at isolated spots or in areas with no contemporary vestiges (as at Dong-duong where there is a ninth-century Cham temple). This clearly suggests that these (bronze) Buddhas were once placed in wooden temples. In addition, Dupont rightly concluded that some stylistic features leave no doubt that these Buddhas belong to Hinayana, which seems to have prevailed throughout Southeast Asia before the end of the seventh century, when the early Sriwijaya inscriptions testify to the presence of Mahayana Buddhism, which henceforward would remain the only form of Buddhism attested in maritime Southeast Asia.

In this context mention should be made of the basic religious dichotomy in Southeast Asia with Theravada triumphant in the mainland part, whereas the Mahayana of the maritime part finally gave way to Islam in Malaysia, Indonesia, and the southern Philippines (the Sulu archipelago and Mindanao). An enquiry into the causes of this dichotomy would raise problems that are outside the scope of this chapter.

These scattered Buddha statues, whatever their importance, give us little insight into the nature and penetration of Buddhist ideas in Southeast Asia. We have considerably more data for some areas, as we have seen in the case of Sriksetra. This is particularly true for the Mon kingdom of Dvaravati which flourished from at least the middle of the seventh century till the fifteenth century and laid the foundations of Buddhism in present Thailand.[21]

Apart from a small number of inscriptions in Mon, there is evidence too of the use of Pali, especially at Nakhon Pathom. Following the publication of Dupont's work, an important inscription was discovered at Vat Sa Morakot at Prachinburi, dated A.D. 761.[22] Although the inscription itself is in ancient Khmer, it contains three verses in Pali. It is the great merit of Mendis Rohanadeera that he was able to identify the Pali verses as belonging to the *Telakatahagatha*. From this inscription the learned author concluded that "it can now be established that the Sri Lankan Theravada literature found its way to Southeast Asia, even before the eighth century A.D. through Dvaravati, and not in the eleventh century though Ramannadesa as had been greatly believed." Although we can fully agree with the general tenor of this statement, there is however one difficulty. As has been argued by Dupont, Coedes, and others, Dvaravati was a typically Mon kingdom, yet the Prachinburi inscription is in Khmer (apart from the Pali quotation). It either belongs to Dvaravati, but was drafted in Khmer because that was the language of the local population or, more probably, can be attributed to one of the early Khmer kingdoms which dominated this part of eastern Thailand in the confused period preceding the campaigns of Jayavarman II.[23] In either case, however, this important document marks the easternmost expansion of Theravada Buddhism up to the twelfth century, when the unification of the Sangha during the reign of Parakramabahu I gave a fresh impulse to the expansion of Theravada.[24]

In addition to the few inscriptions, the numerous ruins and the rich iconography of Dvaravati, with its characteristic style of the Buddha image,[25] testify to its great importance for the expansion of Buddhism. As often happens in such cases, the new faith, once it was fully established, became a focus for further expansion. It not only became the principal faith of the Thai who founded a new kingdom at Sukhothai (Sukhodaya) in the thirteenth century, but also expanded into Cambodia. The importance of Dvaravati in this development can hardly be underestimated.

Already at an early date (c. seventh century) we find inscriptions in Mon, no doubt inspired by Dvaravati in Lopburi, and from the eleventh century farther north in Haripunjaya (Lamp'un). These are votive inscriptions attesting to the expansion of Theravada into northern Thailand. This area also became a great center of Pali studies where important texts, such as the *Jinakalamali* and the *Camadevivamsa*, were composed. It is also of particular interest because of the dated Buddha images.[26]

The unification of the Sangha in the time of Parakramabahu I, even if it did not completely put a stop to its partitionist tendencies, appears to have had great influence in Southeast Asia. Whatever the circumstances of the Sangha may have been in Sri Lanka, it did present an image of unity to the outside world. In addition to increasing the political strength of the island in the second half of the twelfth century, it enhanced its prestige as the center of the (Theravada) Buddhist world. This in turn increased and strengthened relations with large parts of mainland Southeast Asia. It is likely therefore that this intensification contributed to the lasting predominance of Buddhism in the region, where it successfully survived Muslim and Christian pressures, as well as the evils of colonialism. This stands in sharp contrast to developments in maritime Southeast Asia where such pressures led to the almost complete disappearance of Buddhism.

In this connection a few words should be added on the expansion of Buddhism in this region. As we have seen—in contrast to mainland Southeast Asia with its division into clearcut linguistic and cultural units, partly reflected in the various nations—maritime Southeast Asia presents a certain degree of cultural unity between the territories that make up Indonesia. Apart from a few small and historically uninteresting tribal pockets, all the languages spoken in the region belong to the great Austronesian family. There is also some degree of cultural affinity apparent in such fields as customary law. Despite the close relations between many parts of maritime Southeast Asia and South Asia—including Sri Lanka—Theravada does not appear to have exerted any real influence there. On the other hand, it may be said that some forms of Hinduism and Mahayana Buddhism predominated there in the pre-Islamic period.

It is essential to point out at least some of the factors leading to this difference between these two regions of Southeast Asia. Apart from the purely religious differences between Hinayana and Mahayana, which there is no need to discuss here, there are also some socio-economic differences that had political implications. Thus, one of the most characteristic aspects of Theravada is its strong monastic organization with the Sangha as a powerful factor in the state. It is true that the Sangha depended largely on the piety of the king and the ruling class, but the king depended no less on the support of the Sangha. No king could hope to reign for any length of time without such support, which had already been necessary for his consecration. Moreover, as the monks were in constant contact with the population of even the most remote villages—the daily alms rounds gave plenty of opportunities—their influence on the loyalty of the subjects had important implications for the stability of royal authority. The ancient Buddhist ideal of the king being a servant of the people, to which he is bound by an unwritten social contract, had not completely disappeared.

On the other hand, the most distinctive feature of Mahayana is the Bodhisattva doctrine urging both the king and his subjects to achieve progress on the Way towards the perfection of Buddhahood by performing good deeds (*punya*) and increasing knowledge (*jnana*). Already in the intermediate state of a bodhisattva the aspirants acquired superior powers raising them above the state of ordinary people (*prthagjana*). On the other hand, to acquire such a high position there was no need to enter monastic life and discipline; the characteristic *bodhisattva* is a man of the world. For kings, this principle created excellent opportunities: by having themselves identified as a bodhisattva, they could enjoy a special position for their achievements in charity and wisdom. Such ideals entailed duties towards their subjects, but also raised their prestige among the population under their authority.

Although the doctrines of Mahayana go back as far as the first or second century A.D., its influence is not clear before about the seventh century in Eastern India where the great *vihara* at *Nalanda* in particular developed into one of its greatest centers. Already at this early stage we find evidence for the spread of Mahayana doctrines even as far as the island of Sumatra, where the Talang Tuwa inscription of A.D. 684 provides a remarkable example of a king aspiring to Buddhahood.[27]

On the other hand, there are strong indications now that Sumatra was not as deficient in religious monuments as was once thought. Recent research, as foreshadowed in the 1983 SPAFA[28] report, gives the clear impression that both the region of present Palembang and especially that of Jambi were both rich in brick monuments. Those of Muara Jambi, east (i.e., downstream) of the present city of Jambi, datable to the period from the eleventh to the thirteenth century A.D., are particularly numerous and interesting, although frequently problematic. Muara Takus, situated near the confluence of two branches of the river Kampar (Kampar Kanan and Kampar Kiri), has some fairly well-preserved monuments including one large and several smaller *stupas*. Finally, there are interesting groups of Buddhist monuments in eastern Sumatra at Kota Cina near present Medan[29] and at Padang Lawas near Padang Sidempuan.[30] They all attest to the popularity of Tantric forms of Buddhism, often with strong Sivaite influence.

The same holds true for western Sumatra, in particular the Batanghari district of Jambi (province of Riau) and West Sumatra in its narrow meaning (province of Sumatra Barat). Numerous inscriptions, especially of Kings Akarendrawarman and Adityawarman in Old Malay, Sanskrit, and Tamil, have been discovered there, but hardly any remains of buildings and only a few statues. The first is a large composite statue representing Amoghapasa, a Tantric form of the Jina Amoghasiddhi, surrounded by thirteen other deities, including a small Bhairava. As the inscription indicates, these are actually copies of free-standing statues of Candi Jago in East Java, sent to Sumatra by King Kertanagara (1268-92). The second is a huge Bhairava, actually the largest statue ever found in Indonesia, though not as high as the Avukana Buddha,[31] "decorated," if that is the right term, with garlands of sculls, but otherwise nude. At the same time, however, the Bhairava carries a small figure of Amitabha in his crown, usually associated with Avalokitesvara. Whatever the precise identification of the statue may be, it is thought that it represents King Adityawarman himself in a divine but demonic shape, apparently as a magical guardian to one of the roads giving access to the plains of West Sumatra.

As these statues fall outside the chronological limit fixed for this chapter, we may perhaps briefly attempt to determine their significance for maritime communications between South and Southeast Asia. What strikes us most when surveying the different kinds of Buddhist remains in Malaysia and Sumatra is the changing pattern of influences from South Asia. Whereas influences from Andhra Pradesh and Sri Lanka prevail in the earliest period (from the third or fourth century A.D.), Mahayanic influences from northeastern India (Bihar and Bengal) are particularly strong from the seventh to the tenth century. This is also true for Myanmar: influences there from Bengal are strong, particularly in Pagan, whereas those from this island appear to persist in southern areas at Hmaw-za, Pegu, and Thaton. From the eleventh century, however, southern influences, especially those of the powerful Chola empire, are once again apparent. Thus the well-known Buddha statue from Kota Cina is quite South Indian in style, and South Indian influence is even reflected in the use of Tamil in some inscriptions (two from Barus and one from Batu Berpahat near Suruaso). It is, however, difficult to decide whether such influences came straight from South India or via this island. The Tamilnadu was not really noted for Buddhism, although there were important centers of this religion at Kanci and Negapatam. An indication of possible relations between West Sumatra and Sri Lanka is the name Nandanavana which Adityawarman gave to a park near Suruaso, probably following the example of Anuradhapura.

To return to the pre-1000 period, with which this paper is mainly concerned, some attention should now be given to central Java, where

Buddhism in its Mahayana form saw a spectacular development during the time of the Sailendra dynasty. The grandeur and beauty of the monuments built at that time make it difficult to believe that this sudden blossoming of Buddhist creative activity is mainly confined to a period of less than a century (c. A.D. 775-860). The great Borobudur and the enormous temple groups of Candi Sewu and Candi Plaosan, as well as numerous other monuments (such as the candis,[32] Banyunibo, Kalasan, Sari and Sojiwan) and a rich iconography, attest to the wealth of Buddhist culture at that time.

A particular feature of the Sailendra period is the international orientation of the rulers. This is already apparent from the earliest Sailendra inscription of Java, namely the stone of Kalasan which is dated A.D. 778 and is inscribed with a Sanskrit inscription in early Nagari script.[33] From its first verse it follows that the temple was dedicated to the goddess Tara, "who helps the creatures cross (*ya tarayati*) the ocean of suffering without fear." It is quite possible, even likely, that this formulation is an allusion to actual maritime voyages by merchants and pilgrims. *"Tara"* actually means "Star," and stars were the principle means of guidance for sailors crossing the ocean.

Another inscription, dated a few years later (782), informs us that a statue of the *bodhisattva* Manjusri was inaugurated in the presence of a guru from Bengal or Bangladesh (Gaudidvipa),[34] Kumaraghosa by name, who must have crossed the ocean to perform this consecration ceremony in Java.

Again ten years later, in 792, a Sanskrit inscription from the Ratuboko plateau in Central Java on the southern border of the plain of Prambanan, tells us of a monastery (*vihara*) of the Sinhalese monks and named Abhayagirivihara.[35] This famous name takes us at once to this island where the great Abhayavihara with its high *dagaba* is one of the three great stupas of Anuradhapura, which is being restored by the Archaeological Survey of Sri Lanka as part of the Archaeological Triangle Project.

This monastery was, however, also known for the influence of "dissident" monks who followed doctrines other than those of Theravada, apparently belonging in part to Mahayana. Such ideas brought them into conflict with the predominant doctrine centered in the Mahavihara and, on several occasions, monks were expelled from the Abhayagiri and sought refuge in South India and elsewhere. It is possible that the monks appearing in Java were among those forced to leave this island, but why should they have traveled so far? It is therefore more likely that the Sinhalese monks were in Java because they had been invited by the Sailendra king, as had been the case with Kumaraghosa ten years earlier. In any event, this example proves the existence of close relations between at least two of the great Buddhist establishments in Sri Lanka and Java.

To make matters even more complicated, another Sailendra inscription (the Pre-Nagari stone inscription of Candi Plaosan)[36] mentions *gurus* from Gurjaradesa as visitors to the Sailendra court, possibly again to take part in the inauguration ceremony of the principal statue or one of the buildings of this great complex, most of which was built in the middle of the ninth century. This would appear to have been the case from the large, but badly weathered, fragment in the National Museum at Jakarta. A few years ago a much larger part of the same inscribed stone was discovered, but this has not yet been read.[37] As to Gurjaradesa, the reading of which is beyond doubt, one may wonder whether it indicates present Gujerat or else the great empire of the Gurjara-Pratiharas, reigning from the city of Kanauj (Kanyakubja). Gujerat with its ports on and near the gulf of Broach has played an important part in commercial relations with Southeast Asia—as far as we know, this was especially the case in and after the fifteenth century when it contributed considerably to the early expansion of Islam. There is no evidence, however, to show that the country had close relations with Southeast Asia before that time. Furthermore, it was not an area where Buddhism flourished particularly, although the great stupa of Devnimori and some other sites show that Buddhism, no less than Vaisnavism and Jainism, had its place in Gujerat.

Although the identification with Gujerat seems to me to be the most likely of all one cannot exclude the possibility that the inscription refers to relations with the Kingdom of the Gurjara-Pratiharas, which was quite powerful in the ninth century during the reigns of Bhoja and Mahendrapala. The latter seems to have controlled Bihar with its great centers of Buddhism.[38] Whichever interpretation one chooses, the Plaosan inscription indicates the existence of relations between Buddhist centers in northern India (not only in Bengal) and Central Java.

In conclusion, it appears that the Javanese Buddhists of the Sailendra period maintained close relations with other parts of the then-Buddhist world in South Asia. There can be little doubt that Sri Lanka played an important part in these relations. Not only were there direct relations between the Abhayagirivihara and the Ratuboko plateau, but it is likely that the relations with the Indian subcontinent, except perhaps for those with Nalanda and Bengal, usually passed through Sri Lanka. It was convenient for sailors to call at this fertile island before taking the big leap to cross the Gulf of Bengal en route for the Straits of Malacca. They would use the south-west monsoon during part of the year and avoid the coast of Tenasserim, where especially the Mergui archipelago offered an ideal refuge for pirates.

Before leaving the subject of Indonesia, a brief mention may be made of two important data from the end of the period under survey. The first of these data is a short inscription on a rock at Pohsarang, west of the town of Kediri, East Java. It tells us about the planting of a Bodhi Tree on the occasion of some road repairs in Saka 924 (A.D. 1002/3).[39] The term used for "Bodhi Tree" is actually *boddhi warinin*. The curious thing is that the Javanese "*warinin*" is in fact the banyan tree, called *nyagrodha* in Sanskrit, which is related to, yet different from, the Bodhi Tree. Kern, who edited this inscription, quite rightly pointed out that the true Bodhi Tree (*ficus religiosa*) does not grow in Java and that the *warinin* was used as a substitute. However natural this may seem, it is contrary to Buddhist practice according to which Bodhi Trees were invariably grown from branches of the original Mahabodhi at Bodhgaya. I may add that this is the only known case of a Bodhi Tree being planted in Java.

The second of these data is known from Cola inscriptions of the turn of the millennium (the so-called "Leiden plates" of King Rajendra Cola), which mention the foundation by a Sailendra king of a Buddhist temple at Nagipattana (Negapatnam) in c. 1004.[40] This Buddhist temple was in the shape of a high tower which was used by sailors as a landmark until it was demolished in the middle of the nineteenth century. Fortunately, we still have an ancient drawing of the building which shows a superficial likeness to the Satmahal Prasada at Polonnaruva.[41]

Although the foundation of this temple has no direct bearing on the expansion of Buddhism, it clearly shows that this religion was so deeply rooted in ancient Sriwijaya that its kings even ventured to spread it to its very country of origin. It should, however, be added that this was a part of the country in which Buddhism had, on the whole, precious little influence.

The Leiden plates may not indicate that the Buddhist foundation had any bearing upon trade, yet it should not be forgotten that Sriwijaya was above all a trading kingdom whose prosperity depended to a large extent on the ability of its rulers to control shipping through the Straits of Malacca. Sriwijaya no doubt had its own products, carried to the capital from other parts of Sumatra, but the Chinese notices leave no doubt that most of the trade was on transit to Sriwijaya from other parts of the Indonesian Archipelago and the Malay Peninsula.

This far-flung empire may therefore be regarded as a typical example of the close relations between Buddhism and trade. It may be supposed that Buddhism, just like Islam a few centuries later, spread mainly along the trade routes. More than other human activities, trade connects countries to one another, thereby creating possibilities for the expansion of religion. It is likely that Buddhist monks, as we know in the case of Fa-Xian, traveled on merchant ships. Even if these monks were not missionaries in the narrow sense of the term, they would often have given expression to their ideas, if only as a means of paying their way. Just as scholars today sometimes serve as guides to travel companies, learned monks would join commercial ventures and offer spiritual guidance to the traders. It may not be pure speculation to suppose that traders in those far-off times may have felt that the presence of holy men on board ships would have a wholesome effect on the conduct of the sailors or even of the weather-gods. In addition, we should not forget that Buddhism enjoyed the favor of traders from its very beginning (Anathapindika of Savatthi, donor of the Jetavana, is the example which first springs to mind) as well as in subsequent centuries when many of the generous sponsors of the *cetiyas* of Barhut, Bhattiprolu, Bodhgaya, and Sanchi were traders or trading guilds.

Despite the importance of trade in the expansion of Buddhism to large parts of Southeast Asia, we should be careful not to overemphasize this factor. There is a tendency among scholars in the trading nations of Western Europe, such as the Netherlands and the United Kingdom, to point to trade as the only or the principal channel through which religions such as Buddhism and Islam spread, but this is no less dangerous an approach than ignoring the role of trade in the process. As pointed out at the beginning of this chapter, Buddhism is based on what is regarded as a correct understanding of the different processes of life and on accepting the consequences of such insight. It is not a commodity that may be offered for sale by traders. Trade, however, was (or was before the age of mass tourism) the most familiar way in which people of different countries or even continents came into contact with one another, and opened the way to closer relations between different peoples. The presence of pious Buddhists among traders may have inspired in those with whom they came in contact a strong desire to know more about a doctrine aimed at liberating man from suffering in all its forms. It is likely that such a desire would have arisen in the minds of those who had reached a certain level of knowledge and understanding. It is therefore not surprising that learned kings, such as the Devanampiya Tissa and Menander, were among the first non-Indians to grasp the meaning of the teachings of Lord Buddha. For Southeast Asia we have no clear examples of the same development, except for the Kashmiri Prince Gunavarman who would have converted the Queen of Cho-po (Java?) to Buddhism. Although there are no other examples available, it seems likely that this was a fairly regular pattern, suggesting that Buddhism generally spread from the king or the ruling classes to other sections of the population.

It is no exaggeration to say that trade, in particular that related to the Silk Road, though by no means the principal factor in the expansion of Buddhism to parts of Southeast Asia, probably provided or facilitated the efforts which subsequently led to the adoption of Buddhism by large sections of the population of Southeast Asia.

Notes

1. *The Mahavagga,* vol. 1 (Oldenberg, 1929), pp. 23-25, *imam dhammapariyayam sutva virajam vitamalam dhammacakhum udapadi.*
2. Trenckner, *Milindapanho* (London: William and Norgate, 1880), p. 420; translation by Rhys Davids vol. 2 (1894), pp. 373f.; translation by Horner (1964), pp. 2-304. The question whether this passage belongs to the original version of the text (see Horner's Introduction, p. 30) is not strictly relevant in this context; another passage of the same work (p. 88; translation pp. 122 f.) shows that the king, though aware of the truth of Nagasena's arguments, did not "go forth from home into homelessness" on account of his numerous enemies. This, of course, means that Menander did not become a monk.
3. O. Boperachi, "Milinda's conversion to Buddhism: fact or fiction?" *Ancient Ceylon* 7 (1990): pp. 1-16. We should distinguish sharply between becoming a Buddhist (layman), i.e., taking the Three Refuges, and becoming a monk. I fully agree with A.K. Narain, *The Indo-Greeks* (1957), pp. 19-99, who gives some strong arguments to the effect that the tradition of Menander (Milinda) being converted to Buddhism is reliable.
4. N.G. Majumdar, *Epigr. Ind.* 24 (1937): pp. 1-10; D.C. Sircar, *Epigr. Ind.* 26 (1941-1942): pp. 318- 21; *Sel. Inscr.*, I, 2d ed. (1965), pp. 14, 102-6.
5. Trenckner, *Milindapanho* (London: William and Norgate, 1880), p. 268; translation Horner, 86f.
6. See *Dipavamsa*, pp. 6-18: *abhisitto tini vassani pasanno Buddha-sasane* (three years after having been inaugurated a king, he had faith in the religion of the Buddha) in B.C. Law, "The Dipavamsa," *Ceylon Hist. Journal* 7 (1957-1958): p. 171. See also P.H.L. Eggermont, *The Chronology of the Reign of Asoka Moriya* (1956), p. 19. The Kalinga campaign took place in his ninth regnal year.
7. S. Paranavitana, "Tiriyay Rock-Inscription," *Ep. Zeyl.* 4 (1943): pp. 151-60; B. Ch. Chhabra, *Expansion of Indo-Aryan Culture during Pallava Rule*, pp. 109-15.
8. C. O. Blagden, "An Inscription of the Shwedagon Pagoda, Rangoon," *Ep. Birm.* 4 (1936): pp. 15, 20-43, in particular lines B-8 to 13.
9. Ibid., lines 16 to 21.
10. C. Duroiselle, "Excavations at Hmawza," *Arch. Survey of India* (1926-1927): pp. 171-83; U Tha Myat, *Pyu Reader* (n. d.), pp. 25-33.
11. S. Paranavitana, "The Ruvanvalisaya Pillar of Budadasa," *Ep. Zeyl.* 3 (1931): pp. 120-26 and pl. 8; B. Ch. Chhabra, *The Expansion of Indo-Aryan Culture*, pp. 12f. and Fig.2.
12. C. Duroiselle, "Excavations."
13. The connection with "Pallava rule" is, however, not quite clear, as we already noted with reference to the Ruvanvälisäya inscription. On the other hand, the script is closely related to other South Indian scripts and, at least from the seventh century, to that of the Pallavas.
14. B. Ch. Chhabra, *The Expansion*, pp. 20-26.
15. Ibid., p. 23, note 2.
16. Published by S. Paranavitana, *Ep. Zeyl.* 3 (n.d.): pp. 158-61; see also Chhabra, *The Expansion*, pp. 16f.
17. See A. Lamb, "Recent Archaeological Work in Kedah," *Journ. Fed. Mal. St. Mus* 12 (1928); "Report on the Excavation and Reconstruction of Chandi Bukit Batu Pahat," *Fed. Mus. Journ.* 5 (1960); and "Miscellaneous Papers," *Fed. Mus. Journ.* 6 (1961).
18. Thus, unlike the other peoples of mainland Southeast Asia, the Cham belong linguistically and culturally to the great Austronesian (Malay-Polynesian) group; in

addition, the ancient Cham inscriptions are written in a language which is apparently strongly influenced by that of the Old Malay inscriptions of Sriwijaya.

19. The only exceptions are some of the languages of the northern Moluccas (especially Halmahera), of Irian Jaya and of some tribal pockets in the Philippines and West Malaysia. The speakers of such languages are but a tiny minority of the population of maritime Southeast Asia.

20. P. Dupont, "Variétés archéologiques—Les Buddha dits d'Amaravati en Asie du Sud-Est," *BEFEO* 49 (1955): pp. 631-36, Pls. 56-64.

21. There is much literature on Dvaravati, but the basic work is still P. Dupont, *L'Archéologie Mone de Dvaravati*, 2 vols. (EFEO, 1959). See also the detailed review of this work by M.C. Subhadradis Diskul in *Essays offered to G. H. Luce* (1966) vol. 2, and H. G. Quaritch Wales, "Dvaravati in South-East Asian Cultural History," *J.R.A.S.* (1966): pp. 40-52.

22. M. Rohanadeera, "Telakatahagatha in a Thailand Inscription of 761 A.D. New evidence on cultural relations between Sri Lanka and The Dvaravati Kingdom in Thailand, Vidyodaya," *Journal of Social Science* 1 (1987): pp. 59-73.

23. Before the time of Jayavarman II, Cambodia was divided into what the Chinese called Chen-la of the Water and Chen-la of the Land, but both of these were again divided into several principalities. In addition to the works of Coedès, see O.W. Wolters, "Jayavarman II's military power: the territorial foundation of the Angkor empire," *F.R.A.S.* (1973): pp. 21-30.

24. C.W. Nicholas and S. Paranavitana, *A Concise History of Ceylon* (1961), pp. 262-65.

25. See especially P. Dupont, *L'archéologie mône de Dvaravati*, 2 vols. (Paris: EFEO, 1959), vol. 1, pp. 73-78.

26. A.B. Griswold, *Dated Buddha Images of Northern Siam* (1957).

27. G. Coedès, "Les inscriptions malaises de Crivijaya," *BEFEO* 30 (1930): pp. 38-44, pl.3.

28. SPAFA (SEAMEO Project in Archaeology and Fine Arts), Final Report of Consultative Workshop on Archaeological and Environmental Studies of Srivijaya (I-W2a) (Jakarta, 1982).

29. E.E. McKinnon, *Kota Cina: an Important Early Trading Site on the East Coast of Sumatra* (1976).

30. SPAFA, *Final Report of Consultative Workshop on Archaeological and Environmental Studies of Srivijaya*, 1-W2b (1986): pp. 59-66; F.M. Schnitger, *The Archaeology of Hindoo Sumatra* (1937), pp. 16-37; "Forgotten Kingdom in Sumatra" (Leiden: E.J. Brill, 1964), pp. 85-107; Satyawati Suleiman, *Sculptures of Ancient Sumatra (Arca-arca di Sumatra pada Zaman Purba)* (Jakarta,1981); and SPAFA, *Final Report of Consultative Workshop*.

31. F.M. Schnitger, *The Archaeology of Hindoo Sumatra*, pls. 14-16.

32. I am following the current Indonesian practice of designating all pre-Muslim structural monuments as candi.

33. F.D.K. Bosch, "De inscriptie van Keloerak," *Tijdschr. Kon. Bat. Gen.* 68 (1928): pp. 1-64, in particular pp. 57-62.

34. Ibid., pp. 1-56.

35. J.G. de Casparis, "New Evidence on Cultural Relations between Java and Ceylon in Ancient Times," *Artibus Asiae Ed.*, 24 (1961): pp. 241-48.

36. J.G. de Casparis, *Prasasti Indonesia* vol. 2 (1956), pp. 175-206.

37. In addition there are numerous votive inscriptions in the Plaosan complex; see J.G. de Casparis, "Short Inscriptions from Candi Plaosan-Lor," *Dinas Purbakala Indonesia* (1958).

38. B.N. Puri, *The History of the Gurjara-Pratiharas* (1957), pp. 66-69.

39. H. Kern, "De inscriptie van Puh Sarang (Kediri) uit 924 Saka," *Verspreide Geschriften* 6 (1917): pp. 77-82 (original article of 1883).

40. G. Coedès, "Le Royaume de Crivijaya," *BEFEO* 18 (1918): pp. 51-86, especially 54. For the full text of the inscription, the so-called "Larger Leiden Plates," see the edition by K.V. Subrahmanya Aiyer in *Epigr. Indica.* 22 (1933-1934): pp. 213-66, 15 pls.

41. See the reproductions of the drawing in the article by Sir Walter Elliot, "The Edifice Formerly Known as the Chinese or Jaina Pagoda at Negapatam," *Indian Antiquary* 7 (1878): pp. 224-27. A smaller reproduction is found in Subrahmanya Aiyer's article mentioned in note 40 above.

Chapter 3

THE TRAVELS OF MARCO POLO IN THE LAND OF BUDDHISM

Ananda Abeydeera

> *Thus grew the tale of Wonderland:*
> *Thus slowly, one by one,*
> *Its quaint events were hammered out -*
> *And now the tale is done,*
> *And home we steer, a merry crew,*
> *Beneath the setting sun.*[1]

We owe the work that has sometimes been called the Book of Marco Polo to an accident of fate—the imprisonment of Marco Polo and his meeting with another prisoner, Rustichello of Pisa, a courtier and a writer by profession, who was a passionate teller of tales of chivalry and compiler of Round Table romances. Indeed, the book opens with a prologue not unlike the apostrophe used by the *trouvères* to attract their audience's attention. It instantly pinpoints the nature and purpose of the discourse. Rustichello addressed "Great Princes, Emperors and Kings, Dukes and Marquises, Counts, Knights and Burgesses, …[2] a court audience for the most part, avid for descriptions of the "various races of mankind and of the diversities of the sundry regions of the world" and for accounts of "great marvels" written by someone who had seen them with his own eyes. There can be no better definition of the kind of book that was in vogue during the Middle Ages when the exotic wider world was uppermost in people's minds. Marco Polo and his writer were well acquainted with such works, which were as much collections of fables as they were encyclopaedias.

The description of Sri Lanka is found in chapters 173 and 177 of the above-mentioned edition of the original manuscript which was

written by Rustichello in 1298. It was condensed into a single chapter
(168) of the edition of the work that Marco Polo presented to Thiébault
de Cépoy in 1307 and which was published much later by G. Pauthier.[3]
An entire passage about the life of the Buddha is absent from this edition, thereby making it necessary to consult both versions. Marco Polo
apparently made two trips to Sri Lanka: the first in 1284 as official representative of Kublai Khan and the second in 1293 on his journey
home to Venice. Sri Lanka was already a major port of call where ships
took on water and provisions and, although his ship put in there in
1293, it seems that he did not stay long. At no point does he indicate
the location or duration of his two visits, but his account would appear
mostly to refer to his first stay there. He mentions the Khan's mission
in Sri Lanka on only two occasions, and although as ambassador he
must have gone to Yapahuva, the then capital, there is nothing in his
story to confirm this.

Readers are bound to wonder what Marco Polo's role was in his missions outside China. The Mongol Emperor's expectations of his ambassadors, and hence of Marco Polo, emerge clearly in chapter 15, "How
the Lord sent Mark on an Embassy of his Notes," and 16, "How Mark
returned from the Mission whereon he had been sent":

> '... and [the Great Kaan] would say: 'I had far liever hearken about the
> strange things, and the manners of the different countries you have seen,
> than merely be told of the business you went upon;'—for he took great
> delight in hearing of the affairs of strange countries. Mark therefore, as he
> went and returned, took great pains to learn about all kinds of different
> matters in the countries which he visited, in order to be able to tell about
> them to the Great Kaan.'[4]

It is tempting to read these two chapters as pure fabrication
designed to flatter the author of the tale. However, as the writings of
Chinese chroniclers show, it was the custom among Mongol sovereigns
to keep themselves informed about the situation in various countries—
their resources, the customs of the inhabitants, their religions, rites, and
peculiarities. The Chinese accounts were enriched by observations similar to those found in the Book of Marco Polo. Seen in this light, Marco
Polo's description of Sri Lanka is the basis of a report he intended to
make to the Mongol Emperor on returning from his mission.

After a stopover of five months in Sumatra, probably awaiting the
winter monsoon, Marco Polo went to sea once more, and a thousand
miles west of the Nicobar Islands "You come to the Island of Seilan,
which is in good sooth the best Island of its size in the world."[5] As is to
be expected, the dimensions of the island of Sri Lanka are overstated
(2,400 miles in circumference), but he adds: "... in old times it was

greater still, for it then had a circuit of about 3,600 miles, as you find in the charts of the mariners of those seas"[6] and part of the island had been swallowed up by the sea. This theory of the encroaching sea might well come from the Sinhalese tradition which records, with some exaggeration, several floods, in particular one in the third century B.C.: "In the times of King Kelanitissa, one hundred thousand port towns, 970 fishing villages and 400 villages inhabited by pearl divers were submerged, taking with them eleven-twelfths of the territory of Lanka [which formed the domain of the king to the west of the island]."[7]

It is somewhat surprising that Marco Polo should explain the larger dimensions of Sri Lanka on medieval maps in terms of the laws of nature, since the medieval mind was perfectly willing to be convinced not only by what could be observed and proved by natural law, but also by all things extraordinary, marvelous, and supernatural. His explanation is all the more surprising in that it did not resurface until the sixteenth century, admittedly in a more elaborate version, when the Portuguese historian, João de Barros, attributed the new dimensions of the island to a geological process, i.e., the erosion of the land by the ocean:

> According to what the geographers have written about it, it would seem that in those very ancient times, it [the island] was as big as the natives claim it to have been when they say that it was more than 700 leagues in circumference and that the sea had gradually eaten it away; that is probably why he [Ptolemy] said that it stretched to 2 and a half degrees beyond the equinoctial line towards the south.[8]

The annals of the island recount several major floods to explain its modest size and thus avoid contradicting the Indian Brahmins who attached great significance to Lanka, exaggerating its dimensions: "On the other side of this ocean is an island of 100 yojana in surface area."[9] In that way they provided Westerners with evidence substantiating the claims of the geographers of antiquity: "Taprobane may be considered to be a very large island, or, to follow the opinion of Hipparchus, as the beginning of another world."[10]

Marco Polo goes on to describe some of the islanders' customs and such descriptions are often repeated from one chapter to the next: the people of the country spoke a language of their own and were independent; they paid tribute to nobody and had a king of their own. The description of Taprobane in Pierre de Beauvais's *Mappa Mundi* had already indicated that the islanders spoke "a separate language which none understand, and they themselves understand no other," a deduction made from the strange method of trading described by Pliny: "In order to trade with foreign merchants, they spread their products out along the shore and the exchanges take place in silence."[11] The name given by Marco Polo to the King, Sendemain, probably corresponds to a title. The King of Sri Lanka in 1284 was, according to the Sinhalese chronicles, Bhuvanaika Bahu, and in 1293 Parakramabahu IV was on the throne. The historian Paranavitana identifies Sendemain with Chandrabhanu, a title commonly used at the time by the Malays who occupied the region of Jaffna in the north of the island.[12]

The rest of the description of the islanders' customs is not specific to Sri Lanka: "The people are Idolaters and go quite naked except that they cover the middle. They have no wheat, but have rice, and sesamum [sesame] of which they make their oil. They live on flesh and milk and have tree-wine such as I have told you of. And they have brazil-wood, much the best in the world."[13] Marco Polo was especially struck by sights that were unknown in the West, and more particularly the Christian West. Not only had they not heard of the true God in Sri Lanka, but they went about practically naked, a sure sign of sin in the Middle Ages. In this connection, it should be noted, as Atkinson[14] pointed out, that Marco Polo did in fact raise the question of nudity. The indigenous people's reply inverted the equation "nudity equals lust":

> We go naked because naked we came into the world, and we desire to have nothing about us that is of this world. Moreover, we have no sin of the flesh to be conscious of, and therefore we are not ashamed of our nakedness, any more than you are to show your hand or your face. You who are conscious of the sins of the flesh do well to have shame, and to cover your nakedness.[15]

The inhabitants of Sri Lanka did not have bread or wine made from grapes either, which also had religious connotations as they symbolize the body and blood of Jesus Christ. We will return to the religion of the island's inhabitants later, because Marco Polo goes on to devote a whole section of his account to it. The attitude of the indigenous people did not make a good impression on him: "The people of Seilan are no soldiers, but poor cowardly creatures. And when they have need of soldiers they get Saracen troops from foreign parts."[16]

Marco Polo thus corrected the image, firmly planted in people's minds at the time, of a race of "giants." It is true that the naval and military forces of Sri Lanka, whose population had little inclination for warfare, had always been made up of mercenaries, sometimes recruited in India, to reinforce the troops mobilized locally as the need arose. It is true too that the islanders, with their peaceful disposition and softened as they were by Buddhism, a non-violent religion, had only very limited experience of large-scale military operations.

Coming as he did from a feudal society, Marco Polo could only feel contempt for the placidity of the local population such as lords would for villains. It was also by contrast a way of praising the warrior virtues of the Great Khan and the prowess of his armies which he extols at length elsewhere:

> All their harness of war is excellent and costly. Their arms are bows and arrows, sword and mace; but above all the bow for they are capital archers, indeed the best that are known. On their backs they wear armour of cuirbouly, prepared from buffalo and other hides, which is very strong. They are excellent soldiers, and passing valiant in battle.[17]

And now we come to the marvelous: "*So if you will allow me to talk of these things I shall tell you of the most precious thing in the world.*" The Venetian, let us not forget, was interested in luxury goods such as the island's rich store of precious stones: "You must know that rubies are found in this Island and in no other country in the world but this. They find there also sapphires and topazes and amethysts, and many other stones of price."[18] Of course, the Polos were involved in Venetian trade and at that time merchants basically sold expensive products which made them enormous profits; but here the reason for Marco's interest seems to have been quite different in that he wished to create an impact, captivating with descriptions of marvels of which the public never tired.

One particular marvel, worthy of the Lapidaries, is described with considerable talent. It was the ruby owned by the King of Sri Lanka for which Kublai is said to have offered the value of a city: "And the King of this Island possesses a ruby which is the finest and biggest in the world; I will tell you what it is like. It is about a palm in length, and as thick as a man's arm; to look at, it is the most resplendent object upon earth; it is quite free from flaw and as red as fire. Its value is so great that a price for it in money could hardly be named at all."[19] The Khan's emissaries returned without the "jewel" as the King of Sri Lanka refused to part with it: "But the King replied that on no account whatever would he sell it, for it had come to him from his ancestors."[20]

The King's ruby is mentioned in other fourteenth-century travelers' tales. Some attempt may be made to identify it. Ibn Battuta in his *Travels* dates the origin of the royal heritage to the tenth century, in other words, when Arab merchants began to settle in Sri Lanka. But this is probably the date of origin of what turned into a legend. It was, Ibn Battuta tells us, the great Sheikh Abu Abdullah, who taught the path on the mountain of Serendib, who gave rubies to the king. The Sheikh, known as the founder of Shiraz orthodox Sufism, lived in the tenth century: "Nevertheless we set off for the Bay of Bamboos from which Abu Abdullah, son of Khafif, took the two rubies which he gave to the Sultan of this island."[21]

Ibn Battuta provides us with a further, almost anecdotal clue:

It is said that the sheikh, who had one day dived in the presence of the king of these idolaters, emerged from the water with his hands tight shut, and said to the king: "Choose the contents of one of my hands." The king chose what was in the right hand, and the sheikh threw it to him. It was three matchless rubies which remain in the possession of the kings of this country and are set in their crown. These princes hand down the jewels as heritage.[22]

In order to establish his legitimacy the King of Sri Lanka needed a harmonious and protective alliance of three jewels symbolizing the Buddha (awakened one), the *dhamma* (doctrine) and the *sangha* (fraternity), also known as "Trividha Ratna" which in Pali means "three kinds of ruby."[23] Ibn Battuta's three rubies might very well be a reference to Buddhism and the religious power of the king. Rubies, according to popular belief, must be kept in pairs; in this duality resides their power. This tradition apparently accounts for the fact that Ibn Battuta speaks of two rubies and not three in the rest of his account.

In his chapter on precious stones, Ibn Battuta describes another ruby, this one in the possession of the king of the northern region of the island: "I have also seen in the presence of the sultan Arya Chakaravarti a ruby dish as big as the palm of my hand, which contained oil of aloe. I expressed my astonishment at seeing the dish; but the sultan said to me: 'We own objects made of rubies still larger than this.'"[24] This passage from Ibn Battuta is germane to our subject.

A Chinese chronicle written in 1349 describes the occasional dispatch of embassies to Sri Lanka under the Yuan Mongol dynasty to procure jewels and medicinal drugs. On three occasions ambassadors were instructed to negotiate the purchase of the Buddha's sacred alms bowl which was part of the King of Sri Lanka's collection of relics:

> Opposite the altar of the Buddha was placed a great alms bowl made of a substance that was neither jade nor copper nor iron. It was crimson in colour and luminous, and when struck it rang out like glass. So at the beginning of this dynasty [Yuan], ambassadors were dispatched on three separate occasions to bring it back.[25]

The bowl placed before statues of the Buddha contained an offering of water or food. There was one in front of each statue and they were not considered as relics. This report by the Chinese authorities confirms in part Marco Polo's account of the embassy sent to the King of Sri Lanka.

The second part of Marco Polo's tale makes it easier to identify the purpose of his mission in 1284. Missing from some of the manuscripts in Latin,[26] it is located between the description of the "Maabar" coast (coast of Coromandel in the southeast of India) and that of the Malabar coast (southwest India) in the *Société de Géographie* edition. This passage, which is not in the initial chapter on Sri Lanka, has a certain significance, as indicated by the care taken to include it further on. Marco Polo was careful not to neglect anything which might amuse or please, or for that matter to leave out anything important, so he returns to tell us:

> certain particulars which I omitted when before speaking of the island of Zeilan: Now it befel that the Great Kaan heard how on that mountain there was the sepulchre of our first father Adam, and that some of his hair and of his teeth, and a dish from which he used to eat, were still preserved there. So he thought he would get hold of them some how or another, and dispatched a great embassy for the purpose, in the year of Christ, 1284. The ambassadors, with a great company, travelled on by sea and by land until they arrived at the Island of Seilan, and presented themselves before the King. And they were so urgent with him that they succeeded in getting two of the grinder teeth, which were passing great and thick; and they also got some of the hair, and the dish from which the personnage used to eat, which is of a very beautiful green prophyry. And when the Great Kaan's ambassador had obtained the object for which they had come they were greatly rejoiced, and returned to their lord. And when they drew near to the great city of Cambaluc, where the Great Kaan was staying, they sent him word that they had brought back that for which he had sent them. On learning this the Great Kaan was passing glad, and ordered all the ecclesiastics and others to go forth to meet these relics, which he was led to believe were those of Adam.[27]

Buddhists venerate Sri Pada, a footprint they believe to be that of the Buddha. Situated at the top of the summit commonly known as Adam's Peak,[28] Sri Pada has given its name to the whole mountain. The sacred footprint is a hollow form in the rock which only vaguely resembles a human footprint and which is supposed to represent the mark left by the Buddha's foot on one of his visits to Sri Lanka. During the first millennium B.C. the divinities of the Indian world were often only represented by a footprint marking the supernatural presence and its occupation of a sacred place. Buddhists had established a sanctuary there in the third century B.C. and pilgrimages to it were encouraged from around 100 B.C. and continue to this day.[29] Muslims saw the footprint as the mark of their first parent fallen from Paradise, the other foot being placed on the Kaaba in Mecca.

At no point does Marco Polo mention this object of worship. He seems to be quite unaware of its existence: "Furthermore you must know that in the Island of Seilan there is an exceeding high mountain; it rises up so steep and precipitous that no one could ascend it, were it not that they have taken and fixed to it several great and massive iron chains, so disposed that by help of these men are able to mount to the top."[30] This description of the chains that help pilgrims to climb to the summit of

Adam's Peak and which are still there today should not mislead us about
Marco Polo's visit to the mountain.[31] Marco Polo did not know the real
reason for the pilgrimages to Adam's Peak, and drew his own conclusions, placing the tomb of "Sagamoni Borcan"[32] and his relics there. It is
not very likely that the relics, preserved so carefully by the Sinhalese
kings for the power they conferred on them, would have been offered to
the Great Khan. The person who possessed them was not only acknowledged as king, but was also invested with supernatural powers; the procession of the Buddha's Tooth Relic served the additional purpose of
bringing rain and thus prosperity to the land.[33]

The importance attached to rubies as described by Marco Polo
brings vividly to mind the magical and religious role of the Buddha's
Tooth Relic. In fact, we believe that the two elements "relic" and "ruby"
should be inverted. Would Marco Polo's readers have been quite so
impressed if he had said that the relics, which they would in any case
have regarded as worthless if they were not connected with Adam, had
been refused to the Mongol Emperor but that he had been given a
"bowl" in green porphyry and other precious stones? The other relics
were in fact soon forgotten in favor of the dish with such magical powers: "That if food for one man be put therein it shall become enough for
five men." The myth of this bowl dates back to Indian antiquity as a
didactic Tamil novel of the second century A.D. shows: "I have brought
you the magic bowl called 'Cow of Abundance' which once belonged to
Aputra. Each and everyone of you must venerate this divine bowl."[34] It
would have been difficult for Marco Polo to admit that the Khan had
asked for relics of the Buddha at a time when the Christian West
believed him to be favorable to the Christian religion. It was far better to
pretend that he thought they were Adam's relics, which would be far
more acceptable.[35]

Who was "Sagamoni Borcan"? Sagamoni is Sakyamuni, one of the
most common names for the Buddha, meaning the ascetic of Sakya.
Sakya is the princely clan to which he belonged and the Sanskrit word
"muni" which is translated as sage or saint, derives in fact from "mauna"
or silence. Bourkan is the Mongol name for the Buddha. It means a person who will provide proof, a witness and, by extension, a saint.

Up to this point Marco Polo had described the various Buddhist
communities he came across in his travels, recounting with astonishment the extraordinary powers and some of the practices of the "idolaters." He felt he had to include an account of the life of Gotama in his
description of Sri Lanka, and the version he gives is no doubt that of the
Tibetan lamas who lived in great number at Kublai's court. Buddha,
which means "enlightened one," was used only at the end of his life.
Gotama is one of the names of the future Buddha. The passage giving

two of the reasons (old age and death) that impelled Gotama to abandon his life as a prince for that of an ascetic is not included in the manuscript published by Pauthier.

In his account Marco Polo introduced dialogues as well as touches of lyricism which he generally avoided. His conclusion is rather surprising for a thirteenth-century Italian Catholic:

> So what did he one night but take his departure from the palace privily, and betake himself to certain lofty and pathless mountains. And there he did abide, leading a life of great hardship and sanctity, and keeping great abstinence, just as if he had been a Christian. Indeed, and he had but been so, he would have been a great saint of Our Lord Jesus Christ, so good and pure was the life he led.[36]

Even though Marco Polo was fascinated by the life of the Buddha and came close to acknowledging that he was worthy of inclusion in the ranks of the saints, his tone changes when evoking his accession to the status of god and his various rebirths or Jataka. The Jataka, numbering 549, are the subject of very popular stories which are part of the Buddhist literary canon.[37] He also mentions the belief in metempsychosis without really understanding it, which goes some way to explaining the distance he took:

> And they all *declared* him to be a god; and so they still *say*. They *tell* moreover that he hath died four score and four times. The first time he died as a man, and came to life again as an ox; and then he died as an ox and came to life again as a horse, and so on until he had died four score and four times; and every time he became some kind of animal. But when he died the eighty-fourth time they *say* he became a god.[38]

The way in which Marco Polo stressed the origin of his information, e.g. "so they say" or words to that effect like a refrain, is clearly an effort to distance himself from the "idol." In that regard it must not be forgotten that on the occasion of an initial journey in 1266, Kublai had sent the two Polo brothers to Rome to ask the Pope to send him "As many as an hundred persons of our Christian faith; intelligent men, acquainted with the Seven Arts."[39] As they returned to the Khan without the missionaries one may wonder whether they had assumed that role themselves.

Although Marco Polo no longer had any illusions about the possibility of converting the Mongols and could talk articulately with their emperor about Buddhism, he had every reason to fear that on reading his tale Christians might come to doubt the "true God." Did that fear not lead to the omission of this chapter in certain manuscripts? However, Marco Polo stressed the importance of Holy Scripture as the supreme authority and guarantee of the truth, as the judgement of God was the proof *par excellence* of truth:

> The Idolaters come thither on pilgrimage from very long distances and with great devotion, just as Christians go to the shrine of Messer Saint James in Gallicia. And they maintain that the monument on the mountain is that of the king's son, according to the story I have been telling you; and that the teeth, and the hair, and the dish that are there were those of the same king's son, whose name was Sagamoni Borcan, or Sagamoni the Saint. But the Saracens also come thither on pilgrimage in great numbers, and *they* say it is the sepulchre of Adam.
>
> Whose they were in truth, God knowest; howbeit, according to the Holy Scriptures of our Church, the sepulchre of Adam is not in that part of the world.[40]

While it is true that Marco Polo was accused by his contemporaries of being an impostor, it seems that this was more because of the new insight he brought to their vision of the world than because of the fables which were, as we shall see, so much cultural background. Marco Polo was certainly aware that he might not be taken seriously, which explains why he hesitated, oscillating between new facts and fable. He did indeed arouse suspicion, and was in fact accused of lying, but his standing is attested to by the number of times it was felt necessary to repeat and recall his "lies." The missionaries who followed him such as Jourdain de Catala[41] and Odoric of Pordenone[42] used his descriptions as a basis for their own.

Notes

1. Lewis Carroll, *Alice's Adventures in Wonderland*, Bilingual edition (Paris: Aubier-Flammarion, 1970), p. 78.
2. Marco Polo in *Recueil de voyage et de mémoires* (Société de Géographie), vol. 1, p.1. The prologue is not in the later manuscripts published by G. Pauthier.
3. *Le Livre de Marco Polo*, published by G. Pauthier (Paris: Firmin Didot, 1865). The English version used is *The Book of Ser Marco Polo, the Venetian, concerning the kingdoms and marvels of the East*, translated and edited, with notes, by Colonel Sir Henry Yule, R.E., C.B., K.C.S.I., Corr. Inst. France, 3d ed. (London: John Murray, 1903).
4. *Book of Ser Marco Polo*, vol. 1, p. 28.
5. *Book of Ser Marco Polo*, vol. 2, p. 312.
6. *Book of Ser Marco Polo*, vol. 2, pp. 312-13.
7. B. Gunasekara, ed., *The Rajavaliya or a Historical Narrative of Sinhalese Kings from Vijaya to Vimala Dharma Surya II* (Colombo: George J.A. Skeen, Government Printer, 1900; reprint, 1954), p. 23.
8. J. de Barros, *Terceira Década da Ásia* (Lisbon, 1563), bk. 2, ch. 1, f. 26r. Quoted by W.G.L. Randles in *De la terre plate à la terre ronde* (Paris: Armand Colin).
9. "Vâlmîki, Le Ramayana, II, Aranyakânda, Kiskinhâkânda et Sundarakânda," *Sarga* 41: 23-5, tr. A. Roussel (Paris: Adrien Maisonneuve, 1979), p. 371. See also *Sarga* 48: 10-11, 140-41.
10. Pomponius Mela (44 A.D.), *Description de la Terre*, 3, 7. On the exaggerated dimensions attributed to the island, see A. Abeydeera, "Aspects mythiques de la cartographie de l'île de Ceylan," in the collection *L'Ile, territoire mythique* (Paris: Aux amateurs de livres, 1989), pp. 1-17.
11. Ch. Langlois, *La vie en France au Moyen Age*, vol. 3 (Geneva: Slatkine, 1970), pp. 127-28.
12. C.W. Nicolas; S. Paranavitana, *A Concise History of Ceylon* (Colombo: Ceylon University Press, 1961), p. 289. See also S. Paranavitana, *Ceylon and Malaysia* (Colombo: Lake House), p. 122.
13. *Book of Ser Marco Polo*, vol. 2, p. 313.
14. G. Atkinson, *Les nouveaux horizons de la Renaissance française* (Paris: Droz, 1935), p. 70.
15. *Book of Ser Marco Polo*, vol. 2, p. 366.
16. *Book of Ser Marco Polo*, vol. 2, p. 314.
17. *Book of Ser Marco Polo*, vol. 1, p. 260.
18. *Book of Ser Marco Polo*, vol. 2, p. 313.
19. Ibid.
20. Ibid.
21. I. Battuta, *Voyages*, Arabic text accompanied by a French translation by C. Defrémery and B.R. Sanguinetti, vol. 4 (Paris: Imprimerie Nationale, 1922), p. 177. Also *The Travels of Ibn Battuta*, translated into English by Sir Hamilton Gibb (Hakluyt Society).
22. Battuta, *Voyages*, vol. 2 (1914), pp. 81-82.
23. For the allusion to the three jewels, see *Pujavaliya*, "The thirteenth-century literary work of Mayurapada Buddhaputra," in C.H.B. Reynolds, ed., *An Anthology of Sinhalese Literature up to 1815, selected by the UNESCO National Commission of Ceylon* (London: George Allen and Unwin, 1970), p. 190.
24. Battuta, *Voyages*, vol. 3, p. 260.

25. Wang Ta-Yuan, "Notices of Ceylon in Tao i Chich Lüeh," *Journal of the Royal Asiatic Society* 27 (73) (Ceylon): pp. 31-32. Wang Ta-Yuan visited Ceylon in 1432 with the naval expedition of Cheng Ho.

26. See H. von Tscharner, ed., *Der Mitteldeutsche Marco Polo nach der Admonter Handschrift: Deutsche Texte des Mittelalters*, vol. 40, Preußische Akademie der Wissenschaften (Berlin: Weidmannsche Buchhandlung, 1935), pp. 58-59.

27. *Book of Ser Marco Polo*, pp. 319-20.

28. On the Edenic vision of Adam's Peak by a Franciscan, see A. Abeydeera, "Jean de Marignolli: envoyé du pape au jardin d'Adam," *L'Inde et l'Imaginaire, Purusartha No. 11* (Paris: EHESS, 1988), pp. 59-67.

29. See S. Paranavitana, *The God of Adam's Peak*.

30. *Book of Ser Marco Polo*, p. 316.

31. For the chains which help people to the summit, see the miniature in *Le livre des Voyages de Marco Polo*, translated by Robert Frescher, Manuscript 5219 (675 H.F.), folio 133 verso (Paris: Bibliothèque de l'Arsenal).

32. See Paul Pelliot, *Notes on Marco Polo*, 3 vols (Paris: Imprimerie Nationale, 1959-1973).

33. For descriptions of the disappearance and appearance of rain after displays of the Buddha's Tooth Relic, see *The Chulavamsa being the more recent part of the Mahavamsa*, part 2, translated by Wilhelm Geiger (Colombo: The Ceylon Government Information Department, 1953), chap. 83: 5-13, pp. 177-78, and also *The Rajavaliya*, p. 56.

34. Shattan, *Manimékhalaï ou Le scandal de la vertu*, Chant 11: 137, p. 88, translated from the ancient Tamil by Alain Danielou (Paris, Flammarion, 1987); see also Manimekhalai, R.N. Saltore, *Encyclopaedia of Indian Culture*, vol. 3 (New Delhi, Bangalore, and Jalandhar: Sterling Publishers, 1914), pp. 911-14.

35. See the excellent study by J. Witte, *Das Buch des Marco Polo als Quelle für Religionsgeschichte* (Berlin: Hutten-Verlag, 1916), in particular pp. 20-36: "Der Buddhismus, Ceylon, Adam's Grab, Buddhas Lebensbeschreibung, Buddha-Reliquien."

36. *Book of Ser Marco Polo*, vol. 2, p. 318.

37. See *Choix de Jâtaka: extraits des Vies antérieures du Bouddha*, translated from the Pali by G. Terral (Paris: Gallimard, Collection de Connaissance de l'Orient, 1979).

38. *Book of Ser Marco Polo*, vol. 2, p. 318. The emphasis is ours.

39. *Book of Ser Marco Polo*, vol. 1, p. 13.

40. *Book of Ser Marco Polo* vol. 2, p. 319.

41. Fr Jourdain Catalani de Sévérac, *Les Merveilles de l'Asie*, translation with introduction and notes by Henri Cordier (Paris: Paul Geuthner, 1925).

42. *Les voyages en Asie au XIVe siècle du bienheureux frère Odoric de Pordenone, religieux de Saint-François*, published with an introduction and notes by Henri Cordier (Paris: Ernest Leroux, 1891).

Chapter 4

INDUS-GULF RELATIONS
A Reassessment in the Light of New Evidence

Nilofer Shaikh

The present study is intended to examine the role of coastal people and maritime contacts in the third millennium B.C. between South and Southwest Asia. The region saw the rise of urban civilizations at that time. This transformation in Indus is shown here to have been brought about by means of contacts of the Indus people along the routes that were adopted by them at different times. These routes—initially the land routes in pre-Indus times and later the sea route in the Mature Indus time—also brought the Persian Gulf region onto the map of the Indus interaction sphere.

The first evidence of Indus contacts with the Persian Gulf and with Mesopotamia occurred in the Mature period in the latter part of the third millennium B.C. There was a shift in the trade routes from north to south during this period, with increasingly greater reliance being placed on sea routes. So much so in fact that the Indus people extended their activities in the region of Indian Gujarat in the east and sped westward to have direct relations with the Gulf States and through them with Mesopotamia. This extended geographic connection along the coastal maritime route necessitated the establishment of many seaports, enlarged the economic prospect of their material development by placing at their disposal the raw materials and trade benefits of a wider region, and, finally, persuaded them to evolve new commercial mechanisms and the attendant structures. This led to the evolution of all the accoutrements that are associated with the name of the Mature Indus civilization and which include not only agricultural and industrial developments but also administrative measures such as the promulgation of standard weights and measures, a system of numeral notation and writing, the practice of sealing commercial goods, and the opening of far-flung commercial colonies such as Shortughai and Ras-al-Junayz. This extension eastwards of the Indus civilization with direct connection by sea to distant parts not only changed the nature of the Bronze Age civilization in the Indus land but also led to the development of intermediate sites along the Persian Gulf. This activity made them international and there can be no doubt that it was the Indus contacts with Mesopotamia (where objects of Mature Indus origin have been noted) that for the first time involved sea route connections and gave rise to the Persian Gulf.

The sea route connections are mentioned in the Mesopotamian commercial and literary documents of the third millennium B.C. These documents refer to a number of places such as Anshan, Aratta, Dilmun, Gupin, Magan, and Meluhha. Of these, Dilmun, Magan, and Meluhha have been of particular importance to cuneiformists and archaeologists and are usually referred to as being connected by sea. On the basis of archaeological and literary evidence, these three places may reasonably be supposed to correspond to the following modern regions:

- Dilmun: Failaka, Bahrain, and Oman
- Magan: Southern Iraq, the Bampur Valley, and Makran region of Iran
- Meluhha: Indus and the Ghaggar/Hakra Valley

It was this literary and archaeological evidence from Mesopotamia and Indus that persuaded archaeologists to explore the Persian Gulf region. Excavations in Bahrain, eastern Arabia, Failaka, Oman, and Tarut, and research on the existence of the Persian Gulf trade attest to the existence of contacts by sea between the Indus world, the Persian Gulf, and Mesopotamia during the Mature Indus period. It is important to note that sea connections have been traced during the Mature period only, and not before or after it.

The coast from Mesopotamia down the Gulf all along the Arabian Sea to Gujarat is dotted with sites bearing traces of the Mature Indus period. In fact it is because of the Indus-Mesopotamia contacts that these occur in the Gulf area. While presence of Indus objects in Mesopotamia has already been reported by a number of archaeologists, recent findings in Oman and the Persian Gulf have thrown fresh light on such Indus-Mesopotamia contacts. Such material was clearly seaborne through the Gulf area. Objects found in the west and which show evidence of Indus contacts include some of those mentioned in the ancient texts. To date any material reported of western origin in Indus is almost negligible, nor do the texts refer to exports from Mesopotamia to Meluhha. The only findings showing similarity or actual imports include a few cylinder seals from Mohenjo-daro and Harappa, and one from Kalibangan. These seals appear to be of local workmanship rather than imports, even though the style, shape or motif was copied. One cylinder-shaped seal has recently been reported from Sibri belonging to period VIII c. 2000 B.C.[1] and another seal also from Sibri is reported by Santoni,[2] both show different motifs, one with a hunting scene engraved on it, the other made of black steatite with a zebu facing a lion. One round seal found on the surface at Lothal was a late Persian Gulf type Dilmun seal and was probably an import. One other seal has been reported by Srivasta[3] from Dwarka; it may be a Persian Gulf seal but no plate has been published, so that this remains unconfirmed. Other objects that appear to have been actual imports include chlorite vessels from Mohenjo-daro. One of these with a mat pattern was reported from early levels in DK-G south. A similar design is found at Tepe Yahya, where such vessels were manufactured, and in Susa in Iran and Tarut in the Persian Gulf island where they also appear to have been manufactured. Another vessel from Mohenjo-daro has hatched triangles and a chevron design. This too was an import. One vessel of chlorite with a dot-in-circle design was found in the DK-B area four feet below the surface during major excavations at Mohenjo-daro in 1925 but was not reported by Marshall. Such vessels with the dot-in-circle motif were characteristic of Persian Gulf chlorite vessels, called "Serie recente"[4] and may have traveled by sea from the Gulf. The mat and chevron design vessels, which are early and are known as "Intercultural style" vessels,[5] probably came through Tepe Yahya via the southern land route as connections by sea were a later development when Yahya's links and production industry came to an end. One pottery jar was reported from Balakot period II and is considered by the excavator to be a near-eastern import from the Persian Gulf, probably from Umm-an-Nar,[6] being non-Harappan in shape and decoration.

The Persian Gulf sites (Oman and the Persian Gulf are also referred to as Dilmun civilization sites), which have furnished evidence of contacts with Mature Indus, include objects that either show similarity in style or are direct imports. These factors, taken together, both point to the direct export of objects and the exchange of ideas, a further dimension of trade. The Oman and Persian Gulf sites that have produced Indus-related materials are: Umm-an-Nar, Shimal, Ras-al-Ghanada, Ras-al-Junayz, Hilli, Bat, Amlah, Buraimi, Maysar I, Ras-al-Qala, Barbar, Al-Hajjar, Hamad town, Sar, Tarut, and Failaka. The Gulf site evidence shows clearly that the Mature Indus people (also referred to here as Mohenjo-darians) had contacts by sea in the later third and early second millennium B.C. It is equally clear that the Kulli culture of Baluchistan, which was contemporary with the Mature Indus period, had contacts with the Persian Gulf. Although the Gulf sites had been in contact with Mesopotamia and Iran since Ubaid and Jamdet Nasr times, the rise of Gulf sites appears to coincide with the rise of Indus cities in the east. The reverse may be true, but this can only be established through further research.

Sites along the eastern and western coasts and in the interior of the Oman peninsula have furnished objects that show similarity to Indus material, are actual imports or else were manufactured in a third place although they are found in both regions. These items are considered here in a site-by-site fashion.

The excavations at Umm-an-Nar uncovered a residential area and some large collective stone tombs containing goods of foreign origin. These included lapis lazuli beads: the presence of lapis lazuli in the Gulf sites indicates sea-transport from Indus, as lapis mines in Badakhshan had the presence of Mature Indus settlement Shortughai.[7] Moreover, lapis lazuli was an item that some texts reported as having traveled from Meluhha to Mesopotamia and Umm-an-Nar; there may have been a trading center of Dilmun culture on the way. Other objects of Indus origin were etched carnelian beads. Such beads were widely distributed in west Asia; so far the only working of etched beads has been found at Chanhu-daro and Lothal. Other objects which indicate some sort of contact with the Indus are the chlorite vessels with similar mat and dot-in-circle designs as encountered at Mohenjo-daro. The dot-in-circle design (Série récente) is commonly found at Gulf sites and was a product of the Gulf region. A single band of gold is also reported from Umm-an-Nar although the region of origin of the gold is not known. The movement of gold from Meluhha to Mesopotamia is reported in the texts[8] and the possibility that Indus supplied gold may also be inferred from the increase in the quantity of gold objects between the pre- and the Mature periods in the Indus valley. The presence of tin in the artifacts of Umm-an-Nar is also of great significance. Proportions of up to 2 percent of tin have been reported in objects, thereby suggesting deliberate inclusion, there being no sources of tin in the region and in view of the fact that the Gudea period texts also refer to the import of tin from Meluhha. Other resemblances were noted in pottery—these included vessels bearing the elongated bull design of the Kulli culture. Shimal, on the west coast of the Oman peninsula, has furnished evidence of contacts. Objects from a grave included a stone weight of Indus type[9] and a late Indus type jar.[10] This find of Indus weight is important—Dilmun texts used weights of different denomination than Sumer—in that it suggests that the weighing system in use in the Gulf area was in accordance with the weighing system of the Indus. These weights of Indus type are found at various sites in the Gulf region. The Shimal site has also furnished evidence of a chlorite vessel with dot-in-circle design, though the vessel is of a different shape to the Mohenjo-daro vessel; nevertheless, such vessels with dot-in-circle design were a characteristic feature of the Gulf region. There are no other reported traces of Indus contact. Ras-al-Ghanada, located between Abu Dhabi and Dubai, has provided evidence of Indus-type pottery. Archaeometric analysis shows that this pottery was locally manufactured along with local Oman pottery.

The site of Ras-al-Junayz, on the eastern coast of Oman, has furnished evidence of contacts. These include an Indus shard with four pictograms of Indus script incised on it. Kenoyer mentioned that the ware of this shard is similar to jars found at Balakot where they were regarded as containers for exportation. Such ware is also reported from other Oman sites such as Hilli 8, Ras-al-Ghanada, and Maysar. Inspection of the surface at Ras-al-Junayz by a Franco-Italian team yielded further evidence of Mature Indus, including Indus shards among local metal and ceramic products. Tosi chronologically dated this site between the late third and early second millennium B.C. [11] *Fasciolaria trapezium*, a shell which is distributed along the Indus coast and was a common species at Mature Indus sites has also been found here. Whether this was an import or the people themselves collected it is difficult to say, but other items of Indus association recovered from this site included large pottery jars, copper and steatite seals, alabaster vases, metal objects, and an ivory comb.[12] The ivory comb has direct parallels with the Indus ivory combs reported from Mohenjo-daro, Harappa, and Kalibangan. No area other than Indus has produced ivory objects in such large numbers, hence it was the likely area of origin. Moreover, the texts mention the import of ivory combs from Dilmun, an indication that Indus sometimes traded its produce via this place.

The sites in the interior of Oman peninsula have yielded evidence of contacts on the one hand with Indus and southeast Iran, and on the other with Persian Gulf sites and Mesopotamia. Hilli has imparted both local and foreign material. Hilli A afforded pottery designs that are similar to Mature Indus pottery motifs. These include trapezes, hatched designs appearing in combination with floral-zoomorphic elements, dotted fish scales, and palm and pipal leaf. This pottery may not have been an imported item, being probably locally produced, yet the fact remains that common features of motifs indicate an Indus influence on Oman culture. Pipal leaf design is not native to Oman but is a characteristic feature of Indus pottery, hence its presence here manifests Indus contacts with Hilli. Among the zoomorphic motifs, the presence of peacock on pottery, points to connection with Indus. Hilli 8 too had some important ceramic connections with Indus: the rim shard of an Indus-type jar was found here, with red slip outside and dark grey slip inside. Similar ware came from Balakot (which Kenoyer assumed were made for export) and Mohenjo-daro. Other Indus type pottery was found with fingernail decoration. Hilli also yielded pottery having Kulli parallels: such pottery was reported from a tomb and had felines with striped bodies painted in dark brown or buff paste. Also present at Hilli 8 was a cord-impressed pottery in IIf and III. Such cord-impressed pottery is found at Indus sites and has also been recovered from Shortughai and Garden Reg. Other evidence recalling direct Indus parallels include two etched carnelian beads from Tomb A in Hilli north. One bead has exact parallels with beads from Ur cemetery and Lothal. This bead comes under Reads type D. The other has parallels in Ur and Chanhu-daro. One etched bead is also reported from tomb B at Hilli with honeycomb design. Other items from Hilli include beads of agate, shell, frit, and some silver. Another denominator of contacts with Hilli are the chlorite vessels with a single row of dotted circle motif below the rim. Such vessels have also been found on other Oman sites, e.g. Bat, and rectangular compartmented boxes with similar decoration at Hilli, Bat, and Amlah. Chlorite vessels from tomb A at Hilli north and Hilli 3 number some eighty items, of which a hemispherical bowl with dot-in-circle design just beneath the rim has connections with the Indus chlorite bowl and is also found in southeast Iran. Weisgerber[13] believed that these bowls were made in Oman and cited the presence of unfinished vessels at Maysar as an indication of this. Qatarah and Al-Qusais too produced evidence of such bowls. One was found at Telloh, being dedicated by Ur-Baba, son of a merchant Shesh Shesh, to an unknown prince of Lagash and has now been dated to Ur III period.[14] Similar vessels were found at Tepe Yahya IV A and Susa. This item in fact moved from west to east, as only one piece has so far been found at Mohenjo-daro. Tin is also reported in Hilli metal artifacts. An analysis of a sword showed a tin content of 6.5 percent and a mould of a tap hole associated with the remains of a furnace had a tin content of 5 percent. As noted above, there are no sources of tin in Oman, hence it most likely came from the Indus. Buraimi, another site near Hilli, in the Oman peninsula, has also furnished evidence of Indus contacts. Here some Kulli-type pottery, i.e., a grey canister with forward tumbling caprids, horned heads, and triangles, was found. Maysar I furnished evidence of an important triangular stone prism. This three-sided seal had on one side a short-horned bull with lowered head and probably a manger in front. Such prism-shaped seals have been found in Mohenjo-daro and one in Harappa. During Caspers[15] has tried to connect these prism seals with the Aegean world where such prisms are found. Ceramic evidence from Maysar I includes cord-impressed and fingernail decoration pottery; the latter takes the form of careful straight cuts in the clay before firing. It is characteristic of Mature Indus pottery and is also reported from Shortughai.

The Oman sites not only point to connections with the Indus Valley, but have a marked relationship with southeastern Iranian sites and bear evidence of Mesopotamian burials and pottery dating from Jamdet Nasr times onwards. Indus contacts appear to have been confined to the Mature Indus period only. Cleuziou[16] was of the opinion that the Oman Peninsula and eastern Iran had active cultural contacts in the second quarter of the third millennium B.C. and that these links were stronger with Indus in the early second millennium B.C. This in fact reflects and supports the textual evidence which indicates strong relations between Magan and Sumer in the Ur III period, while Dilmun was referred to principally as having trade links with Magan. In the Larsa period, Dilmun prospered while Meluhhan trade was directed through it, and links with southeastern Iran appear to have fallen off. The evidence of plano-convex bricks of the Early Dynastic period in Oman at Hilli 8 further supports the textual evidence that this region was Dilmun, which was referred to in respect of the import of raw materials during the Early Dynastic Period.

Further up the Gulf, archaeological investigation has revealed the Dilmun culture which was known as Barbar in Bahrain and Failaka. This Dilmun culture now includes the Persian Gulf area and the Oman Peninsula. Ras-al-Qala, on the northern shores of Bahrain Island furnished some significant evidence to clarify the chronology of the Gulf sites in relation to others. The site furnished evidence of seven sites buried one on top of the other. The lowest of these contained chain-ridged pottery and a few Persian Gulf seals, round-shaped and with primitive design, closely resembling those of Indus. The boss at the back was a high boss with single groove at right angles to the perforation. These seals are known as Early Dilmun or Persian Gulf seals. City No. 2 above the earlier one had Barbar pottery known as red-ridged pottery and Late Persian Gulf seals which are also called Dilmun seals. These seals had at the back a wide boss with triple grooves and four incised dot-in-circles. These seals were round-shaped unlike Indus which were square or Mesopotamian which were cylindrical. About 300 Late Persian Gulf seals are reported from Bahrain and Failaka. Ras-al-Qala has produced some very interesting ones. One round seal with a small high boss and single grooved line, had a typically Indus motif, i.e., a short-horned bull with five Indus pictographs. This seal was found at the basal foundation of the earliest City No.2 wall gateway. Another round seal had a bull and Indus script, and a boss matching that of early seals. Such seals are a clear indication of the presence of Indus merchants in Bahrain. Similar seals, round-shaped and with early boss and Indus-related motifs have also been reported from Ur. Further evidence suggesting foreign connections at Ras-al-Qala includes scraps of copper and bun-shaped copper ingots. These have also been found at Mohenjo-daro, Lothal, and Susa. Spherical and cubical stone weights are reported from Bahrain; analysis has shown a mere 1 percent of variation with their Indus counterparts.[17] Seven such weights were found in Ras-al-Qala. Other items of Indus origin at Ras-al-Qala include ivory tusks and fragments. This site has also furnished evidence of a linga-shaped gamesman of which an identical parallel was found at Mohenjo-daro. Some lapis lazuli beads and fragments of chlorite bowls with dot-in-circle design are other items of exchange. At Barbar in Bahrain, Temples I and II also produced some Indus-related objects. Lapis lazuli was reported which included three conical gamesmen, two cylindrical beads, and pendants. The pendants were similar to those found in Indus valley. Ivory objects included two small pieces sawn off from larger ones, and a part of a flat object decorated with dot-in-circle motif, perhaps part of an ivory comb from Temple II. Ivory was an import item from Meluhha; its presence at Gulf sites and its extensive use in Indus indicate its movement from east to west via the sea route. Five etched carnelian beads are reported from a group of Sar Buri tumuli on the west coast of the Island of Bahrain. Ratnager had remarked on the puzzling absence of etched beads on the Barbar sites on the sea route.[18] However, these recent reports mention their presence on the Bahrain and Oman sites along the sea route. Metal objects too are reported from Barbar. The temple complex provided evidence of a copper-bronze dove and the handle of a mirror modeled as a nude male figurine in the late third millennium contexts. Similar mirrors have been found on the Mehi Kulli culture site in Baluchistan.

The main burial chamber of the Jefferson tumulus at Hamala town, northwest of Bahrain, contained a copper-bronze goblet and a metal horned goat standing on a low base with a loop attachment soldered to one side, suggesting it is a pin or a broach. During Caspers[19] compared this to Mohenjo-daro copper-bronze animals. The Al-Hajjar complex in Bahrain yielded evidence of a triangular prism seal. On two sides of this seal there was an animal design and on the third side some Indus script. The animal design consisted of a short-horned bull with lowered head. During Casper found, however, that the script was different from that commonly found on Indus seals. [20] This may reflect the seal cutter's grasp of the Indus script, as he may have written something different to what is usually found on Indus seals. A stone weight of the Indus type was found at Hamad town in Bahrain. [21] Considering the Gulf region to be the Dilmun of the texts, it is clear that Dilmun adopted the Indus weighing system which was also adopted at Ur to measure articles according to the Dilmun standard, as attested by the presence of Indus-type weights at Ur dating from the Ur III period.

Mughal's excavations at Sar in Bahrain have thrown fresh light on Indus-Gulf relations. Sar has yielded large numbers of chlorite vessels with dot-in-circle designs similar to the Mohenjo-daro vessels reported earlier. Mughal assigns these vessels with Dilmun-type seals to the late third and early second millennium B.C. The seals found at Sar include both early and late types which are thought to have been made locally but betray some influence of Mesopotamian and Indus art motifs.[22] They were found in a burial complex, being distributed among the graves in such a way as to reflect the persistence of early seals as heir-looms. Both types of seals were found with ceramics, steatite/chlorite vessels, and metal types characteristic of the Barbar I-III period dated in Mesopotamian terms to Ur III-Old Babylonian times. Other objects of Indus origin at Sar are agate, carnelian, and shell beads. The presence of bronze objects also points to the import of tin—as mentioned above, tin traveled from east to west, along the sea route.

Archaeological investigation on Tarut, north west of Bahrain, yielded evidence of the Ubaid to Barbar period. Intercultural-type vessels of chlorite were found here, similar to those found in Iran, Indus and Mesopotamia. Such early vessels were produced mainly at Tepe Yahya and Shahdad and were traded between all three regions. But recently Kohl[23] opined that these intercultural-style vessels were also produced at Tarut; analysis of the different vessels showed variations, and both unworked as well as complete vessels were found here. Tarut has also imparted evidence of worked and unworked lapis lazuli, alabaster vessels, and metal objects. At Tarut there is also evidence of late chlorite vessels with the dot-in-circle motif.

Further north at Failaka in the bay of Kuwait, large numbers of seals and Barbar remains were found. Reported here were also intercultural-type vessels with hut or temple facade motif, mat or weaving motif, similar to those found at Mohenjo-daro, thus indicating a common origin for both. Lapis is reported from Failaka thus confirming its movement westwards along the sea route. Seals are also found at Failaka; one cylinder-shaped seal bears Indus script. About 200 round-shaped seals are reported, but few of them have typical Indus motifs. Such seals are reported by Kjaerum.[24] One round seal had four Indus signs on the face. Another seal with a Dilmun-type boss had Indus pictographs and a short-horned bull on the front. Tell Abraq in the Gulf has also yielded Indus-type seals, pottery, and Indus weights.[25]

Conclusion

These new findings at the Gulf sites have conclusively shown that during the Mature Indus phase the sea route was gaining in importance in comparison with the land routes. In pre-Indus times the latter was in fact the only trade route linking the Indus region to Iran, Afghanistan, and Central Asia. No direct overland trade connections in the pre-Indus period have so far been evidenced with Mesopotamia. Mesopotamian trade with Indus is attested in the Mature Indus phase, mainly by the sea route: this is borne out by the presence of objects of Mature Indus origin in the Persian Gulf. These include etched carnelian beads, lapis lazuli, cubical stone weights of the same denomination as Indus, ivory and shell objects, Kulli-type pottery, Indus-type seals, triangular prisms, Indus motifs on Persian Gulf seals, Indus script on Persian Gulf round seals, and so forth. All these are definite evidence of the Mature Indus presence in the Gulf for trade purposes. As in Mesopotamia, no pre-Indus objects have been recovered here. The pre-Indus connections were all overland with Afghanistan, Iran, and Turkmenia. These links, combined with the requirements of the Mesopotamians, led to the establishment of intermediary settlements in Afghanistan and Iran along the lines of Mundigak, Shahr-i-Sokhta, and Tepe Yahya. All three went into decline when the Mohenjo-darians or the Mature Indus people began to forge ahead in their civilizational advance by capturing the world trade market. They now made a direct approach to the mineral-rich areas they had noted in their advance to Shortughai in northeast Afghanistan which must have taken place at a time when the markets of Mundigak, Shahr-i-Sokhta, and Tepe Yahya could no longer meet the expanding needs of the Mature Indus people. This led to the staggering of the northerly overland and southern routes; in particular the sea route assumed importance for the first time. This advance of the Mature Indus people brought them into direct contact with Mesopotamian civilization, which was rich in different facets of cultural maturity, including literacy, science, mathematics, and astronomy. Naturally the two civilizations mutually affected one another. The Mohenjo-darians unquestionably maintained their individual character and developed particular aspects of their innate genius. However, it is quite clear that the Indus civilization now focused increasingly on the coastal region and probably came to rely more on sea trade than on the land route connections with the north. The land route nonetheless retained some importance. It continued to act as a channel for the import of raw materials from the hinterlands. The rise and development of the Indus civilization should henceforth be viewed in terms of this directional flow. Its sudden growth to maturity can be credited not only to the fact that it controlled the rich mineral and forest resources of the northerly hills right up to Shortughai, but also to its direct approach to the civilization of West Asia by sea route.

For the first time this Bronze Age civilization extended into Gujarat in the east and right up to Sutkagendor in the west. Such coastal expansion was an absolutely new feature in the development of the mature Indus civilization, not only imparting but receiving influences from the west by sea. This sea connection was probably responsible for the new trends in the Mature Indus civilization. Mohenjo-daro in fact lay close to the center of the new expansion. This shift in routes led to a complete change in the character of Indus. Direct contact with the Gulf countries led to a new phase of expanding trade and prosperity both for Mohenjo-darians and the people of the Gulf. The presence of Mohenjo-darians in this region is attested by the presence of their seals and other goods. As long as the two trade links remained intact, Mohenjo-darians would continue to flourish. This shift in the pattern of the trade routes was obviously a landmark in the development of this civilization as well as of the Gulf countries. The pre-Indus land route connections did not bring about any fundamental change in the pre-Indus cultures; such a change occurred in the Indus delta country only with the rise of Mohenjo-daro. The Indus people were directly involved with the saltwater ecosystem for the first time.

We may well inquire as to who the Mohenjo-darians were. They may have been seamen who exploited the coastal environment and brought about some major transformations. They had the Kot Dijian character and the Baluchi character and another character too. As long as they traded overland, their character did not change; but the development of the southern sea route trade with the West led to changes in their character. This was apparent in the rise of their cities and towns, with their planned architectural layout and fortifications with bastions. They became a stratified society with a full-time craft specialization. In addition, there was an overall uniformity in material culture, as well as large-scale import and export of raw materials and finished products, and the introduction of seals, weights, measures and above all writing.

Similarly the Gulf countries also rose to maturity. It is here on the coasts that further research should be conducted to throw fresh light on the origins of Indus-Gulf civilizations. Mohenjo-daro continues to clutch the secrets of the origin of Indus civilization in its unexcavated depths— these southern areas still harbor untold riches for archaeological research.

Notes

1. A.H. Dani, *Recent Archaeological Discoveries in Pakistan* (UNESCO, 1988), pl 9.
2. M. Santoni, "Sibri and the South Cemetery of Mehrgarh: Third Millennium Connexions between the Northern Kachhi Plain (Pakistan) and Central Asia," in *SAA 1981*, edited by B. Allchin (Cambridge, 1984): pp. 52-60.
3. K.M. Srivasta, *Bahrain Indus Valley Connection*, unpublished report (Delhi: South Archaeological Congress, 1986).
4. Miroschedji (1973).
5. P.L. Kohl, "The Balance of Trade in South Western Asia in the Mid-Third Millennium B.C.," *Curr. Athr.* 19 (3) (1978): pp. 463-92.
6. G.F. Dales, "The Balakot Project: Summary of Four Years Excavation in Pakistan," in *SAA 1977*, edited by M. Taddei (Naples, 1979): pp. 241-74.
7. H.P. Frankfurt, "The Early Periods of Shortughai (Harappan) and the Western Bactria Culture of Dashly," in *SAA 1981*, edited by B. Allchin (Cambridge, 1984): pp. 170-5.
8. S.N. Kramer, *The Sumerians* (Chicago, 1970).
9. Ash (1978).
10. E.C.L. During Caspers, "A Copper-Bronze Animal in Harappan style from Bahrain: Evidence of Mercantile Interaction," *JESHO* 30 (1) (1987): pp. 30-46.
11. M. Tosi, "A Possible Harappan Sea Port in Eastern Arabia: Ras-al-Junayz in the Sultanate of Oman. Peshawar," paper presented at the First International Conference on Pakistan Archaeology (1986).
12. Ibid.
13. G. Weisgerber, "Makan and Meluhha Third Millennium B.C.: Copper Production in Oman and the Evidence of Contact with the Indus Valley," in *SAA 1981*, edited by B. Allchin (Cambridge, 1984): pp. 196-201.
14. S. Cleuziou and B. Vogt, "Tomb A at Hilli North (UAE) and its Material Connections to South-East Iran and the Greater Indus Valley," in *SAA 1983*, edited by J. Schotsmans and M. Taddei (Naples, 1985): pp. 249-77.
15. E.C.L. During Caspers, "A possible 'Harappan' contact with the Aegean World," in *SAA 1983*, edited by J. Schotsman and M. Taddei (Naples, 1985): pp. 435-52.
16. S. Cleuziou, "Oman Peninsula and its Relation Eastward during the 3rd Millennium," in *Frontiers of the Hindu Civilization*, edited by B.B. Lal and S.P. Gupta (New Delhi: Indian Archaeological Society, 1984), pp. 371-94.
17. J.G. Shaffer, "Harappan Commerce: An Alternative Perspective," in *Anthropology in Pakistan*, edited by S. Pastner and L. Flam (Indus Publications, 1982), pp. 166-200.
18. S. Ratnagar, *Encounters: The Westerly Trade of the Harappan Civilization* (Delhi: Oxford University Press, 1981), p. 130.
19. E.C.L. During Caspers, "Copper-Bronze Animal."
20. E.C.L. During Caspers, *Triangular Stamped Seals from the Arabian Gulf and Their Indus Valley Connection* (Instituto Universitario Orientale, Annali 43, 1983), pp. 661-70.
21. M.R. Mughal, personal correspondence with the author.
22. M.R. Mughal, *The Dilmun Burial Complex at Sar: The 1980-82 Excavations in Bahrain* (Bahrain: Ministry of Information, 1983).
23. P.L. Kohl, "The Lands of Dilmun Changing Cultural and Economic Relations during the Third to Early Second Millennium B.C.," in *Bahrain through the Ages: The Archaeology*, edited by Shaikha Haya Ali Al Khalifa and M. Rice (London: KPI eds., 1986), pp. 367-75.
24. P. Kjaerum, "The Stamp and Cylinder Seals," vol. 1 of *FailakalDilmun: The Second Millennium Settlements*. Jutland Archaeological Society Publication 17 (1) (1983).
25. C.C.L. Karlovsky, personal correspondence with the author.

Chapter 5

THE SOUTHERN SILK ROAD
Archaeological Evidence of Early Trade between India and Southeast Asia

Ian C. Glover

Introduction

In the popular imagination the term "Silk Road" conjures up memories of the great caravan trail by camel and pack horse from Loyang in Northern China across the high arid plateaux of Central Asia to Iran, India, southern Russia, and the Near East. But there were other routes, and scholars working in Southeast Asia are more concerned with the trails south from Yunnan into Vietnam, Thailand, Laos, and Myanmar, and of course the great "Sea Road" from the coastal ports of southern China along the Vietnamese coasts, round Cape Ca Mau into the Gulf of Thailand, to the Straits of Malacca, and the porterage routes across the peninsula linking this trade with the shipping routes across the Bay of Bengal to India and the west.

As an archaeologist working in western Thailand over the past decade I have been particularly concerned with the evidence for the start of trade contacts between India and Southeast Asia. I believe that there is now evidence to show that regular commerce across the Bay of Bengal began much earlier than we have hitherto believed, and that we have to look back into prehistory, using the methods of field archaeology, to identify its earlier stages and understand its logic.

When we speak, in historical terms, of contacts between India and Southeast Asia we think first of "Indianization," that massive and complex process which, starting perhaps about the beginning of the Christian Era, led to the transfer of so many aspects of Indian culture eastwards across the Bay of Bengal. This is an immense field of research which I can only just touch on since my primary concern is to examine the archaeological evidence in Southeast Asia for the very beginning of this process, and to seek an explanation for it.

The influence of Indian Hindu-Buddhist civilization in Southeast Asia from the middle of the first millennium A.D. is undeniable and found almost everywhere except in the remote and forested interior of the mainland or in the eastern islands of Indonesia and the Philippines. From this time on there was an increasing adoption of Hindu and Buddhist cults and, as archaeological finds witness, numerous religious monuments and icons, the latter imported from India or modeled on Indian prototypes. We have evidence for the use of Indian scripts and languages, at least for political and religious propaganda; and some ambiguous external historical sources, Chinese and Indian which record the process of Indianization. These data are presented and analyzed in numerous books and articles, of which I refer specifically to Coedès, Wolters, Wheatley, Mabbett, and Ray.[1] Before the mid-first millennium A.D., however, the data are much more meager, and until quite recently there were very few material items of undoubted Indian or Mediterranean manufacture found in Southeast Asia in contexts which suggested (for the specific context of deposition and recovery was always imprecise) that they reached there before the early centuries of the Christian era. However, the acceleration of archaeological survey and excavation in Southeast Asia, and particularly in Thailand, over the past twenty years has produced quite a number of pieces: beads, bronzes, seals, coins, an ivory comb, ceramic vessels and so on, of western origin which can help us to extend back to at least the middle of the first millennium B.C., the physical evidence for regular exchange systems spanning the Bay of Bengal. This should not really surprise us since the scale of Indianization in the first millennium A.D. was so vast that scholars have long argued that it must have been preceded by an extended period of regular, but less intense (and archaeologically less visible) contacts.

There are also arguments being put forward from the evidence of the new archaeological work in Southeast Asia that some indigenous societies of the region, particularly those with developed metallurgy and extensive flooded-field rice agricultural systems, were already developing stratified, territorially organized, semi-urbanized "states" in northern Vietnam and northeast Thailand, quite independently of stimulus or diffusion from China or India.[2] Certainly it is clear that traditional societies throughout most of western Southeast Asia were undergoing a dramatic process of restructuring from early in the first millennium A.D. This included demographic, political, and mercantile centralization, with the appearance of true urban forms which, when they became quite evident on the ground, were organized into kingdoms formally subscribing to Indian principles of polity.

Indo-Roman Trade

That Indianization in Southeast Asia was closely linked to trade seems clear from the elusive Indian historical and mythological sources,[3] much of which was by sea.[4] Voyaging to Suvarnabhumi or Suvarnadvipa, the fabled Lands of Gold was, according to the Indian historical accounts, a hazardous undertaking and "shipwreck, ordeal by scorching sun, tempest, hunger and thirst, as well as plagues of serpents and insects" were among the perils to be expected by travelers. It is clear that these were speculative mercantile voyages for commercial profit, financed by merchant guilds in many parts of India. Kautilya, in the *Arthasastra*, that famous manual of advice for achieving worldly success, originally compiled in the fourth century B.C., ranks the pursuit of profit above all other goals of life, even the paths of virtue and love. As a later writer put it: "Who goes to Java, never returns. If by chance he returns then he brings back enough money to support seven generations of his family." Most of the existing Indian texts seem to have been compiled, in their surviving forms, only in the early centuries of the Christian era but are thought to reflect a reality of Indian-Southeast Asian voyaging established in the late centuries of the pre-Christian era. In them Suvarnabhumi is reported both as a place for profitable trading and as a field for Buddhist proselytization. At least three missionaries, Gavampti, Sona, and Uttara, are named in the text *Sasanavamsappadipika*; the last two are said to have been despatched by the Emperor Asoka to convert the people of Suvarnabhumi soon after the third Buddhist council in the middle of the third century B.C.

I emphasize these Indian historical sources because, in the context of Southeast Asian prehistory, it is important for us to appreciate that the late prehistoric period saw the expansion of a complex and powerful mercantile system into an area in which trade networks certainly existed; but for which the most appropriate models are the ethnographically-known reciprocal exchange cycles of eastern Melanesia-Kula, Vitiaz Strait, Mailu, and others.[5] Ray argues that the middle of the first millennium B.C. saw the rise of specialized trading communities (*vanijas* and *setthis*) in the middle Ganga Valley dealing in salt, textiles, metals, and pottery.[6] Money was increasingly coming into use and this was associated with the spread of the new cults of Buddhism and Jainism which accepted the accumulation and reinvestment of wealth; this concept was quite alien to the culture of the Vedic period in which reciprocal exchange of the "prestige goods" type was the normal method of distributing exotic and luxury items. Long-distance trade between the agricultural hinterland of the middle Ganga Valley, the ports such as Tamralipti (Tamluk) in the Ganga Delta, and those at the mouth of the Narmada Valley such as Broach (Barygaza of the *Periplus*) developed rapidly at this time, and the gemfields and gold-rich deposits of south India were quickly integrated into this trade.

By the early part of the Christian era these trade routes reached out to bring together the previously rather disparate Southeast Asian exchange systems, linking them into a vast network stretching from Western Europe via the Mediterranean Basin, the Persian Gulf, and the Red Sea to India, Southeast Asia and China. This period saw the first appearance of what has been called the World System—the economic integration by trade of most of the inhabited globe, excepting the Americas and Australasia, and its significance for the subsequent development of Southeast Asian societies cannot be ignored.

Before examining the archaeological evidence for these early links between the mainland of Southeast Asia, particularly Thailand and India, I must briefly consider the development of commercial trading systems further west and specifically those linking the Indian subcontinent with the civilizations of the Mediterranean Basin, and also the emergence of simpler exchange systems within the greater area of Southeast Asia, from Thailand and Vietnam in the north, to the islands of the Philippines and Melanesia in the south and east.[7] Ray presents the evidence for the development of trading systems down the east coast of India,[8] and other authors present up-to-date accounts of specialized aspects of Indo-Roman trade, so I will be brief and general in this section and try to emphasize the implications of this trade for contacts across the Bay of Bengal.

Indo-Roman commercial undertakings seem to have been highly organized and are quite well documented in Classical writing dating from the second century A.D. even though there is much uncertainty about details. Revisions are regularly proposed for dating the growth of this trade from the evidence provided by the excavation of archaeological sites,[9] which help to amplify the historical sources. I would also argue that virtually all new data on this trade are likely to come from archaeology, which has barely started to research the problem, rather than from literary and historical sources, which seem to be finite and mostly known.

The great expansion of Southeast Asian, and particularly of Island-Mainland exchange, which is evident in later prehistory is, I believe, closely connected with this Indo-Roman commerce. It can be explained in part, at least, by a rising demand for exotic and prestigious items of consumption and adornment in the sophisticated urban civilizations of the Mediterranean Basin, India, and, of course, China; I refer to that "splendid and trifling" trade in spices, perfumes, precious stones and pearls, silks and muslin, tortoise-shell, ivory and rhinoceros horn, dyes and unguents, ghi, lac, and so on scorned by the high-minded Gibbon for undermining republican virtues.

As an example of the demand for exotic products in the west we need only to look at the spice trade,[10] and particularly at the trade in cloves—the unopened flower-buds of the plant, *Eugenia aromatica*: *kuntze*, whose home was restricted (until the late eighteenth century A.D.) to the small islands of Ternate, Tidore, Motir, Makyan, and Bachan in the Moluccas.[11] Cloves were known in China in the third century B.C., and were described by Pliny in Rome in the first century A.D.[12] At the production end, the trade in cloves, nutmeg, and mace transformed Moluccan society from scattered kin-based communities of hunter-gatherers and shifting cultivators to stratified coastal trading states and petty empires. As Ellen points out, "It was the spice trade which was partially responsible for the Indianization of Southeast Asia and which facilitated the spread of Islam. It was responsible for the growth and demise of numerous states on the commercial routes from the Indies to the Mediterranean … and led to the first serious involvement of Europeans in Southeast Asia and the formation of colonial empires there."[13] So this Western demand for an aromatic flower-bud of rather little value to the native peoples of the Moluccas transformed, in the long run, the economic and political face of Asia. Of such small things are empires built.

Of course there was trade too in everyday raw materials to supply workshop centers servicing the trade, and foods such as sugar and rice, as well as in timber, metals and metal ores, and in manufactured products such as pottery, textiles, sewn boats, glassware, and steel. But the volume of these was probably not great, for ships were small[14] and it is almost certainly true that the demand for low-bulk, high-value luxuries drove the trade.

In India there is abundant physical evidence of this trade in the form of Mediterranean amphorae and Italic Arretine ware on the South Indian coast, Roman gold coin hoards throughout South India, numerous Classical intaglios and seals throughout southern India and Sri Lanka, and Mediterranean lead in the Satavahana coinage of Central India.[15] In the Mediterranean, although Asian imports have largely disappeared (slave girls and elephants) or decayed beyond recognition (silks and cotton, wood and lacquer), or are difficult to source (gold, gemstones), we have a remarkable reminder of this trade in the form of an exquisite Indian ivory figurine from the first century A.D. found buried under the ash of Pompeii.[16]

But what we lack in identifiable artifacts is more than made up by the wealth of textual data. For instance, we have detailed contemporary and product-specific descriptions of the structure of the trade in the *Periplus*, in Strabo's and Ptolemy's *Geographies*, and Pliny's *Natural History*. The material available has enabled historians such as Warmington, Miller, and Raschke, and archaeologists such as Wheeler to develop a comprehensive and, on the whole, convincing structure for the trade between India and the Roman world as it existed at the beginning of the Christian era.[17] These exchange systems were more developed than the ones I have described for Southeast Asia and approximate to Renfrew's "Middleman Trading" and "Port of Trade" modes.[18] And in many cases, particularly at the western ends of the trade routes, these were entrepreneurial ventures, undertaken for commercial profit, facilitated by the use of coinage, and underwritten by accumulated capital.

Eastwards from India, however, the data, historical and archaeological, becomes much more sparse. Indeed, Wheeler was unwilling to extend to Southeast Asia the well-structured trading systems which he could describe for India and the Erythrean Sea. He attributed the few Western-derived items found up to that time in Thailand and Vietnam to what he called "drift," by which apparently he meant movements of objects through intermittent, short-distance reciprocal exchange networks.[19] Certainly Wheeler did not believe that the well-organized mercantile commerce of the Indian Ocean extended at that time across the Bay of Bengal. Raschke too is doubtful whether commercial links between India and Southeast Asia were on a regular basis until well into the first millennium A.D., that is to say between about the third to sixth centuries A.D.[20] The Western items they refer to are, of course, the famous Pong Tuk lamp from a monastic site on the north bank of the Mekong River in western Thailand, a coin of Antoninus Pius, some inscribed gemstones, rings, medallions and statuary from India, and the Mediterranean seals at Oc-eo and other locations in Vietnam.[21] Since then quite a few other finds have been made or recognized and these are enough, I believe, to permit us to argue that regular exchange links between India and Southeast Asia commenced earlier than Wheeler or Raschke allowed. It is unclear, however, whether we can refer to this as trade, specifically a commercial exchange entered into for financial profit, or an extension of the "Big Man" prestige goods reciprocal type of economy which is so well-documented for recent Melanesia, and postulated below by me for earlier societies within Southeast Asia as well as for many other parts of the prehistoric world.[22]

Since Wheeler wrote, further finds of Western artifacts, for the most part casual, unprovenanced discoveries, have been documented in Southeast Asia, and later I list these and then present in a little more detail the recent evidence from the site of Ban Don Ta Phet in Thailand, which has produced the most abundant evidence to date for early Indian links with Southeast Asia.

Later Prehistoric Exchange Systems and Maritime Transport in Southeast Asia

In writing about the beginning of this process in Southeast Asia, I use the term "Later prehistory" which I find usefully vague in light of our poor control over regional chronologies, but by which I mean more or less the last millennium before, and the first few centuries after, the opening of the Christian era. This coincides roughly with Bayard's "General Period C" on the mainland of Southeast Asia,[23] but many of the technological and social criteria by which they define the period on the mainland—the use of iron, the development of intensive wet rice farming, and increased social ranking—are as yet undocumented in island Southeast Asia.

I think that it can now be accepted that by the middle of the third millennium B.C. substantial improvements had been made in maritime technology in Southeast Asia, and that long distance voyaging in double- or single-hulled outrigger canoes and plank-built boats was taking place. This period saw the expansion of pottery-using, agriculture, and probably of Austronesian-speaking peoples throughout island Southeast Asia.[24] This is particularly well-exemplified on the eastern margins of our region by the rapid colonization of many previously uninhabited islands in the western Pacific, such as Fiji, New Caledonia, New Hebrides, Tonga, and Samoa. Westward voyaging from Southeast Asia at this time is less obvious; indeed the real evidence is negligible. The distribution of Munda (a language related to Mon-Khmer in the Austroasiatic family), cord-impressed pottery, and shouldered adzes in eastern India—in Assam, Bengal, parts of Uttar Pradesh, Bihar, and Orissa—is more likely to be the result of a long-established and continuous distribution of related cultures from South China and Vietnam, through Thailand and Burma into India, than the product of maritime or even land-based trade routes. There is no evidence I know of for direct long-distance trade between Southeast Asia and India before the Iron Age, which in eastern India begins about 750 B.C. and a couple of hundred years later in Thailand according to present, albeit rather poorly supported, chronologies.[25]

The only hard evidence, up to now, for Western maritime connections with Southeast Asia is the so-called Indonesian Presence in East Africa and Madagascar. Received opinion, supported by new archaeological work, seems to put this as late as the middle of the first millennium A.D., the Early Historic period for many western Indonesian cultures.[26]

In an earlier paper, I summarized the evidence for the emergence of localized exchange networks in Indonesia in the neolithic and early metal age periods (roughly from mid-third to late first millennium B.C.), and Peacock did the same for western Malaysia.[27] More recent evidence from the mainland of Southeast Asia also demonstrates the development of this localized exchange in raw materials and exotic products in the second millennium B.C. The social context in which these exchanges took place is still obscure, but I envisage it to be in the form of "Boundary Reciprocal" or "Down-the-line" exchange of the sort formalized by Renfrew.[28] In particular we can point to the presence of arm-rings (and the raw material for making them) from such marine shell species as Trochus and Tridacna at inland sites in Central Thailand such as Kok Charoen, Ban Kao, Ban Na Di, and Tha Khae (Natapintu); and Obluang in the northwest (Santoni et al); exotic stone for arm-rings at Ban Na Di and other sites in the northeast (Higham and Kijngam); hard volcanic stone suitable for making polished adzes from the hills of the Thai-Cambodian border into the coastal lowlands (Pisnupong); and the import of lead, tin, and copper ores and metal to sites such as Ban Chiang and Non Nok Tha, also in northeast Thailand (Pigott and Natapintu; Bennett). Similar evidence is available for the late neolithic Phung Nguyen and early bronze age Go Mun cultures of Vietnam (Ha Van Tan).[29]

New Archaeological Finds from Southeast Asia Bearing on Trade with the West

Quite a few of these items are, like the earlier discoveries mentioned above, casual finds without good provenance, but increasingly material is coming from controlled excavations where the finds can be dated and related to other material in burials, habitation refuse, and so on. Taking some of the casual finds first, we should note the following discoveries in Thailand.

A copper coin of the western Roman Emperor Victorinus (A.D. 268-70), minted at Cologne, was found at U-Thong in western Thailand (Landes),[30] and is preserved in the National Museum there.

The site of Khlong Thom (also known as Khuan Lukpad or "bead mound") in Krabi Province, southern Thailand has become famous for its rich collection of glass and semi-precious stone beads, and rather notorious for the means by which most were acquired. In an attempt to salvage some reliable information, several programs of survey and limited excavation were conducted by Thai and foreign archaeologists between 1973 and 1986. Veraprasert and Bronson document the history of investigation of the site and list and illustrate some of the finds.[31] Among the ones which particularly concern me here are a number of etched agate and carnelian beads—a carnelian bead in the form of an animal, probably a lion, resembling, though smaller, the one discovered by us at Don Ta Phet (see below); glass "collar beads" similar to those from Arikamedu; a defaced Roman coin, apparently not datable;[32] and at least two, perhaps many more (Bronson pers. com.), Roman carnelian intaglios. Two of these portray the Goddess Tyche or Fortuna, and a pair of fighting cockerels. Both are common Roman types and can be dated to the late first to early second centuries A.D.[33]

Bronson also refers to other intaglios with scenes of elephants, a lion, the god Perseus, an unidentified woman, and some seals with Pallava inscriptions. Some of these seals are purely Classical while others are undoubtedly Indian.[34] Most are kept in the Wat Khlong Thom in the care of Abbot Phrakru Arthorn Sangwornkij. Amongst the glass from Khlong Thom, Veraprasert refers to rim fragments of a blue glass container "very similar to Roman glassware," and both Veraprasert and Bronson document the evidence for the local manufacture of glass and stone beads in addition to those presumably imported as finished pieces. Bronson describes the site as more of a specialized manufacturing center than an entrepôt; a place where expatriate (Indian) craftsmen worked under the protection of an enterprising local ruler, importing some raw materials (glass cullet and agate blocks) as well as finished goods (beads and seals). There is also evidence for tin smelting, perhaps for export to tin-short India. The activities at Khlong Thom lasted over several centuries and not all of them can be ascribed to the very early days of trade across the Bay of Bengal. And the isolation of the site from major population centers and urban sites with monumental architecture makes it difficult to fit it into existing categories such as "port of trade," "central place for exchange," and so on. Bronson sees Khlong Thom more as a "Colonial Enclave" in Renfrew's scheme,[35] as some type of early offshore technology park set in a tropical wilderness and, in doing so, he highlights the unusual features of the site as well as how little we really know about the structure of trade between India and Southeast Asia at this time.

Increasing numbers of etched beads are being reported in Thailand, particularly from museums in the south. These include single specimens from Ban Chiang and Saraburi and about twenty-five from the region around U-Thong.[36] However, few of these have been verified by archaeologists really familiar with Indian stone beads and, in some cases, these have turned out to be banded glass beads.

Artifacts found in Malaysian archaeological sites which are undoubtedly derived from the west are few and ambiguous, both as regards their provenance and identification. The most significant site is Tanjung Rawa, Kuala Selinsing, Perak on the west coast of Peninsular Malaya.[37] The site appears to have been a low island at the mouth of the Selinsing River, perhaps a fishing and trading settlement of pile houses over a muddy bank seasonally flooded. Finds include wooden coffins, or "boat" burials; abundant pottery, some of which parallels that from the proto-historic "Funanese" trading port of Oc-eo on the Vietnamese coast and the Pontian boat burial (see below); glass, stone and shell beads and bracelets, fragments of dammar, gold and tin ingots; and items of jewelry, pieces of glass cullet, and etched beads which most probably are western.[38] More specific finds include an Indian gold ring with a Hindu motif, a carnelian seal bearing a Sanskrit inscription dated palaeographically to the fourth-fifth century A.D., and glazed Chinese ceramics. Radiocarbon dates suggest that the site was occupied from at least the third to the seventh or eighth centuries A.D. and are generally in agreement with the archaeological finds. The Kuala Selensing site is comparable to Khuan Lukpad at Krabi in its big range of exotic material, most of which is surely dated to the early to mid-first millennium A.D., but some could just as easily be several hundred years earlier if we had more information about the specific context of discovery.

The Pontian boat burial,[39] which contained Oc-eo style high-fired combed grey ware ceramics has recently been dated by radiocarbon to the second century A.D. This dating suggests that some of the Kuala Selinsing material may be rather earlier than the radiocarbon dates indicate.[40] Finally, I must mention the site of Bukit Tengku Lembu in Perlis which contained fragments of a high-fired polished black pottery which has variously been described as "Greek" and Indo-Roman Rouletted Ware.[41] Unfortunately this material, while it certainly seems to have been made in antiquity west of the Bay of Bengal, lacks a good context, having been dug out by farmers seeking fertilizer, and is not very precisely described or illustrated.

Indonesia has also produced some artifacts traded from the west, such as the few shards, and at least three virtually complete vessels of Indo-Roman Rouletted Ware of the first century A.D. which were recognized in the National Museum, Jakarta, by Walker among pottery belonging to the Buni grave complex on the north coast of Java.[42]

Then there have been some occasional finds from well-excavated and published sites in Thailand, Burma, and Indonesia. Among these we should first note an Indian ivory comb from the moated settlement at

Chansen in Central Thailand. This comes from a good context in Period II which the excavators, Bronson and Dales[43] dated to between the first and third centuries A.D. This piece is now on exhibition in the National Museum, Bangkok.

Excavations at Beikthano in Central Myanmar[44] have provided convincing evidence for a town with a palace and stupas based on Indian Buddhist models. Among the finds are one etched bead (see the discussion below) and a number of Indianizing Pyu coins. The excavator with the aid of four radiocarbon and stylistic comparisons with various Indian architectural prototypes dates the site to the first-fifth centuries A.D.; but the coin evidence[45] suggests that Beikthano was occupied well into the eighth century A.D.

In west Bali, Indonesia, the site of Gilimanuk has been excavated over a number of years by Soejono,[46] and has produced the most abundant evidence yet for the introduction of iron, copper, and bronze tools and ornaments in Indonesia, and for contacts with the west in the form of glass and semi-precious stone beads.[47] The site has been dated to the turn of the Christian era.[48] But the most exciting recent discoveries in Bali come from the work of I.W. Ardika at a number of sites on the north coast, just below the modern village of Sembiran.[49] There, in levels below structures and occupational debris which he relates to the trading port mentioned in the ninth century A.D. Julah inscription, he has found abundant traces of an earlier coastal settlement associated with substantial quantities of the Indo-Roman rouletted ware, a shard of Wheeler's Type 10 stamped and polished black ware from Arikamedu, and one shard with characters written in Karoshti, a script previously known mostly from Northwest India and Pakistan, but not being found in some frequency along the Ganga Valley and at trading stations in Bengal and Southern Thailand.[50]

In February 1993, during a joint excavation with Vietnamese archaeologists, one shard of this rouletted ware was found at the base of an excavation at Tra Kieu, the ancient Cham capital of Simhapura in Central Vietnam.[51]

Further east in Indonesia and even into New Guinea, recent excavations have produced a few copper and bronze tools and ornaments from datable contexts, and these suggest that small quantities of metal were being taken east along well established trade routes from at least the second century B.C.[52] This evidence suggests to me that the spread of the fifteen Heger 1 bronze drums and fragments which are now documented from eastern Indonesia[53] could have been quite early. Spriggs and Miller[54] suggest the third century A.D. as a likely date for this "late Tonkin" group of Heger 1 drums, and this is entirely plausible.

Finally, I should mention another category of evidence—animal bones—which were found in a series of prehistoric deposits in caves which I excavated in the eastern part of the small island of Timor in Indonesia in 1966-1967. In levels dating from the middle of the third millennium B.C., and over the next 4000 years, I found the remains of animals foreign to this isolated and biologically impoverished island: pigs, monkeys, civet cat, phalangers, dogs, goats, cattle, deer, and horses. The presence of goat bones, almost certainly of immature domesticated goat (Capra hircus), in several caves from the late second or first millennium B.C. onwards, were a surprising discovery.[55] Goats (other than the Serow (*Capricornis sumatraensis*), which is distributed throughout the mountains from the Himalayas east to China, and south to Sumatra) have never before been reported from archaeological sites in Southeast Asia. It has been thought that the spread of this animal is quite recent and was associated with the expansion of Islam with its preference for goat meat rather than the despised but traditional Asian pig; but the evidence from Timor shows that they were introduced into the seasonally dry eastern islands of Indonesia much earlier than this. We have to look west for the sources for these goats and the logical place is Peninsular India where goats appear in small numbers in Indus Valley Culture sites, and rather more frequently in the chalcolithic cultures of Maharashtra, and in southern neolithic cultures, between the mid-second and first millennium B.C.[56]

Although not all are so securely dated, the newer finds described above add substantially to the body of material demonstrating contacts between Southeast Asia and the Indo-Roman world from at least the last few centuries B.C. into the early centuries of the Christian era.

Finally, in this section I want to present some of the relevant material from a late prehistoric Iron Age site in western Thailand which has been excavated on quite a large scale between 1975 and 1985 and which has yielded a large corpus of finds deposited over a very short time in the early fourth century B.C. A lot of this material is directly relevant to the question of exchange between India and Southeast Asia and, I believe, helps to put the process of Indianization into better focus.

The Cemetery of Ban Don Ta Phet

The archaeological site of Ban Don Ta Phet lies between Kanchanaburi and U-Thong in west-central Thailand. The village is on a low mound rising above low swampy ground which is today under rice and sugar cultivation. Antiquities were found there by school children in September 1975 and excavations were undertaken by the Thai Fine Arts Department between November 1975 and May 1976. A number of funerary deposits were identified, richly equipped with iron tools and weapons, bronze vessels, and jewelry made from bronze, bone, ivory, glass and semi-precious stones.

After the Thai work of 1975-1976, two other excavation seasons were undertaken in 1980-1981 and 1984-1985, jointly by the Institute of Archaeology, London, and the FAD, in which further funerary deposits were revealed with a generally similar range of furnishings. As several preliminary reports are available or are in preparation,[57] I will not repeat the details here. Five radiocarbon dates were determined on organic temper (mainly rice) in pottery. Taking center point figures for these dates, which are statistically the same age, from the calibrations in Stuiver and Pearson[58] we get a mean of 350-390 B.C., and at the moment this seems the best "single" date to recommend.

There are two categories of finds at Ban Don Ta Phet which provide the evidence for exchange between India and Thailand at this time. These are beads and some of the bronze vessels. Other items which occur in abundance at the site, such as low-fired earthenwares, and the forged iron tools and weapons, are entirely local, even parochial in character.

Beads from Ban Don Ta Phet

More than 3000 beads of glass and semi-precious stone were found at Ban Don Ta Phet, generally in the lower part of each funerary deposit, and mostly at the western end; glass and stone beads were together but erratically spread.[59] It is worth noting that a substantial number (8.5 percent) of the glass beads, including most of those made from a translucent clear to greenish glass were in the form of natural mineral crystals of the cubic, octahedral, rhombic, dodecahedral, tetragonal, and hexagonal prism systems. This suggests that the bead makers were quite familiar with natural gemstones and were perhaps imitating them for a provincial market.[60] From the point of view of contacts with the West, the most interesting of the glass beads are large, translucent green six-sided prisms. Parallels for these shapes in glass are hard to find in the archaeological literature.[61] Beck illustrates two similar prismatic glass beads from Marshall's excavations at the Bhir mound, Taxila (fourth-third century B.C.);[62] surface collections from Ahichchhatra, Kausambi, and Narhan in northern India contain a few such beads,[63] and some were found at Oceo[64] and in collections said to come from Ban Chiang in northeast Thailand that are displayed in the Suan Pakkard Palace collections in Bangkok. The Indian parallels for these beads are suggestive, for in form and color they are remarkably similar to the famous beryl crystals of south India that were so popular in the Buddhist cultures of north India as well as the Roman world, and which attracted the attention of Pliny the Elder.

To my knowledge, very few of these translucent pale green hexagonal beads have so far been found at other Southeast Asian sites (Oc-eo,

Ban Chiang, and the Pasemah megaliths in south Sumatra are the only other locations I know of) and there is no evidence of glass manufacturing at this time east of India, so there is a probability that these "glass beryls" were made in India and traded into Southeast Asia.[65] This suggestion makes more sense when the evidence from the etched stone beads and bronzes is taken into account.

Of the 3,000 or so beads found in the three seasons at Ban Don Ta Phet, more than 600 were made of hard, semi-precious stone such as agate, carnelian, rock crystal, and nephrite. By far the most common were spherical carnelians, then small facetted carnelians, cylindrical and barrel-shaped banded agates, small unmodified rock crystals, and small cylinders of jade. All of these beads were drilled for suspension with cylindrical holes 1.0–1.5 mm. in diameter and it has recently been argued that the striations inside the drill holes demonstrate the use of diamond-tipped drill bits such as the ones more recently used by the Cambay bead makers.[66] The facetted lozenge-shaped carnelians were cut and polished on some sort of wheel, and the spherical and barrel-shaped beads were polished to a very high surface finish. Lamb has already commented on the technical mastery shown by the makers of early Southeast Asian hardstone beads.[67] Bellwood discusses the distribution of these plain spherical and facetted carnelians within Southeast Asia and summarizes the arguments for, and against, their ultimate source in India.[68]

Probable though it may be that the plain carnelian and agate beads were imported, this is difficult to prove given their ubiquity and simple forms. But among these stone beads there is a particular variety known to archaeologists as "etched beads," about which there must be less doubt. More than fifty etched beads were found during the three seasons at Ban Don Ta Phet and about an equal number have come from looted sites in the region around U-Thong town, a smaller number from Krabi as noted above, and a few from sites in central and north-east Thailand.[69]

Most of these belong to the well-known Type 1 etched beads as characterized by Beck, Mackay, and Dikshit, on which a white design is etched or stained on the natural red or greyish-black of the polished stone surface.[70] The technique of etching the surface layers of agate and carnelian extends back to the Harappan civilization of the western part of South Asia in the third millennium B.C. and although etched beads were traded west to Mesopotamia at this time,[71] none of the distinctive Harappan beads have so far been discovered east of the Ganga-Yumna Doab.

Etched beads went through periods of popularity and relative decline in India[72] although it is unlikely that this very specialized craft died out altogether. After the Harappan period they reappeared in the Ganga Valley between about 600 B.C. and A.D. 200,[73] and then came back into fashion among Muslim medieval communities, particularly in the region from Iran to Sind, although etched beads have been found as far west as Crimea and the Caucasus. The etched beads from Ban Don Ta Phet most closely match those of the second Indian period, as Chin You-di recognized.[74]

Apart from Ban Don Ta Phet and the region around U-Thong, very few etched beads have so far been recognized or published from Southeast Asia and despite the relative lack of systematic excavation in most countries, it is my feeling that they will always be rather rare east of India. However, it should be noted that many more are turning up in Burma, some from early historic cities. In Thailand, I know only of about twenty-five other examples.[75]

Apart from the etched beads, there is one large, and a broken back half, of carnelian pendants carved in the form of a leaping lion which is almost certainly Indian in origin. A similar, but smaller lion pendant was found at Khlong Thom, and small crouching lion pendants are commonly found in the Buddhist reliquaries of the Gandhara Civilization; see, for example, the crystal lion from the Dhamararajika stupa at Taxila.[76] Numerous other examples of such lions are to be found in museums with good collections of Gandharan material although few are provenanced and dated. Before representation in human form was acceptable (a tradition which developed only from the first century A.D.), Buddha was often shown by one of his attributes such as the footprint, the umbrella of royalty, the empty throne; or the lotus, bull, or elephant to recall the circumstances of his conception and birth, or as a deer to remind devotees of the sermon in the deer park at Sarnath.[77] However, a particularly common representation was of Buddha as a lion, a reference to him as Shakysimha, or Lion of the Shakya Clan. It is highly possible that the lion bead from Ban Don Ta Phet is an early Buddhist icon, and as such probably the earliest witness to Buddhist ideas and values yet recognized in Southeast Asia.

Finally, I should mention another sort of bead again, probably an import, but this time from Vietnam. This is a pale green nephrite[78] two-headed animal pendant found inside a bronze bowl in context 324 in the 1985 season at Ban Don Ta Phet. One other bead of this type has been found at or near U-Thong, and is in the National Museum, Bangkok.[79] Such pendants are a characteristic, even diagnostic, artifact of the Sa-Huynh Iron Age Culture of the central coastal region of Vietnam.[80]

We can summarize the evidence for the beads from Ban Don Ta Phet thus: some, if not all, of the glass and semi-precious stone beads were acquired by exchange from the Buddhist civilizations of northern India. The presence of objects of Buddhist veneration (even though the context of deposition cannot be said to be that of established Buddhist religious practice) gives some credence to the traditional Indian historical accounts, as preserved for instance in the Mahavamsa and the Sasanavamsappadipika, that Buddhist missionaries such as those said to have been despatched to Suvarnabhumi by the Emperor Asoka were active in Southeast Asia at this time, or even before the reign of Asoka.

Bronze vessels from Ban Don Ta Phet

Bronze was used for three categories of grave furnishings at Ban Don Ta Phet: for containers, bird figurines, and for ornaments such as bracelets, anklets, and small bells. The latter are either very simple forms ubiquitous in Southeast Asia or found only at Ban Don Ta Phet. Some of the bronze vessels, however, present strong evidence for contacts with India, as has already been pointed out by Rajpitak and Seeley.[81] Nearly 300 bronze containers were found in the ninety or so funerary deposits excavated during the three seasons. A full classification of the vessels has not yet been made, but it is clear that there is considerable variation in size, form, and presumably function. There are flat-bottomed cylindrical and waisted canisters, more-or-less hemispherical bowls in various sizes, and a few unique pieces such as a stepped, truncated cone, or stupa-like form, and a large bucket or *situla* with thick walls which is made with a high-lead, low-tin bronze.[82]

The composition and manufacturing methods have already been mentioned earlier in this paper, and are rather fully discussed by Rajpitak and Seeley, and in Rajpitak,[83] so I will only summarize the main points here. Most of the vessels were made of a high-tin bronze (23-28 percent Sn), cast with thin walls, and were then hot-worked, quenched, and annealed to varying degrees. Some vessels had bands of fine incised decoration below the rims and a few included scenes of people, houses, horses, cattle, and buffaloes which remind one of processional scenes on, for example, the famous Kulu vase in the British Museum. Rajpitak and Seeley suggested that this intractable alloy was chosen because of its resemblance to yellow gold when freshly polished, and they point to occasional finds of high-tin bronze bowls in India with similar properties, such as those from Adichanallur in Tinnevelly District, Tamil Nadu; Coimbatore in the Nilgiri Hills, and Taxila where Marshall found a number in the Mauryan strata at the Bhir mound.[84] They refer to an interesting observation made by Nearchus when he traveled through this region with the Macedonian army in the fourth century B.C. and preserved in Strabo's *Geography* that the local people used "brass that is cast, not the kind that is forged …" with the strange result that "when they fall to the ground they break to pieces like pottery." Such a description fits equally the bowls from the Bhir mound at Taxila and those from Ban Don Ta Phet. Copper-tin alloy artifacts are rare in India (which is deficient in tin) at this period and true brass (copper-zinc), which is not so brittle, was only just coming into use. Taking these points into account, and the already demonstrated links between Thailand and northern India, it would seem possible that these high-tin cast bronze vessels (which are outside the normal range of Indian metallurgy) were imported from Southeast Asia.

Fragments of high-tin bronze vessels and bracelets have also been identified at a number of localities in Thailand,[85] and quite recently high-tin bronze bowls with shallow engraved scenes of animals in procession, people, house structures, and lotus leaves radiating from the base of the bowl have been recovered from a site disturbed by tin mining at Khao Jamook near the Thai-Burmese border in Ratchaburi province, west of Bangkok.[86] These are remarkably similar to the bowls from Ban Don Ta Phet, and the Kulu Vase from Gundla in northwestern India. Batchelor[87] also documents a number of high-tin, hemispherical bowls which have been found over a number of years in the tin gravels of western Malaya. Unfortunately, these cannot be dated.

Knobbed-base vessels from Ban Don Ta Phet

Most of the bronze bowls are undecorated and flat or gently curved inside, but a number—perhaps twenty to thirty including fragments—are finished on the inside of the base with a series of concentric circles surrounding a conical boss which is sometimes cast integrally with the vessel, and sometimes riveted on.[88] I know of only one other example of this type of vessel from Southeast Asia, a bronze bowl in the Guimet Museum collections which is reported to have come from the Than Hoa Province of North Vietnam, but in India it occurs in a modified form on at least one of the Nilgiri high-tin bronze bowls now in the British Museum (Breeks); on a silver dish from Taxila (Marshall); and it is replicated in pottery in the "knobbed ware" first identified at Sisulpalgarh, an early historic town site in Orissa (Lal).[89] In the past thirty years or so, this distinctive ceramic form has been recognized at over a dozen sites in Bengal, Orissa, and the Ganga Valley. It occurs in a variety of fabrics but seems to be most common in a late phase of Northern Black Polished Ware which can be dated to the last centuries before the Christian era.

The function of these knobbed-base vessels is not at all clear; for the most part, the excavators in India have been satisfied to describe the form, attributing them to a fabric class, noting their stratigraphic context and, if we are lucky, including an illustration. It is far from certain if they are confined to certain types of functional contexts such as burials or ritual deposits in religious buildings, or whether they were a rare but purely utilitarian form. The Nilgiri bowls almost certainly come from megalithic graves,[90] and the splendid black granite bowl from near Taxila in Pakistan, which is now in the British Museum, was found in 1861 in the center of a ruined masonry building between Shahr Dheri and Usman Khattar north of Taxila, by two zamindars while digging for treasure.[91] Almost certainly this was a foundation deposit for a stupa.[92] Whatever the function of the ceramic and metal vessels it is difficult to believe that this stone vessel would have been made for a secular or utilitarian purpose.[93]

It is difficult to believe that these formal similarities arose quite independently in the two areas. Rather, I believe that they provide yet further evidence for the penetration of Indian material culture style into Southeast Asia. If we seek an explanation for the meaning of the base knob and concentric circles, then I think that this should be seen as a commonly understood mandala, a schematic cosmological symbol representing perhaps Mt. Meru and the surrounding oceans. These containers, whether of bronze, stone, or pottery did not serve as everyday cooking, serving, or food display vessels, but served some special purpose for ritual and funerary use only. They are witness to the adoption in Thailand, by some groups, of Indian moral, philosophical, and political concepts. The finds on which this argument is based can be dated with reasonable certainty to the last few centuries B.C. and reinforce the position of Ban Don Ta Phet as the earliest "Indianizing" site so far recognized in Thailand.

Textiles from Ban Don Ta Phet

A few textile fragments and threads were found adhering to bronzes at Ban Don Ta Phet and most of these for the joint London-FAD excavations have been examined by Chiraporn Aranyanak of the Conservation Laboratory of the National Museum, Bangkok, a specialist on ancient textile fibers. Although her work is far from complete she has told me that she has been able to identify hemp, the fiber derived from *Cannabis sativa* as the most common material used, and cotton, from a single thread adhering to a bone fragment (sf.604) from context 46. The identification of cotton, the earliest I believe yet identified in Thailand, strengthens the evidence for early links with India for this is where the cotton plant (*Gossypium sp.*) was originally domesticated in the context of the Harappan Civilization of the third millennium B.C.

Summary

The presence of various categories of material at Ban Don Ta Phet imported from India by the fourth century B.C., together with the other evidence for mutual exchange between northern and eastern India, Thailand, Malaysia, and Indonesia strongly suggests that Buddhist missionaries were already active, indeed were established, in Southeast Asia before the Christian Era and perhaps even before the reign of the Emperor Asoka. Wheeler was correct to argue a generation ago on the basis of the evidence that the few items at that time known to be derived from India or the Roman world came there through Èdrifti rather than through organized commercial relationships; but enough evidence is now at hand to refute this interpretation and to show that Southeast Asia was already part of a world trading system linking the civilizations of the Mediterranean Basin and Han China.

Thus, for one section of the southern Silk Road from China to the Near East and Europe, recent archaeological work has been able to show that the network of trade, which in later centuries transmitted silk, porcelains, and high quality manufactured goods from China to the West—and bullion, for the most part, from west to east—was already established at the very beginning of the Buddhist Era and before the coalescence of the Warring States of China into a single mighty empire. Whether silk itself was being shipped south from China at this time is not yet clear. We have had hints from sites in Thailand[94] that silk may have been known in Southeast Asia at this time, but the identifications are not yet sufficiently secure to be sure of this. Even if silk is found in well-dated prehistoric contexts in Southeast Asia, this does not necessarily mean that it was an import at that time from the north since silk cultivation itself may have been long established in the region; but only further archaeological research and laboratory examination will make this clear.

Notes

The fieldwork on which much of this article is based on what was done in co-operation with the Fine Arts Department of Thailand and I particularly want to thank the various Directors General and Mr. Pisit Charoenwongsa, formerly of the Division of Archaeology, for their very great help. The research was supported by the British Academy, the Hayter and Gordon Childe Funds of the University of London, the Evans Fund of Cambridge, the Society of Antiquaries of London, and the British Museum. I am especially grateful to the late Kalyan P. Gupta, Dr. Himanshu Ray, K.N. Dikshit, Rafiq Mughal, Surapol Natapintu, Robert Knox, and Elizabeth Errington for their help in tracking down various Indian parallels for the material from Ban Don Ta Phet, and calling my attention to new discoveries.

1. G. Coedès, *The Indianized States of South-East Asia,* edited by W.F. Vella and translated by S.B. Cowing (Canberra: Australian National University Press, 1968). I.W. Mabbett, "The 'Indianization' of South-East Asia: Reflections on Historical Sources." *Journal of South-East Asian Studies,* 8 (1 and 2) (1977): pp. 1-14, 143-61. H.P. Ray, "Early Maritime Contacts between South and South-East Asia." *Journal of South-East Asian Studies,* 8(1) (1989): pp. 42-54. O.W. Wolters, *Early Indonesian Commerce: a Study of the Origins of Srivijaya* (Ithaca: Cornell University Press, 1967). P. Wheatley, "Nagara and Commandery: Origins of the South-East Urban Traditions" (Department of Geography Research Papers, University of Chicago, 1983), pp. 207-8.
2. J.C.H.S. Davidson, "Urban Genesis in Viet-Nam." In R.B. Smith and W. Watson, eds., *Early South-East Asia* (Oxford University Press, 1979), pp. 304-14; D.T. Bayard, "A Tentative Regional Phase Chronology for Northeast Thailand." *South-East Asian Archaeology,* at the 15th Pacific Science Congress, Otago University Studies in Prehistoric Anthropology 16 (1984): pp. 87-128. Moore, E.H., "Moated Sites in Early North East Thailand." *B.A.R. International,* Series 400 (1988): pp. 150-53.
3. Wheatley, "Nagara and Commandary," p. 264
4. H.P. Ray, "Early Maritime Contacts;" "In Search of Suvanabhumi: Early Sailing Networks in the Bay of Bengal." In: P. Bellwood, ed., *Indo-Pacific Prehistory, 1990,* vol. 1 (Canberra and Jakarta: Indo-Pacific Prehistory Association, 1991): pp. 557-65; and "Early Coastal Trade in the Bay of Bengal." In: J. Reade, ed., *The Indian Ocean in Antiquity* (London: Routledge, forthcoming).
5. Brookfield and D. Hart, *Melanesia: A Geographical Interpretation of an Island World* (London: Methuen, 1971), pp. 314-31. J. Miksic, *Archaeological Research on the 'Forbidden Hill' of Singapore: Excavations in Fort Canning, 1984* (Singapore: National Museum, 1985), pp. 1-35 presents a useful synthesis of the growth of external trade in the region around the Malay Peninsula from later prehistory to the nineteenth century A.D.
6. Ray, "In Search of Suvanabhumi."
7. I do not deal with the connections from Southeast Asia to China, only with those to the west, although it is worth noting here that recent surveys and casual discoveries in Thailand and Java have produced a surprisingly large number of Chinese, primarily Han-style artifacts, and we shall soon have to take this new data into account.
8. Ray, "Early Coastal Trade in the Bay of Bengal."
9. V. Begley, "Arikamedu Reconsidered." *American Journal of Archaeology* 87 (1983): pp. 461-81; and V. Begley and R.D. De Puma, eds., *Rome and India—the Ancient Sea Trade* (Madison, Wisc.: University of Wisconsin Press, 1991); and W. Wijaya-

pala and M.E. Prickett, *Sri Lanka and the International Trade.* Catalogue for an Exhibition of ancient imported ceramics found in Sri Lanka's archaeological sites (Colombo, Department of Archaeology, 1986).

10. J.I. Miller, *The Spice Trade of the Roman Empire, 29 B.C.–A.D. 641* (Oxford University Press, 1969).

11. I.H. Burkill, *The Economic Products of the Malay Peninsula.* (London: Crown Agents, 1935): pp. 976-80

12. R.E. Eicholz, ed., *Pliny's Natural History,* Book 37, Loeb Classical Library Volume 8 (London: Heinemann, 1962).

13. R.F. Ellen, "The Trade in Spices." *Journal of the Indonesian Circle* 12 (1977): p. 25

14. G.W.B. Huntingford, ed., *The Periplus of the Erythaean Sea* (London: The Hakluyt Society, 1980): app. 4.

15. Begley and De Puma, *Rome and India*; N. Seeley and P. Turner, "Metallurgical Investigations of Three Early Indian Coinages: Implications for Metal Trading and Dynastic Chronology." In: B. Allchin, ed., *South Asian Archaeology 1981* (London: Cambridge University Press, 1984); P. Turner, *Roman Coins in India.* Occasional Paper No. 12 (London: Institute of Archaeology, 1989); and R.E.M. Wheeler, *Rome Beyond the Imperial Frontiers* (Harmondsworth: Penguin, 1954).

16. E.C.L. During Caspers, "The Indian Ivory Figurine from Pompeii—a Reconsideration of its Functional Use." In: H. Hartel, ed., *South Asian Archaeology, 1979* (Berlin: Dietrich Reimer Verlag, 1981): pp. 341-53.

17. E.H.Warmington, *The Commerce Between the Roman Empire and India* (Cambridge University Press, 1928); J.I.Miller, *The Spice Trade of the Roman Empire, 29 B.C.-A.D. 641* (Oxford University Press, 1969); M.G.Raschke, "New Studies in Roman Commerce with the East," in *Aufstieg und Niedergang der Romischen Welt,* vol. 2, no. 9 (Berlin and New York: de Gruyter, 1978), pp. 604-1378; R.E.M.Wheeler, *Rome Beyond the Imperial Frontiers* (Harmondsworth: Penguin, 1954).
I think that a good argument could be made for the introduction of iron into Southeast Asia from eastern or Peninsular India in the mid-first millennium B.C. However, I will not try to develop this further here since we have very few well-dated and described early Iron Age sites in Southeast Asia. Ban Don Ta Phet is almost certainly not one of the earliest sites with iron in Thailand—iron bracelets on well-stratified burials at Nil Kham Haeng are dated to about 700 B.C. (V.C. Pigott, *Recent Excavations at Nil Kham Haeng and the Archaeometallurgy of Copper Production in Central Thailand.* 3d International Conference of South-East Asian Archaeologists in Western Europe, Brussels [December 1990]), and there is at the moment a lack of comparability between the iron tools and weapons from Ban Don Ta Phet and Ongbah Cave (P. Srensen, "Prehistoric Iron Implements from Thailand." *Asian Perspectives,* vol. 16, no. 2 (1974): pp. 134-73)—the only two sites in Thailand yielding a large number of well-preserved iron artifacts—and those from southern and eastern India.

18. C. Renfew, "Trade as Action at a Distance: Questions of Integration and Communication." In: J.A. Sabloff and C.C. Lamberg-Karlovsky, eds., *Ancient Civilization and Trade* (Albuquerque: University of New Mexico Press, 1975): pp. 3-60.

19. Wheeler, *Rome Beyond the Imperial Frontiers,* pp. 206-7

20. M.G. Raschke, "New Studies on Roman Commerce with the East." In: *Aufstieg und Niedergang der Romischen Welt,* vol. 2, no. 9 (Berlin and New York: de Gruyter, 1978): p. 653.

21. In the original description of the lamp from Pong Tuk (Thailand), Coèdes (G. Coèdes, "The Excavations at P'ong Tuk and their Importance for the Early History of Siam." *Journal of the Siam Society* 21 [1928]: pp. 195-209) compared it to Roman

lamps of the first century A.D. from Pompeii; Picard (Picard, C., "La Lampe Alexandrine de P'ong Tuk [Siam]." *Artibus Asiae* 18 [1955]: pp. 137-49) argued, on the basis of many examples, that it is a Ptolemaic lamp from an Alexandrine workshop of the late centuries B.C., but most recently Brown and Macdonnel (R.L. Brown, and A.M. MacDonnel, "The Pong Tuk Lamp: a Reconsideration." *Journal of the Siam Society* 77 (2) [1989]: pp. 9-20) have strongly suggested that it is late Roman or Byzantine from the eastern Mediterranean, dating to between the first to fifth/sixth centuries A.D. National Museum, Bangkok. For information on the Mediterranean seals, see L. Malleret, *L'Archéologie du Delta du Mekong*, 2-3 (Paris: Publications de l'École Française d'Extrême-Orient, 1960-1962).

22. H.C. Brookfield.and D. Hart, *Melanesia: a Geographical Interpretation of an Island World.* (London: Methuen, 1971), pp. 314-31; Renfrew, "Trade as Action at a Distance;" and A. Sherratt, "Resources, Technology and Trade: an Essay in Early European Metallurgy." In: G. de G. Sieveking, et. al, eds., *Problems in Economic and Social Archaeology* (London: Duckworth, 1976), pp. 557-81.

23. Bayard, "A Tentative Regional Phase Chronolgy for Northeast Thailand;" and C.F.W. Higham and A. Kijngam, "Prehistoric Investigations in Northeastern Thailand." *B.A.R. International Series* 231 (1984): pp. 13-21.

24. P. Bellwood, *Prehistory of the Indo-Malaysian Archipelago* (Sydney: Academic Press, 1985), chap. 7

25. I should make it clear early in this discussion that not all citations of "fact" and opinion concerning early Indian trade with the West can be fully referenced in this paper or it would come to resemble that invaluable and monumental compendium by Raschke, "New Studies in Roman Commerce with the East" with its 674 pages and 1791 endnotes.

26. M. Hitchcock, "Research Report on Indonesian and Tanzanian Maritime Links." *Indonesia Circle* 59 & 60 (1993): pp. 62-67.

27. I.C. Glover, "The Late Prehistoric Period in Indonesia." In: R.B. Smith and W. Watson, eds., *Early South-East Asia* (Oxford University Press, 1979), pp. 167-84; and B.A.V. Peacock, "The Later Prehistory of the Malay Peninsula." In: R.B. Smith and W. Watson, eds., *Early South-East Asia* (Oxford University Press, 1979), pp. 199-214.

28. Renfrew, "Trade as Action at a Distance," pp. 41-42.

29. A.N. Bennett, "The Contribution of Archaeometallurgical Studies to South-East Asian Archaeology." *World Archaeology* 20 (3), (1989): pp. 329-51; Higham and Kijngam, "Prehistoric Investigations in Northeastern Thailand," pp. 63-70; S. Natapintu, "Archaeological Evidence from Ban Tha Kae and Some Notes on Ancient Settlements in Lower Central Thailand." In: Bhuthorn Bhumathon, ed., *The Archaeological Site of Ban Tha Kae* (in Thai) (Bangkok: Fine Arts Department, 1984), pp. 1-12; V.C. Pigott, and S. Natapintu, "The Thailand archaeometallurgy project." *Muang Boran Journal*, 10 (4) (1984): pp. 126-27; and P. Pisnupong, "Aspects of Stone-Working at Khok Phanom Di" (M.A. thesis, Otago University, Department of Anthropology, 1988); M. Santoni, J.P. Pautreau, S. Prishanchit, "Excavations at Obluang, Province of Chiang Mai, Thailand," in I.C. and E.A. Glover, eds., *South-East Asian Archeology 1986* (Oxford, BAR S-561), pp. 37-54.

30. C. Landes, "Pièce d'époque romaine trouvée à U-Thong, Thailande." *Journal of Silpakorn*, 26 (1) (1982): pp. 113-15.

31. Most publications on Khlong Thom are in Thai and others are unpublished reports available only in Bangkok. At the time of-writing, the most accessible publications are M. Veraprasert, "Khlong Thom: an Ancient Bead and Manufacturing Location and an Ancient Entrepot." In: *Seminar in Prehistory of South-East Asia* (Bangkok:

SEAMEO Project in Archaeology and Fine Arts [SPAFA Final Report], 1987), pp. 323-31; and B. Bronson, "Glass and Beads at Khuan Lukpad, Southern Thailand." In: I.C. and E.A. Glover, eds., *South-East Asian Archaeology 1986* (Oxford: BAR S-561. 1990), pp. 213-30. The former refers to the more significant accounts written in Thai, except that of Srisvohat, A., "Ancient Beads in the Southern Part of Thailand." In: Phongphaiboon Suthiwongsa, ed., *Encyclopedia of Southern Culture*, 10 vols., in Thai (Songkhla Institute of Southern Studies, Sri Nakaraintaravirot University, 1987): pp. 3212-43, which contains by far the best illustrations.

32. Veraprasert, "Khlong Thom," p. 328; and B. Bronson, pers. com.

33. Martin Henig of the Institute of Archaeology, Oxford, has seen the photograph of these seals and has kindly provided me with these identifications. The seal showing Tyche he compares with the following; nos.102-5, p. 15 in M. Henig and M. Whiting, eds, "Engraved Gems from Gadara in Jordan. The Sa'd Collections of Intaglios and Cameos," no. 6 (Oxford University Committee for Archaeology Monograph, 1985) and to nos. 602-4 in G. Sena Chiesa, *Gemme del Museo Nazionale dei Aquileia* (Padua, 1966). The 'fighting cocks' seal he refers to Sena Chiesa (1966): no. 1341, p. 1341.

34. Bronson, "Glass and Beads at Khuan Lukpad."

35. Renfrew, "Trade as Action at a Distance," p. 43

36. I.C. Glover, "Early Trade between India and South-East Asia—a Link in the Development of a World Trading System." *Occasional Paper* No. 16 (Hull: University of Hull, Centre for South-East Asian Studies, 1990; 2d revised edition).

37. I.H.N. Evans, "Excavations at Tanjong Rawa, Kuala Selensing, Perak." *Journal of the Federated Malay State Museums* 15 (23) (1932): pp. 79-134; Sir J. Lowenstein, "The Origins of the Malayan Metal Age." *Journal of the Malayan Branch of the Royal Asiatic Society*, 39 (2) (1956): p. 74; Peacock, "The Later Prehistory of the Malay Peninsula," pp. 210-11; and N.K. Shuhaimi, "Recent Research at Kuala Selinsing, Perak." In: P. Bellwood, ed., *Indo Pacific Prehistory 1990*, vol. 2 (Canberra and Jakarta: Indo-Pacific Prehistory Association, 1991): pp. 141-52.

38. I.H.N. Evans, "Notes on the Remains of an Old Boat from Pontian, Pahang." *Journal of the Federated Malay States Museums* 12 (16) (1927): pp. 93-96; "On Ancient Remains from Kuala Selinsing, Perak." *Journal of the Federated Malay States Museums* 12 (22) (1928): pp. 121-31; "Further Notes on Remains from Kuala Selinsing, Perak." *Journal of the Federated Malay State Museums* 12 (25) (1928): pp. 79-134, "Excavations at Tanjong Rawa;" and Shuhaimi, "Recent Research at Kuala Selinsing."

39. Evans, "Notes on the Remains of an Old Boat;" and G. Sieveking, "The Iron Age Collections of Malaya." *Journal of the Malayan Branch of the Royal Asiatic Society*, 39 (2) (1956): pp. 93-94.

40. Since there is no free charcoal in the site which we can associate with the burials, and thermoluminescence dating did not give consistent and reliable results, we had to look for a new source of datable material and this has been provided by the organic temper (mainly rice) in one of the pieces of pottery of what we call "Fabric A." The possibility of directly dating the pottery was first seen by Dr. Ian Freestone of the British Museum Research Laboratory while he was investigating the weathering of the quartz grains which gave the problems with TL dating, and one date (BM-2016) was produced in 1981 but later recalculated by the laboratory to 2190±230 BP (BM-2016R). But because of the small sample of carbon available and type of counter used by the BMRL, this result had the unacceptably large standard error of Å 230 and it was clear that only mass-spectrometry accelerator dating could give us good enough results with this sort of material. The Oxford Radiocarbon Accelerator Unit accepted four samples for dating in 1987.

41. P.D.R. Williams-Hunt, "Archaeological Discoveries in Malaya, 1951." *Journal of the Malay Branch of the Royal Asiatic Society*, 15 (1) (1952): pp. 186-88; B.A.V. Peacock, "The Kodiang Pottery Cones: tripod Pottery in Malaya, with a Note on the Bukit Tengku Lembu Blackware." *Federation Museums Journal* 13 (1964): pp. 4-20; and B. Bronson, "The Later Prehistory and Early History of Central Thailand." In: R.B. Smith and W. Watson, eds., *Early South-East Asia: Essays in Archaeology, History and Historical Geography* (Oxford University Press, 1979): p. 330.

42. M. Walker and S. Santoso, "Romano-Indian rouletted pottery in Indonesia." *Asian Perspectives*, vol. 20, no. 2 (for 1977) (1980): pp. 228-35.

43. B. Bronson and G.F. Dales, "Excavations at Chansen, Thailand, 1968 and 1969: a Preliminary report." *Asian Perspectives*, vol. 15 (for 1972) (1978): pp. 28-30, fig. 7.

44. U. Aung Thaw, *Report on the Excavations at Beikthano* (Rangoon: Ministry of Culture, 1968).

45. J. Cribb, "The Date of the Symbolic Coins of Burma and Thailand—a Re-examination of the Evidence." *Seaby Coin and Medal Bulletin* 75 (1981): pp. 224-26.

46. R.P. Soejono, "The Significance of the Excavations at Gilimanuk (Bali)." In: R.B. Smith and W. Watson, eds., *Early South-East Asia* (Oxford University Press, 1979), pp. 185-98.

47. Ratna Indraningsih, "Research on Prehistoric Beads in Indonesia." *Bulletin of the Indo-Pacific Prehistory Association* 6 (1985): pp. 133-41

48. B. Bronson and I.C. Glover, "Archaeological Radiocarbon Dates from Indonesia: a First List." *Indonesia Circle* 34 (1984): p. 41.

49. I.W. Ardika and P. Bellwood, "Sembiran: the Beginnings of Indian Contact with Bali." *Antiquity* 65 (1991): pp. 221-32.

50. Ray, "Early Coastal Trade in the Bay of Bengal."

51. M. Yamagata and I.C. Glover, "Excavations at Buu Chau Hill, Tra Kieu, Vietnam 1993." *Journal of South-East Asian Archaeology* 14 (1994): pp. 48-57.

52. W.R. Ambrose, "An Early Bronze Artefact from Papua New Guinea." *Antiquity* 62 (236) (1988): pp. 483-91; and I.C. Glover, "Archaeology in Eastern Timor, 1966-67." *Terra Australis* 11 (Canberra: Australian National University, 1986): 153 and plate 36

53. D.D. Bintarti, "Prehistoric Bronze Objects in Indonesia." *Bulletin of the Indo-Pacific Prehistory Association* 6 (1985): pp. 64-73; A.J. Kempers and M. Bernet, "The Kettledrums of South-East Asia." *Modern Quaternary Research in South-East Asia* 10 (Rotterdam: Balkema, 1988): p. 240; and M. Spriggs and D. Miller, "A Previously Unreported Bronze Kettledrum from the Kai islands, Eastern Indonesia." *Bulletin of the Indo-Pacific Prehistory Association* 8 (1988): pp. 79-89.

54. Spriggs and Miller, "A Previously Unreported Bronze Kettledrum," p. 86

55. Glover, "Archaeology in Eastern Timor," p. 205

56. A.T. Clason, "Wild and Domestic Animals in Prehistoric and Early Historic India." *The Eastern Anthropologist* 30 (3) (1977): pp. 241-89.

57. You-di Chin, *Ban Don Ta Phet: Preliminary Excavation Report, 1975-76* (in Thai) (Bangkok: National Museum, 1976); I.C. Glover, "Ban Don Ta Phet and its Relevance to Problems in the Pre- and Protohistory of Thailand." *Bulletin of the Indo-Pacific Prehistory Association* 2 (1980): pp. 16-30, "Excavations at Ban Don Ta Phet, Kanchanaburi Province, Thailand 1980-81." *South-East Asia Studies Newsletter* 10, (1983): pp. 1-3, "Ban Don Ta Phet: the 1984-85 Excavation." In: I.C. and E.A. Glover, eds., *South Asian Archaeology 1986* (Oxford: BAR S-561): pp. 139-84; and I.C. Glover et al., "The Cemetery of Ban Don Ta Phet, Thailand: Results from the 1980-81 Excavation Season." In: B. Allchin, ed., *South Asian Archaeology 1981*, (Cambridge University Press, 1984), pp. 319-30.

58. M. Stuiver and G.W. Pearson, "High Precision Calibration of the 14C Time Scale, A.D. 1950–500 B.C." *Radiocarbon*, vol. 28, No. 2B (1986): pp. 805-38.

59. A comparative study of early Thai and Indian glass beads has been undertaken by Kishor Basa as part of his Ph.D. thesis in London (K.K Basa, *The Westerly Trade of South-East Asia from c. 400 B.C. to c. A.D. 500 with Special Reference to Glass Beads.* (Ph.D. diss., London: Institute of Archaeology, UCL, 1991). I would like to acknowledge his help in the preparation of this article. See also K.K. Basa, et al., "The Relationship between Early South-East Asian and Indian glass." In: P. Bellwood, ed., *Indo-Pacific Prehistory 1990*, vol. 1 (Jakarta and Canberra: Indo-Pacific Prehistory Association, 1991): pp. 366-85; and I.C. Glover and J. Henderson, "Early Glass in South and South-East Asia and China." In: R. Scott and E. Moore, eds., *China and South-East Asia—Art, commerce and Interaction* (London: Percival David Foundation of Chinese Art, forthcoming) for a discussion of the comparative chemical compositions of early Indian and Southeast Asian glass.

60. Glass beads simulating natural emerald or beryl crystals seem to be rare in museum collections from the Mediterranean world. To date, we have only found two in the holdings of the Department of Greek and Roman Antiquities of the British Museum. One (BM 81-7-9-8) is 33.9 cm long by 23.3 cm in diameter and is made of a translucent watery green glass and appears to have been drilled for suspension, as a natural gemstone would be. Only the surface weathering and refractions from the hydration layers clearly showed that it was made of glass. It was accessed to the museum in 1881, and the catalogue entry, difficult to read, suggests that it comes from Amrit on the Syrian coast just south of Tarkis. The other piece (BM 87-7-6-25 from Tyre) is smaller, darker, more weathered but also is clearly made in the form of the hexagonal crystal of the beryl group, see W. Schumann, *Gemstones of the World* (London: N.A.G., 1977): pp. 90-96.

61. P. Francis, *Glass Beads of India* (Lake Placid, New York: Lapis Route Books, 1982).

62. H.C. Beck, "The Beads from Taxila, New Delhi." *Memoire of the Archaeological Survey of India,* no.65 (1941): Pl. IX, 3 and 12

63. K.K. Basa, pers. com

64. L. Malleret, *L'Archéologie du Delta du Mekong*, 2-3 (Paris: Publications de l'École Française d'Extrême-Orient, 1960-1962): p. 43.

65. A preliminary report on the composition of the glass from Ban Don Ta Phet and comparisons with Indian and other early Southeast Asian glass has been presented in Basa et al., "The Relationship between Early South-East Asian and Indian glass." Henderson and Glover are currently analyzing more glass from Arikamedu and have further unpublished composition analyses on glass from Ban Don Ta Phet and these will be presented in a future report.

66. During her examination of the drill holes in the agate and carnelian beads from Ban Don Ta Phet, Williams (L. Williams, "A New Approach to the Study of Bead-making Workshop Practices with Special Reference to Carnelian and Agate Beads from Ban Don Ta Phet, Thailand." [B.A. Report, University of London, Institute of Archaeology, 1984]) observed distinctive regular concentric grooves which she was unable to replicate using either metal or stone drill bits with abrasive sands. Leonard Gorelik has suggested that such marks, which he had observed on ancient beads from Mantai in Sri Lanka and Arikamedu in South India and on beads made by contemporary Cambay craftsmen, and which he had replicated in his own experiments, could only have been produced by the use of diamond-tipped drills. The case for this at Mantai and Arikamedu is set out in A.J. Gwinnett and L. Gorelik, "Evidence for the Use of a Diamond Drill for Bead-making in Sri Lanka, c. 700–1000 A.D." *Scanning Electron Microscopy* 11 (1986): pp. 473-77. In a telephone message

in November 1990, Dr. Gorelik told me that he had identified the use of a diamond-tip drill to the eighth century B.C. on material from Yemen.

67. A. Lamb, "Some Observations on Stone and Glass Beads in early South-East Asia." *Journal of the Malayan Branch of the Royal Asiatic Society* 38 (1965): pp. 87-124.
68. P. Bellwood, "Archaeological Research in Minahasa and the Talaud Islands, Northeastern Indonesia." *Asian Perspectives* XIX (22) (1978): pp. 240-88; and P. Francis, *Indian Agate Beads* (Lake Placid, New York: Lapis Route Books, 1982).
69. Every time I visit Thailand I have been shown more etched beads in private collections and provincial museums, and a detailed study of the range of their forms and techniques of manufacture would be timely. My preliminary observations suggest that Thai etched beads are not simply a random sample of the range of South Asian beads, so either Indian beadmakers produced for and exported to a discriminating market, or there was a yet undiscovered eastern center of manufacturing etched beads. Many etched and other decorated beads have recently been identified in Myanmar although none from dated excavated context, see U. Aung Myint and E. Moore, "Beads from Myanmar (Burma): Line Decorated Beads amongst the Pyu and Chin." *Journal of the Siam Society* (forthcoming); and, of course, there is a separate tradition of Tibetan etched (*dzi*) beads, see J.D. Allen, "Tibetan Dzi beads." *Ornament* 6 (2) (1982): pp. 57, 60-1.
70. Carnelians, which in the raw state are more often salmon pink than red, have usually been roasted to strengthen their color through oxidization, see G. Possehl, "Cambay Beadmaking." *Expedition*, vol. 23, no. 4 (1981): pp. 39-47; and Francis, *Indian Agate Beads*, p. 2, and the black agates may also have been darkened by boiling them in a sugar syrup followed by oxidation of the organic solution which readily penetrates the microscopic fibrous structure of the chalcedony group of quartz minerals. Most books on gemstones (e.g. M. Bauer, *Precious Stones*, translated by L.J. Spencer, from 1904 edition [New York: Dover, 1968], pp. 522-23, and Schumann, *Gemstones of the World*, p. 136) indicate that this technique, known for some time in Rome, was introduced from there to Idar-Oberstein in Germany about 1820. But examination of etched agates from Thailand and India shows that it was regularly practiced in antiquity. H.C. Beck, "Etched Carnelian Beads." *Antiquaries Journal* XII (1933): pp. 384-98; E. Mackay, "Decorated Carnelian Beads." *Man* (September, 1933): pp. 143-46; and M.G. Dikshit, *Etched Beads in India* (Deccan College Monograph Series 4).
71. J. Reade, "Early Etched Beads and the Indus-Mesopotamia Trade." Occasional Paper, No. 2 (1979).
72. Beck, "Etched Carnelian Beads," pp. 387-88 and pl. LXXI.
73. R.C. Gaur, *Excavations at Atranjikhera* (Aligarh Muslim University, Centre of Advanced Study, Department of History, 1983): fig. 4.
74. Chin You-di, "Nothing is New." *Muang Boran Journal* 4 (4) (1978): pp. 6-16.
75. At least two etched beads (one white on black agate and one white on red carnelian) were illustrated by Veraprasert in a presentation made to the Research Conference on Early Southeast Asia in Nakorn Pathom in April 1985, but they are not included in the versions of this talk (Veraprasert, "Khlong Thom;" and "Khlong Thom: an Ancient Bead and Manufacturing Location and an Ancient Entrpot." In; I.C. Glover et al., eds., *Early Metallurgy, Trade and Urban Centres in Thailand and South-East Asia* [Bangkok: White Lotus, 1992]: pp. 149-61). They are probably among those illustrated in Srisvohat (1987). An unpublished etched agate from Ban Chiang was seen in the site museum there in January 1985. It is a spherical black agate bead, 2 cm. in diameter with three 'latitudinal' white bands, a type common at Don Phet (see, for instance, Glover et al., "The Cemetery of Ban Don Ta Phet," fig. 46,

no. 73). This Ban Chiang bead is catalogued as 189/2515 (1972) p. 437, and was donated to the museum by Prakru Vimolpamyakorn, the Abbot of Wat Bothi Sri Narai at Ban Chiang, and is said to have been found in the excavations in the monastery compound. It is almost certainly from the Late Period at Ban Chiang which White (J. White, "A Revision of the Chronology of Ban Chiang and its Implications for the Prehistory of Northeast Thailand" [Ph.D. diss., University of Pennsylvania, 1986], p. 279) now dates to 300 B.C.–A.D. 300, and should be nearly enough contemporary with the occurrence of this type at Ban Don Ta Phet. In Southeast Asia and outside Thailand and Myanmar, etched beads are even rarer. Evans ("On Ancient Remains from Kuala Selinsing," p. 123; and "Further Notes of Remains from Selinsing," p. 139) reports what seem to be several etched agate and carnelian beads from the ancient settlement at Tanjong Rawa, Kalumpang Island, Kuala Selinsing, Malaya; a few have been found on the island of Palawan in the Philippines (R.B. Fox, *The Tabon Caves* [Manila: Monograph No. 1 of the National Museum, 1970]: col. Pl.1a); three were excavated at Leang Buidane Cave in the Talaud Islands of north-central Indonesia (Bellwood, "Archaeological Research in Minahasa and the Talaud Islands, pp. 275-76 and fig.10); one has been published from the excavations at the early city of Beikthano in Central Myanmar (Aung Thaw, *Report on the Excavations at Beikthano*, fig.76) and many more surface finds from Myanmar have been documented by Aung Myint and Moore, "Beads from Myanmar." One cylindrical etched carnelian was found in Tomb 13 at Shizhaishan (Zuo Ming, "Etched Carnelian Beads Found in China." *Kaogu 1974* 6 [1974]: pp. 382-85) and another was found in Tomb 24 at Lijiashan (Zhang Zhenqi, "An Analysis of the Bronze Culture in the Area of Dian Chi Lake, Yunnan Province." *Southern Ethnology and Archaeology* 1 [1987]: p. 110), both in Yunnan Province, South China. These examples are rather securely dated to the Western Han period (175-118 B.C.) and are very similar to two of the beads from burial context 73 at Ban Don Ta Phet (Glover et al., "The Cemetery of Ban Don Ta Phet," fig. 46), and to many in northern India (see Jamal Hassan, "The Distribution and Type of Beads in the Gangeatic Valley." *Puratattva* 11 [for 1979-80] [1982]: p. 133).

76. J. Marshall, *Taxila: an Illustrated Account of the Archaeological Excavations*, vol. III (Cambridge University Press, 1951): pl. 496

77. A.K. Coomaraswamy, *Introduction to Indian Art*, 2d edition (Delhi: Munshiram Manohalal, 1966), pp. 30-1

78. These "bicephalous" pendants are usually called jade in the literature but, to my knowledge, no previous finds have so far been mineralogically identified. In 1985 we were fortunate in having one small broken fragment from the handle of the pendant from Ban Don Ta Phet, and this was identified as actinolite by Dr. D.R.C. Kempe of the Department of Mineralogy of the British Museum (Natural History). Actinolite is an amphibole and includes nephrite, one of the two jade minerals, and Dr. Kempe comments that "it is safe to call this jade" (pers. com. 14.3.1985). As mentioned in the text these pendants are a diagnostic artifact of the Sa-Huynh Iron Age Culture of Central Vietnam; at least one has been found in context at Xuan An, a Dongson Culture site in the southern part of the Red River Valley (Chua Van Tan, "Nouvelles recherches préhistoriques et protohistoriques au Vietnam." *Bulletin de l'École Française d'Extrême-Orient* 68 [1980]: pp. 113-54; and Ha Van Tan and Trinh Duong, "Khuyen tai hai thu va quan he Dongson – Sa Huynh" [Two-headed animal earrings and the relationship between Dongson and Sa Huynh]. *Khao Co Hoc* 4 [1977]: pp. 62-67). I was told in January 1987 that eighty to one hundred such animal pendants have now been found in that country where they are dated from the last few centuries B.C. to the second century A.D. One glass pendant of

this type was found in a site in the Tubon Valley and is now in the Danang Provincial Museum. Apart from the two specimens from Thailand, two have been found in the Philippines where they are included in the ethnic category of the *ling-ling-o* ornament (W.G. Solheim, "Remarks on the Lingling-O and Bi-cephalous Ornaments." *Journal of the Hong Kong Archaeological Society* 10 [1982-1983]: pp. 107-11; R.B. Fox, *The Tabon Caves* [Manila: Monograph No. 1 of the National Museum, 1970], fig.37a and pp. 126-31), and one was recorded in the 1930s as a cult object of the Yami people of the island of Botel Tobago (Orchid Island) off the southeastern coast of Taiwan (T. Kano, "Kotosho Yami no yagi suhai ni tsuite" [About Goat Worship of the Yami of Botel Tobago]. *Jinruigakuzashi* 45 [in Japanese] [1930]: pp. 41-45).

79. Chin You-di, "Nothing is New," fig. 2a and p. 12
80. Chua Van Tan, "Sahuynh, a Civilization Type of the Metal Age in Vietnam." In: *Recent Discoveries and New Views on some Archaeological Problems in Vietnam* (Hanoi: Institute of Archaeology, Committee of Social Sciences, 1979): pp. 30-1
81. W. Rajpitak and N. Seeley, "The Bronze Bowls from Ban Don Ta Phet: an Enigma of Prehistoric Metallurgy." *World Archaeology*, 11 (1) (1979): pp. 26-31.
82. This vessel (Glover, 1989, fig. 25) is so far unique to Thailand and most closely resembles some objects in bronze and pottery from the contemporary Dongson Culture of North Vietnam, whence I believe it was imported.
83. Rajpitak and Seeley, "The Bronze Bowls from Ban Don Ta Phet," pp. 27-30; and W. Rajpitak, "The Development of Copper Alloy Metallurgy in Thailand in the Pre-Buddhist Period, with Special Reference to High-tin Bronze" (Ph.D. diss., Institute of Archaeology, London, 1983).
84. A. Rea, *Catalogue of Prehistoric Antiquities from Adichanallur and Perumbair* (Madras Government Museum, 1915); J.W. Breeks, *An Account of the Primitive Tribes and Monuments of the Nilgiris* (London: William H. Allan, 1873); and Marshall, "*Taxila.*"
85. A.N. Bennett and I.C. Glover, "Decorated High-tin Bronzes from Thailand's Prehistory." In: I.C. Glover, ed., *South-East Asian Archaeology 1990*, (Hull University, Centre for South-East Asian Studies, 1992): table 2.
86. Bennett and Glover, "Decorated High-tin Bronzes;" and K. Lualamai, "2000 Years Old Bronze Bowls from Ratburi," *Khan Chong* (in Thai) (Bangkok: Silpakorn University, 1986).
87. B.C. Batchelor, "Post 'Hoabinhian' Coastal Settlement Indicated by Finds in Stanniferous Langat River Alluvium near Dengkil, Selangor, Penninsula Malaya." *Federation Museums Journal* (n.s.) 2 (1978): pp. 1-55.
88. There is some variability in the size and specific form of the bronze knobbed-base vessels at Ban Don Ta Phet. Generally they have steep, almost vertical sides curving to a flat base, with some thickening in the center of the base and at the rim. The walls are exceptionally thin, less than 0.5 mm. in some cases, and the vessels appear to have been turned or ground on a rotary device. The number and design of concentric circles varies also, but seven circles are commonly found, sometimes with a "dot and circle" motif between the larger rings. A detailed study of the variability and manufacturing methods employed on these vessels has been started and will be included in a final report on the site.
89. J. Marshall, *A Guide to Taxila*, 3d. reprint edition (Karachi, Department of Archaeology, 1960), pl. VII; and B.B. Lal, "Sisulpalgarh 1948, an Early Historical Fort in Eastern India." *Ancient India* 5 (1948): p. 89 and pl. XLIV B
90. R. Knox, "Jewellery from the Nilgiri hills: a Model of Diversity." In: J. Schotsmans and M. Taddei, eds., *South Asian Archaeology* (Naples: Instituto Universitario Orientale, 1985): p. 525

91. E. Errington, "The Western Discovery of the Art of Gandhara and the Finds of Jamalgastu" (Ph.D. diss., London: School of Oriental and African Studies, 1987); and R. Mitra, "On Some Bactro-Buddhist relics from Rawal Pindi." *Journal of the Asiatic Society of Bengal* 31 (1862): pp. 175-79.

92. This circular black granite vessel (BM 1867, 4-27,1) was found in 1861 together with a crystal hamsa or goose (BM 1867, 4-27,2) which was said to be resting on the center cone of the bowl, and an inscribed piece of gold leaf, some 3 inches long known as the "Taxila scroll." The first two pieces were given by Cunningham to the British Museum in 1867 but the scroll was declared lost although not before a transcription was made and later published. It reads "(Gift) of Sira, depositing a relic of the Lord in the hamsa of her mother, the hamsa of her father. Might it become its place when a corporeal birth comes" (Errington, *The Western Discovery of the Art of Gandhara*, pp. 177-78). The British Museum attributes these pieces to Cunningham's Tope 32 of the Gangu group (Taxila), but Errington (ibid.) argues that they more probably came from another site, perhaps the Taxila Stupa 41, further west between Shahr Dheri and Usman Khattar. But whatever the specific location, there seems to be no doubt that the granite bowl was a Buddhist reliquary or ritual vessel of some type from the ruins of a religious building.

93. Sri K.N. Dikshit of the Archaeological Survey of India, in a letter dated 22.1.85, suggested that the pottery knobbed-base bowls may have been "used by Buddhist monks as a special type of bowl from the sixth century B.C. to the beginning of the Christian Era."

94. Higham and Kijngam, "Prehistoric Investigations in Northeastern Thailand," pp. 126-27.

Chapter 6

AN INSCRIPTION IN MEMORY OF SAYYID BIN ABU ALI

A Study of Relations between China and Oman from the Eleventh to the Fifteenth Century

Liu Yingsheng

The history of relations between China and Oman has been the focus of the work of Hirth and Rockhill in their studies on Zhao Rukua's work *Chu-Fan-Chi*,[1] particularly in regard to geographical place-names in Oman. We know that Wong Man was no doubt Oman, while Wu Ba was probably Mirbat, and Nu Fa was Zufar. Later in the 1930s, Chinese scholars like Zhang Xingliang and Feng Chengjun accepted some of the ideas of Hirth and Rockhill and made contributions of their own to this subject.[2] The Japanese scholar, Yajima Hikoichi, in an excellent article, identified some Omani place-names mentioned in Chinese literature and related them to those in Muslim geographical works.[3] Furthermore, recent publications of Chinese geographical works from the early Ming period contain some valuable studies on this topic.[4]

Only a few Omanis such as Sinbad, known as Obaidah Abdullah bin Al-Qasim and who visited China, have left their names in the historical literature. I propose to reexamine an inscription of the Mongol-Yuan period relating to an Omani in China, and to give a description of his life.

The name of this Omani in Chinese is Bu A Li (Abu'Ali). There are three different sources regarding his life. The first is a chapter about Ma Ba Er (that is Ma'abar/Cola in India) and Ju Lan (Quilon in India), in *Yuan Shi* (A History of the Yuan Dynasty). The text reads:

In A.D. 1281 the envoys of the Mongol-Yuan Government started their mission to *Ju Lan* [Quilon] from *Quan Zhou* [Zaytun]. After three months at sea, they reached Seng Jia Yie [a mistake in transcription for *Seng Jia Na*, which derives from Simhala, that is Sri Lanka]. As they no longer had the monsoon winds and were in need of supplies, they sailed to Ma'abar. Instead of sailing they wanted to travel through Ma'abar to Quilon. A minister of Ma'abar called Bu A Li [Abu'Ali] told them that he himself would like to serve Qubilai Qaghan and be his servant. He had sent an envoy called Zha Ma La Ding [Jamal al-Din] to China. The *Da Bi Zhe Chi* [a mixed Chinese-Mongolian word, meaning great secretary] had reported this news to the Sultan of Ma'abar. The Sultan had become angry on hearing this. He had confiscated Abu'Ali's money, property and slaves, and had even wanted to kill him.[5]

The second text is a paragraph from a chapter in *Gao Li Shi* (History of Korea) written by the Korean historian Zhe Linzhi in 1451, which says "a prince of Ma Ba Er [Ma'abar] called Bo Ha Li had come into conflict with his king and escaped to the Mongol-Yuan Empire. The Emperor [namely Yuan Cheng Zhong] married him to a Korean girl."[6] This description was copied in other Korean sources. It was the Japanese scholar, Jitsuzō Kuwabara, who connected the two references, and identified Bu A Li (Abu'Ali) of Yuan Shi with Bo Ha Li of the Korean source.[7] But he was mistaken in continuing to identify Bo Ha Li (Abu'Ali) with a prince of Kish called Fakhr-al-Din Ahmad, who was sent to visit China by the Mongol prince in Iran, Li-Khan Qazan. Another Japanese scholar, Karashima Noboru, recently made the same mistake.[8]

The third source concerning Abu'Ali is an inscription in memory of Sayyid bin Abu'Ali. The inscription is no longer extant but fortunately it was recorded by its author, Liu Minzhong, in his collected works *Zhong An Ji:*

The real name of Bu A Li [Abu'Ali] in Chinese was Sa Yi Di [Sayyid]. His home town was a city called *Ha La Ha Di* in Chinese. His forefathers had emigrated to a coastal territory called Xi Yang [Western Ocean] in Chinese where they settled as merchants. The father of Sayyid called Bu A Li [Abu'Ali] had enjoyed the trust of the king of that territory. The king was one of five brothers, and Abu'Ali had been called the sixth brother, and had been ordered to rule over some tribes. So he became very rich and had a hundred servants and concubines. His bed was made of ivory and he owned a lot of gold ornaments. When Abu'Ali died, he was succeeded by Sayyid. The King called him by his father's name Abu'Ali. So only a few people knew that his name was Sayyid.[9]

Ten years ago, the Chinese scholar Chen Gaohua correctly proved that "Xi Yang," where Abu'Ali's forefathers had settled, was Ma'abar of India.[10] Consequently, these three sources concern the same person. But where was the hometown of this Abu'Ali? Chen Gaohua said that he was unable to answer that question.

According to my own research, the name of the hometown of Abu'Ali's family, "Ha La Ha Di," was the Chinese transcription of the ancient Omani port city, Qalhāt.[11]

The name of Qalhāt appears many times in medieval classical Chinese literature but, of course, in various forms. For example, in Zhao Rukua's *Zhu Fan Zhi,* a lot of Arabic place names are mentioned. One of them is called "Jia Li Ji." Peliot thought that it was a Chinese transcription of Qalhāt,[12] a thesis with which I agree. Again in *Da De Na Hai Zhi* (A Regional Description of Hai Nan Island compiled in the Da De Period), there is a list of countries from whence ships came to Hai Nan for trade. In this list, next to the name "Kuo Li Mo Si" (that is no doubt Hormuz), there is a place called Jia La Du.[13] It is clear that this Jia La Du is another Chinese transcription in the Mongol Yuan period of Qalhāt. Phonetically it is very close to Marco Polo's Calatu. In the fifteenth century, Qalhāt was called "Jia La Ha" by Chinese sailors. In the famous navigational chart of Zheng He, four shipping lines from different places on the west coast of India were drawn to Jia La Ha, together with their courses and compass directions.[14] From this chart we can also find a series of place names near Muscat, such as Tiwi, Quliqat, and Turtle Island. But the editor of the chart put Jia La Ha (Qalhāt) in the wrong place on his map.

So now we know that these three sources not only referred to the same person, but that person was an Omani. On the basis of this material, a short account of his life can now be given.

Sayyid was born in Ma'abar (Cola) on the east coast of India in A.D. 1251. The date of his family's move from Qalhāt to India is not known. His forebears worked in Ma'abar as middlemen and traders with both the Gulf countries and China, and kept in frequent contact with both areas. So they were well aware of political changes in China and Western Asia. The Mongol conquest in the east and the west gave his family and other Moslem merchants in India an opportunity to extend their trade. Their ships were well received in Quan Zhou (Zaytun) by the local Mongol-Yuan officers. Although his mission to China before 1281 displeased the King of Ma'abar, Sayyid continued to send envoys to Qubilai Qaghan every year, and also to the Mongolian princes such as Abaqa and Qazan in Persia. When the envoys of Mongolian governments in China and Iran stopped in Ma'abar, Sayyid always prepared ships for them beforehand, and provided them with supplies. But his mercantile interests and the demands of his social position in Ma'abar conflicted with each other, and he was to lose the King's confidence.

Realizing Sayyid's position to be in danger, Qubilai Qaghan sent a minister by the name of A Li Bie (Ali Beg) as head of a group of envoys to Ma'abar in 1291, and brought a letter inviting him to China. Sayyid left his wives, children, relatives and property in Ma'abar, and with a hundred servants and the Mongol-Yuan envoys he escaped to China (rather than his hometown of Qalhāt). He probably arrived in Dai Du (Beijing) the following year, 1292. Qubilai Qaghan received him with respect, granted him clothes made from brocade, allowed him to marry a young Korean lady, and gave him a house in which to live. In this way, he was also able to keep in contact with the Korean royal family.

When Temur succeeded to the throne in 1294, Sayyid was given the titles of Zi De Dai Fu (Qualified and Moral Minister of the Mongol-Yuan empire), Zhong Shu Yu Cheng (Right Minister of the Central Government), and Sheng Yi Fu Jian Deng Chu Xing Zhong Shu Sheng Shi (Consultant of the Government of Fu Jian Province). On several occasions, the new emperor granted him large sums of money. When his Korean wife died in 1298, Temur Qaghan married him to another girl.

In the winter of 1299, Sayyid died in Beijing at the age of forty-nine. He had a son and two daughters in China. When the news of Sayyid's death reached Temur Qaghan, he ordered the Government to meet the costs of his funeral arrangements and issued another imperial edict to protect Sayyid's family. His body was transported to Quan Zhou (Zaytun) through official post stations and buried there. The inscription on his tomb was written by the most famous scholar of that time, namely Liu Minzhong. He wrote the text in accordance with an imperial edict from Temur Qaghan.

This is my contribution to the history of relations between the Chinese and the Omanis.

Notes

1. F. Hirth and W. W. Rockhill, *Chao Ju-Kua, His Work on Chinese Arab Trade in the 12th-13th Centuries, Entitled Chu-Fan-Chi.* Studies on Zhao Rukua's work (St. Petersburg, 1911). See Feng Chengjun, ed., *Zhu Fan Zhi Jiao Zhu* (Description of Various Countries) (Shanghai, 1956).
2. Zhang Xingliang, *Zhong Xi Jiao Tong Shi Liao Hui Bian* (Sources on Communications between China and Western Countries), vol. 2 (Beijing, 1977; reprint), p. 273; Feng Chengjun, *Zhu Fan Zhi Jiao Zhu*, p. 59.
3. Yajima Hikoichi, "The Ports of South Arabia as named in the Sailing Route Book by Kia Tan." *Oriental Studies*, vol. 31 (1935): pp. 34-49.
4. Gong Zhen, *Xi Yang Fan Guo Zhi* (Description of Western Lands). Edited with notes by Xiang Da (Beijing, 1982; reprint), pp. 33-5; Huang Shengzeng, *Xi Yang Chao Gong Dian Lu.* (Description of Tributes Paid from Western Countries to the Chinese Court), edited with notes by Xie Fang (Beijing, 1982), pp. 103-5.
5. Yuan Shi, chap. 210, pp. 4660-70.
6. Zheng Linzhi, *Zheng He Hang Hai Tu* (The Chart of Zheng He), drawn by Mao Yaunyi in the late Ming Dynasty, edited with notes by Xiang Da (Beijing, 1957; reprint), pp. 514-15.
7. Jitsuzō Kuwabara, *Hojuko no jiseki* (Achievements of Pu Shougeng) (Tokyo, 1935); and *Pu Shougeng Kao*, Chinese translation by Chen Yujing (Beijing, 1954), pp. 88-9.
8. Karashima Noboru, "Trade Relations between South India and China during the 13th and 14th centuries," in *East-West Maritime Relations*, vol. 1 (Tokyo: Study Group for East-West Maritime Relations, the Middle Eastern Cultural Center in Japan, 1989), p. 74.
9. Liu Minzhong, *Zhong An Zian Sheng Liu Wen Jian Gong Wen Ji* (published in the late Yuan period), chap. 4. The claim by Liu Minzshong that five brothers ruled Ma'abar was supported by Marco Polo.
10. Chen Gaohua, "Ying Du Ma Er Wang Zhi Bo Ha Li Lai Hua Xin Kao (A New Study of the Visit of Prince Bo Ha Li of Ma'abar of India to China)." In: *Nan Kai Da Xue Bao* (Academic Journal of Nan Kai University, 1980): 4.
11. Peliot, *Notes on Marco Polo* (Paris: Imprimerie Nationale, 1959), p. 138.
12. Ibid.
13. The fragment of *Da De Nan Hai Zhi* is kept in Beijing Library, see Chapter 7, p. 21; *Da De* is one of the titles of the sixth Mongol Emperor Temur who reigned, from A.D. 1297 to 1307 (he was the grandson of Qubilai Qaghan).
14. Zheng He, *Zheng He Hang Hai Tu* (The Chart of Zheng He), drawn by Mao Yaunyi in the late Ming Dynasty Edited with notes by Xiang Da (Beijing, 1982; reprint), Chart No. 20. Some other Omani place-names located between Zuo Fa Er (Zufar) and Ma Shi Ji (Muscat) are given on this chart.

Chapter 7

THE MONGOL EMPIRE IN THE THIRTEENTH AND FOURTEENTH CENTURIES
East-West Relations

Bira Shagdar

The Nomadic Society of the Mongols

The geographical position of Mongolia in the heartland of Central Asia was the main environmental factor that determined both the internal development and the external situation of the country. It was an essential factor that had much to do with the shaping of a unique nomadic civilization. On the other hand, the vast mountainous steppe zone of Mongolia is part and parcel of the two major regions of world civilization, i.e., Central Asia and the so-called Eurasian steppe belt stretching from the Danube and the Mediterranean up to the Great Wall of China. For centuries Mongolia had been at the crossroads of world communication. Two major roads, the "Great Silk Road," and the Eurasian steppe corridor, the "Silk Road of the Steppes," linked Mongolia with the centers of civilization in the East and the West.

Mongolia is regarded as a *locus classicus* of Central Asian nomadism, which, by the early thirteenth century, had reached the peak of its development, and produced an advanced socio-economic and political system in Mongolia.

Ghengis Khan and the Foundation of the Mongol State

It was historically important that the advent of Temüjin, Ghengis Khan, (1162- 1227)[1] coincided with the period in which Mongol society went through substantial change. The general situation of the country offered a good opportunity to those who aspired to power and glory in the steppe. It was Ghengis Khan who distinguished himself through his will-power and aptitudes, and made the best use of the situation that prevailed in Mongolia at that time.

It was in 1206, after having successfully waged several decisive battles against his most powerful rivals, that Ghengis Khan convened a Quraltai, the Council of Mongol nobility, at the head of the Onon River. At this Quraltai he was finally granted the status of ruler of all the Mongols, with the rank of Khan and the title of Ghengis.[2] The event meant, in fact, the birth of a new state—a unified Mongolia that stretched a thousand miles from east to west, all the way from the Khin-gan Mountains to the Altai Range, and more than six hundred miles from north to south, from Lake Baikal to the southern range of the Gobi along the Great Wall.

In 1206-1211, Ghengis Khan was engaged in the establishment and reorganization of a civil and military administration in the country. According to a Sino-Mongolian inscription of 1346, in the fifteenth year of the reign of Ghengis Khan, i.e., 1220, the capital city of Qaraqo-rum had been founded in the valley of the Orthon River.[3] Thus Ghengis wished to rule his empire from Mongolia.

Shortly after the creation of a strong political and military machine in his own country, Ghengis Khan embarked on the path of expanding his power. However, it is difficult to say whether, from the outset, he had any serious intention of conquering the settled civilizations that surrounded Mongolia. His priority of subjugating other countries shows that having settled his internal affairs, he began, firstly, to incorporate all other nomadic peoples living outside Mongolia in his state. It is true that on two occasions Ghengis Khan had campaigns orga-nized against the Chin empire of China (in 1210 and 1214-1215). By doing so he wished to demonstrate his might and fame rather than to subjugate China. He soon put an end to the war against China and continued bringing the nomadic tribes, wherever they could be found, under his control, throughout the Eurasian steppe areas. He conquered practically all the nomadic peoples of Turkic origin up to the north-eastern edge of Persia.

In 1219-1224, Ghengis Khan successfully carried out his campaigns against the empire of Kharism-Shah 'Ala'al-Din Muhammad, which at that time was on the decline due to internal discord and feuds. As a result, all the lands of the empire with their ancient cities of Samarkand, Bukhara, Urgench, Utrar (Otrar), Nishapur, and Merv, among others, were brought under the rule of the Mongol Khan. But soon the Mongol cavalrymen, headed by Ghengis Khan's generals who had pursued the defeated Kharism-Shah, returned home the long way to Mongolia via the Caucasus, following a route north of the Caspian Sea.

It is unlikely that Ghengis Khan had devised a clearly formulated war strategy, it is more probable that he just preferred to carry out his intentions immediately. If his wide-ranging conquests are judged by their real outcome, it becomes clear that he did not really intend to build a world empire in the true sense of the word. His main aim was to subdue all his rivals so that all the nomadic peoples existing throughout Central Asia became his subjects. The most suitable pasture lands which were occupied by the nomadic peoples were in the east-west directions from Mongolia, but not from north to south.

The campaigns Ghengis Khan launched against the countries of Central and Western Asia were not followed by regular land-occupation by the Mongols, and when Ghengis Khan returned home, he took his army with him, leaving behind only a few military governors as representatives of his power and his tax collectors. Mongol authority was, therefore, not felt so strongly in the countries of Central and Western Asia during the reigns of Ghengis and his immediate successors. It was exerted more in the form of sporadic raids to collect tributes and to punish those who showed disobedience. This situation continued practically until the reign of Möngke Khan, who finally created an effective administrative system for ruling the domains in Central Asia.

It should be noted that the traditional form of submission typical of all steppe empires must have corresponded to Ghengis Khan's general conception. According to this, it was more important to master the peoples as appanage (*ulus*) rather than to govern the territories of the conquered countries. With regard to sedentary societies, Ghengis preferred to ensure the economic exploitation of those countries by establishing a system of tax collection and of receiving tributes. Keeping this in mind, he distributed the conquered peoples among his four sons. The empire of Ghengis Khan was more a nomadic confederation than a world empire which ruled, in the real sense, the countries of sedentary civilizations.

The World Empire of Ghengis Khan's Successors

Contrary to Alexander the Great whose Graeco-Asian Empire did not even survive his death, Ghengis Khan left a great empire capable of functioning both in time and space. Many of his successors were from his own family and continued his imperial policies. During their reigns the Mongol nomadic empire became the largest empire that has ever existed in world history, stretching from the Far East to Eastern Europe, and including most of Asia, as well as a good deal of Europe.

Ghengis Khan's successors, although declaring their adherence to the commandments of their great predecessor, had in fact departed from his fundamental principle of staying outside "civilization" and not sacrificing the ideals of the nomads for the sake of others. Ögedei (1229-1241), Güyük (1246-1248), and Möngke (1251-1259) went on expanding their empire by way of conquering great sedentary societies.

There is no doubt that this unprecedented territorial expansionism by the Mongol nomads caused much misfortune and distress to humanity. However, the bloodshed and destruction of settled civilizations must not have been as terrible and unimaginable as some terrified and horrified contemporaries naturally tried to depict in their descriptions of the invasions of unknown peoples.

The world empire of the Mongols can be divided into five major parts, mainly based on the following geographical division: Mongolia itself as the center of the empire, beginning with the rise of Ghengis Khan and ending with the death of Möngke Khan in 1259; the Yuan Dynasty in China, beginning with the enthronement of Khubilai; the IL-Khans in Persia; the Golden Horde in Russia; and the Chagadai Khanate in Middle Asia. Despite the fact that the Mongol Empire represented a conglomeration of extremely varied peoples and countries and socio-economic structures, it had many common features and important similarities that made it a coherent entity almost for the whole period of its existence. On the other hand, it cannot be denied that there were specific differences and incompatibilities between the sub-divisions of the Empire that were, in the end, the cause of its disintegration.

Having conquered a world empire, the Mongols were confronted with the most difficult task—a task which had never been attempted before by any society, nomadic or sedentary. The complexity of the problem was due, not so much to the immense size of the territory involved, as to the fact that it was difficult to reconcile, within the framework of one empire, two worlds so entirely different one from the other (the nomadic and the sedentary).

Nevertheless, Ghengis Khan and his successors managed to set up the organization of a world empire that was capable of maintaining its unity for dozens of years after its foundation. They ensured the supremacy of the members of Ghengis Khan's clan for several generations in the Khanates, which had eventually become independent but still remained allied to the central part of the empire. What had been done in this respect? Yeh-lü Chu-tsai, a noted Khitan adviser to Mongol Khans, is said to have repeated the old Chinese proverb to Ögedei: "Although the Empire can be conquered on horseback, it cannot be ruled from a horse."[4]

There is no doubt that the Mongol Khans realized this fact when they were faced with the problem of governing their world empire. The problem as to whether or not the Mongols should part with their nomadic way of life was really a vital issue for them. Anyhow, it should be said that the first successors of Ghengis Khan had decided to make a historical attempt to govern the great empire by means of creating an administrative system that combined the traditional nomadic, political, and military institutions with the centralized, bureaucratic administrative structure of the Chinese and Persian-Central Asian models. It seems to mean that the Mongols resolved, anyhow, not to dismount from their horses, but to combine, in their own way, the two types of civilization— the nomadic and the sedentary. Let us consider what they could do in this respect and what was the final result of their historical experiment.

With the conquest of many countries and direct contact with the great sedentary civilizations, the Mongols had not only to revise the nomads' age-old feelings of primordial antipathy and estrangement towards their counterparts—cultivators or settled peoples—but also to come seriously to terms with the significance of the advantages of the sedentary civilizations, useful for their empire-building efforts. First of all, the Mongols had borrowed and adapted cultural gains, including the art of writing and literature. In their attempts to substantiate ideologically their political supremacy, they resorted not only to their own Shamanistic belief, but also to different religious and political concepts and postulates from other countries. To give but one illustration, *The Secret History of the Mongols* propagated a concept of the heavenly origin of the "Golden Clan" of Ghengis Khan. It is said in the book by the words of Alan-goa herself, the legendary foremother of the Golden Clan, concerning the story of the birth of Bodoncrar, who was believed to be the genuine ancestor of Ghengisids, as follows:

> Every night, a bright yellow man entered by the light of the hole at the top or [by that] of the door top of the tent and rubbed my belly. His light was wont to sink into my belly. When he went out, like a yellow dog he was wont to crawl out by the beams of the sun or moon … If one understands by that, it is evident [that] its sign is [that] "They are sons of Heaven …"[5]

This quotation reveals the basic concepts, regarding the origin of Ghengisids, which was a final result of the lengthy process of cross-meeting and fertilization of indigenous and alien religious and political views on the genesis of khanship against the background of the nomadic civilization in Mongolia. These concepts are those of Heaven and of Light.

Here lies a unique example of how a great syncretic idea came into being as an outcome of meeting different traditions and cultures. It is true that the worship of Heaven was initially characteristic of Shamanism, and it must be regarded as an indigenous belief of nomadic peoples. It was this worship that was the bedrock of the old Mongolian political conception of Khanship; but it does not exclude that the Heaven-sanctioned Khanship conception of the Mongols might, in the final phase of its evolution, have been inspired by the highly developed political doctrine of the Chinese, the doctrine of the mandate of heaven (*t'ien-ming*).[6] As the above quotation shows, Ghengis Khan could be considered to have descended from "the son of Heaven." Moreover, we can go still further in order to discover another stratum of influence, this time, the influence of a more distant civilization, namely the Iranian, or to be more exact, the Zoroastrian-Manichaen concept of Light which might have inspired the Mongols to elaborate their own version of an immaculate conception of Alan-goa by means of Light.[7]

The sources witness that Ghengis Khan and his successors widely propagated the idea of their celestial mandate and their extraordinary origin, and referred, on every occasion, to the might of Everlasting Heaven.

Despite the cruelty that accompanied the conquests, religious fanaticism was, however, alien to the Mongols. They pursued a policy of religious tolerance in their multinational empire. And it is difficult to think that this policy was determined simply by the indifference or ignorance of the Mongols, as some scholars suppose. Rather, it was a premeditated policy necessitated by "holding the soul" of their subjugated peoples belonging to different ethnic groups and beliefs.

Coming to the political structure of the Mongol Empire, reference has to be made to some traditional institutions of nomadic society which acquired special significance, having been, in many instances, modified in conformity with new requirements. By this period the Quraltai, the oldest form of political institution of the nomads, assumed much more importance than had ever been the case before. It had become a real assembly of élite Mongol leaders—princes and nobles—acting on the basis of old traditions and customs, to handle most important matters of state, like the acclamation of a Khan, questions of war, and establishment of law and policy.

The Mongol Empire was created through military conquest, and the Mongol Khans regarded the army as the most basic amongst all the imperial institutions. It was military supremacy that provided the political domination of the Mongol Khans. The military organization, based on a decimal system, had not only been sustained for generations of Khans, but had served as the model of the army constructed by later followers and pretenders to the right of the members of Ghengis Khan's family throughout Central Asia. A new important element of the Mongol army structure during the post-Ghengis Khan period was the institutions of Tamma. Tamma forces were originally established by order of the central imperial government for the purpose of maintaining conquered territories. Some Tamma armies ultimately became the nuclei of the permanent military forces of the empire's subsidiary Khanates, such as Hülegüs's IL-Khanate in Persia.[8]

The Mongols were the first to innovate a worldwide network of communications that in fact linked East and West, thus facilitating the movement of peoples and ideas. A horse relay postal system was introduced by Ögedei in 1234.[9] He began by setting up post stations (*jam*) in his own domain. This was further extended by his brothers, Chagadai and Tului and his nephew Batu, to include the lands under their direct rule; it was a very important mechanism which made it possible to link the empire's center in Mongolia with its other parts. The structure of the system was based on the building of a post station at stages equivalent to a day's journey; that is about 25-30 miles. The stations held stocks of horses and fodder for those who traveled. Normally, messenger traffic was about 25 miles a day, but express messengers could go much faster, 200-300 miles per day.[10]

Based on the travel accounts of contemporary travelers, like the famous friars John of Plano Carpini and William of Rubruck, we can reconstruct the route along which the horse relay post stations had functioned. The two missions followed more or less the same route. They passed through Eastern Europe, proceeded by way of Kiev into Mongol-ruled territories in Russia, in which Sarai on the Volga, the Ordu of Batu, was an important passing point. Further on, the travelers crossed the country of the Kanli Turks north of the Aral Sea and, following the Syr Darya, passed through the towns of Yanikant (near modern Kazalinsk in Kazakhstan), Barchin (near Kizil Orda), and Otrar. From northern Khwarism they moved into the old Kara-Khitai territory south of the Balkash, crossed the Chu, Ili, and Emil rivers, then through Omyl (now Tacheng in Sinkiang), and by way of Lake Ulyungur and the river Urungu. They passed the Altai mountains and entered into western Mongolia, the region between Kobdo and Uliastai. From there they proceeded due east, crossed the Khangai range and reached Qaraqorum, the capital of the Mongol Empire.[11] In this way John of Plano Carpini's mission covered a distance of almost three thousand miles, in three-and-a-half months. All across Central Asia and Mongolia they rode Central Asian or Mongol horses, suitable for lengthy travel in the steppe-mountainous regions, coping with a severe climate and changing their mounts regularly at the post-stations set up all along the route. Thus, with the creation of the Mongol Empire a new great Eurasian road was opened linking Mongolia with Europe. This road could be called a Mongol Örtege Road or a Mongol horse relay post station road that ran in its Central Asian part parallel to the famous Silk Road which led from the western point of Gansu towards Lob Nor and then along the foot of the Kunlun all the way to Khotan, Yarkand, Kashgar, and up to the Near East. Although one cannot assert as categorically as did Henry Howorth, when he wrote that the Mongols, for a while, made the desert as safe as the Queen's Highway, it is true they maintained and protected communications between East and West effectively and by so doing greatly contributed to history and obtained closer contact between peoples and cultures. No doubt that the Mongols, having monopolized East-West relations, not only gave a new lease of life to the traditional Silk Road, but also played a key role in the way it functioned.

As regards the practice of ruling great sedentary societies like Persia and China, the Mongols invented some original institutions and offices which not only functioned efficiently in various parts of the empire, but left a noticeable mark on the civil administration and government of conquered countries. One of the key institutions in the Mongol's administration of the empire on the local level was the office of the *"daruqaci."* The institutional system of *"daruqaci"* had been set up in all the Mongolia-ruled regions of Eurasia-Persia, China, and Russia.

The Mongol Khans had also introduced various forms of taxation in the regions of their empire. They had to procure the best way of economic exploitation of the conquered peoples all over the empire. To take the original Mongolian taxation, for example, it could be divided into tribute (*alba*) and levy (*qubciur*). Both *alba* and *qubciur* were paid in kind. With the conquest of the sedentary population of Persia and Central Asia, *qubciur* acquired a rather different context, and it became the term used for a poll tax, either flat rate or graduated, imposed on the conquered sedentary peoples.

The first three successors of Ghengis were staunchly in favor of maintaining Mongolia as the center of their empire. In this respect the reign of Möngke was the most important period in the history of the empire. It was during his reign that the Mongol Empire not only expanded greatly, but eventually acquired a clear organizational form. Möngke Khan managed to create an efficient administrative system for ruling the empire from the center in Mongolia. He established the supremacy of the Great Khan in Qaraqorum over any prince, regardless of his lineage, and over any clan or family alliance. The Great Khan had to preside over a strong bureaucratic structure staffed by supranational personnel which included, besides the Mongol themselves, Uighurs, Khitans, Chinese, Central Asians, and Persians. Möngke Khan introduced an institution of viceroys for governing the conquered territories; Mongol princes, instead of being granted people as their appanage, were assigned to specific territorial domains. Möngke Khan appointed five viceroys who were responsible for the administration of their domains and personally accountable for that administration to the Great Khan. Henceforth, the Great Khan acted as the supreme overlord. Of the five appointees, three were Möngke's brothers.

By the time of the reign of Möngke, the Mongols, who had been a small, imperceptible nomadic people, had become, for all practical purposes, the rulers of the then-known world. Mongolia had become the vortex of great events and innovations. Embassies from all over the world, including the European kingdoms and the Vatican, undertook the long voyage to the Mongol court. It was characteristic of Möngke Khan, just as his predecessors, that he was tolerant enough to let activists of different religions attend his court, proposing their services, and he was ready to accept advice and help from experts.

It was thanks to experts and defectors from civilized countries that the Mongol Khans could set up an efficient administrative system created in order to rule their world empire.

Almost all the great world religions had become well known to the Mongols during that period. Under Möngke the Nestorians held a privileged position. As witnessed by William of Rubruck, the Franciscan friar who met Möngke Khan, the Mongol Khan's official attitude towards different religions was as follows: "We Mongols believe that there is but one God, by Whom we live and by Whom we die, and towards Him we have an upright heart ... But just as God gave different fingers to the hand, so has He given different ways to men."[12] That was a truly pluralistic policy as regards religions and ideas.

Mongolia had for a while become a meeting place of different peoples, cultures, and religions. During the reign of Möngke Khan, the city of Qaraqorum became the true center of the world empire. It was a cosmopolitan city, where one could meet Armenians, Buddhists, Chinese, Christians, Europeans, Hungarians, Muslims, Russians, and others. The city was linked to all parts of the empire by the wide network of roads connecting the horse relay post stations.

Contemporary travel accounts give lively descriptions of the artistic activities within Qaraqorum and the open display of works of art. Friar William of Rubruck was greatly impressed by the Khan's palace and a large tree at its entrance made of silver by Master William of Paris. He writes that the Khan's palace resembled a church, with a middle nave and two sides beyond two rows of pillars and three doors on the south side. There were two quarters in the city: one for the Saracens (Persians), where there were bazaars and where many traders gathered, the other being the quarter of the Catalans, Chinese who were all craftsmen. There were also large palaces belonging to the court secretaries and twelve Buddhist temples, two mosques, and one Christian church.[13] According to another source, under the reign of Ögedei, foundations to a Buddhist edifice were laid, which was completed by Möngke. A great stupa covered with a tall pavilion constituted rooms around which the statues of various Buddhas were arranged, completely in accordance with the indication of the sutras.[14]

The city was enclosed by a mud wall and had four gates. At the east gate, millet and other kinds of grain were sold; at the west gate, sheep and goats; at the south gate, cattle and wagons; and at the north gate, horses.[15]

The Mongol Empire and East-West Relations

With the creation of the Yuan Empire in China, the center of gravity of the Mongol Empire had shifted to foreign countries, mostly to China and Persia.

It is characteristic that during the reign of the Yuan emperors, East-West relations had attained the highest degree of development. Scholars may argue whether there was a Pax Mongolica or not. Whatever the political and military consequences of conquests may have been, the fact is that the period of the Mongol Empire had, in one way or another, facilitated a wide-scale exchange of material and cultural wealth between peoples and countries. Complicated processes of blending, merging, and mutual influence of all kinds of social, political, and cultural traditions and values took place within the Empire's boundaries.

During the Mongol Empire, thanks to the safety of the trade routes and the generosity of traders, intercontinental and international trade increased as never before.[16] By the end of the thirteenth century, fabrics were even being imported from Egypt, and through Venetian traders, from Europe.[17] Persian, Sogdian, and Central Asian merchants were most active in developing trade throughout the Empire. The Mongol and Turkic nomads served mostly as caravan drivers and guides, and supplied the merchants with means of conveyance—camels, horses, food, and accommodation all along the route. Different kinds of fabrics, including cotton, silk, and brocade, were imported into Mongolia from China.

Merchants prospered, particularly during Khubilai's reign. They imported camels, horses, carpets, medicines, and spices and exported Chinese textiles, ceramics, lacquer ware, ginger, and cassia.[18] Overseas trade between China and India, Southeast Asia, and Persia had been developing.

One has to underline the significance of the exchange of intellectual innovations between East and West. In 1267 Khubilai invited the Persian astronomer, Jamal al- Din, to China to make known his discoveries. He brought along diagrams of an armillary sphere, sundials and astrolabe, a terrestrial globe, and a celestial globe, as gifts for the court. He also presented a new, more accurate calendar, known in Chinese as the Wan-Nien Li (calendar for Ten Thousand Years), as a gift to Khubilai.[19]

Four years later, in 1271, Khubilai finally established an Institute of Muslim Astronomy. There, the Chinese astronomer, Kuo Shou-ching (1231-1316) used the Persian diagrams and calculations to build his own instruments and to devise his own calendar, the Shou Shih Li (Calendar Delivering the Season), which with minor revisions was employed throughout the Ming Dynasty.[20]

Muslim medicine also enjoyed great popularity in China under Mongol rule. Khubilai, himself afflicted with gout and other ailments, was particularly hospitable to physicians. In 1285, 1288, and 1290, he dispatched envoys to South India to seek not only precious goods but also skilled craftsmen and doctors. Two branches of the Kuan-hui ssu (Imperial hospitals), composed primarily of Muslim doctors, were established in K'ai-P'ing and in North China to treat the Emperor and the court. Khubilai also sought to obtain medicines from Korea. Thirty-six volumes of Muslim medicinal remedies were placed in the court library. Khubilai established an Imperial Academy of Medicine (Ch. *T'ai-i-yuan*) which laid down the criteria for the selection of instructors of medicine and supervised the training of physicians and drafting of medical texts.[21] Western Asian surgery greatly impressed the Chinese, because physicians from the Near East who performed all sorts of difficult operations are frequently mentioned. Some of them were not Muslim but Nestorian Christians, like Ai-hsieh (1227-1308) whose Chinese name is a rendering of Syriac Isa, Yehoshua, or Jesus.[22] He was not only a famous physician but also served for some time as a Court astronomer under Khubilai Khan, prior to the arrival of Jamal al-Din. He reached high offices at Khubilai's court and was honored posthumously by having his biography included in the Yuan Dynasty history.[23]

The Mongols are known to have used Chinese and Central Asian experts in the field of engineering and technology from the beginning of their conquest. Some Muslim experts were involved also in hydraulic engineering works in China. Sayyid Ajall Shams-al-Din, the Muslim engineer who was the Governor of Yuunan, did much for the irrigation of the K'un-ming Basin.[24] There was another great Arab engineer called Shams (1278-1351). He was the author of a treatise on river conservation, the *Ho-fang t'ung-i* (Comprehensive Explanation of River Conservation), published in 1231. Shams's grandfather had come to China in the wake of the Mongol conquest of Arabia and settled in China. Apart from hydraulic engineering, Shams is described in his biography as having been an expert in astronomy, geography, mathematics, and musical or rather acoustic theory.[25]

The creation of the world empire had greatly broadened the geographical outlook of the populations. Travelers and merchants were the main disseminators of first-hand information about diverse countries and peoples. The Mongols and their Empire had not only become the focus of world interest, but they themselves had accumulated extensive knowledge of the countries and peoples they had incorporated in their empire. *The Secret History of the Mongols* displays not only a remarkably accurate knowledge of the geography of Mongolia itself, but also contains fairly accurate information on foreign countries, their towns, and peoples.

The Europeans who visited Mongolia and China, like John of Plano Carpini, Friar William of Rubruck, Marco Polo, and others, had transmitted a wealth of information on Mongolia and other Asian countries to their countrymen; while the Arab and Persian travelers had introduced the countries of Central Asia and the Middle East to the Mongols and the Chinese. A world map drawn during the Mongol rule in China, probably based on the information derived from Muslim sources, gives a fairly accurate rendering of Asia and Europe.[26]

It should be noted that East-West relations during the period of the Mongol Empire were not at all a one-way movement. With the foundation of the IL-Khanate by Hulegu (1256-1265), Persia and Iraq, together with much of Anatolia, had been finally brought under Mongol control. Hulegu, as did his brother Khubilai, decided to settle in the center of the sedentary society, Persia. He set up his capital at Maragheh in Azerbaijan. The IL-Khanate existed for seventy years. The position of IL-Khans was that of a subject realm to the Great Khanate. The prestige of the Great Khans, particularly that of Khubilai, was immense, and the connection between China and Persia remained strong and friendly under Mongol rule. This factor greatly favored the development of the relations between the two great centers of civilization.

Under Mongol rule, the East Asian or, to be more exact, the Mongol-Chinese impact on Persia and the Middle East became stronger than ever before. In Persia, as in China, the Mongols were confronted with a flourishing culture. The Mongol conquest, particularly in its initial stage, had caused great damage to this culture, simply because a great number of intellectuals and artisans were annihilated or forcefully deported to Mongolia and China. As a nomadic people, the Mongols could not offer anything culturally superior in exchange for what they had destroyed. However, what could be regarded as a positive point in favor of the Mongols was the fact that they played an active intermediary role in introducing some East Asian elements into Persian culture and religion. To take the case of religion, the single homogeneous Islam had undergone drastic changes; prior to the Mongols, of the two Islamic sects, the Sunni and the Shiah, the former dominated in Persia. Under the Mongols the Shiite sect took the upper hand and Persia became a Shiite state. Moreover, the policy of religious tolerance pursued by the Mongols directly resulted in the revival of non-Islamic traditions in Persia. The persistent Mongol attempt in Persia to establish a political alliance with the Christian West against the Mamelukes led to increased sympathy towards Christians. On the other hand, the Christian powers, the popes in particular, never ceased to hope that the Mongols would become converted to Christianity. There were good reasons for this as Nestorian Christians were known to be influential in the IL-Khanate. Some of them served the IL-Khan's Court as Mongol ambassadors to the countries of Europe. For instance, Rabban Sauma and Mark—the two Uighur Nestorian Christians whom Khubilai Khan first sent to Jerusalem as his envoys for the purpose of collecting information about the country, but under the pretext of making a pilgrimage to sacred places—were granted the Golden Gerege (Emperor's Credentials). When they arrived at the IL-Khanate, they were received with great honor as personal ambassadors of the great Khan.

In the 1280s, Rabban Sauma was sent by Arghun as his envoy to Europe, where he visited Constantinople, Rome, Paris, and London; he had an audience with the kings of those countries and handed them letters and gifts from the IL-Khan. Subsequently under the name of Yaballaha III, Mark became Catolicos—supreme head—of all the Nestorian churches of Asia, his seat being within IL-Khanid territory.

The most intriguing aspect of religious life under the IL-Khans was the fact that Buddhism, which was quite a new and alien faith for the bulk of the population, enjoyed a brief period of official favor. That was a distant reflection of the general religious policy of the Mongol Empire. Hulegu, who had close contact with his brother Khubilai, displayed sympathy towards Buddhism; his successors, especially in the reign of Arghun, tolerated Buddhism more and more. The preferred form of that faith, as in Yuan China, was a variety of the Lamaistic Buddhism of Tibet. Thus some kind of Tibetan religious and cultural influence had reached Persia through the Mongols. Nevertheless, material evidence of Mongol-Tibetan Buddhism in Persia is very scant, for Buddhist monuments were destroyed or converted for Islamic use after the conversion of the Mongol rulers to Islam. Only a few Buddhist ruins subsist near Maragheh.

Perceptible East Asian or Mongol Buddhist and Chinese influence is visible in some examples of Persian painting of the Mongol and post-Mongol periods, as in the case of a pair of miniatures in Miscellany Collection H. 2152 of the Topkapi Library, made for the Timurid prince Baysungur and mainly composed during the IL-Khanid and Timurid period. The two miniatures were classified by those who had collected works of various origins in Miscellany albums as the "work of masters of Hitay,"[27] namely Mongolia and China.

It was under the impact of Buddhist art in the reign of the IL-Khans that figurative painting, previously neglected in Islamic painting, was first introduced into Islamic countries, particularly Persia. The characteristics of the "school of Hitay" aroused the admiration of Muslim artists. The Muslims found occasion to become acquainted with this school in the Mongol period, when Buddhist princes invited *baksi* (Buddhist masters) to build temples in Samarkand, Khurasan, and Azerbaijan. In general, it must be said that the Persian miniature was quite a new form of painting that emerged during the period of Mongol rule.

The IL-Khans are known to have patronized and promoted sciences, particularly astronomy. The famous philosopher and astronomer, Nasir al-Din Tusi (1201-1274), was one of Hulegu's advisers. Under their guidance, large observatories were built, some of which are still extant. The most famous observatory was in Maragheh which in addition to the studies conducted there, show that astronomy was far more advanced in Persia than in Europe.

Historiography enjoyed no less attention and patronage on the side of the IL- Khans who were naturally interested in immortalizing their "great deeds" and those of their predecessors. For that purpose, they mobilized the connoisseurs of old times and historians of different nations, and made available their archives and official chronicles for those who wrote history. Under these circumstances, historiography in Persia reached its apogee, and historians took advantage, more than anyone else, of acquainting themselves with other cultures and peoples. This is illustrated by two famous works of the period of the Mongol Empire, namely, *Tarikh-i Jahan-Gusha* (The History of the World Conqueror) by the Ata Malik Juvaini (1226-1283) and *Jami-altawarikh* (The Compendium of Histories) by Rashid al-Din (1247-1318). Both authors held high political positions in the IL-Khanate and witnessed or took part in many important events in their day. Juvaini began working on his book during his residence in Qaraqorum in 1252-1253 at the suggestion of his "faithful friends and pure-hearted brothers"[28] from the court of Möngke Khan. He must have completed his work shortly after 1260 and it was to be the first history of the non-Islamic world that appeared in Persian historiography. He wrote of the Mongols on the basis of their oral and written sources which he probably collected during his stay in Qaraqorum. He was one of the great Islamic apologists of the universal policy of the Mongol Khans.

Rashid al-Din wrote his book in 1300-1311 by order of the IL-Khans-Ghazan and Öljeitu. His *Compendium of Histories* was the world's first real universal history. Rashid al-Din had a unique opportunity of obtaining the assistance of scholars from different nations resident at the IL-Khan court. The history of India was written with the help of the Kasmiri hermit, Kamalashri, and the history of China with the assistance of two learned Chinese, on the basis of a book compiled by three Buddhist priests.[29] It is not known what Europeans supplied Rashid al-Din with material for the history of the Franks, but there is no doubt that he used European sources.

Pride of place was given in the book to the history of the Mongols, based almost exclusively on native sources. The author could avail himself of the assistance and favor of influential Mongols, such as Pulad-chinksank, the representative of the Great Khan at the IL-Khanate courts, and Ghazan Khan himself whose knowledge of history was surpassed by that of Pulad alone.

We have every reason to think that all those details included in his book must have been retold or especially prepared for him by his Mongol colleagues from such Mongol sources as the famous *Altan debter* (Golden Book), which was always preserved at the treasury of the Khan in the hands of the oldest emirs.[30] Some scholars assume that the first draft of *Jami-altawarikh* was not originally written in Persian, and goes back to a Mongolian version, most probably compiled by Pulad-chinksank and other Mongol genealogists.[31]

One cannot underestimate the role played by Pulad-chinksank in composing the *Jami-altawarikh*. He was a great Mongolian historian who might in turn have collaborated with other Mongolian and East Turkish connoisseurs of history. He held the high rank of chancellor at the court of Khubilai Khan and was sent to the IL-Khanate as the Great Khan's envoy and was appointed emir and commander-in-chief of the army in Iran and Turan. He died in 1312 or 1313.

Thus, as W. Barthold noted, Rashid al-Din's work took the form of a vast historical encyclopedia, such as no other people, either in Asia or Europe, possessed in the Middle Ages. The very possibility of the creation of such a work with the assistance of learned men of all nations shows what might have been the results, under more favorable circumstances, of the Mongol invasion, which had connected the most distant civilized peoples with one another.[32]

No matter how great the contact and mutual influence of peoples and cultures might have been during the period of the world empire of the Mongols, they could not actually change the nature of great civilizations, either in Yuan China or in IL-Khanid Persia. Moreover, the highly developed civilizations in conquered countries went on developing, having successfully overcome all obstacles and damage. The nomadic conquerors who had settled in conquered countries were assimilated everywhere in varying degrees by existing local civilizations. In the IL-Khanate, unlike in Yuan China, the Mongols had adopted the main local religion of Islam. This factor removed the most conspicuous point of difference between the heathen conquerors and their subjects and did much to foster the assimilation of the Mongols into the Muslim population. The fate of the Mongols in Persia and Middle Asian countries turned out quite differently in contrast to those in Yuan China. They were not driven out of those countries, but they could not return to their homeland and so remained there forever, having been assimilated with the local populations, especially with the Muslim Turks to whom they were close both ethnically and linguistically.

Although the Mongol conquest was mainly military and political rather than cultural or religious, in contrast to Roman, Buddhist, or Islamic conquests, worldwide Mongol expansionism had much more far-reaching consequences in many spheres of the lives of various peoples than expected.

The Mongols of those days had not played an exclusively negative role in history—as empire-builders they greatly encouraged and facilitated the meeting and intermingling of peoples and cultures on a worldwide scale. It seems to me that the great historical experience—both negative and positive—that humanity had accumulated at that time should receive serious consideration henceforth, all the more so in that it could be useful for the development of mutual understanding and co-operation between peoples and countries in our time.

Notes

1. The date of birth of Genghis Khan is not quite certain. See P. Pelliot, *Notes on Marco Polo*, vol. 1 (Paris, 1959), pp. 281-8; O. Lattimore, "Genghis Khan and the Mongol Conquests." *Scientific American*, vol. 209, no. 2 (1963).
2. *The Secret History of the Mongols*, translated and edited by F. W. Cleaves (Cambridge, Mass.: Harvard University Press, 1982), vol. 1, p. 141, para. 202. See *The History of the MPR* (Ulan Bator, 1989), vol. 1, pp. 170-91.
3. F. W. Cleaves, "The Sino-Mongolian Inscription of 1346," *HJAS*, vol. 15, nos. 1-2 (1952).
4. The quotation is taken from Lue Kwanten, *Imperial Nomads* (Leicester University Press, 1979), p. 142.
5. Cleaves, *The Secret History*, par. 21, p. 142.
6. Igor de Rachewiltz, *Some Remarks on the Ideological Foundations of Ghengis Khan's Empire* (Paper on Eastern History No. 7 March 1973), pp. 21-26.
7. Sh. Bira, "On the Traditional Historiographical Mutual Relationship between India and Mongolia," in *Mongolia and India*, edited by Sh. Bira (Ulan-Bator, 1989), pp. 30-3; and *The Secret History of the Mongols* is a great historical and cultural monument" (in Mongolian), *Bulletin, The IAMS News Information on Mongol Studies*, no. 2 (6) (Ulan-Bator, 1990): pp. 11- 13.
8. D. Morgan, *The Mongols* (Oxford: Basil Blackwell, 1986), p. 73.
9. Cleaves, *The Secret History*, par. 281, p. 142.
10. A. Ricci, *The Travels of Marco Polo* (London, 1931), p. 157.
11. Igor de Rachewiltz, *Papal Envoys to the Great Khans* (London, 1971), pp. 95-96.
12. See de Rachewiltz, *Papal Envoys*, p. 136; See de Rachewiltz, *The Mission of Friar William of Rubruck*, translated by P. Jackson with David Morgan (London, 1990), p. 236.
13. de Rachwiltz, *The Mission of Friar William*, p. 221.
14. Cleaves, "The Sino-Mongolian Inscription of 1346."
15. de Rachwiltz, *The Mission of Friar William*, p. 221.
16. P. Ratchnevsky, *Ghenghis Khan: His Life and Legacy*, translated and edited by Thomas Nivison Haining (Oxford: Basil Blackwell, 1991), p. 205.
17. Ibid, p. 199.
18. M. Rossabi, "The Muslims in the Early Yuan Dynasty," in *China under Mongol Rule*, edited by John D. Langlois Jr. (Princeton University Press, 1981), pp. 270-77.
19. J. Needham, *Science and Civilization of China*, vol. 3 (Cambridge University Press; reprint 1979), p. 49.
20. H. Franke, "Sino-Western Contacts under the Mongol Empire," *Journal of the Royal Asiatic Society*, vol. 6 (Hong Kong, 1966); M. Rossabi, *Khubilai Khan: His Life and Times* (Berkeley, Los Angeles, and London, 1988), pp. 125-26.
21. Jutta Rall, *Die Vier grossen Medizenschulen der Mongolen-Zeit* (Wiesbaden: Franz Steiner Verlag, 1970), pp. 30-1.
22. Franke, "Simo-Western Contacts," p. 60.
23. Ibid.
24. Needham, *Science and Civilization of China*, vol. 1, p. 141.
25. Franke, "Simo-Western Contacts," p. 61.
26. W. Fuchs, *The Mongol Atlas of China by Chu Su pen* (Peking: Monumenta Serica, Monographs, 1946).
27. E. Esin, "A Pair of Miniatures from the Miscellany Collections of Topkapi," *Central Asiatic Journal* vol. 21, no. 1 (1977): p. 15.

28. Juvaini, *The History of the World-Conqueror*, translated by J.A. Boyle, vol. 1, (Manchester University Press, 1958), p. 5.
29. W. Barthold, *Turkestan Down to the Mongol Invasion*, second edition translated from Russian by A.R. Gibb (London, 1958), p. 45.
30. Rashid ad-Din, *Jami-altawarikh*, vol. 1, part 1 (Moscow-Leningrad: The Russian Translation, 1952), p. 18.
31. A. Zeki Velidi Togan, "The Composition of the History of the Mongols by Rashid ad-Din," *Central Asiatic Journal*, vol. 7, no. 1 (March 1962): p. 64; see Sh. Bira, *Mongolskaya Istoriographiya XIII-XVII vekov* (Mongolian Historiography of the 13th-17th Centuries) (Moscow, 1978), pp. 133-37.
32. Barthold, *Turkestan Down to the Mongol Invasion*, p. 46.

Chapter 8

A BRUNEI SULTAN OF THE EARLY FOURTEENTH CENTURY
A Study of an Arabic Gravestone

Chen Da-sheng

Introduction

As a Chinese scholar, I was lucky to be able to join the Maritime Silk Routes Expedition organized by UNESCO. As a member of the international team of scholars, I sailed on the the expedition ship, the Fulk-al-Salamah, from Oman to China, stopping in Pakistan, India, Sri Lanka, Thailand, Malaysia, Indonesia, Brunei, and the Philippines. I took part in the international seminars held in each of these countries during the expedition. I cannot describe here all the events from which I benefited during this scientific expedition, so I shall confine myself to those that particularly concerned my own studies and which took place in Brunei Darussalam.

Along the portion of the Maritime Route Expedition I followed, Brunei, which is not a Member State of UNESCO, was also the only country which did not have official diplomatic relations with the People's Republic of China. There is, however, a very long history of relations between the two countries. The earliest Chinese records of Brunei date back to the period of the Liang Dynasty (A.D. 503-557). Since that time, various names for Brunei can be found in different Chinese documents, such as Po-li, Bo-ni, Fo-ni, Po-lo, and Wen-lai among others. Most scholars agree that all these names refer to the north-western part of Borneo Island and the region around Brunei Darussalam.[1]

My interest in Islamic inscriptions on the gravestones of Brunei had been aroused for sometime, due to the discovery of a Chinese gravestone of A.D. 1264.[2] This was the earliest evidence of Chinese Muslim remains in South and Southwest Asia and particularly attracted my attention as it is the gravestone of a certain "Mr. Pu," who had gone to Brunei from Quanzhou, the town where I myself lived from 1976 to 1985. (During those years I worked in the Foreign Maritime Museum, and since then I have been studying the Arabic and Persian inscriptions and Islamic history of that region).

During my stay in Brunei, I visited five Muslim cemeteries in Bandar Seri Begawan with Mr. Hâjî Abdul Rahîm bin Hâjî Ahmad, curator of the exhibition section of the Brunei Museum, and his colleagues PG. Hâjî Mohd Yamîn PSJ and PG. Hâjî Abd Momîn. Professor Liu Yingsheng from Nanjing University (China), also a member of the UNESCO International Expedition, accompanied us. We visited the sites of the Jalan Residency cemetery (which is the site of the Chinese gravestone of A.D. 1264), the Royal Grave Yard, the Jalan Brunei Tutong cemetery, the Mausoleum of Sultan Bolkiah, and the tomb of Sultan Sharîf Alî at Kota Batu.

Identification of a Brunei Sultan Gravestone

While I was visiting the Brunei Museum and glancing through the contents of the *Brunei Museum Journal,* I came across two photographs of an Arabic gravestone. I was struck by the similarity of that gravestone to those I had frequently seen in Quanzhou. At first I was surprised and wondered why the *Brunei Museum Journal* would publish an Arabic inscription excavated in Quanzhou. However, after I had read it in detail, I was even more surprised because the gravestone in question was not found in Quanzhou, but in Brunei. The paper was entitled "Tomb of Maharaja Brunei" and presented by Metassin bin Hâjî Jabah and Suhaili bin Hâjî Hassan.[3] They mentioned that the gravestone was found at the Residency/Dagang cemetery near the town center and that it was made of granite. However, although I could only judge from the photographs in the *Journal,* my experience suggested that the gravestone was made of diabase, not granite, and that the inscription was carved in Quanzhou, not in Brunei. In order to confirm this first intuition I asked to see the gravestone itself. Thus, the day before I left Brunei, thanks to the aid of Mr. Awang Sumadi bin Sukaimi, chief cultural officer of Brunei, I was able to see the gravestone in an underground storeroom of the Brunei Museum. The gravestone was indeed made of diabase, not granite. I was also told that no such mineral exists in Brunei.

The gravestone measures 68.5 cm in height, 39 cm in width, and 9 cm in thickness; the top is in the shape of a pointed bow; the bottom has a rectangular tenon which is easily erected upon a stone base with a mortise; both sides are polished and decorated with a band in concave relief and are engraved with Arabic inscriptions: seven lines on the front and four lines on the back.

Mr. Jibah provided a full text of the Arabic inscriptions on both sides, except for one word at the end of the third line of the front. The text was transcribed by two Egyptian scholars, Mr. Abdulla Abdul Hamid al-Attar, Director of the Coptic and Islamic Antiquities Secretariat, Ministry of Culture, and Mr. Yehiya Abdul Alim, Secretary at the Museum of Islamic Art, Division of Stones, Welfare and Proofs, Bab el-Khalk, Cairo. Mr. Jibah also presented an English translation of the text by Mr. Hâjî Muḥammad Siraj, senior religious propagation assistant, Dakwah and Tabligh Centre, Bandar Seri Begawan, Brunei Darussalam. Most of the text in Arabic was correctly transcribed except for a few words. As regards the front, I suggest that the word at the end of the third line missed by Mr. Jibah is "yusamma," meaning "he was called." The word "al-Alm" in the second line should be "al-Ālim" meaning "a learned man." On the back, the last line was wrong. In order that the reader may understand the text better, I shall give a full version of the Arabic inscriptions, as well as a complete English translation as follows:

The Arabic inscriptions

Front:

Back:

ا (١) هذا قبر المرحوم الشهيد

ب (١) كل نفس ذائقة

(٢) السلطان العالم العا

(٢) الموت وانما توفون

(٣) دل المويد المظفر يسمى

(٣) اجوركم يوم القيامة

(٤) مهاراجا برنى تغمده

(٤) فمن زحزح عن النار

(٥) الله بالرحمة والر

(٦) ضوان وصلى] الله

(٧) على محمد وآله اجمعين

English translation:

Front:

1, This tomb belongs to the late martyr
2, Sultan, a learned and just man
3, a protector and conqueror. He was called
4, Mahârâjâ Brunî. Forgive him
5, Allâh with His grace and pleasure.
6, May Allâh bless
7, Muhammad and all his descendants.

Back:

1, Every soul must taste
2, of death; and ye shall only be paid your hire
3, upon the resurrection day.
4, But he who is forced away from the fire[4]

Neither the date nor the name of the deceased was given in the inscription, although there were several titles for the person, such as "Mahârâjâ" meaning "great king" and "Brunî" meaning "Brunei." Mr. Jibah pointed out that "history tells us that there is no such name as 'Mahârâjâ' for a Sultan in Brunei." What does the term "history" mean here? I believe it might mean "the Genealogical Tablet (Batu Tarsilah) of the Sultans of Brunei."[5] One could argue that if the real name of the deceased was not engraved on the stone, it could hardly be verified with the Genealogical Tablet of the Sultans of Brunei. In addition, the Genealogical Tablet of the Sultans of Brunei only covers twenty-nine generations of the Sultans of Brunei and the earliest rule of Sultan Muhammad Shâh only dates back to A.D. 1363.

Situation of Arabic Stone Carvings of Quanzhou

Before we go to the heart of the discussion I wish to present some essential information pertaining to the study of the stone carvings of Muslims in Quanzhou. In earlier times, Quanzhou used to be a major trading port, especially from the mid-ninth century to the mid-fourteenth century. Foreigners came to Quanzhou from all over the world and settled there. Among them, Muslims were the most numerous. They built mosques and cemeteries in the city and around the suburbs. When the ancient city wall of Quanzhou was demolished during the 1920s and 1930s a great number of stone carvings in Arabic and Persian were excavated. In 1957, photos of seventy-seven Arabic and Persian inscriptions were published by Wu Wen-liang, of which seven were fully translated and eighteen were partially translated into Chinese.[6] In the 1970s and 1980s a number of other stone inscriptions in Arabic and Persian were found and deposited in the Foreign Maritime Museum of Quanzhou. In 1984 the author published *Islamic Inscriptions in Quanzhou*, which catalogued 168 Arabic and Persian stone inscriptions found in Quanzhou up to 1981, with full translations and appropriate textual research.[7] Recently, in a new book entitled *Corpus d'Inscriptions Arabes et Persanes en Chine: Vol. 1, Province de Fujian*, I increased the number of inscriptions by twenty, covering those found at Quanzhou since 1982.[8]

Most of the Arabic and Persian stone inscriptions in Quanzhou date from the Song and Yuan Dynasties (A.D. 961-1368). Most were excavated at the foot of the ancient city walls built between A.D. 1352 and 1398 and the remainder were found among the Muslim cemeteries in the south and east suburbs. They are divided into two categories according to their use: mosque structures and tomb structures. The former include lintel stones, decorated stones, and historical recorded stones of mosques. The latter include gravestones, grave-carving-stones, facing-stones, and lintel-stones of qubba. The inscriptions are mainly in Arabic and a few are mixed with Persian and Chinese. They indicate the names of mosques; the founders or renovators and dates of establishment and renovation of mosques; the names and dates of the dead; and the origins and status of the deceased and quotations from the Korân and Hadîth. These stone inscriptions provide material which is particularly valuable for the study of the history of Islam and the foreign maritime trade of Quanzhou. The collection of Arabic and Persian stone inscriptions of the Quanzhou Foreign Maritime Museum is the richest of all the museums in China.

A Comparative Study of Brunei Sultan and Quanzhou Fâṭimat Gravestones

Generally, when faced with the fact that there is no date and name of the deceased, epigraphers have to identify a gravestone using methods of comparison. Here I suggest a comparison with the gravestones found in Quanzhou.

Regarding the material of the gravestone, as I mentioned above, the one found in Brunei was made of diabase. Brunei does not have such a mineral, while diabase is common in Quanzhou. Of the 111 gravestones with Arabic inscriptions found in Quanzhou, 91 were made of diabase and the other 20 of granite. The former date from around A.H. 670-764 (A.D. 1272-1362).[9]

Regarding the shape and style of the gravestone, the pointed bow on the top, the bands in concave relief, and the rectangular bottom tenon were exactly the same as those of gravestones found in Quanzhou. As in Brunei, the carving techniques used on the gravestone were similar to those found in Quanzhou. The proportions of the height, width, and thickness too were similar to those in Quanzhou. Below is a comparative list of the gravestone in Brunei and the dated gravestones in Quanzhou:

Table 8.1   Comparative list[10]

Site	Height	Width	Thickness	Material	Date
Brunei	68.5	37.5	9.5	diabase	
Quanzhou					
No. 32	69	42	10	diabase	A.H. 689/A.D. 1290
No. 33	72	39	9	diabase	A.H. 698/A.D. 1299
No. 34	61	39	9	diabase	A.H. 700/A.D. 1301
No. 35	61	39	12	diabase	A.H. 701/A.D. 1301
No. 37	83	44.5		diabase	A.H. 702/A.D. 1302
No. 38	56	36		diabase	A.H. 704/A.D. 1304
No. 39	91	49	9	diabase	A.H. 703/A.D. 1303
No. 41	62	36.5	8	diabase	A.H. 704/A.D. 1304
No. 43	75	50	10	diabase	A.H. 715/A.D. 1315
No. 45	74	43	9	diabase	A.H. 721/A.D. 1321
No. 46	56	36.5	8	diabase	A.H. 722/A.D. 1322
No. 48	53	30.5	7.5	diabase	A.H. 725/A.D. 1325

As regards paleographic identification, I believe the inscription on the gravestone in Brunei to be similar to that on the gravestone of Fâtimat bin Nainâ A̲ḥmad, who died in Quanzhou on the 13th of Rama̲dân, A.H. 700 (22 May A.D. 1301. see No. 34 in above table).[11] I also believe that both the Brunei Sultan gravestone and the Fâtimat gravestone were inscribed by the same people. The gravestone of Fâtimat is also made of diabase, the top is in the shape of a pointed bow, both sides are polished and decorated with a band in concave relief, and both sides are engraved with Arabic inscriptions: seven lines on the front and four on the back. All the characteristics mentioned for the Fâtimat stone are the same as those of the Brunei gravestone, except that in the case of the former, the bottom was broken. However, from the broken bottom we can see it was a rectangular tenon which is similar to that of the bottom of the Brunei gravestone. If the words of the two inscriptions are compared the writing is identical. For example:

Table 8.2

Words in Arabic	In Lines of Stone	
	Brunei	Quanzhou
هذا قبر المرحوم	1	1
الس	2	2
تغمده الله بالرحمة والرضوان وصللى] الله على محمد وآله اجمعين	4-6 6-7	3 7

Compared with other Muslim gravestones found in Brunei, one particular feature has attracted my attention—though no gravestone of either the first or the second Sultan has been found in Brunei, all inscriptions on the gravestones of the Sultans of Brunei since the third generation of the Genealogical Tablet (Batu Tersilah) were written mainly in Jawi except for quotations from the Korân, Hadîth, or some very common Islamic verses. Moreover, those inscriptions have not provided any explanation of the meaning of Mahârâjâ. However, not only was this Sultan's gravestone inscribed wholly in Arabic, but it also gave a special explanation of Mahârâjâ as "He was called Mahârâjâ Brunei."

This thorough comparison of the style, shape, and proportions of the Brunei and Quanzhou gravestones, reinforced by the Arabic paleographic study, leads me to believe that the Brunei Sultan Mahârâjâ gravestone of diabase was engraved in Quanzhou about A.H. 700/A.D. 1301, then transported to Brunei for a Brunei Sultan.

Further Supporting Evidence

There were two other relics found in Brunei concerning the relations of Brunei and Quanzhou. One I mentioned above, the Chinese gravestone of a Muslim, Mr. Pu in A.D. 1264, which was made of granite. Franke and Ch'en T'ieh-fan said: "The tombstone is not made from local material and the Chinese inscription can only have been engraved in China. Even in the nineteenth century, inscribed tombstones were shipped from China to South-East Asia."[12] Shariffuddin and Hâjî Ibrahîm pointed out that granite gravestones were used by the Chinese.[13] In fact, it appears that although granite is also one of the minerals to be found in Brunei, the Malay do not like to use it to make gravestones. I agree with Wolfgang Franke that the gravestone of Mr. Pu was engraved in Quanzhou and shipped to Brunei.

Another relic is a top-stone of a tomb-cover lying on the northern side of the tomb of Sultan Muḥammad Jamalul Alam in the royal grave-yard. It is like a stone erected upside-down. Unfortunately, it was too late and quite dark when I found the top-stone. I had no time to measure its size nor to identify the material it was made of. I could merely take pho-tos of it, but I believe it to be made of diabase or granite, not sandstone as was usually the case with the Malay. One cross section faces the sky and is cut out in the shape of pointed bow with a motif of a full moon floating upon a cloud. Both ridge sides of the stone are polished without any inscription. The other cross section is deeply covered. When I inquired as to whether they had seen similar top-stones before, both Hâjî Abdul Rahîm and Mohd Yamin replied in the negative. Indeed, they had never come across similar top-stones during their visits to the ancient cemeter-ies of Brunei, nor were there any in the collections of the Brunei Museum.

However, this type of top-stone is very familiar to me, as I have seen many similar ones in Quanzhou. Many examples can be found in my publication entitled *Islamic Inscriptions in Quanzhou*.[14] They are all of the same shape with the same decorative motif and all belong to the period before A.D. 1352 when the ancient city wall was built.

Here I should like to introduce the Ispâh Rebellion and to explain its importance as far as the Muslim population of the region was con-cerned. Towards the end of the Yuan Dynasty, Muslims in Quanzhou raised an army of Ispâh which was involved in a war among the local powers of Han nationality in Fuzhou, Xinghua (Putian), Huian, and Quanzhou. The war lasted ten years (A.D. 1357-1366) and was called the Ispâh Rebellion by historians.[15] In 1366, the army of Ispâh was wiped out by the army of Chen You-ding (Han army of Fujian province) in two military engagements at Xinghua City and Quanzhou City. After the capture of Quanzhou, the army of Chen You-ding closed the city for three days, wantonly robbing and killing the Muslims among the popu-lation. It was recorded that "in the fight all foreigners ['Xi-yu-ren'] were wiped out, some Chinese were killed by mistake because of the colour of their hair and high noses, and the tombs of Muslims were plundered."[16] Only a few Muslims who lived outside the city escaped to remote places, mountain areas, or coastlands and hid their identity in order to survive. From then on foreign merchantmen ceased coming to Quanzhou because the seaport activity was at a standstill. Furthermore, Muslims in Quanzhou subsequently went through a difficult period. As a result it is not easy to find any Arabic inscriptions dating from later than A.D. 1366 in Quanzhou. A few Arabic gravestones from after A.D. 1366 have been found in the villages where the Muslim descendants now live, but they are different in style, shape and paleography and have different motifs from those of the period before A.D. 1366.

Genealogy of the Sultans of Brunei

In Brunei I was given some information on the genealogy of the Sultans of Brunei: "A Family Tree of the Sultans of Brunei Darussalam"[17] and "Sultan-Sultan Brunei."[18] According to the genealogy the present Sultan Hassanal Bolkiah is the 29th Sultan of Brunei and has ruled since 1967. Sultan Muḥammad Shâh was the first Sultan to establish a Muslim kingdom in Brunei in 1368.

The genealogy of the Sultans of Islamic Brunei is based on several historical sources and legends.

Chinese sources

A Chinese record in *Ming-shi* mentioned that in the fourth year of the Hong-wu Era (A.D. 1371), two Chinese envoys, Zhang Jingzhi and Shen Zhi, visited Brunei and met the Brunei King who was called Ma-he-mo-sha (Maḥmûd Shâh).[19] Huang Xing-zeng (A.D. 1490-1540) mentioned that in the fourth year of the Hong-wu Era (A.D. 1371), the King of Brunei Ma-mo-sha (Maḥmûd Shâh) sent an envoy named Yi-si-ma-yi (Ismaᶜîl) to the Ming court. He presented credentials and a letter which were decorated with gold and silver and brought local products from Brunei as a tribute.[20]

Jawi inscription

The Genealogical Tablet (Batu Tarsilah) of the Sultans of Brunei was engraved in the 2d Ẕu-l-ḥijjah A.H. 1221 (10 February 1807). Mr. Shariffuddin and Mr. Ibrahim did textual research on it and pointed out that some sentences on the tablet "seem to suggest that it is either Sultan Muḥammad or Sultan Aḥmad who took a Chinese wife from Chinabatangan. Another version has it that Sultan Muḥammad took a Johore princess while Sultan Aḥmad, the second Sultan, was a Chinese who came down from Chinabatangan."[21]

Legend among local Muslims

During the early 1360s, Raja Awng Alak Betatar, ruler of Brunei, married Puteri Johor, the daughter of Seri Teri Buana Sang Nila Utama, King of Temasik (Old Singapore) known in Brunei as the Kingdom of Johor. It was during the visit to Temasik that the Raja converted to Islam. The ruler of Temasik invested him with the title, Paduka Seri Sultan Muḥammad Shâh.[22]

The Genealogical Tablet (Batu Tarsilah) of the Sultans of Brunei was made late in A.H. 1221/A.D. 1807 and it would appear that the author also referred to the Chinese records and legends of the local Muslims. Ostensibly Brunei scholars took the Genealogical Tablet (Batu Tar-

silah) as the Genealogy of the Sultans of Brunei because they lacked earlier documents or evidence. In fact no other record dating from before
the period of Sultan Muḥammad Shâh has been found in Chinese, Jawi,
or Malay pertaining to the establishment of the Muslim kingdom in
Brunei. It is a recognized fact that many countries in Southeast Asia trace
their own history from Chinese documents. I checked two very significant Chinese works entitled *Zhu-fan-zhi* and *Dao-yi-zhi-lue*. The former
was written by Zhao Ru-kuo in A.D. 1225[23] and the latter by Wang Da-
yuan in A.D. 1349.[24] Both authors lived in Quanzhou and both books
recorded information on Brunei, in particular on local traditions, customs, products, and Chinese traders in markets. However, no information was given on the religion of the country. The author would argue
that the situation of Islam in Brunei before Sultan Muḥammad Shâh is
not clear because of the lack of Islamic records on the subject, but we
cannot state that a Muslim kingdom had not existed in Brunei before
Sultan Muḥammad Shâh.

Regarding the advent of Islam in Brunei, Hâjî Matussin bin Omar,
director of the Brunei Museum, pointed out that he preferred a much
earlier date, perhaps around the thirteenth century.[25]

Some names of Muslims in Brunei are mentioned in an earlier Chinese document *Song-shi* (Chronology of Song) recorded in the "Chapter of Bo-ni (Brunei)" that in the second year of Tai-ping-xing-guo (A.D.
977), King of Brunei, Xiang Da sent an envoy, Shi-nu (Sina ?), an assistant envoy Bu-ya-li (Abu ᶜAlî), and Judge Ge Xin (Kâsîm) to China.
They brought a letter from the king for the court of China which
mentioned a Chinese merchant named Pu Lu-xie who arrived in Brunei
that year.[26] According to Purcell, Pu Lu-xie stands for Abu Alî.[27] Hâjî
Matussin bin Omar pointed out that the above extract suggests that
Muslim traders from China were visiting Brunei, and may have been
subsequently responsible for the introduction of Islam.

Monumental evidence for the acceptance of Islam in other parts of
Southeast Asia has been found in Phan-rang (Champa) dated A.D.
1039,[28] Leran (near Surabaya in East Jawa) dated A.D. 1082, Pasai
(Sumatra) dated A.D. 1297, and Trengganu (the Malay Peninsula) dated
A.D. 1303.[29] Besides the above evidence, Dr. Othman Mohd Yatim in
his book quoted a study conducted by Abdul Latif Hâjî Ibrahîm in
1979. Ibrahîm identified a gravestone discovered in one of the cemeteries, near Jalan Residency, in Bandar Seri Begawan, Brunei. It marked the
grave of a woman named Makhdarah, who died in A.H. 440 (A.D.
1048). Yatim also indicated that the importance of this woman has yet
to be ascertained.[30] Yatim has not published the photo of the gravestone
since and the author has not seen the paper written by Ibrahîm.[31] Surprisingly, Mr. Matussin bin Omar did not mention this in his book in

1981, and nobody told me about it during my visit to Brunei. Nothing more can be said about this gravestone at this juncture.

Conclusion

What is the significance of the discovery of the Arabic gravestone of Sultan Mahârâjâ Brunei? It has provided very important evidence concerning the history of the Muslim Kingdom established in Brunei during the late thirteenth and early fourteenth century. As mentioned above, there are sources in Chinese that record names of Muslims in Brunei. There is also some monumental evidence of the presence of Islam found in the countries of Southeast Asia around Brunei between the late tenth and early fourteenth centuries. However, this only attests to the presence of Muslim traders, and to the fact that Islam had spread to Brunei and the countries around it before the rule of Sultan Muḥammad Shâh. It does not mean that Muslim kingdoms actually existed. The Arabic gravestone of Sultan Mahârâjâ Brunei presented evidence that a Muslim kingdom already existed in Brunei about A.H. 700 (A.D. 1301). It sheds new light on the study of the early history of the Muslim kingdoms established in Brunei, and even in Sumatra if we take into consideration the Arabic gravestone of Sultan Malik al-Salleh of A.D. 1297 found in Pasai (Sumatra). Scholars agree, in general, that the first Muslim kingdom established in Southeast Asia was in Pasai (Sumatra) because of the discovery of the gravestone of Sultan Malik al-Salleh in A.D. 1297. However, this new identification raises some old questions: Where was the first Muslim kingdom established in Southeast Asia? Was Islam introduced from Johor into Brunei or from Brunei into Johor? Were Peninsular Malaysia and the Indonesia Archipelago influenced by Islam mainly from Arabia, Persia, and India, or from China, or from both? What role does Brunei play in the spread of Islam in Southeast Asia?

Professor Lombard believed that the discovery of the Arabic inscriptions in Quanzhou will not only enrich our knowledge of Islam in China, but also renovate our knowledge of Islam in the Orient.[32] The author would like to say that the finds of Arabic inscriptions in Brunei obliges us to acknowledge the history of Islam in Brunei and, furthermore, in Peninsular Malaysia and the Indonesia Archipelago.

Notes

1. Zhou Nan-jing, "Hui-gu zhong-guo yu ma-lai-xi-ya wen-lai wen-hua jiao-liu de li-shi" (A Study of the History of the Cultural Exchange between China and Malaysia and Brunei), in *Zhong- wai wen-hua jiao-liu-shi* (History of the Cultural Exchange between China and the Rest of the World), edited by Zhou Yi-liang (Zhengzhou: He-nan ren-min chu-ban-she, 1987), p. 399.
2. Wolfgang Franke and Ch'en T'ieh-fan, "A Chinese Tomb Inscription of A.D. 1264, Discovered Recently in Brunei," *Brunei Museum Journal,* vol. 3, no. 1 (1973): pp. 91-99.
3. *Brunei Museum Journal,* vol. 6, no.1 (1987): pp. 10-15.
4. The text stopped here and this sentence was not complete. The completed text is a quotation from the Qu'ran 3:185, and the following text is "and brought into Paradise is indeed happy; but the life of this world is but a possession of deceit."
5. A. Sweeney, "Silsilah Raja-Raja Brunei," *Journal of the Malaysian Branch of the Royal Asiatic Society,* vol., 41, no. 2 (Dec. 1968): pp. 1-82; and P. M. Sharifuddin and Abd. Latif Hâjî Ibrahîm, "The Genealogical Tablet (Batu Tersilah) of the Sultan of Brunei," *Brunei Museum Journal,* vol. 3, no. 2 (1974): pp. 253-64.
6. Wu Wen-liang, *Quan-zhou zong-jiao shi-ke* (Religious Inscriptions in Quanzhou) (Beijing, 1957). Wu's book included inscriptions of other religions.
7. Chen Da-sheng, *Quan-zhou yi-si-lan-jiao shi-ke* (Islamic Inscriptions in Quanzhou) (Fuzhou, 1984).
8. Chen Da-sheng and Ludvik Kalus, *Corpus d'Inscriptions Arabes et Persanes en Chine: Tome 1, Province de Fujian* (Paris: Librairie Orientaliste Paul Geuthner, 1991).
9. Chen Da-sheng, *Quan-zhou yi-si-lan-jiao shi-ke*; Chen Da- sheng, "Recherches sur l'Histoire de la Communauté Musulmane de Quanzhou (Fujian-Chine)" (M.A. thesis at E.H.E.S.S., Paris, 1989), 204 pages and 30 plates.
10. The numbers in the list follow those given by Chen Da-sheng, in *Quan-zhou yi-si-lan-jiao shi- ke.*
11. Chen Da-sheng, *Quan-zhou yi-si-lan-jiao shi- ke,* pp. 16-17, fig. 34-1, 2.
12. Wolfgang Franke and Ch'en T'ieh-fan, "Chinese Tomb Inscription," p. 94.
13. P.M. Sharifuddin and Abd. Latif Hâjî Ibrahîm, "The Genealogical Tablet," p. 253.
14. Chen Da-sheng, *Quan-zhou yi-si-lan-jiao shi- ke,* figs. 89, 97, 118, 120, 121.
15. Chen Da-sheng, "Guan-yu Yuan-mo Quan-zhou Yi-si-lan-jiao yan-jiu de ji-ge wen-ti" (On the Several Problems of the Study on Islam in Quanzhou towards the End of the Yuan Dynasty) in *Yi-si-lan-jiao zai Zhong-guo* (Islam in China) (Yinchuan, 1982), pp. 140-5, 168-74.
16. "Li-shi" (An Amorous Story) in *Qing-yuan Jin-shi zu-pu* (Genealogy of the Jin Lineage in Quanzhou), manuscript edited by Jin Zhi-xing (Quanzhou, 1555).
17. *Selamat Datang / Welcome,* edited by Broadcasting & Information Department, Brunei Prime Minister's Office (Brunei Darussalam, 1987), p. 9.
18. Disusun Dan Diterbitkan Oleh Jabatan Pusat Sejarah, Kementerian Kebudayaan Belia Dan Sukan (Negara Brunei Darussalam, 1990).
19. Zhang Ting-yu, *Ming-shi* (Chronology of the Ming Dynasty) (Beijing, 1739; re-printed in 1974, vol. 325: "Wai-guo liu" [Foreign Countries 6], "Bo-ni" [Brunei]).
20. Huang Xing-zeng, *Xi-yang chao-gong dian-lu* (Tributes from the Western Countries), c. 1520 (Reprinted in Beijing, 1982), p. 56.
21. P.M. Sharifuddin and Abd. Latif Hâjî Ibrahîm, "The Genealogical Tablet," pp. 254, 257, footnote 9.
22. William L.S. Barrett, *Brunei and Nusantara: History in Coinage* (Brunei, 1988), p. 2.

23. Zhao Ru-kuo, *Zhu-fan-zhi* (Notes on Foreign Countries), Quanzhou, 1225, edited and annotated by Feng Cheng-jun (Beijing, 1956), vol. 1, "Bo-ni-guo" (Brunei), pp. 76-80. Refer to F. Hirth and W.W. Rockhill, *Chau Ju-kua: His Work on the Chinese and Arab Trade in the Twelfth and Thirteenth Centuries, Entitled Chu-fan-chi* (St. Petersburg: Imperial Academy of Sciences, 1911).

24. Wang Da-yuan, *Dao-yi-zhi-lue* (Information on Foreign Maritime Countries), Quanzhou, 1349, edited and annotated by Su Ji-qing (Beijing, 1981), pp. 148-51, "Bo-ni" (Brunei).

25. Matussin bin Omar, *Archaeological Excavations in Protohistoric Brunei* (Brunei, 1981), pp. 1-2.

26. Tuo Tuo, *Song-shi* (Chronology of Song), vol. 489 (Beijing, 1345; reprint 1977). See also W.P. Groeneveldt, "Notes on the Malay Archipelago and Malacca," in *Miscellaneous Papers Relating to Indo-China and the Indian Archipelago*, reprinted for the *Straits Branch of the Royal Asiatic Society*, Series II, vol. 1, (London, 1887), p. 230.

27. V.W.W.S. Purcell, *The Chinese in South-East Asia* (London, 1951), p. 25.

28. Paul Ravaisse, "Deux inscriptions coufiques du Campa," *Journal Asiatique* Series II, vol. 20 (Paris, 1922): pp. 247-89.

29. S.Q. Fatimi, *Islam Comes to Malaysia* (Singapore: Malaysian Sociological Research Institute, 1963), pp. 38-50, 64-68. The gravestone of Leran belongs to a Muslim woman named Fâtimah. The gravestone of Pasai is at the grave of Sultan Malik al-Salleh.

30. Othman Mohd Yatim, *Batu Aceh–Early Islamic Gravestones in Peninsular Malaysia* (Kuala Lumpur, 1988), p. 62.

31. Abdul Latif Hâjî Ibrahîm, "Penemuan Batu Nisan Bertarikh 440 Hijrah (1048 Masehi) di Brunei," *Dewan Budaya* Kuala Lumpur, Dewan Bahasa dan Pustaka (Oct. 1979), pp. 6-9.

32. Denys Lombard, "Compte-rendu de CHEN Da-sheng, Quanzhou Yisilangjiao shike (Islamic Inscriptions in Quanzhou [Zaitun])," in *Archipel*, no. 31 (Paris, 1986): pp. 195-96.

Chapter 9

CARAVANSERAIS ALONG THE GRAND TRUNK ROAD IN PAKISTAN
A Central Asian Legacy

Saifur Rahman Dar

The famous Grand Trunk Road or *Shahrah-i-'Azim* connecting Calcutta (India) with Peshawar (Pakistan) has been in existence for the last 2,500 years. It has been variously described as "the muse of history,"[1] or "a broad scratch across the shoulders of India and Pakistan."[2] As the greatest highway in the world,[3] it has been compared with the Pilgrim's Way in England, the Appian Way in Rome, and Jada-i-Shah of the Achaemenians.[4] The strategic value of this grand highway and the correctness of its alignment have stood the test of time for more than 2,500 years. The rising British power withstood the ferocious war of independence—the so-called Mutiny of 1857—thanks to this well-planned and well-maintained Grand Trunk Road (GTR).[5]

All along this highway, there once stood forts (*qila*), fortified towns (*qila band shehr*), army halting posts (*parrao or chhaoni*), caravanserais, *dak*-posts (*chowki*), milestones (*kos minars*), stepped wells (*baoli*) and, of course, shady trees for the convenience of travelers and passers-by. The present chapter deals briefly with a survey of existing remains of these facilities along the part of the GTR which runs through present-day Pakistan. This survey was carried out by the author during the years 1987-1989. The area interested me for three reasons:

(i) It covered one fifth of the total length of the GTR.
(ii) Part of the Silk Road passing through Pakistan also corresponds to the GTR,[6] and

(iii) The portion of the GTR passing through Pakistan certainly comprises the most varied and difficult geographical and geological land mass ever encountered by a road builder[7] or a merchant, or even a soldier.

History

No one knows when the GTR started. Presumably, it came into existence as soon as vehicular traffic started developing as a complement to river communication. There were numerous such major roads connecting different parts of the vast country. Panini, the famous grammarian (500 B.C.), mentions the existence of an Uttarpatha (Northern Road) as well as a Dakshinapatha (Southern Road).[8] There was also Vannupatha: the Road from Bannu from the Middle Country passing through a desert. Uttarpatha probably was the same as Kautilya's Haimavatapatha running from Vallika (Balkh or Bactria) to Taxila. Kautilya also gives detailed advice as to different types of roads which a king should build. These include the roads linking different national or provincial centers, those leading to military camps and forts, and roads for chariots, elephants, and other animals together with their respective widths and how to maintain them.[9] There is a mention of trade routes (water routes and land routes) and it was the duty of the emperor to maintain them and keep them free from harassment by the king's favorites, robbers, and herds of cattle.[10] The width of a royal highway and those within a *droonamukna* and a *sthaniya* or a harbor town were fixed at eight *dandas* or forty-eight feet.[11] The Royal Road of the Mauryans at the beginning of the 3rd century B.C., according to Magasthenes, used to run in eight stages from Purushupura (Peshawar) in the northeast to Pataluputra, the Mauryan capital, in the extreme east.[12] Sarkar has given details of these eight stages, three of which fell within today's Pakistan, namely Purushupura to Takshasila, Takshasila to Jhelum, and Jhelum to Alexander's Altars on the Beas River.[13] To help travelers on this Road, directions and distances were indicated with the help of stone pillars fixed every 10 stadia or one *kos*.[14] These correspond to the medieval *kos minar* or modern milestone. It is quite possible that Chandra Gupta took this idea of a Royal Road from the *Jada-i-Shah* of the Achaemenians and this, along with other factors, became instrumental in bringing in the Persian influence which we encounter in Mauryan art. There were charitable lodging houses (*dharma vasatha*) inside the cities for heretical travelers, ascetics, and Brahmins[15] but there is no mention of similar facilities alongside the highways. Chandra Gupta's grandson Asoka improved upon this road system, as he proudly claims in one of his edicts, by planting trees, digging wells every half *kos*, and building *nimisdhayas* all along the Royal Road.[16] The word *nimisdhayas* has been variously interpreted[17] but is usually translated as rest-house. Sirkar has accepted it to mean a *sarai* or hostelry.[18] If so, this is the earliest reference to halting stations provided on high roads. Still, Asoka was certainly not the originator of such facilities on the highways because he admits that such comforts were provided by previous kings as well. Earlier Kautilya had advised kings to provide sources of water (*setu*), land routes and waterways (*varisthala-patha*), groves (*arama*), and the like.[19] Besides, from various *jataka* stories, we learn that each caravan was led by a caravan leader, the Sarthavaha, who would decide where to make halts for the night showing thereby that there were no fixed and permanent halting stations on the way.[20]

The introduction of *baolis* (or *vapis*)—stepped walls along the high roads in the subcontinent of Pakistan and India—is attributed to Central Asian people. It is believed that in the second century B.C., the Sakas, in their second wave, introduced here two types of wells—Sakandu and Karkandhu—the former being the stepped well whereas the latter was the Persian wheel.[21]

Kanishka definitely had control over the Uttarapatha which then formed a part of the Silk Road which now, thanks to the Roman Empire, turned towards the sea coast near Barbaricon or Barygaza. The presence of numerous Indian carved ivories and other works of art from western marts discovered at Begram[22] near Hadda testify to this. Various Chinese pilgrims from the fifth to the seventh centuries A.D. also used various land routes to enter northern Pakistan—Fa Hien (c. A.D. 400) and Sung Yun (c. A.D. 521) through Udyana (modern Swat), and Hieun Tsang (seventh century A.D.) through Balkh-Taxlia.[23] This also shows that these roads must have been quite busy in those times. It was along these routes that Buddhism and the influence of Gandhara art in particular and art of India in general penetrated Central Asia and far into mainland China.[24] These Chinese travelers did not mention the existence of proper inns anywhere on this high road though such facilities had existed within the limits of cities since the time of Kautilya.[25] Perhaps they never needed to stay in such places, as they normally stayed in Buddhist monasteries which they found on their way.

Even during early Muslim rule in the subcontinent we have very little knowledge as to how the ancient highways worked and what roadside facilities existed for the comforts of travelers prior to the coming of the Mughals. The first specific reference to roadside inns or *sarais* is found during the reign of Muhammad bin Tughlaq (A.D. 1324-1351) who contracted *sarais*, one at each stage, between Delhi and his new capital Daulatabad.[26] From Shams Siraj Afeef, author of *Tarikh-i- Firoze*

Shahi, we also learn that his successor, Firoze Shah Tughlaq (A.D. 1351-1387), built several buildings including 120 hospices and inns, all in Delhi, for the comfort of travelers.[27] In these *sarais*, travelers were allowed to stay and eat free of charge for three days. After this fashion, Mahmud Baiqara (A.D. 1458-1511) built numerous beautiful *sarais* in Gujrat for the comfort and convenience of travelers.[28] Almost simultaneously, Sikandar Lodhi (A.D. 1488-1517) of Delhi also built *sarais*, mosques, *madrassahs*, and bazaars at all such places where Hindus had their ritual bathing sites.[29]

But it was Sher Shah Suri who revived the glory of the Royal Road of Chandra Gupta Maurya and at the same time excelled in providing roadside facilities to the travelers to such an extent that today the Grand Trunk Road and Sher Shah Suri have become synonyms. He ensured that the road journeys between all important centers in his empire, particularly between Sonargaon in Bengal and Attock Banares on the Indus River, were safe and comfortable. He realigned the Grand Trunk Road and Sonargaon at Rohtas, widened it, planted fruit-bearing and shady trees at the sides, constructed *sarais* every 2 *kos*,[30] and introduced *kos minars* and *baolis* at more frequent intervals in between two *sarais*. Along some other roads, Gaur to Oudh and one from Benaras, for example, besides *sarais* and fruit-bearing trees, he also planted gardens.[31] It has been recorded that, in all, Sher Shah built 1,700 *sarais* throughout the length and breath of his empire. In some history books the total number is exaggerated to 2,500.[32] Nadvi has estimated that there were 1,500 *sarais* between Bengal and the Indus alone. From some history books, we get a fair idea as to how these Suti *sarais* looked and how they were maintained. Briefly, these were state-run establishments used both as *dak*-posts and as resting places for travelers. In these *sarais*, free food and lodging were provided to all, irrespective of their status, creed, or faith.

Islam Shah (Saleem Shah) succeeded his father, Sher Shah Suri, and ruled from A.D. 1545 to 1552. Along the road to Bengal, he added one more *sarai* in between every two built by his father. Following traditions established by his father, he continued to serve food, both cooked and uncooked, to travelers.[33] In Pakistan, the *Kachi Sarai* at Gujranwala (now demolished except for its mosque) and the so-called Akbari *Sarai*, adjacent to Jahangir's Mausoleum are attributable to the Suri period, the latter to Islam Shah Suri.[34] During the reign of Akbar the Great (A.D. 1558-1605) the system of having halting places (*sarais, dak-chowkis*, and *baolis*) along important roads was further developed and perfected. Not only did the emperor himself build numerous new *sarais* at different locations, but his courtiers followed suit.[35]

Jahangir (A.D. 1605-1628), in particular, issued orders that the property of all such persons who die without issue be spent on the construction of mosques and *sarais*, the digging of wells and tanks, and the repairing of bridges. Simultaneously he ordered the landlords of all such far-off places where roads were not safe, to construct *sarais* and mosques and dig wells so that people were encouraged to settle near these places. Jahangiri *sarais* are said to have existed eight *kos* apart from one another. Jahangir ordered these *sarais* to be built of stone and burnt brick (*pakka/pukhta sarais*) and not of mud (*kacha sarais*). In each of his *sarais* there were proper baths and tanks of fresh water and regular attendants. Mulberry and other broad-leaved trees were planted at various halting stations between Lahore and Agra.[36] Jahangiri *kos minars*—such as one each at Manhiala near Jallo and at Shahu Garhi in Lahore—were between twenty and thirty feet high. *The emperor's courtiers too built rabats.*[37] Besides repairing the old bridges, Jahangir also constructed several new ones over all such rivers and nullahs which came in the way of his highways.[38] On the highway leading to Kashmir, he built permanent houses at different stages so that he need not carry tentage with them.[39]

Shah Jahan's period (1628-1658) is renowned for its building activities. The emperor busied himself with constructing and embellishing royal buildings in Agra, Delhi, and Lahore. His courtiers followed suit.[40] Several of his nobles, such as Wazir Khan, are renowned for patronizing building activities. The construction of roads and *sarais* did not lag behind, though these never had the same attention they received from Jahangir. The bridge of Shah Daula on Nullah Deg on the way from Lahore to Eminabad is definitely a construction from Shah Jahan's period.[41] Wazir Khan *sarai* (now extinct) was built near his grand public *hamam* inside Delhi Gate. Lahore was also constructed during this period.

Despite this increased activity, the road between Lahore and Kabul—the most important of all highways in ancient India—never had enough *sarais* at the desired places. Consequently, travelers had to contend with many difficulties while traveling on this section. It was Aurangzeb Alamgir (1659-1707) who realized this. He ordered that, in all parts where there were no *sarais* and *rabats*, permanent (*pukhta*) and commodious *sarais* should be constructed at government expense. Each new *sarai* was required to comprise a bazar, a mosque, a well, and a *hamam*. Older *sarais* were equally properly attended to and were soon repaired whenever necessary.[42] Some of his noblemen, such as Shaista Khan also built new *sarais*.[43] Khan-i-Khanan, a Wazir of Shah Alam Bahadur (1707-1712) had ordered that each city must have a *sarai*, a mosque, and a hospice constructed in his name.[44] He even despatched funds for that purpose. Amirud Din Sambhli, a courtier of Muhammad Shah (1719-1748), built a beautiful *sarai* in Sambhal.[45] Nawab Asif Jah, during the reign of the same king, built a caravanserai and bridge in Deccan.[46] Hussain Ali Khan of Barha built a *sarai* and a bridge in his locality.[47]

After the death of Muhammad Shah in A.D. 1748, the Punjab suffered a severe political setback. Central power declined and provincial Subedars of Lahore fought incessantly against invading Durranies and Marathas and the rising power of the Sikhs. Roadways were no longer safe and *sarais* were unattended to. In A.D. 1799, the Punjab was entirely taken over by the Sikhs. Their rule is a story of inverse development as far as architectural activities are concerned. In a state of political anarchy that characterized most of the eighteenth and nineteenth centuries, the highways became the wounded arteries of national life which drained the blood from the economic body of the country. I do not know if ever during this anarchical period a new *sarai* was constructed or orders were given to repair the old ones.

When the British occupied the Punjab in 1849, they did not fail to realize that it had always been the gateway to the whole of the subcontinent, and that the Grand Trunk Road was of special significance to this area in particular and to the whole subcontinent in general.[48] If the danger from the northwest was to be checked and local reserves of fighting men were to be tapped properly to reinforce the British army, this highway must be kept in first-rate condition and further improved. The first twenty-seven years of their reign, therefore, were spent in realigning this highway, making it metaled, constructing bridges, causeways and culverts wherever needed, and building their own *sarais*. It has been said that the terrain as followed by this highway in the Punjab is perhaps the most difficult and varied ever met by a road-builder. The story of the reconstruction of this highway has been graphically told by K.M. Sarkar in the work quoted above. The new road thus reconstructed hardly differed from the original alignment of the Mughal Highway. More often than not, it followed the former alignment, while at other places it ran parallel to it. Almost all old stations on the GTR such as Sarai Kachi (Gujranwala), Gakharr Cheema, Wazirabad, Gujrat, Kharian, Sarai Alamgir, Rewat, Margalla, Sarai Kala, Sarai Hasanabdal, Begum-ki-Sarai, and Peshawar, still occupy strategic positions on the new GTR. A few others such as Sarai Sheikhan, Eminabad, Khawaspura, Rohtas, Sarai Sultan, Sir Jalal, and Sarai Pukka are not far from it. One has to read the account of the Mughal Highway as given by William Finch[49] and compare it with the British Highway as rebuilt from 1849 to 1886[50] and see how, right from the beginning, the route from Kabul to Peshawar and from Peshawar to Lahore, from most ancient to modern times, has practically never changed. The network of the routes in medieval India and Pakistan and the Mughal period and even today passed the cities built during the Sultanate period, bearing in mind the course of ancient routes. If something has changed, it is the institutions of *sarais*. Better roads, improved means of communications, better transport facilities, lack of time available to individuals, and fast-moving life obliterated the need for caravans to move in groups, the necessity of having night stopovers on the way, short halts for shade under fruit-bearing trees or beside stepped wells, and for taking direction and distances from huge *kos minars* on the way. The course of the modern GTR has shifted slightly towards the south here and there because traveling in the cool shade of the Himalayan foothills is no longer necessary.

This is the reason why all old *sarais, baolis, kos minars*, and even ancient bridges have become derelict and are vanishing quickly. It is time for the department concerned to step forward and save these historical landmarks.

Features and Functions of Mughal *Sarais*

Thus, although the initial alignment of the present-day GTR in Pakistan may date back to a very remote age, provision of various kinds of facilities for travelers on this highway started quite late. We have seen how our information on the subject prior to the coming of the Mughals in the sixteenth century A.D. is scanty and incomplete. However, with the coming of the Mughals, the vista of our information, visual and literary, broadens considerably. We now have a well-established empire, with emperors eager to provide their empire with a solid foundation based on a well-organized road system, safe and quick communication, and safe and comfortable road journeys for armies, caravans, and individuals. We now have sufficient, though still not ample, information on how the system worked. Besides, we still have sufficient structural remains scattered all over the country to assist us in visualizing the entire system and interpreting its various functions. Here is a brief account of the system from A.D. 1526 to 1886.

Transport system

To begin with, it should be clear that from the Mauryan to the Mughal periods, traveling within the country, both for local people as well as foreigners, was regulated and controlled through a system of passports (*mudra*) duly issued and sealed by the Superintendent of Passports (Mudradhyaksha). At various points, there were inspection houses manned by the Superintendent of Meadows (Vivitadhyaksha) who would examine the traveling document of each party passing through that post. What these Inspection Houses looked like, we have no idea.[51]

Suri sarais

The first clear picture of a *sarai*—as an institution and a building— emerges during the reign of Sher Shah Suri and his son Salim (Islam) Shah

Suri (A.D. 1539-1552). Suri *sarais* were built a distance of two *kos* apart with stepped wells (*baolis, vapis, van* or *vao*) and *kos minars* at more frequent intervals between every two *sarais*. Structurally, a *sarai* comprises a space, invariably a square space, enclosed by a rampart with one gateway called *darwazah*. As these ramparts were built with sun-dried bricks, they were referred to in later years as *kacha sarais* and compared to *pakka* or *pukhta sarais* of the Mughal period which were built of burnt bricks or stone blocks. Each *sarai* had rows of cells (*khanaha*) on all four sides. There were special rooms, one in each corner, and invariably in the center of each wall as well. These were called Khanaha-i-Padshahi, i.e., King's House or Government House reserved for state personnel on the move. There were separate *khanaha* or cells for Muslims and non-Muslims—each served by attendants of their respective faiths. Inside each *sarai* there was a mosque and a well. Revenue-free land (*madad-i-ma'ash*) was attached to each *sarai* to meet the salaries of the staff and other contingent expenditure.[52]

The *sarai* acted both as a wayside inn for travelers and an official *dak-chowki*. Each *sarai* was run by an official called *Shahna* or *Shiqdar* with a number of caretakers (*nigehban* or *chaukidar*) to assist him. There was an *imam* of the mosque and a *muezzin* to call to prayer. Hot and cold water, together with bed-steads (*charpai*), edibles (*khurdani*), and grain and fodder for the horses (*dana-i-asp*) were provided by the Government (*Sarkar*) free of charge. A physician was stationed at every *sarai* to look after the health of the people of the locality. Bakers were also settled in the *sarais*.[53]

Although there are many *sarais* attributed to the Suri period, only one definite Suri *sarai* of the type described above is reported in Pakistan. It was in Gujranwala and was called *Kachi Sarai*. It was extant until the 1950s but has since vanished except for its mosque. The model laid down by the Suri kings was never forgotten by later rulers. What we can observe in later period *sarais* is only an improved reflection of the prototype of Suri *sarais*.

Rabats, sarais, and dak-chowkis

According to Arthur Upham Pope, *rabats* were fortified frontier posts which, during the early Islamic period, were set up as a necessary defense against hostile non-Muslim peoples.[54]

While discussing the recently discovered Ghaurid period Mausoleum of Khaliq Wali at Khati Chour, Holy Edwards, an American scholar, pronounced this unique fortress-like mausoleum as being a *rabat* in its original conception. She has described a *rabat* as a small military outpost on the frontier of a kingdom or state that also accommodates small groups of travelers. If we accept this definition, we have this exceptional example in Pakistan.

Many scholars, on the other hand, regard *rabat* and *sarai* as one and the same thing. But there is a minute difference between the two. In Ma'sr-ul-Umara, we learn that Shaikh Farid Murtaza Khan Bukhari, a courtier of Jahangir, built several *rabats* and *sarais*.[56] Maulana Nadvi[57] has made it clear that *sarais* were built alongside the highways for temporary stopovers by travelers whereas *rabats* and *khanqahs* (hospices) were built inside cities where people could stay for a longer period. These can be considered as guesthouses (*mehman khana*) or some type of hostelry—although they have never been mentioned under this title.

The *Sarais* of Sher Shah served both as *sarais* and *dak-chowki* and for that purpose two horses were kept in every *sarai* to convey news to the next station.[58] However, some scholars regard caravanserais as distinct from *sarais*-cum-*dak-chowkis*. The former concept developed in Pakistan, northern India, and Gujrat only in the fifteenth century. Caravanserais were invariably private establishments or created by endowments, whereas *dak-chowkis* were state properties. The *dak-post*-cum-*sarai* were usually smaller in size than the *sarais*. Postal messengers and noblemen (Mirzas) were not supposed to stay in caravanserais which were usually reserved for middle-class people, businessmen, and merchants. In caravanserais, again, the clients were charged moderately but not so in *sarais*-cum-*dak*-posts. Caravanserais in cities were usually established by endowments by individuals, organizations, and even by governments but gradually these tended to become rent-yielding properties.

Purpose

The Mughal rulers took upon themselves the responsibility of building roads and bridges and providing halting stations along the way because such arrangements were beneficial militarily, economically, and socially. An efficient road system, with well-supplied halting stations, secure highways, and well-protected fortified places—as these *sarais* always were—guaranteed easy passage for armies to guard their frontiers. It also encouraged the caravans and merchants to move along with their valuable merchandise from one place to another with a feeling of security. Establishment of *sarais* also provided people of the area with ample opportunities for employment and services. Major cities and towns subsequently developed around many *sarais* built in isolated places. Of course, in times of war and invasion, the villages and cities located on more frequented routes suffered a lot too. *Sarais* and *dak-chowkis* helped develop an efficient system of postal communication. Buildings which were just *dak-chowkis* were also constructed at certain places. One such *dak*-post, recently repaired under the supervision of the author, can be seen next to the roadside near Wazirbad. The *sarais* with their monumental gateways, *baolis* with their towering pavilions, and *kos minars* with cylindrical masonry columns, 20-30 feet high, guided travelers and caravans to their destinations and helped them cover long distances. Resting places and road-markers such as *sarais, kos minars,* and *baolis* were actually an outcome of the development of a centralized state.

Types

A cursory classification of existing remains of known caravanserais along the GTR from Peshawar to Delhi reveal at least five types according to their architectural features and functions:

The Fort-cum-Sarai

Every *sarai* was basically fortified in a sense that its gates or gate were closed at night and that its four wells usually had no other outlets except the main gate or gates. The earliest type we come across had only one gateway and four solid cornered bastions. *Sarai* Damdama, Mathura, of the sixteenth century but of pre-Mughal days, with solid pentagonal bastions, is one such example. No such example has survived in Pakistan. The Gakhar period Sarai Rewat, usually called Reway Fort near Rawalpindi can perhaps be classified in this category because it has merlons on the walls, high enough to conceal a soldier behind each, and rows of single cells below without having a veranda in front of each cell as is usual in all *sarais*. But it is unique in that it has three gates instead of one as in the pre-Mughal era.

The Wayside Sarai

This was perhaps the most common type seen along the roadsides running between big cities or urban centres. It differs from the fort-cum-*sarai* in two respects. It always had two gateways and usually a few larger rooms (Khanaha-i-Padshahi) in the four corners with side walls. The Akbar period *sarai* at Chapperghat, south of Kanauj,[59] Sarai Nur Mahal in India, Begum-ki-Sarai (of the Akbar or Jahangir period, though with a single gateway), and Sarai Kharbuza (Jahangir period) near Rawalpindi, in Pakistan, are good examples. In such *sarais*, there was usually a bazar, a mosque, and a well—all within the four walls of the *sarai*.

The town-sarai or rabat

This type of *sarai* was built as an integral part of an urban center. The Agra Gate Sarai at Fatehpur Sikri and Sarai Ekdilabad, District of Etawa (Shah Jahan period) in India are perhaps good examples. The Sarai Wazir Khan adjoining Delhi Gate in Lahore[60] with its colossal public *hamam* is one example in Pakistan. But its full plan is difficult to exhume today owing to the erection of modern buildings on the site. At least one scholar has interpreted the original building of Khaliq Wali Tomb at Khati Chaur as a *rabat* with the meaning of a military border post-cum-*sarai* (see above: *rabat-sarai* and *dak-chowkis*).

The custom-clearing sarai/sarai with double compound

The Badarpur Sarai near Delhi, with its two compounds, joined together through a common gateway, is unique. Here, entry to the bigger *sarai* would be through its northern gate, where the traveler waited before being allowed to pass into the adjoining smaller *sarai* through the connecting door and went out through the southern gate of the smaller *sarai* after his documents had been checked and clearance obtained. No such type has ever survived in Pakistan.

The mausoleum-cum-garden sarai

This type comprises *sarais* attached to a garden or mausoleum. The Arab *sarai* attached to Humayan's tomb in Delhi and the so-called Akbari Sarai attached to Dilamiz Garden (later the Jahangir's Mausoleum) at Shahdara near Lahore are such examples. The mosque of Sarai Akbari certainly belongs to the Suri period, though its rows of cells and three gates belong to the Shah Jahan period. One of the gates provides access to the mausoleum-garden of Jahangir.

The farood gah or royal halting station

Though this is not a typical caravanserai, it belongs to that category because it also served as a temporary halting station, though only for royalty. A typical example of such a halting station is the Wah Garden together with its *hamam* and an attached *farood gah* or resting-house. The Hiran Minar near Shaikhupura together with its royal residence, a vast tank and double story pavilion[61] can also be regarded as such though it provided a temporary halt for the emperor and his entourage but for an altogether different purpose, namely hunting, shooting, and recreation.

Gateways

The earliest *sarai* of the Suri period, or even earlier, had only one gateway in one of its four walls. This type continued during the Akbar period as shown by the Arab Sarai at Delhi and Begum-i-Sarai at Attock with only one entrance gate. Normally, Mughal period *sarais* had two monumental gateways—one located in front of the other in two walls facing each other. Akbari Sarai at Shahdara, Sarai Kharbuza near Rawalpindi, and Pakka Sarai near Gujar Khan are such examples. Two nearer examples in the Indian Punjab are the Jahangir period *sarai* at Fatehbad[62] and another at Doraha.[63] A gateway seldom had a fixed size in relation to the size of the *sarai* itself. It was usually built high and monumental so that it was visible even at a distance, thereby serving the same purpose as that of a *kos minar*. As seen in the case of Fatehabad and Doraha Sarais, the gateways were invariably decorated with variegated designs set in a mosaic of glazed tiles. Unfortunately, no such decoration has survived in any of the *sarais* recorded in Pakistan. These gateways were often two stories with enough rooms to accommodate the *shiqdar* or *shahna* and *nigehban/ chowkidar*. See for example the gateways of Akbari Sarai, Sarai Pakka, and Sarai Sheikhan. The main gateway of Sarai Rewat in its eastern wall looks as if it has two storeys but actually it is a single-storey structure without an elaborate system of attached rooms.

Shapes

As a rule, all *sarais* were square in shape. However, in certain cases and depending on the lie of the ground, one side was slightly larger than the other. In Pakistan, Sarai Kharbuza (420' x 420'), Begum-ki-Sarai (323' x 323'), and Sarai Pakka (300 x 300 paces) are examples of perfect squares. The Gakkhar period *sarai* at Rewat (323.6' x 321.6') and Sarai Sultan (560' x 540') are almost square. Sarai Akbari at Shahdara (797' x 610') is oblongish, whereas Sarai Kala near Taxila is a perfect rectangle (137.5' x 375') with a single (?) gate in its eastern wall. This shape was by choice and not dictated by the terrain. The only other example of a perfect rectangle that has come to my knowledge so far is Raja-ki-Sarai (Agra) with its two gateways set in two shorter walls and one in a longer wall. The gateway of Sarai Kala has been set in one of the long walls. On the Ferozepur Road, near the Central Jail, there used to be a Jahangir period *sarai* called Sarai Gola Wala,[64] which is reported to have been octagonal in layout like some Persian *sarais*.[65] The Sarai Agra Darwaza ar Fatehpur Sikri is irregular in shape.

Disposition of Cells

Inside a *sarai*, living quarters comprised cells which were invariably of uniform size in all four walls. In front of each cell there was usually a veranda to provide protection from sun and rain as well as to admit indirect light into the cells. No window or ventilator was allowed inside the cell. Sarai Rewat is the exception where there is no veranda in front of the cells. The corner rooms (octagonal or round) were usually set inside the corner bastions and were always larger than the normal cells. These were used by dignitaries or even used as stores. Like ordinary cells, corner rooms too were not provided with a window or ventilator. However, the corner rooms of the Begum-ki-Sarai are exceptions to this rule. Here, all four corner rooms have openings. The openings in two octagonal corner bastions along the western wall provide a beautiful view of the mighty Indus river. The corner rooms of this *sarai* are the most elaborate. Each is a suite of one large elliptical hall with a veranda in front, an octagonal room at the back, two side rooms, and a set of two staircases leading to the roof. We see the comparable arrangement at Sarai Rewat and Sarai Kharbuza. Only Sarai Sultan near Rohtas has a set of larger rooms in the center of the eastern and western walls like the ones in Doraha Sarai already quoted. Sometimes, in one of the corner rooms, a Turkish *hamam* was installed such as in Doraha Sarai just referred to. These *hamams* inside a *sarai* were first introduced by Jahangir and copied by some later rulers. But no *sarai* with a *hamam* has been reported in Pakistan. Only Damdama Sarai, Mathura, had solid pentagonal corner towers. All others are either octagonal or circular and are always hollow. The corner tower rooms at Akbari Sarai are square with chambered corners from within and each has a set of two small adjoining oblong rooms. Sarai Kharbuza near Taxila, on the other hand, has two octagonal rooms one set behind the other in each corner. The back room is actually a corner bastion protruding outside the walls of the *sarai*.

Mosque, bazar, and well inside a Sarai

If there were two gates to a *sarai*, there was often a bazar in the center of each *sarai* running from gate to gate.[66] It probably comprised of shops of makeshift materials as no permanent structure has ever been discovered inside a *sarai*. In Pakistan, probably, the Sarai Rewat, Serai Kharbuze, Akbari Sarai at Shahdara, and Sarai Sultan, Rohtas had this arrangement. Elsewhere only at Agra Gate Sarai, Fatehpur Sikri was there a row of permanent shops, but then these were along the outer facade of the *sarai* and not inside it.[67]

Somewhere in the open courtyard, a mosque was provided for the faithful such as in Pakka Sarai, Begum-ki-Sarai,[68] Sultan Sarai, and Sarai Kharbuza. At times, such a mosque was constructed in the middle of the western wall of the Sarai—as in Akbari Sarai, Sarai Rewat, and Sarai Kala. At the last site, it is slightly off-center. The mosques inside the sarais ranged from a single-domed chamber (as in Sarai Pakka and Sarai Kharbuza) to imposing three-domed structures as seen in Sarai Akbari and Sarai Rewat. Sarai Pakka is unique in that it originally contained two mosques, one for men in the courtyard (it was intact until 1968 when I studied it for the first time but has now been rebuilt completely) and another for women in the western wall (now in complete ruins). Except in the case of *sarais* close to urban centers, mosques were excluded from the four walls of a *sarai* such as Chapperghat Sarai.

Invariably, close to the mosques inside the *sarai* was a burnt-brick well such as in Pakka Sarai, Sarai Sheikhan, Sarai Kharbuza, and Sultan Sarai. Wells catering for the needs of Begum-ki-Sarai, Akbari Sarai, and Sarai Rewat can be found outside the four walls of the *sarais* proper. The well inside Sarai Kharbuza was in the form of a *baoli* or *vao*. As in case of Sarai Sultan and Sarai Pakka, *baolis* are sometimes found immediately outside a *sarai*.

Staircases

At the main gateways, staircases of two stories were usually provided on either side. Usually staircases were also provided at one or both sides of the special rooms (Khanaha-i-Padshah) or the corner bastions such as at Pakka Sarai and Begum-ki-Sarai.

Parapets

Parapets were usually in the form of medium-sized battlements such as in Begum-ki-Sarai or Sarai Rewat. The merlons in the case of Rewat give it the appearance of a fortress. But at other places, such as Sarai Kharbuza and Sarai Pakka, the parapets are simple and plain.

Inscriptions

No proper inscription has been found in any of the surviving *sarais* in Pakistan. Only some scribbling belonging to different periods has been reported from Begum-ki-Sarai at Attock.[69] Outside Pakistan, two Persian inscriptions are known from Sarai Ekdilbad, near Etawa, commemorating the simultaneous construction of a *mauza* (village/town), a *sarai*, and a garden by Shah Jahan.[70] Sarai Amanat Khan, built in 1640-1641 by Ahmanat Khan himself, the famous calligrapher of the Taj Mahal, also bears a dedicatory inscription on the west gate.[71] Sarai Nur Mahal near Phillour (East Punjab, India), the most impressive of all *sarais* in the Punjab built by Empress Nur Jahan, also bears a dedicatory inscription with two dates A.H. 1028 (A.D. 1618) and A.H. 1030 (A.D. 1620).[72]

Hamams

Turkish *hamams* of the Roman *thermae* type were a speciality of the Mughals and were introduced by them into the subcontinent. Their palaces (Lahore Fort), gardens (Shalamar, Lahore, and Wah Gardens at Hasanabdal), and even some of their *sarais* (Sarai Itamadud Daula at Doraha), were provided with elaborate *hamams*. It was Jahangir (A.D. 1605-1628) who introduced *hamam* into *sarais*. This practice was continued by others. In none of the *sarais* in Pakistan is such a *hamam* known to have survived. However, we have a beautiful and colossal public *hamam*, attached to, though structurally detached from, Sarai Wazir

Khan, inside Delhi Gate, Lahore. It has now been renovated. Wah Gardens, a place officially known as Farood Gah-i-Shahinshah-i-Mughalia or the Resting Place of the Mughal Emperors and therefore to be considered as a category of *sarai* or temporary residence, has an elaborate *hamam* of which only the foundations have survived.[73]

Distances

There is some confusion as regards the exact distance between two *sarais*, *baolis*, and *kos minars* of the Mughal period. The difficulty is due to the conversion of a *kos* or *kroh/krosa* into English miles. The former appears to have been measured differently at various times. We know from Sarwani that Sher Shah built his *sarais* at a distance of two *kos*.[74] His son Salim Shah added one more *sarai* in between every two built by his father. Thus making the distance between two *sarais* equal to one *kos*. Sarkar, on the other hand, states that Suri *sarais* were situated 10 *kos* apart[75] whereas *sarais* of Jahangir's period according to his own decree were 8 *kos* apart on the road from Agra to Lahore.[76] Following this, the East India Company established *Dak* bungalows on the highways at 10 mile intervals.[77] But, on the other hand, we know from Akbar Nama that the distance between Sarai Hasanabdal and Sarai Zainuddin Ali on the way to Attock was 4.25 *kroh* and 5 *mans* (app. 5 *krohs* as usually accepted) which is usually estimated to equal 10.5 English miles.[78] Now, the Akbari *kroh* has been estimated to equal 5,000 *ilahi gaz* (of 30" length) or 4,250 English yards.[79] As the distance between Peshawar and Lahore is about 264 miles, there must have been at least 26 *sarais* between these two stations, of which 20 can easily be recognized or presumed to have existed.

Attendants

Nicholas Withington (1612-1616) while writing about a *sarai* between Ajmer and Agra talks about "hostesses to dress our victuals if we please."[80] Peter Mundy also talks about female attendants in *sarais*.[81] However, no such reference has ever been made by a native writer. Perhaps they refer to female attendants, who together with their males were appointed to cook food for travelers in these sarais and about whom Khafi Khan has written that all Bhatiaras and Bhatiarnain of India are the descendants of these very cooks (*nan-bais*).[82]

Charges

We know that in the early days of the *sarais,* both accommodation and food were free. During the Mauryan period, there used to be charitable lodging houses under government control wherein free accommodation was granted to heretical travelers and to ascetics and Brahmins, whereas artisans, artists, and traders were required to lodge with their co-professionals in what can be called as guest-houses attached to their places of work.[83] During Feroze Shah Tughlaq's reign, travelers were provided with free board and lodging for three days. However, some of the *sarais,* especially those created out of endowments, tended to become rent-earning establishments. Sarai Wazir Khan, inside Delhi Gate, Lahore was certainly one such example whose income, together with that of the grand *hamam* nearby, supported Wazir Khan's Mosque.[84] We also learn from some early western travelers that the charge per room around 1634 was about 1 to 3 pice and 3 dams per day inclusive of stabling for horses and cooking space.[85]

Caravanserais Remains

Our knowledge of caravanserais along the Grand Trunk Road between Calcutta and Agra-Delhi is perfunctory. However, under Mughal rule—particularly from Jahangir onward—we are not that poor as regards written information and even actual remains, particularly for the part of ancient GTR that stretched from Agra to Lahore and onward to Peshawar. We have an almost perfect alignment of the road from Agra to Lahore as it existed in 1611 and described by William Finch. He lists the following important stations on this section: Agra, Rankata, Bad-ki Sarai, Akbarpur, Hodal, Palwal, Faridabad, Delhi, Narela, Ganaur, Panipat, Karnal, Thanesar, Shahabad, Ambala, Aluwa Sarai, Sirhind, Doraha (Sarai), Phillaur-ki-Sarai, Nakodar, Sultanpur, Fatehpur (Vairowal), Hogee Moheed (Taran Taran?), Cancanna Sarai (Khan-i-Sarai), and Lahore.[86]

Ruins of some interesting *sarais* are still traceable in that part of the GTR which once passed through Haryana and the East Punjab in India. These include Nur Mahal Sarai near Phillaur built by Empress Nur Jahan; the Sarai at Ghauranda between Panipat and Karnal; Sarai Amanat Khan on the Taran Taran-Attari Road built by Amanat Khan, the calligrapher of the Taj Mahal; Dhakhini Sarai south of the village of Mahlian Kalan on the Nakodar-Kapurthala Road; Doraha Sarai at Doraha south of the Ludhiana-Khanna Road; and Sarai Lashkari Khan twelve kilometers west of Khanna on the GTR in the Ludhiana district.[87]

Sarai Amanat Khan is probably the last existing stretch of the GTR, before the latter enters into present-day Pakistan via Burj and Raja Tall in India to Purani Bhaini in Pakistan and then straight to Manhala Khan-i-Khanan after the name of Abdul Rahim Khan-i-Khan, the famous general of Akbar and Jahangir. Our journey along the GTR in Pakistan begins here. Here once stood the Sarai Khan-i-Khan, most probably the Cancanna Sarai already mentioned by William Finch. This *sarai* is no more. But, outside the village, a Mughal period *kos minar,* one of a pair in the locality, still provides positive evidence of the ancient GTR. One of the two *kos minars* at Manhala has recently disappeared. The other is also not safe as it has a big hole whereby it could collapse without the slightest malevolent human interference.

From Manhala of Khan-i-Khana, the road used to go to Brahman-abad where an interesting *baoli* with a small pavilion is now in very poor state and will soon be filled in if no remedial action is taken. From here, the road goes to Mahfuzpura Cantonment where an elegant *baoli* with a double-ringed well and an imposing two-story domed pavilion has given the site its present name of Baoli Camp. It has been recently repaired by army personnel. Then the road goes to Shahu Garhi where the best-preserved *kos minar* near the railway line is being encroached upon by modern dwellings. Shahu Garhi is only a few minutes away from Chowk Dara Shikoh and then to the Delhi Gate for entry into the Walled City of Lahore. Here just beside the gate was Sarai Wazir Khan next to a grand public *hamam* also built by Wazir Khan.

Retracing our steps to mainland India, from Sarai Amanat Khan there was a shorter route which bypassed Lahore and directly reached Eminabad passing through Amritsar in India and Pull Shah Daula in Pakistan. At the latter site we have one of the best-preserved of all Mughal period bridges. This bridge was built on Nala Dek by the famous saint, Shah Jahan. We shall come back to this bridge later.

The Walled City of Lahore marked the starting point of three routes: the road to Delhi and Agra from Delhi Gate on the eastern side, the road to Multan to the south side from the Lahori Gate, and the road to Peshawar from the north side through the Khizri or Kashmiri Gate.

The ancient route to Multan has not so far been studied properly. A hurried survey by the author brought to light a number of remains of ancient *sarai* along this road, one each at Sarai Chheamba, Sarai Mughal, Sarai Harappa, Sarai Siddhu, and Sarai Khatti Chaur—the last named *sarai* is different from the *rabat* at the same site as mentioned above. The Mughal-period *sarai* at this site was partially excavated by the author during the conservation of the Mughal-period mosque which is probably part of the *sarai.*

The present study is confined to the GTR going towards the north. For this purpose, the ferry passage over the River Ravi was from the Khizri Gate over to Shahdara—the King's way to Lahore.

The precise course of the ancient GTR between Shahdara and Gujranwala is not clear at all points, but it was certainly a little north of the present course. At Shahdara, we have the best-preserved *sarais* in all Pakistan. Originally built during the Suri period as its mosque still testifies, the present edifice with its three magnificent gateways dates back to Shah Jahan's period. As it was sandwiched between two great monuments—the Mausoleum-garden of Jahangir and the Mausoleum-garden of Asif Khan—it served both and hence was saved for posterity.

From Shahdara, the road moves northward passing through Rana Town where, until they were both filled in in 1987, there were two *baolis* next to the present GTR. From Rana Town, it takes a turn to cross Nullah Deg at Bahmanwali/Chak 46. The crossing is still marked by an ancient bridge and the ruins of a *sarai* nearby. From here it went straight to Sarai Shaikhan (also called *Pukhta Sarai*), where a magnificent paneled gateway and an ancient well stand in ruinous condition. From Sarai Shaikhan the road goes to Tapiala Dost Muhammad via Kot Bashir (Chhaoni site and a *baoli*) to Dera Kharaba (*baoli*), Tapiala Dost Muhammad (mausoleum) for the onward journey to Pull Shah Daula with an ancient bridge on Nallah Deg, and monuments at Baba Jamna. It continues on to Gunaur, Wahndoki (ancient mound), and Eminabad, where a number of monuments—ancient bridge, *baoli*, mosque, and tank—give the area some sanctity. Finally, it reaches Kachi Sarai at Gujranwala.[88] This *sarai*, built of mud brick in the characteristic Suri fashion, was intact until about half a century ago. Today, it has totally vanished, leaving behind its central mosque. The *baoli* of the *sarai* has also been filled in. The huge vacant area nearby for army encampments (*parao*) has also been covered with modern constructions. From Eminabad to Gujranwala, I examined a few *baolis* and a portion of the ancient GTR, with brick-paved berms during my survey in 1987. From Gujranwala, it passes through Gakkhar Gheema, Dhaunkal (*baoli*, ancient mosque), and Wazirbad (*dak-chowki*), crosses Nullah Palkhow and the River Chenab, and reaches Gujrat. The *dak-chowki* at Wazirbad has recently been repaired by the author, but the Akbar-period fort and *baoli* and a public *hamam* inside the fort at Gujrat, are seriously threatened. Gujrat was an important station on the ancient GTR as it is on the present-day national highway. From here emanate four roads to Kashmir via Bhimber (where there is a *sarai* still today), to Lahore via Eminbad just described, and to Lahore by a loop road via Shaikhupura (with a hunting ground at Hiran Minar and an elegant *baoli* at Jandiala Sher Khan), Hafizabad, and then to Rasul Nagar. The fourth road goes to Peshawar via Khawaspura on Bhimber Nullah, passes through a village called Baoli Sharif (*baoli*), Kharian with two *baolis*, a British-period *sarai* (now partially filled in), on to Sarai Alamgir (*sarai* and mosque), and crosses the Jhelum River to reach Jhelum city with the Mangla Fort some miles north of it. From here the ancient road deviates a little to the south and goes to the Rohtas Fort with two *baolis* and an ancient mosque within the fort. Sarai Sultan with a small *baoli* on the opposite bank of the River Kahan is fully occupied by a modern village—its main gate and the *baoli* are also endangered. Midway between Sarai Sultan and Domeli still stand the remains of a huge *baoli* but without a pavilion—it is called Khoji *baoli*.

From Sarai Sultan to Sar Jalal or Jalal Khurd, the path of the ancient road is not clear. It certainly passed through Khojki (*baoli*) and Domeli where there are hot water springs and another *baoli* (reported) nearby. But where did the ancient road cross the hot water springs mountain? We are not sure. In historical accounts, at least four stations have been mentioned, namely Rohtas Khurd, Saeed Khan, Naurangabad, and Chokuha between Rohtas and Jalal Khurd. Rohtas Khurd may correspond to Sultan Sarai, but identification of the others remains uncertain. At Jalal Khurd (modern Sar Jalal) we come across the ruins of a *sarai* (?), an ancient *pakka* tank, and a Tughlaq-period mosque. From here, the ancient road led to Rewat passing on the way through Dhamyak (grave of Sultan Muhammad Ghori), Hattiya, Mahsa, and Pakka Sarai off Gujar Khan. The Pakka Sarai has survived on the high bank of a hilly torrent.[89] It has a well and two mosques inside it and a small *baoli* outside. At Kallar Sayyidan too, two *baolis* have been reported. From here the road reaches Rewat Fort which actually marks the site of a pre-Mughal Sarai with a grand mosque inside it. At Rewat, the modern GTR joins up with the ancient road again.

The course of the ancient road from Rewat to Sarai Kharbuza, once again, is not clear. We once had two square stone *baolis* within the fork of the Islamabad-Rawalpindi Road near Rewat, now filled in, and that is all. There are usually two stations in European accounts, namely Lashkari and Rawalpindi. The ancient road probably bypassed present-day Rawalpindi to the north and went straight first to the Pharwala fort and then across the Soan River to Golra Sharif. Two *kos minars* once stood near Golra railway station. These are still on the record of the Department of Archaeology as protected monuments but are there no more. Onward at Sarai Kharbuza near Tarnol and Sangjani we meet the remains of a *sarai* with a *baoli* and mosque inside it.[90] From Sarai Kharbuza, an off-shoot of the GTR went north through Shah Allah Ditta over the mountain to Kainthala for the onward journey to Dhamtaur near Abbotabad as a short cut to Kashmir. At Kainthala we still have a *baoli* with fresh drinking water and the remains of an ancient road and an ancient site called Rajdhani, a seat of government.

From Sarai Kharbuza, the main GTR goes to Margala Pass where the modern GTR meets it and Attock. At the Margala Pass and under the shadow of the towering Nicholson monument, we still have a considerable stretch of stone-paved road with a Persian inscription from the period of the Mughal Emperor Aurangzeb Alamgir (1658-1705). The stone slab has now been removed and preserved in the Lahore Fort. The historic Giri Fort is not far from the Margalla Pass. From Margalla, the modern GTR joins the ancient one at least as far as Hasanabdal. On the way there are the dilapidated remains of a *sarai* at Sarai Kala of which only the gateway and mosque remain. At Sarai Kala we meet the remains of an ancient bridge on Kalapani. From this bridge onward, the alignment of the ancient road is marked by the magnificent Laoser Baoli within the Wah Cantonment, the remains of the beautiful Wah Gardens with a Farood Gah-i-Shahinshah-i-Mughalia—that is to say, the Resting Place of the Mughal Emperors built by Jahangir (1605-1628)—and then another square *sarai* at Hasanabdal with a sacred tank and two mausoleums. From Hasanabdal onward the road goes to Burhan where once stood to be Sarai Zainud Din Ali (not yet located), to Hattian (Saidan Baoli), to Kamra (Chitti Baoli), Behram Baradari (small walled garden), Begum-ki-Sarai (*sarai*, mosque, and a square *kos minar*), and finally Attock where there is still an impressive fort from the Akbar period (1556-1605) with a Persian inscription and an ancient well, a *baoli* on the bank of Dakhnir Nullah south of Rumain, and the pillars of a boat-bridge from the Akbar period on the Indus River.

Beyond Attock, the ancient road probably used to run northward as does the modern GTR, although the path of the ancient GTR between Attock and Peshawar is not very clear. Very few historical landmarks have so far been recorded between these two historic cities. I know of only one ancient stepped well or *baoli* just beside the modern GTR near Aza Khel Payan (Pir Payai railway station), between Nowsherhra and Peshawar. Khushhal Khan Khattack's garden-pavilion at Vallai near Akora Khattack was also probably not far from the path of the ancient GTR. Otherwise, a few more *baolis* have recently been located between Peshawar and Attock by a team from Peshawar University but they are mostly modern. No report has so far been published. The only definite landmark in this region is the famous Sarai Jahan Aura Begum at Peshawar built by Princess Jahan Aura, daughter of Shah Jahan (1627-1658), who after the death of her mother became the First Lady of the Empire. Her *sarai* is popularly known as Gop Khatri as it was built on top of an ancient site of the same name which dated from the second century B.C. The gateway to this *sarai* is currently being repaired. Very few original cells have been preserved. Qila Bala Hisar in the same city also provides a landmark and fixes a point on the GTR for the onward journey to Kabul. Beyond that point, there are only three more landmarks: Jamrud (Fort), Ali Masjid (famous for its Buddhist Stupa), and Landikotal (Shapoola Stupa). Whether there are remains of any *sarai, baoli, kos minar*, or *dak-chowki* between Peshawar and Jalalabad, I am not sure. No published information is available, but the author is hopeful that a survey may reveal some interesting information.

This section is a brief account of the ancient course of the Grand Trunk Road (and its halting stations) which has marked the history of the whole of Northern India as it is today. Along this road marched not only the mighty armies of conquerors, but also the caravans of traders, scholars, artists, and common folk. Together with people, moved ideas, languages, customs, and cultures, not just in one, but in both directions. At different meeting places—permanent as well as temporary—people of different origins and from different cultural backgrounds, professing different faiths and creeds, eating different food, wearing different clothes, and speaking different languages and dialects would meet one another peacefully. They would understand one another's food, dress, manners and etiquette, and even borrow words, phrases, idioms and, at times, whole languages from others. As a result of this exchange of people and ideas along this ancient road and in its caravanserais, beside the cooling waters of the stepped wells and in the cool shade of their pavilions, waiting at the crossroads and under the shadows of the mighty *kos minars*, the seeds of new ways of life, new cultures, and new peoples took root. This was the role of this mighty highway that connected Central Asia with the subcontinent of Pakistan and India. The devastation wrought by invading armies has been forgotten. Merchandise bought and sold has been lost. But the seeds of cultural exchange sown along this road have taken root and given shape to new cultural phenomena that have determined the course of life today along these routes. Here lies the value of the ancient Grand Trunk Road and the halting stations on it.

Notes

1. K.M. Sarkar, *The Grand Trunk Road in the Punjab: 1849-1886* (Lahore: Punjab Government Record Office Publications, 1926), p. 8, (Monograph No. 1).
2. John Wiles, *The Grand Trunk Road in the Punjab: Kyber to Calcutta* (London: 1972), pp. 7-16. Rudyard Kipling, as quoted by Wiles (p. 8), described this road as a mighty way "bearing, without crowding India's traffic for 1,500 miles such a River of life as nowhere else exists in the world."
3. Sir James Douie, *North West Frontier Province, Punjab and Kashimir,* p. 126, see Sarkar, *Grand Trunk Road*, p. 7.
4. H.L.O. Garret in Sarkar, *Grand Trunk Road*, Prefatory Note.
5. John Wiles, *Grand Trunk Road*, p. 7.
6. The part of the Silk Road which passed through Pakistan corresponds to the Grand Trunk Road from Peshawar to Lahore. However, at Lahore, instead of going straight to Delhi, it bent southward and, while embracing the present-day National Highway, it used to terminate at Barbaricon near Karachi and joined the Sea Route. Alexander the Great also followed the same road up to the River Beas. Later invaders, almost without exception, followed the same road to reach the coveted throne of Delhi.
7. Sarkar, *Grand Trunk Road*, pp. 7-8.
8. See Preface by V.S. Agrawala in Moti Chandra, *Trade and Routes in Ancient India* (New Delhi, 1977), p. vi.
9. Ibid., p. 78; Also see R.P. Kangle, *The Kantiliya's Arthasastra,* reprinted with Urdu translation by Shan-ul-Haq Haqqi, and *Muqadama* by Muhammad Ismail (Zabeeh Karachi, 1991), bk. 4, sec. 116, pp. 17-26 (Hamavata Path), and bk. 2. See 22.31 for width of roads.
10. Kangle, *Kantiliya's Arthasastra*, bk. 2, sec. 19.19 and 38.
11. Ibid., sec. 22, pp. 1-3. *Asthaniya* was located at the center of 800 villages, whereas a *dronamukha* was at the center of 400 villages (sec. 19.
12. It was on account of and along this Royal Road that Megasthenes could travel to lands never before beheld by Greek eyes. It was maintained by a Board of Works (See Megasthenes' Indika, Fragments 3, 4 and 34, in J.W. McCrindle, *Ancient India as described by Megasthenes and Arrian* (London, 1877), pp. 50, 86. XV. I. II. According to Megasthenes, this Royal Road was measured by *scheoni* (1 *scheonus* = 40 *stadia* = one Indian *yojana* = 4 *krosas* or *kos*) and its total length was 10,000 *stadia*, i.e., about 1,000 *kos.* He also states that there was an authoritative register of the stages on the Royal Road from which Erastothenes derived his estimates of distances between various places in India.
13. Sarkar, *Grand Trunk Road*, p. 2.
14. Megasthenes' Indika. Ten stadia are usually regarded as equal to 2,022.5 yards or one *kos* of 4,000 *haths*—according to some, 8,000 *haths*. These pillars were meant to show the by-roads and distances. There is great difference of opinion as to what the correct measure of one *kos* or *krosa* is—some regard it as less than 3 miles while others regard it as equal to 1.75 miles (2.8 kilometers). Traditionally and within our own memory, a *kos* was about 2.5 English miles (4 kilometers). For details see Radha Kumud Mookerjee *Asoka*, 3d ed. (Delhi, 1962), p. 188 wherein he regards 8 *kosas* equal to 14 miles i.e., 1 *kos* = 1.75 miles. Also see Moti Chandra, *Trade and Trade Routes in Ancient India* (New Delhi, 1977), p. 78.
15. Kangle, *The Kautiliya Arthashastra*, bk. 2, sec. 56.5.
16. "On the high roads, too, banyan trees were caused to be planted by me that they might give shade to cattle and men, mango-gardens (*amba-vadikya)* were caused to

be planted and wells to be dug by me, at each half *kos* (*adhakosikyani*) *nimisdhaya* were caused to be built, many watering stations *(aparani)* were caused to be established by me, here and there, for the comfort of cattle and men." See the Seven Pillar Edicts, part 7, as on Dehli-Topra Pillar in Radha Kumud Mookerji, *Asoka*, pp. 186-93. Also see Dr. R. Bhandarkar, *Asoka*, 2d ed. (Calcutta, 1932), p. 353.

17. "*Nimisdhaya*" (Skt. *nisdya*) has often been translated as "rest-house." Luder, however, translates it as "Steps down to water." Hultzseh also follows Luder. But Woolner and some others do not accept this meaning and are probably right. See also discussion on this word in E. Hultzseh, *Corpus Inscription Indicarum*, vol. 1.

18. Sarkar, *Grand Trunk Road*, p. 2.

19. Mookerji, *Asoka*, p. 189, note 3.

20. Moti Chandra, Trade, p. ix. He talks about wells and trees but not the "rest houses" built by Asoka, p. 79. He probably agrees with Luder as regards the meaning of "*nimisdhaya*" as "stepped well," i.e., *baoli.*

21. V.S. Agrawala, suggests that, as Kangs were the originators of a canal system in Central Asia in the seventh century B.C., Sakas (Scythians) from the same region introduced stepped wells or *baolis* in the second century B.C.

22. B. Rowland, *Art in Afghanistan. Objects from the Kabul Museum* (London: Allen Lane the Penguin Press, 1971), p. 21.

23. Moti Chandra, *Trade*, p. 19.

24. Saifur Rahman Dar, "The Silk Road and Buddhism in Pakistani Contexts," *Lahore Museum Bulletin*, vol. I, no. 2 (July-December 1988): pp. 29-53.

25. Moti Chandra, *Trade*, p. 84. The silence of these travelers about these facilities can be easily explained. As devout Buddhists, thay always preferred to stay in Buddhist monasteries which were numerous in those days. Their doors were always open to travelers—pious and lay alike.

26. Muhammad Qasim Farishta, *Tarikh-i-Farishta,* trans. Abdul Hayee Khawaja (Lahore, 1974), part I, p. 136. See also Maulana Abdul Salam Nadvi, *Rafa-i-Ama ke kam,* Darul Musanafeen, series no. 93 (Azim Garh: n.a.), p. 40. In Briggs' translation of Farishta's history, however, there is no mention of a *sarai* on the Delhi-Daulatabad road or elsewhere. Instead, Muhammad Tughlaq is reported to have planted shady trees in rows along this road to provide travelers with shade, while poor travelers were fed on this road at public expense. He is also said to have established hospitals for the sick and almshouses for widows and orphans; see Muhammad Qasim Farishta, *History of the Rise of the Mahomedan Power in India till the Year 1612*, English translation by John Briggs, 4 volumes (1829; reprint Delhi: Low Price Publications, 1990), vol. 1, pp. 236 and 242.

27. Shams Siraj Afeef, *Tarikh-i-Feroze Shahi,* Urdu trans. by Maulvi Muhammad Fida Ali Talib (Karachi: Nafees Academy, 1965), p. 23. See also R. Nath, *History of Sultanate Architecture* (New Delhi: Abhinav Publications, 1978), p. 59. From Muhammad Qasim Farishta we learn that Firoze Tughlaq not only repaired the caravanserais built by his predecessors but also built 100 *sarais* of his own; see Muhammad Qasim Farishta, *History of the Rise of the Mohamedan Power in India*, vol. 1, pp. 267-70. He also built several other public amenities such as dams, bridges, reservoirs, public wells, public baths and monumental pillars. He set aside lands for the maintenance of these public buildings.

28. Abdul Salam Nadvi, *Rafa-i-Ama ke kam*, p. 40 quotes *Mirat-i-Sikandari,* p. 75, for this information.

29. Nadvi, *Rafa-i-Ama ke kam*, p. 40. Also Qasim Farishta, *History of the Rise of the Mohamedan Power in India*, vol. 1, p. 186.

30. Abbas Khan Serwani, "Tarikh-i-Sher Shah" in *History of India as told by its Historians*, edited by H.M. Elliot and John Dowson, vol. 4 (London, 1872), pp. 417-18. See also Rizqullah Mushtaki, *Waqiat-i-Mushtaki*, in the same volume; Zulfiqar Ali Khan, *Sher Shah Suri: Emperor of India* (Lahore, 1925); and Hashim Ali Khan (alias Khafi Khan), *Mutakhabut-Tawarikh,* Urdu translation by Muhmud Ahmad Faruqui, vol. 1 (Karachi: Nafees Academy, 1963), pp. 127-28. The more important roads include the Grand Trunk Road from Sonargaon to the Nilab (Indus River) and those from Lahore to Multan via Harappa and from Agra to Mandu. On the Multan-Lahore Road, there still exist two *sarais*, namely Sarai Chheemba close to Bhai Pheru (Phul Nagar) and Sarai Mughal near Baloki Headworks. Another *Pakka Sarai* attributed to Sher Shah Suri was standing as late as 1964, almost in front of the present-day Harappa Museum. A considerable length of an ancient road, still shaded by old trees and called *Safan Wali Sarrak,* extends on either side of this *sarai.* This *sarai* has now been excavated and reported briefly. See Richard H. Meadow and Jonathan Mark Kenoyer, *Harappa, 1994-95: Reprints of Reports of the Harappa Archaeological Research Project* (December 1995), sec.: "Harappa Excavation 1994," p. 13, fig. 13. Though usually these *sarais* are attributed to Sher Shah Suri, on the authority of the author of Ma'asrul Umara, we learn that Khan Dauran Nusrat Jang and Qaleej Khan Torani built several *sarais* on the road from Lahore to Multan (see note 40 below). Another road linked Lahore with Khushab and onward to the Kurram Valley on the way to Afghanistan. Two beautiful *baolis* or stepped wells still exist on this road, one each at Gunjial near Quaid Abad and Van Bachran near Mianwali; both are attributed to Sher Shah Suri. See Saifur Rahman Dar, "Khushab-Monuments and Antiquities," *Journal of the Research Society of Pakistan*, vol. 15, no. 3, part 2 (Lahore, August 1978). There are three interesting *baolis* in the picturesque Son Valley marking some ancient routes linking Khushab with the Salt Range.

31. Shaikh Rizqullah Mushtaki, "Wakiat-i-Mushtaki," in Elliot and Dowson, *History of India*, vol. 4, appendix G, p. 550.

32. Elliot and Dowson, *History of India*, p. 417, footnote 2. This figure occurs in one of the manuscripts of Serwani, whereas Sher Shah is reported as having constructed 2,500 rather than 1,700 *sarais*. This they attribute to ignorance on two fronts, namely that the total distance between Bengal and the Indus is 2,500 *kos,* and there was a *sarai* at each instead of every second *kos.* This tradition can be considered as partly true if it refers to the reign of Salim Shah Suri (A.D. 1545-1552), who is said to have added one more *sarai* between every two *sarais* built by his father. Shaikh Rizqullah Mushtaki, "Wakiat-i-Mushtaki," appendix G, p. 550, also puts Suri *sarais* after one rather than two *kos.* See also Farishta, *Tarikh-i-Farishta,* vol. 1, p. 228, as quoted by Maulana Abdul Salam Nadvi, *Rafa-i-Ama ke kam,* p. 41.

33. Nadvi, *Rafa-i-Ama ke kam*, p. 41. Also Qasim Farishta, *Tarikh-i-Farishta*, vol. 1, p. 332; and Khafi Khan, *Muntakhab-ul-Lubab,* translated by Muhammad Ahmad Faruqi (Karachi: Nafees Academy, 1963), part 1, p. 135.

34. Dr. M.A. Chaghatai, *Tarikhi Masajid-i-Lahore* (Lahore, 1976), pp. 29-31.

35. Abul Fazl, *Ain-i-Akhbari,* vol. 1, p. 115. Among such philanthropists were the widow of Shaikh Abdul Rahim Lukhnavi and Sadiq Muhammad Khan Harvi, who built *sarais* at Lukhnau and Dhaulpur respectively.

36. *The Tuzk-i-Jahangiri* or *Memoirs of Jahangir,* translated by Alexander Rogers, edited by Henry Beveridge (Lahore: Sang-e-Meel Publications, 1974), vol. 1, pp. 7-8, 75, and vol. 2, pp. 63-64, 98, 103, 220, 249; see also Sarkar, *Grand Trunk Road,* p. 49.

37. Sarkar, *Grand Trunk Road,* p. 43. Also see *Tuzk-i-Jahangiri* (Lahore: Nawal Kishore Press, n.d.), p. 5. Such courtiers include Halal Khan, Khawajasara, Saeed Khan Chagatta, the Subedar of Punjab, Shaikh Farid Murtaza Khan Bokhari, and Amir

Ullah Vardi Khan. See Samsamud Daula Shahnawaz Khan, *Ma'asrul Umara*, Urdu translation by Muhammad Ayub Qadri (Lahore: Urdu Markzi Board, 1968), pp. 205, 407, 408, 639 under names quoted here: vol. 1, p. 205 (Amir Ullah); p. 407 (Halal Khan); vol. 2, p. 408 (Saeed Khan Chagatta); and p. 639 (Farid Murtaza Khan Bukhari). *Sarais* were built along the roadside whereas *rabats* were located inside the cities.

38. Rogers and Beveridge, *Tuzk-i-Jahangiri,* p. 77 (Azim Khan). Beside *sarais,* Jahangir also ordered the preparation of *bulghur-khana* (free eating houses) where cooked food was served both to the poor residents as well as travelers; see also A. Rogers and H. Beveridge, *Tuzk-i-Jahangiri,* vol. 1, p. 75.

39. Ibid, p. 406 and Khafi Khan, *Muntakhab-ul-Lubab,* p. 302. Jahangir also mentions the existence of several other *sarais* in his empire, mostly in the Punjab such as Sarai Qazi Ali near Sultanpur, Sarai Pakka near Rewat, Sarai Kharbuza near Tarnaul (also marked on Elphinston's map), Sarai Bara, Sarai Halalabad, Sarai Nur (Mahal) near Sirhind, Sarai Alwatur or Aluwa, and a grand *baoli* built by his mother at a cost of Rs. 20,000 at Barah. See Rogers and Beveridge, *Tuzk-i-Jahangir,* vol. 1, pp. 63, 98, and vol. 2, pp. 64, 103, 219, 220, 249.

40. For example, Azim Khan built a *sarai* in Islamabad (Mathura) whereas Khan Dauran Nusrat Jang and Qaleeg Khan Torani built *sarais* every 10 kos on the road from Suraj to Burhanpur and several *sarais* on the road from Lahore to Multan respectively. See Kahn, *Ma'asrul Umara,* vol. 1, p. 179 (Azim Khan), p. 758. See too previous note.

41. Tariq Masud, "Pull Shah Daula," *Lahore Museum Bulletin,* vol. 3, no. 2 (July-December 1990).

42. Nadvi, *Rafa-i-Ama ke kam,* p. 44

43. Shaista Khan, the Emir Umara of Aurangzeb, also built several *rabats,* mosques and bridges (*Ma'asrul Umara,* vol. 2, p. 705).

44. Nadvi, *Rafa-i-Ama ke kam,* p. 44.

45. Kahn, *Ma'asrul Umara,* vol. 1, p. 358.

46. Kahn, *Ma'asrul Umara,* vol. 3, p. 882. Also see Nadvi, *Rafa-i-Ama ke kam,* p. 45.

47. Kahn, *Ma'asrul Umara,* vol. 1, p. 358, and Nadvi, *Rafa-i-Ama ke kam,* pp. 44-45.

48. Sarkar, *Grand Trunk Road,* p. vii.

49. William Foster, ed., *Early Travels in India, 1583-1619* (London, 1921; Lahore, 1978), pp. 167-68.

50. Sarkar, *Grand Trunk Road,* chap. 3-4, pp. 13-45.

51. Moti Chandra, *Trade,* p. 81, and Abul Fazl, *Ain-i-Akbari,* vol. 1 (Nawal Kishore Edition), p. 197 (under *Ain-i-Kotwal).*

52. Shaikh Rizqullah Mushtaki, "Wakiat-i-Mushtaki," in Elliot and Dowson, *History of India,* vol. 4, appendix G, p. 550; Ishwari Prasad, *The Life and Times of Humayun* (Bombay: Oriental Longmans, 1955), pp. 168-69; and Dr. Hussain Khan, *Sher Shah Suri* (Lahore: Ferozsons Ltd., 1987), pp. 332-40. Also see note 32 above.

53. Dr. Hussain Khan, *Sher Shah Suri,* p. 333.

54. Arthur Upham Pope, *Persian Architecture: The Triumph of Form and Colour* (New York: George Braziller, 1965), p. 238.

55. Khan, *Ma'asrul Umara,* vol. 2, p. 639 (see Farid Murtaza Khan Bukhari).

56. Nadvi, *Rafa-i-Ama ke kam,* p. 45.

57. Dr. Hussain Khan, *Sher Shah Suri,* p. 333.

58. Ebba Koch, *Mughal Architecture: An Outline of Its History and Development (1576-1858)* (Munich: Prestel-Verlag, 1991), p. 67, fig. 65.

59. Catherine B. Asher, "Architecture of Mughal India," in *The New Cambridge History of India,* vol. 14 (Cambridge, 1992), p. 225.

60. Rogers and Beveridge, *Tuzk-i-Jahangiri,* vol. 2, p. 182.

61. Subash Parihar, "Two Little-known Mughal Monuments at Fatehbad in East Punjab," *Journal of Research Society of Pakistan,* vol. 38, no. 2 (Lahore) (April 1991): pp. 57- 62.

62. Subash Parihar, "The Mughal Sarai at Doraha–Architectural Study," *East and West,* vol. 37 (Rome, December 1987): pp. 309-25.

63. Nur Ahmad Chishti, *Tehqiqat-i-Chishti* (Lahore: Al-Faisal Printers, 1993), pp. 764-66.

64. Arthur Upham Pope, *Persian Architecture,* p. 238.

65. Ebba Koch, *Mughal Architecture,* p. 238.

66. *Indian Archaeology, 1980-81,* A review (1983): p. 67.

67. There is some controversy as regards the vaulted roof structure in the courtyard of Begum-ki-Sarai. For some it is a mosque, while for others it is not. On either side of the double row of chambers, there are two open platforms, both accessible from within the chamber. Thus, in the western wall, there are three openings in place of a *mehrab*. This has led some to believe that this structure is a *baradari* or pavilion rather than a mosque. See Lt. Col. K.A. Rashid, "An Old *Serai* Near Attock Fort," reprinted from *Pakistan Quarterly,* vol. 12, no. 3 (Summer 1964): Plate 4. But this is certainly not true. In such deserted places, such as at Begum-ki-Sarai, a mosque was a must. The platform to the west of the Prayer Chamber and three openings in the western walls appear to have been a British-period innovation. Misuse of mosques by British residents for some mundane purpose is not an unknown phenomenon. The use of the famous Dai Anga Mosque, Lahore, as a residence by Mr. Henry Cope, and use of the verandahs of the Badshahi Mosque, Lahore, as a residence for British soldiers, are well-known examples.

68. Lt. Col. K.A. Rashid, "The Inscriptions of Begum Sarai (Attock)," *Journal of Research Society of Pakistan,* vol. 1 (Lahore, October 1964): pp. 15-24.

69. *Epigraphica India* (1953 and 1954), pp. 44-45.

70. Wayne E. Begley, "Four Mughal Caravanserais Built During the Reigns of Jahangir and Shah Jahan," *Muqarnas,* vol. 1 (1983): p. 173.

71. Subash Parihar, *Mughal Monuments in the Punjab and Haryana* (New Delhi: Inter-India Publications, 1985), p. 19.

72. Bahadur Khan, "Mughal Garden Wah," *Journal of Central Asia,* vol. 11, no. 2 (December 1988): p. 154, illust. p. 158.

73. "Tarikh-i-Sher Shah," in Elliot and Dowson, *The History of India,* p. 140.

74. Sarkar, *Grand Trunk Road,* p. 48-49.

75. *Memoirs of Emperor Jahangir,* trans. by Major David Price (Delhi, n.d.), p. 157.

76. Subash Parihar, *Mughal Monuments,* p. 19 and Sarkar, *Grand Trunk Road,* p. 48-49.

77. *Akbar Nama,* vol. 3, p. 378, as quoted by Manzul Haque Siddiqui, *Tarikh-i-Hasan Abdal* (Lahore), pp. 64-65.

78. Manzar-ul-Haque Siddiqui, *Tarikhai-i-Hasan Abdal,* p. 65.

79. William Foster, ed., *Early Travels,* p. 255 and footnote.

80. R.C. Temple, ed., *The Travels of Peter Mundy,* vol. 2 (London: Hakluyt Society, 1914), p. 121; as quoted by William Foster, *Early Travels,* p. 225 (footnote).

81. Hussain Khan, *Sher Shah Suri,* p. 33, and Khafi Khan, *Muntakhab-ul-Lubab,* vol. 1, p. 127.

82. R.P. Kangle, *Kautiliya Arthashatra,* bk. 2. sec. 56, paras. 5-6.

83. Catherine B. Asher, *Architecture of Mughal India,* p. 225.

84. Foster, *Early Travels,* p. 225, and Temple, ed., *The Travels of Peter Mundy,* vol. 2.

85. Foster, *Early Travels,* pp. 155-60, and Subash Parihar, *Mughal Monuments,* pp. 19-26 (footnote 16).

86. Subash Parihar, *Mughal Monuments*, pp. 19-26. Hugel clearly refers to the road Filor-Nakodar-Sooltanpur-Fatehbad-Noorooddeen Suraee (near Taran Taran), Khyroodden Suraee (near Rajah Ku)—Manihala-Taihar (*baoli* nearby)—Lahore as the "old Badshahee Road." See Baron Charles Hugel, *Travels in Kashmir and the Punjab* (1845; reprint Lahore: Qausain, 1976), Pocket Map.

87. Waheed Quraishi, "Gujranwala: Past and Present," *Oriental College Magazine* (Lahore, February-May 1958), p. 20. The first to mention this *sarai* in 1608 was William Finch under the name "Coojes Sarai." Present-day Gujranwala city actually encompasses the sites of the three ancient *sarais* and a settlement namely Sarai Kacha, Sarai Kamboh, Sarai Gujran, and a village called Thatta; see Waheed Quraishi, p. 21.

88. In 1607, Jahangir visited this *sarai* and described the site as "strangely full of dust and earth. The carts reached it with great difficulty owing to the badness of the road. They had brought from Kabul to this place *riwaj* (rhubarb), which was mostly spoiled" (*Tuzk-i-Jahangiri,* translated by A. Rogers, vol. 1, p. 99).

89. Sarai Kharbuza is marked on Elphinston's map. Jahangir visited it in 1607 and described it in these words: "On Monday the 10th, the village of Kharbuza was our stage. The Ghakhars in earlier times had built a dome here and taken a toll from travellers. As the dome is shaped like a melon it became known by that name" (*Tuzk-i- Jahangiri*, translated by A. Rogers, vol. 1, p. 98).

Chapter 10

MARITIME TRADE FROM THE FOURTEENTH TO THE SEVENTEENTH CENTURY
Evidence from the Underwater Archaeological Sites in the Gulf of Siam

Sayan Prishanchit

Introduction

The catchword in today's transport field is *convenience*. Journeys to distant continents which might be thousands of miles away can be made within hours in aircraft that have been developed to achieve supersonic speed. However, the high cost of air freight discourages traders from using it to transport heavy and bulky cargo which is more economically moved by sea-faring vessels—a mode of transport which has been utilized by merchants for thousands of years. Ships can sail at much higher speeds and can carry tens of thousands of tons in this modern era, but they also continue to provide housing and office space for all of those who sail on them in much the same way that they have in the past. All the activities of daily life can still be pursued on board.

There is evidence to suggest that sea traders from afar were present in the river plain in central Thailand and along the coast of the Gulf of Siam down to the Malay Peninsula from the fourth or fifth century on. During the seventh to eleventh centuries, when human settlement became more common, with the Davaravati Kingdom controlling much of central Thailand and the Srivvijaya Kingdom's territory covering the

Malay Peninsula and the Indonesian Archipelago, evidence of maritime trade routes includes ceramics from China, glass and stone beads from India and Persia, and cult icons, all of which had been transported to the region by these maritime traders and introduced to the indigenous peoples. These items were found in abundance especially at settlements along the coasts such as U-Thong, Nakhonchaisri, Kubua in central Thailand and Cahiya, Nakhon Si Thammarat, Yarang (in Pattani), and Narathiwat in the south. Discoveries of these exotic goods have so far occurred on land and unfortunately no wreck site dating to those periods has yet been discovered in those areas.

During the twelfth and thirteenth centuries, Chinese merchants seemed to dominate the Southeast Asian market. There were many more junks traveling in Thai territorial waters and even penetrating deeper inland up the main waterways such as the Tha Chine river and the Mae Klong river. Chinese written records provide accounts of maritime traffic.

Many traders settled in the region and spread knowledge of ship building technology and sailing techniques to the local population. Later, these foreign traders became important for their roles as foreign affairs and international commodity officials. Chinese documents recorded that during the years 1289 and 1290 there was an ambassador from Suwannabhum presented at the court in Peking, and that in the next year, 1291, the Mongol court received the ambassador from the Sukhothai Kingdom. Subsequently, there were official trading expeditions between the two countries from time to time. The documents also recorded many shipments of gifts to the Emperors of China in those years.[1]

Following the inauguration of Ayutthaya City as the capital of Siam in 1351, there were more records describing maritime trade: Siam imported ceramics, silks and satin from China, on the one hand, and, on the other hand, she exported timber products, ivory tusks, scented wood, sampan wood (Acacia sp.), leather, and lead as well as Sangkhalok ceramics and other pottery to other Southeast Asian countries. Every junk had far to sail regardless of its exact destination. Not only trade goods but also life's necessities such as food and water, medicine and items of everyday use such as cooking and storage containers, as well as sources of recreation were stored on board.

There was no guarantee that a ship setting off on a sea voyage would ever reach its destination and the perils of sea travel in those days are reflected in the number of shipwrecks extant on the sea-bed, especially in the gulf of Thailand. Some parts of these wrecks are still intact and in relatively good condition because of the preserving nature of their watery resting places. Now, centuries later, they live in expectation of our generation and its successors that they will reveal more knowledge about the past.

Underwater Archeological Sites in the Gulf of Siam

The Gulf of Siam has been an important territorial waterway and the scene of much sea traffic for centuries. In geographical terms, gulfs are reputed for their calm waters, but it is impossible to predict every storm that occurs there. Likewise, despite its popularity as a sea route since ancient times, the Gulf of Siam has also been the theatre of many storms, which have taken unlucky vessels to their unenviable end.

Since 1977, the Underwater Archaeological Project, under the Archaeology Division, Fine Arts Department, Thailand, has undertaken surveys, excavations, and other research on wreck sites off the coast of the Gulf of Siam. Eight shipwrecks dating back to the period from the fourteenth to the seventeenth centuries were found, namely: Sattahip, Rang Kwien, Pattaya, Ko Kradat, Si Chang 1, Si Chang 2, Si Chang 3, and Samui. Furthermore, there are six other sites which have undergone surveys and yielded material evidence, namely the sites of Presae, Bang Ka Chai, Ko Rin, Samae Sarn Channel, Hin Lak Bet, and Don Hai; but the ships themselves have not yet been located,

Archaeological objects and features from the sites mentioned above provide the most important evidence currently available for the study of the history of maritime trade between China and Southeast Asian countries. Tangible evidence, which can prove or disprove written records, also serves a possibly more useful purpose by shedding more light on the subject through the revelation of other aspects involved and the scope required to synthesize the information in an attempt to uncover the realities of previous times.

Evidence of Maritime Trade from the Gulf of Siam

Types of evidence include the ship's structure, merchandise, and other artifacts as summarized below.

Ship

The most important clues are found in a study of the body of the ship itself. It is necessary to regard the ship as a mobile home, an office, a means of transport, a conveyer of cargo, and also sometimes as a factory. Evidence of the physical components of the ship found in the Gulf of Siam can summarily be described here:

The Sattahip Wreck

This is also called the Ko Khram Wreck, located at 38-43 meters (126-143 feet) below mean sea level in the channel off Ko Khram ("Ko" is a

Thai word meaning "Island"), which faces Sattahip bay, Chonburi province. This is the first underwater archaeological site that the Fine Arts Department, with the cooperation of the Royal Thai Navy, surveyed and excavated, between 1975 and 1977.[2] The structural components such as wood planks from the hull, bull-heads, and ribs were discovered in the sand. The species of wood used to make this structure were identified as pegs and bolts and were made of Terminalia mucronata (sp.), Terminalia (sp.), and Garcina cornea (sp.).[3]

The vessel was built by using an even-edge-joined building technique with a double-planked hull. Wood pegs and bolts were used to hold the planks together. The cargo walls were fastened to the wooden deck planks with iron nails and split bamboo flooring lined the wooden deck. Presumably, the Sattahip vessel is a flat junk and has no keel. The deck was approximately 8 meters wide and 32 meters long.

The Rang Kwien Wreck

This is known as the Nga Chang Wreck or Chinese Coin Wreck among the amateur divers, as ivory tusks and Chinese coins (its main cargos) were discovered in abundance at the time they visited it. It is located at a depth of 21 meters (80 feet) in the Ko Khram Channel about 10 kilometers west of Bang Sa-re Bay and about 800 meters from the Rang Kwien Islet.[4]

Although surveys and excavations of this wreck site were carried out over four successive years (1978-1981), only a few pieces of the ship's structure were found such as the keel, wood planks from the hull, ribs, and the carved decorated pieces for the aft-deck. In addition, there is a Chinese bronze mirror piercing the keel as a lucky amulet to prevent disasters, reflecting a traditional belief and preference among Chinese shipbuilders and sailors.

The even-edge-joined building technique was applied in the construction of this vessel and the round-headed wooden pegs were used to fasten the planks to the ribs. The ship is thought to be 25 meters long.

The Pattaya Wreck

This wreck is located at a depth of 26 meters (90 feet) in the channel between the south beach of Pattaya City and Ko Lan, Chonburi province. The site is situated near the shore of the most popular beach in Thailand. Therefore, it has often been disturbed by tourists, amateur divers, and treasure hunters over a long period of time. There are traces of destruction of the site by means of explosives and most parts of the vessel have been seriously damaged. Structural remains suggest that the Pattaya vessel had a triple-planked hull which was fastened with wooden pegs. The structure was constructed of Shorea (sp.) and Diterocarpus (sp.)

wood. The vessel comprises multiple cargo holds, each of which was separated from the other by split bamboo walls.[5]

The Ko Kradat Wreck

This vessel sank in 3 meters (5-8 feet) of water on the coral reef near Ko Kradat, Trad province. The wreck has often been disturbed by treasure hunters and has been badly damaged. Survey and excavation work in 1978 brought to light part of an even-edge-joined-double-planked hull, the planks of which were fastened by wooden pegs and bolts made of Terminals (sp.) wood. The junk at Ko Kradat was presumably a local Southeast Asian construction based on the Terminalis (sp.) which is found only in Southeast Asia and Africa, but not in China.[6]

The Si Chang 1 Wreck

This wreck is located at a depth of 31 meters (100 feet), 3 kilometers west of Ko Si Chang at the mouth of Chao Phraya River. The Underwater Archaeological Project, Fine Arts Department, Thailand, in cooperation with the Institute for Maritime Archaeology and the Western Australian Museum, undertook surveys and excavations of this wreck site between 1983 and 1985.[7] The result of research yielded many interesting aspects from the remains of the vessel including:

1. *Keel*
   A very long piece of 200 mm thick wood with a trapezoid cross section; the shorter side of the parallel side is facing upward.
   1.1 *Wooden plank floor*
      Dipterocarpus (sp.) wood was cut into short planks measuring 800-850 mm long and 150-300 mm wide. These planks, found in the cargo holds, were presumably the floor lining.
   1.2 *Inner hull planks*
      These planks are made of Shorea (sp.) and were fastened together with round headed wood pegs in an even-edge joined fashion.
   1.3 *Bottom lining planks*
      Soft wood (pine) planks, each between 200 and 300 mm wide, were used to line the bottom of the vessel between its ribs.
2. *Ribs*
   Only three pieces of ribs were found. They are made of Shorea (sp.) and Dipeterocarpus (sp.) wood.

2.1 Bulkhead
The bulkhead is made of Shorea (sp.) wood and was laid attached to the ribs.

A study of the structure of the Si Chang 1 Wreck suggests that the vessel had a keel, and all its components were fastened together with wooden pegs and bolts made of Cassia fistula (sp.). However, the nationality of the owner or the origin of the ship was still unknown.

The Si Chang 2 Wreck
The vessel is located at a depth of 25-27 meters (85-90 feet). The Underwater Archaeological Project of the Thai Fine Arts Department cooperated with the Institute for Maritime Archaeology and the Western Australian Museum in undertaking surveys of the wreck site in 1982, 1985, and 1986. The site was actually excavated in 1987. Only parts of the vessel submerged in sand, including sections of a double-planked hull and bottom planks fastened together with wooden pegs and metal nails, have survived. The keel of the vessel could not be found.

The Si Chang 3 Wreck
This vessel is located at a depth of 24 meters (80 feet), approximately 7 kilometers northwest of the northern end of Ko Si Chang. The Underwater Archaeological Project of the Thai Fine Arts Department cooperated with the Institute of Maritime Archaeology and the Western Australian Museum in undertaking surveys of this wreck site in 1986. The result of the research has yielded many interesting aspects of the vessel's remains, including:

1. Keel
The keel of this vessel is made of three pieces of wood measuring up to 15 meters in length.

1.1 Hull planks
The hull of the vessel was constructed by using a double-planking technique in an even-edge-joined fashion. The inner hull planks were fastened together with round-headed wooden pegs. Metal nails were used for the outer hull planks made of Terrieta (sp.) and Herieta (sp.) and were also used to fasten both layers of the planks together. Ships built according to this technique were common throughout Southeast Asia.

1.2 Bulkheads
Nine bulkheads were found in situ, tightly fastened above the ribs, situated across the keel.

1.3 Maststep
This is a very thick, rectangular piece of wood situated across the keel, fastened tightly to the bulkhead. On the upper surface of the bulkhead, there are two rectangular dug-out pits for fixing the mast support poles.

The Si Chang 3 Wreck is presumably a small vessel with a deck measuring approximately 6 meters in width and 24 meters in length.

The Samui Wreck

This ship is located at a depth of approximately 19 meters (60-65 feet) in the channel halfway between Ko Tean and Ko Samui.

The wreck has been plundered as have many of the sites mentioned above; however, the results of the excavation in 1984 provided evidence of a double-planked wooden hull. Wood planks about 180-200 mm thick were fastened directly to the ribs. The keel of the ship has not been located. This vessel is presumably a flat bottomed junk, the deck of which measures about 18 meters in length and approximately 4-5 meters in width.

Merchandise

Remains of cargo provide important clues in the historical study of maritime trade because the items can often be traced to their place of origin, and sometimes suggest their intended destinations. Orders from western countries requesting their Southeast Asian representatives to purchase timber products and organic goods from ports in the Ayutthaya Kingdom regularly included rice, leather, sampan wood, buffalo horns, scented krishna (Eagle wood), rattan, palm sugar, teak wood, lacquer sap, wax, ivory tusks, honey, areca nut, brown cane sugar, lead, tin, glazed stoneware (Sangakhalok ware), and earthen ware.

Because these wrecks have been lying on the sea bed for many hundreds of years, most of the organic remains (which decay easily) have vanished from their sites. Although only minute fragments of these organic products remain in a most dilapidated state, conditions of preservation under the sea are much better than on land. This evidence is considered important as it indicates the nature of the cargo transported in these times. The remains of merchandise discovered at the wreck sites in the Gulf of Siam are described below.

Organic materials

1. Ivory
A big shipment of ivory (about 25-30 pieces) was found in the Rang Kwien Wreck in the 1981 excavation. Most of the pieces

are large. The diameter at the thick end measures 1,500-1,700 mm. They were neatly laid in a group on round-headed tie supports. The condition of these ivory pieces was so bad that salvage possibilities were not considered promising and the pieces were consequently left in situ. Furthermore, ivory was found in smaller amounts accompanying other products in the Sattahip and the Si Chang 2 wrecks.

2. **Sampan wood: *Acacia (sp.)***
   Samples of sampan wood were found in all of the Si Chang group wrecks.

3. **Leather**
   Only small pieces of leather were found in the Rang Kwien wreck; however, their poor condition and the size of each piece provided samples which were inadequate for species-determination analysis.

Inorganic materials

1. **Ceramics**
   The large number of items included in this category makes up the greater part of the merchandise found. Moreover, ceramic products tell stories of their own when considering factors such as source materials, potting techniques, decoration, and kilns. Some pieces even bear the name of the artist or the reign of the emperor who supported the industry. Ceramics found at the wreck sites in the Gulf of Siam can be divided into four groups according to their origin or place of manufacture.[8]

   1.1 *Thai Ceramics*
      Sangkhalok wares, the celadon-type of glaze applied to white-clay stoneware produced by the Si-Satchanalai and Sukhothai kilns, north central Thailand, were the most common type of Thai ceramics found at almost all the wreck sites. For example, large quantities were found in the Sattahip wreck, the Prasae site, and the Ko Kradat wreck, and some pieces were also found in the Samui wreck. Chaliang ceramics, a celadon-type group glaze on dark-body stoneware originating from the Ban Ko Noi Kiln site, Si-satchanalai, were found in the Rang Kwien wreck. Many heavy storage containers and utility wares such as brown glazed four-eared jars, mortars and large bowls from the Mae Nam Noi kilnsite were found in the Sattahip wreck, the Si Chang 1, 2, and 3 wrecks, and the Ko Kradat and Pattaya wrecks, at the Don Hai site and other coastal sites.

1.2 Chinese ceramics

Many grades of Chinese ceramics were exported. Those which were found at the wreck sites in the Gulf of Siam can be described as follows:

a. *High quality blue and white porcelain known as Kraak ware*
This porcelain was produced at the royal Qing-Te Chen kilns in Jiangxi province, South China during the reign of Emperor Wan Li (1573-1619) at the end of the Ming Dynasty. A large number of these wares were found in the Si Chang 1 wreck.

b. *Medium to low quality blue and white wares known as Swatow ware*
Swatow ware is named after the town on the Southeast coast of China, Chin Cheuw, in Guangdong province. Chinese ceramics in this category were dated from the Ming Dynasty, in the second half of thirteenth century, to the Qing Dynasty, the eighteenth century. This type of ware has been found throughout Southeast Asia and was found in the Samui, the Ko Kradat, and the Si Chang 1 wrecks as well as at the Ko Rin site.

c. *Celadon ware*
These ceramics were popular export goods from the Longquan kilns in Zhejiang province, South China, during the Yuan Dynasty. Celadon ware was found in abundance in the Rang Kwien wreck and some also in the Samui wreck.

1.3 Vietnamese ceramics or Annamese ware

Most of the Vietnamese ware is glazed stoneware; however, many types of ceramics originating from Vietnam can be categorized as follows:

a. *Brownish celadon glazed ceramic*
Hundreds of this type of Vietnamese ware, comprised of plates and bowls, were found in the Sattahip wreck. Colours of glaze range from brownish green to yellowish green. One can see the ring mark left on the inner bottom of these bowls when glaze was wiped off to prevent it from fusing with the glaze above it during the firing process.

b. *Under-glazed blue and white design on buff stoneware body*
This type of ceramic was found in abundance in the Rang Kwien wreck and some in the Si Chang 3 wreck.

    c. Buff-colored glazed ceramics

        This type was found in abundance in the Rang Kwien wreck.

  1.4 Pottery of unknown origin

        Fluted kendis were found in large numbers in the Si Chang 1 wreck and some were also salvaged from the Sattahip wreck and the Ko Rin site.

2. Metal

Artifacts made of metal include:

2.1 Lead

    Lead was found in the form of ingots. These ingots are of various shapes, the most common of which being a short cone. However, cylindrical and lime fruit-size, spherical ingots were also found. Ingots were discovered in abundance in the Pattaya, the Sattahip, and the Si Chang 1 and 3 wrecks. Ancient lead production sites were discovered in the Si-Sawat, Thong Pha Bhume, and Sagkhla-buri areas in Kanchanaburi province.[9] Lead ingots found at those sites and in the wrecks are similar in shape and size.

2.2 Iron

    Iron was imported both as a raw material and as finished products. Large cooking pans were found in the Rang Kwien wreck and knives were excavated from the Don Hai site. Heaps of smelt iron were located in the Pattaya wreck's cargo holds.

2.3 Chinese cash coins

    Thousand of coins weighing many tons were discovered in the Rang Kwien wreck. Many of them were fused together in lumps while many others had retained their original shape, indicating that they were once tied together with silk cords. The coins were cast from an alloy of copper/tin bronze and contain a high percentage of lead.[10] Each coin has a reign mark. The majority of the coins found in the Rang Kwien wreck were dated from the Song dynasty, and some were from the Tang, Yuan and some are similar to those of the Qing Dynasty. The fact that money was used as a means of exchange in the maritime trade is a proposed hypothesis. Given the fact that the sheer number of coins discovered is so enormous (quite apart from their value), and that from the thirteenth century to the reign of King Rama IV of Bangkok in the nineteenth century, the acceptable form of currency for maritime trade in Southeast Asia was Chinese cash coins, it is possible that the Rang Kwien vessel was carrying such coins for trading purposes.

Additional Archaeological Evidence

Another missing piece of our puzzle in that the sites are devoid of any evidence of the skeletons of the sailors or maritime merchants who must have died many hundred of years ago. Unlike today's ships, the junk, with less superstructure, had an open deck, with the result that when the vessel appeared to be doomed, the passengers would have been able to jump clear in time to save their lives. If individuals then failed to survive, their corpses would have been carried away by currents or eaten by sea creatures.

Food

A round-bottomed pot filled with eggs was salvaged from the Si Chang 3 wreck. A medium-sized four-eared storage jar containing fish products was found in the Si Chang 1 wreck. In the Pattaya wreck, a storage jar containing rice was also discovered and poultry bones were found in the Samui wreck.

In many wrecks, areca nuts and round-bottomed pots called palm-sugar pots were found—sugar is considered to have been a staple food for seafarers and also a trading commodity. Furthermore, a couple of bronze fish hooks were found in the Rang Kwien wreck and presumably the sailors used to fish during the voyage.

Kitchen utensils

Many round-bottomed earthenware cooking wares and wood charcoal stoves were found in all the wrecks and at their associated sites. Earthenware pottery which can shrink or expand while cooking over the fire, is brittle and easily damaged. Therefore, a good supply had to be carried in stock especially because of the added hazard of the rocking motion of the ship. Mortars, mixing bowls, and whetstones, which are utensils used in every Southeast Asian household, were also found in the wrecks.

Musical and Signaling Instruments

A bronze gong, a bell, and a tunning peg for string instruments were found in the Rang Kwien wreck. A pair of cymbals was found in the Samui wreck. The bronze gong and bell were presumably used as signaling instruments to communicate on board the vessel.

Jewelry

A pair of gold bracelets decorated with precious stones and made by an artisan in the early Ayutthaya period, as well as a straight jeweled hair pin and ivory ring were found in the Ramg Kwien wreck. A gold pendant decorated with rubies was found in the Sattahip wreck.

Games

Three chessmen were found in the Si Chang 1 wreck.

Miscellaneous

Excavation at the wreck sites uncovered many other items of daily use belonging to both sailors and merchants of the past, such as bronze key sets, musket rifles, and bronze lime jars.

Discussion and Conclusion

Underwater archaeological sites are considered to be one of the most important sources of information for the history of our nation and for that of humanity as a whole. The amount of information depends on the circumstances of recovered wrecks and objects: a wreck can reveal its own history and age, as well as the number of times, and where, it docked. We are able to study the lifestyles, technology, beliefs, means of transport, and especially the maritime trade of our forefathers by examining personal items such as clothing and jewels, cult icons, and items of everyday use, such as fishing tackle, storage containers and cooking utensils, food, weapons, and merchandise.

We can now comprehend the history of the maritime trade from archaeological evidence as given in the following summary:

Ships

There were two types of cargo junks sailing in the Southeast Asian sea between the fourteenth and the seventeenth centuries: the flat-bottomed junk and the keeled junk. The techniques and materials used in ship building indicate that these ships, which are not very large, were locally built Southeast Asian vessels and not real Chinese junks.

Merchandise

The artifacts revealed during the excavations, such as ivory tusks, leather pieces, lead ingots, sampan wood, Chinese ceramics, Vietnamese ceramics, Sangkhalok (Thai) wares, and iron cooking pans and utensils, are among the categories mentioned in the documentation records.

This material evidence from the Gulf of Siam provides a comprehensive, if not yet clear, knowledge of maritime trade in Southeast Asia from the fourteenth to the seventeenth centuries. Gaps occur in the records as only a few wrecks and sites have been discovered. The survey and excavation process has progressed slowly and with great difficulty, and entails risks to those involved in this environment so unfamiliar to man. Perhaps a more serious problem arises from the looting and destruction by treasure hunters who are stimulated by antique dealers, collectors, and interior decorators. The pieces which are most difficult to obtain command the highest prices on the antique market. Artifacts from archaeological sites both on land and underwater can now be found in hotel lobbies, well-appointed houses, antique shops, furniture shops, and gift shops. The smuggler approaches a site unscrupulously, and other artifacts and features without a high market value are intentionally destroyed in the plunder to ease the way to this ultimate prey, in many cases by means of explosives.

This kind of behavior must be discouraged. Mere possession of an antique item whereby the owner can show off his affluence is, in effect, an encouragement to the destruction of archaeological sites. At present, there are no wreck sites available in a suitable state for our successors to study. As an archaeologist who also works in the conservation field, the author would like to mention that wreck sites—as a source of cultural heritage—have a value which goes beyond the reconstruction of our history; in fact, the history of humanity is at stake. Although these wrecks were found in Thai territorial waters, the movable nature of the crafts themselves and the many places from which their cargo originated means that we can be certain neither of the nationalities of the owners and the crew on board, nor of their last port of call or destinations.

The public is now being made aware of the destruction of the natural environment. Many agencies are promoting and attempting to restore the balance of the natural ecological system. The coral reefs which represent another marine resource in critical state are at present under the protection of legislation and active agencies. The concept of the cultural environment has not yet been fully perceived. However, ethnical values should be promoted because archaeological artifacts and features are individually very significant. Time and tide cannot return, though they do leave us some evidence. If destroyed, that evidence will be impossible to replace.[11]

Notes

1. S. Promboon, *The Sino-Thai Relationship in the Tribute System from 1282 to 1858* (in Thai) (Bangkok, 1982).
2. P.C. Howitz, "Two Ancient Shipwrecks in the Gulf of Thailand," in *Journal of the Siam Society*, vol. 65, no. 2 (1977).
3. J.N. Green, personal communication (1990); and S. Prishanchit et al., *Borankhadi Si Khram I: Underwater Archaeology in Thailand* (1988).

4. V. Intakosi, "Rang Kwien and Samed Ngam Shipwrecks," in *SPAFA Digest*, vol. 4, no. 2 (Bangkok, 1983): pp. 3-34.

5. P.C. Howitz, *Two Ancient Shipwrecks*; J.N. Green and R. Harper, *The Excavation of the Pattaya Wrecksite and Survey of Three Other Sites* (Thailand, 1983).

6. J.N. Green, R. Harper, and S. Prishanchit, *The Excavation of the Ko Kradat Wreck Site, Thailand* (Western Australian Maritime, 1980).

7. J.N. Green, R. Harper, and V. Intakisi, "The Ko Si Chang 1 Shipwreck Excavation 1983-1985: A Progress Report" in *International Journal of Nautical Archaeology*, vol. 15, no. 2 (186): pp. 105-22.

8. S. Prishanchit et al., *Borankhadi Si Khram 2: Ceramics from the Gulf of Thailand* (1989).

9. P.C. Howitz, ed., "Discussion on the Ancient Shipwrecks Discovered in the Gulf of Thailand," in *Journal of Archaeology*, special issue (in Thai) (Bangkok: Silapakorn University, 1978).

10. K. Chambhosi, "Chinese Cash Coins from the Rang Kwien Shipwreck," in *Silpakorn Journal*, vol. 26, no. 2. (in Thai) (Bangkok: Fine Arts Department, 1982).

11. Further suggested reading: R. Brown, *The Ceramics of South-East Asia: Their Dating and Identification* (Singapore: Oxford University Press, 1977); N. Chandavit, *Chinese Ceramics from the Archaeological Sites in Thailand* (Bangkok: Special publication of the Fine Arts Department, 1986; Thailand: Fine Arts Department. 1987). *Sangkhalok Si-Satchanalai* (Bangkok: Amarin Printing Group [Special publication in Thai], 1987); D.L. Goldschmidt, *La porcelaine* (Fribourg: Office du Livre, 1978); J. Guy, *Ceramics Excavation Sites in South-East Asia: A Preliminary Gazetteer* (Research Centre for South-East Asian Ceramics and the Art Gallery of South Australia, University of Adelaide, 1987); M. Hadimuljono, *Some Notes on Thai Ceramics Discovered in South Sulawesi, Indonesia* (paper presented at the SPAFA Technical Workshop on Ceramics, Bangkok and Chiang Mai, Thailand, 1985); P.C. Howitz, *Ceramics from the Sea: Evidence from the Ko Kradat Shipwreck Excavated in 1979* (Bangkok: Silpakorn University, Faculty of Archaeology, 1979), and "The Joint Thai-Danish Project on Underwater Archaeology during 1975-1979," in *Thai-Danish Relations: 30 Cycles of Friendship* (Bangkok: The Royal Danish Embassy to Thailand, 1980), and Howitz (ed.), "Discussion on the Ancient Shipwrecks Discovered in the Gulf of Thailand," in *Journal of Archaeology* (Bangkok: Silpakorn University; Special issue in Thai); V. Intakosi, "Rang Kwien and Samed Ngam Shipwrecks," in *SPAFA Digest* , vol. 4, no.2 (Bangkok, 1983): pp. 3-34; C.L. Ketal and M. Van der Pijl (eds.), *The Ceramics Load of the Witteleeuw (1963)* (Amsterdam: Rijks Museum, 1982); S.T. Komolabutra, *B. II-Marine, nos. 50-138, 1684-1699 Archives Nationales de France* (original in French, translation in Thai) (Bangkok: Silpakorn University, Fine Arts Department, 1981); P. Y. K. Lam. et al. *A Ceramics Legacy of Asia's Maritime Trade* (S.E.A. Ceramic Society, West Malaysia Chapter, Oxford University Press, 1985); M. Medley, *The Chinese Potter: A Practical History of Chinese Ceramics* (New York: Oriental Ceramic Society of Hong Kong. 1979). *South-East Asian and Chinese Trade Pottery.* (Hong Kong); S. Prishanchit, *Relative Dating of Ceramics from the Ko Kradat Shipwreck* (Bangkok: Silpakorn University, Faculty of Archaeology. B.A. Research paper, 1980) (In Thai.), and "Recent Discoveries on Sangkhalok Wares," in *Silpakorn Journal* (Bangkok: Silpakorn University).

Chapter 11

THE BAN ON THE EXPORT OF CERTAIN ARTICLES FROM THE LEVANT TO THE MEDITERRANEAN PORTS DURING THE FIFTEENTH AND SIXTEENTH CENTURIES

Zeki Arikan

Trade with the Levant was of great importance for Europe in the Middle Ages.[1] It was also through the countries of the Levant that trade was conducted with India, Persia, and even China. The settlement of the Turks in Asia Minor coincided with a period of economic expansion. Asia Minor then became a very important staging post between the Orient and the Mediterranean. From that time on, the great trade route passing through the Mediterranean ports to the Mongol Empire experienced a phenomenal development. The Seljuk sultans of Asia Minor built great caravanserais along the roads at an average distance of twenty kilometres from each other.[2] They also concluded agreements with the Venetians and the Genoese for the transit of merchandise between Asia Minor and the Mediterranean. Venetian vessels began to put in at Antalya, which became an economic and commercial center in the region. According to Ibn Battuta, "it is one of the world's finest towns; and it is equal in size and splendor to the most magnificent, most populated and best-built cities. Each class of its inhabitants is entirely separated from the others."[3]

At that time, the commerce of Antalya was based mainly on trade between Egypt and Anatolia. From Egypt came spices, linen, and sugar.

In exchange, wood and pitch were exported for shipbuilding, together with slaves and all the products of the heartland of Asia Minor: wax, oak apples, tragacanth from the mountains of Pisidia, and alum, which was brought from Kütahya in a journey that took fifteen days.[4] The town certainly enjoyed direct contacts overland with India and Persia at the period.[5] Pepper and indigo were plentiful in the Antalya market as were fabrics of all sorts—cloth from Châlons, Narbonne, and Lombardy; and plush, which came from Cyprus.[6] The town was a major redistribution center where merchants from East and West met to exchange their goods.

The foundation of the Turkish principalities in Western Anatolia around the beginning of the fourteenth century created a new economic and commercial situation. The principality of Aydin, which occupied an important position in the valley of the Maeander, reached as far as the two great ports of Ephesus and Izmir. The ports of New Phocaea, Izmir, Ayasuluğ (Ephesus, Altoluogo), Scalanuova (Kušadasi), and Miletos (Balat) were of considerable economic importance for the Italian merchants. Among the wares most sought after by the traders from the West, mention must be made of alum, hemp, wax, horses, and cereals. Alum was in fact vital for the European textile industry.[7] Of the ports, the most important was Ayasuluğ with its outport of Scalanuova. Ayasuluğ was, consequently, an important market for slaves and horses, as well as a center for the production of cereals such as wheat, millet, barley, and rice. The town was also the principal outlet for the alum from Kütahya.[8] The usual imports were cloth, tin, amber, wine, and soap. The cloth sold in the market was from the factories of Narbonne, Perpignan, and Toulouse. No tarif was levied on imports except in the case of wine and soap.[9]

As Ottoman domination extended over the Balkans and Asia Minor during the fifteenth century, European ships reached the ports of the Levant. The Ottomans signed commercial agreements with the Genoese and the Venetians. The Aegean continued to be one of the busiest areas of the eastern Mediterranean. The Ottomans certainly continued to maintain the caravanserais built during the Seljuk period. The regions of Asia Minor and Rumelia were criss-crossed by a network of roads connecting Central Europe with the main centers of the Ottoman Empire.[10] The Ottomans established a well-organized internal market. According to the regulations (*kanunname*), the system of duties and taxes applied to the products sold on the markets was also well established.[11] However, Ottoman production of raw materials and manufactured goods did not fully meet the demand. The State was therefore required to import a number of commodities. Regulations issued by Mehmet II setting the customs duties for Istanbul and Galata list the following among other imported items: cloth, fabrics, cloth of gold, silks, material woven from flax and hemp, various spices, lynx, sable and marten pelts, leather from Russia, bow-grips, bows, shields, steel, tin, cinnabar, mercury, white lead, and so forth.[12] At the end of the fifteenth century, the Porte levied a customs duty of 4 percent on foreign merchants and a duty of 1 percent on Muslims.

In the first half of the sixteenth century, the conquests of Selim I and Suleyman the Magnificent made the Ottoman Empire a major economic as well as a great political power. The Ottomans were masters of all the Muslim Mediterranean ports (excluding those in Morocco) and also of the ports that provided outlets to the Red Sea and the Persian Gulf. They also controlled the Black Sea and the caravan routes from northern Iran.[13] It should be remembered that the Black Sea was completely closed to Europeans after the fall of Constantinople. The attempts of the Western powers to obtain access to the Black Sea always met with a Turkish refusal since much of the produce of the Black Sea coasts was earmarked for the supply of Istanbul. Around the year 1550, Rüstem Pasha, the Grand Vizier, asked Suleyman the Magnificent to ban all exports out of the Black Sea area since it was "the storeroom of Istanbul."[14]

The conquest of Egypt and the Arab countries enabled the Ottomans to control the ancient spice and pepper routes from the Indian Ocean through the Persian Gulf and the Red Sea. It is well known that the trade in spices and pepper played a very important role in international commerce. After the great discoveries, Europe obtained these precious commodities directly from Asia. The gradual rerouting of the trade from India and the Far East via the Cape of Good Hope completely upset the price of spices in Europe. But the latest research clearly shows that the opening-up of the Cape route did not put an immediate end to the Mediterranean trade in pepper.[15]

As Robert Mantran said,[16] age-old habits were not changed in a few years, ancient trade routes were not diverted from one day to the next, the contacts and staging-posts established by merchants, tradesmen, and their intermediaries were not destroyed. For much of the sixteenth century, a not inconsiderable quantity of goods from India continued to arrive at Basra and Suez.[17] The Mediterranean ports of the Ottoman Empire remained centers for the marshalling and redistribution of goods. The wars between the Ottomans and the Portuguese also helped the routing of the spice trade to the Mediterranean. Venice, which provided a great market for pepper, was only slightly affected by the discovery of the Cape route. In short, it is certain that the Near East remained open to the spice trade until the Dutch established complete control over the Indian Ocean.[18]

We may say that the Levant trade had not yet lost its importance as a result of the great discoveries, and the Ottoman Empire remained the principal customer for Western goods. The Italian merchant cities still accounted for the largest volume of maritime trade in the eastern Mediterranean. Venice preserved a very strong position even after the sixteenth century and was therefore able to retain most of its economic and commercial advantages. Among the principal goods imported by Venice, we may mention the following articles in particular: medium- and high-quality cloth, luxury fabrics, paper, window glass, and mirrors. From the Levant, the Venetian and European merchants imported leather, spices, wool, cotton, silk, wax, and alum. A major international trade developed in wheat, a matter to which we shall return. To the exports already mentioned should be added fruit and vegetables from the Gulf of Izmir.[19]

The political situation in the first half of the sixteenth century brought about a rapprochement between the Ottoman Empire and France. In the context of a political and military alliance between Suley- man the Magnificent and François I, the first "Capitulations" were nego- tiated in 1536 between Ibrahim Pasha, the Grand Vizier, and the ambassador, Jean de la Forêt, but they do not appear to have been rati- fied.[20] On the other hand, the 1569 Capitulations granted to the French laid the legal and economic basis for the French presence in the territory of the Ottoman Empire. The King's subjects would pay "the ordinary dues in accordance with the customary entry provisions" and would be placed under the protection of their ambassador and their consuls resid- ing in Istanbul, Alexandria, Tripoli in Syria, and Algiers. The French merchants obtained from the Sultan the right to pay only 3 percent cus- toms dues. French merchants began to supplant the Venetians in trade with the Ottoman Empire, particularly after the war of 1570-1573. French merchants held first place among the European traders—they brought cloth, paper, and ironmongery and returned home with leather, wool, silks, and spices. The Capitulations were renewed in 1581 and again in 1604.[21]

Following the French, the English soon won a large share of the international trade of the Levant. They obtained their own capitulations from the Sultan in 1580, and in 1581 set up the Levant Company which coordinated the activities of their merchants.[22] The trade of the Levant Company was built mainly on the sale of English cloth, particularly in Izmir and Aleppo. The Dutch joined the other two European nations at the beginning of the seventeenth century, obtaining capitulations in their turn and achieving remarkable commercial successes. It should be noted that Amsterdam became the main spice center towards the end of the seventeenth century, although the Dutch did not actually possess a Levant company. A Board of Governors was established in Amsterdam, consisting of six deputies and a clerk, all of whom were merchants. This

Board appointed the consuls for the various ports of the Levant.[23] It also determined how many convoys were required and their strength, and settled any disputes between the merchants.[24]

The above is an overview of the Ottoman Empire's commercial relations with the outside world and more specifically with the ports of the Mediterranean. It must, however, be emphasized that Western merchants had to take account of many export prohibitions decreed by the Ottoman administration. These measures were generally adopted for military reasons and were mostly aimed at protecting domestic consumption. These "strategic commodities"[25] included weapons, horses, gunpowder, gold, silver, copper, lead, iron, sulphur, hides, and leather as well as cereals, vegetables, wax, wool, and cotton. We frequently find edicts in the Registers of Important Affairs (Mühimme Defterleri) concerning prohibition of the export of the above-mentioned articles. The names of all such strategic commodities occasionally appear on a list with a reminder that their sale to "infidels" is prohibited; for example, the prohibited articles are enumerated on a page of a Register of Important Affairs: *Küffara verilmesi memnu olan meta bunlardir.*[26]

Concerning these articles, the first thing to note is the trade in wheat, which played a special part in commercial relations between the Ottoman Empire and the countries of the Mediterranean. Venice, Ragusa, and other Mediterranean States had purchased wheat in the Levant for centuries. Around the middle of the sixteenth century, demand for wheat suddenly became exceptional.[27] In fact, Western demand for wheat was part of an enormous flow of trade to and from the Levant, a flow which expanded and developed in the middle of the sixteenth century.[28] Wheat occupied a strategic position in the Levant trade as early as the end of the fourteenth century—one of the first actions of Bayazid I after annexing Antalya to the Ottoman State was to ban the export of wheat to the Mediterranean from that port.[29] It is known that, before the siege of Constantinople, Mehmet II had given permission to Venice to import wheat from the Levant on condition that it remained neutral.[30] Wheat thus became a political tool in the hands of the Ottoman sultans.

Around the middle of the sixteenth century, the Mediterranean world had a population of 60 to 70 million inhabitants.[31] Feeding the population became an increasing problem which was not easy to solve. The cities of Italy in general and Venice in particular were important consumers; this was why the West fetched its daily bread from the ports of the Levant. As a purchaser of grain and many other natural products, the West possessed in the eastern Mediterranean a store of commodities, the prices of which were kept low by the Ottoman Government by means of strict legislation.[32]

The Ottoman Empire possessed three large granaries: Egypt; the plains of Thessaly, Thrace, and Bulgaria; and the Romanian lands. The latter very soon ceased to supply the Mediterranean, their produce being monopolized by the enormous market of Istanbul.[33] The bulk of the produce of Asia Minor was likewise reserved for the consumption of Istanbul. Indeed, there were many ports along the coasts of the Black Sea, the Sea of Marmara, and the Aegean from which merchandise could be shipped to the capital.[34] Istanbul was in fact the first city of the Ottoman Empire in terms of population—according to the research carried out by Robert Mantran, the population of the capital of the Ottoman Empire at the end of the sixteenth century could be put at 700,000 inhabitants.[35] Its population and that of its suburbs in the following century could be estimated at 700,000 to 800,000, making it the first city of Europe and the Near East in the seventeenth century as it was in the sixteenth.[36] A problem was posed by the provisioning and upkeep of the strong force of janizaries, *spahis*, various military corps, and sailors, all paid and maintained by the State, who were present in Istanbul.[37] The city was thus a major center of consumption and so a large part of the production of the Ottoman Empire was directed to Istanbul for the maintenance of the capital's enormous population.

As we said above, Turkish wheat was in great demand around the middle of the sixteenth century. The first reason for its success was undoubtedly its low price, which was all the more important in that poor harvests rarely coincided from one end of the Mediterranean to the other.[38] Braudel speaks of a "boom" in Turkish wheat between 1548 and 1564 due to the crisis in Italian agricultural production.[39] Turkish wheat was transported throughout the western Mediterranean at that time. Shipments increased from all the western ports to the Levant.[40] And yet, the great days of Turkish wheat exports were brief.[41] After 1555, there were shortages of wheat at different times in Egypt, Istanbul, and Syria. Prices rose continually. In November that year there was no bread available for three days in Istanbul.[42] The first volume of the legal registers of Manisa contains a very important note on this shortage: "*Sene 963'de ifrat ile kaht olub Manisa'da bu – dayin kilesi yüz akça ve yalilarda yüz kirk akçaya satilub….*"[43]

Another note in the same register refers to a terrible drought: "*Sene 966 … kat'a yağmur yağmayub nisana değin âsümandan zemine bir katre akmayub tamam kuraklik olub yeryüzünde nebatat olmadi….*"[44]

In 1555, for the first time, the Ottoman Empire banned the export of Turkish wheat to the Mediterranean ports.[45] The Porte renewed this ban in 1560-1561 and even for some years after that. The imperial edicts published by Ahmet Refik ordered the local authorities to take vigorous measures to prevent purchases by Christians.[46] In addition to the documents published by Ahmet Refik, there are many orders in the Registers of Important Affairs on the same subject—it is repeatedly stated that the imperial will excludes all sales of wheat to infidels: "*Deryaya ve küffar-i haksara tereke verilmeğe asla riza-yi şerifim yoktur.*"[47]

The Turkish galleys seized many Venetian and Ragusan vessels, which returned home with no cargo. However, Western merchants who smuggled wheat received general support from the local authorities. The contraband wheat was brought out to the large western ships in caïques or *Karamürsel* where gold and silver solved many apparently intractable problems.[48] The export of grain also appeared to be closely linked to the structure of an agricultural economy under the Timar system.[49] Most of the sellers of wheat were Timariots or high officials. Rüstem Pasha, the Grand Vizier, who traded wheat illicitly, sold nearly 1,800 *carri* (or 36,000 hectoliters) to the Ragusans in 1550-1551, of which 600 came from his estates at Salonika.[50] The imperial edicts, which we have mentioned, invariably accused the Sanjakbeys, *kadis*, and Timariots of hoarding grain in order to engage in commercial speculation.[51]

As we have indicated, the export ban not only related to wheat but covered other articles and goods from the Levant. The main problem was the supply of the raw materials required by producers. Craft working was the almost universal system of production in the Ottoman Empire.[52] The corporations, which were strictly controlled by the central authorities, were both manufacturers and vendors. They practiced their trades within the framework of the regulations promulgated by the state. This was why the export of the raw materials essential to Ottoman industry and crafts was prohibited. Leather, hides, wool, and cotton were products in general use, being the raw materials of tanners, dyers, weavers, and others. The imperial candleworks in Istanbul, placed under the authority of an aga and an administrator, employed 100 workers. It produced all the candles required by the Sultan's mosques, the Sultans themselves, the old and new seraglios, and those of the viziers and notables.[53] The regulations for the supply of the candleworks (*mumhane*) at Üsküb are also worth mentioning. Here the income from the works was assigned to the *subaşi* and the law insisted that all producers of wax should sell their produce solely to the works in question.[54]

In 1571 (979), the Porte ordered the *lala* of Izmir to seize a Ragusan ship with a cargo of skins, cotton, and wax.[55] There are many documents dealing with the same subject, from which it is quite clear that all sorts of prohibited raw materials were sold to Western merchants in the ports of Izmir and their surroundings. The local authorities, such as the *kadi* and the administrator, were often responsible for combating fraudulent practices connected with the sale of goods.[56] The Ottoman Empire also wished to prevent the flight of gold and silver to Iran and India.[57] In addition, the sale of copper to Iran was entirely prohibited.[58]

In conclusion, we may say that in order to protect domestic demand or for military reasons, the Ottoman State did not permit Western merchants to export certain strategic articles. However, these prohibitions were not always absolute. Export licenses were granted when the production levels were high enough. What is certain is that smuggling was very active in the eastern Mediterranean.[59]

Notes

1. W. Heyd, *Yakin Doğu Ticaret Tarihi*, translated by E. Ziya Karal, vol. 1 (Ankara, 1975).
2. O. Turan, "Selçuk Kervansaraylari," *Belleten.* 39 (1946): pp. 471-503; see X. de Planhol, *De la plaine pamphylienne aux lacs psidiens. Nomadisme et vie paysanne* (Paris, 1958), p. 89.
3. *Voyages d'Ibn Battuta*, Arabic text accompanied by a translation by C. Defremery and B. R. Sanguinetti, vol. 2 (Paris, 1854), pp. 258-59.
4. Heyd, *Yakin Doğu Ticaret Tarihi*, p. 608.
5. de Planhol, *De la plaine pamphylienne*, p. 92.
6. Heyd, *Yakin Doğu Ticaret Tarihi*, p. 608.
7. S. Faroqhi, "Alum production and alum trade in the Ottoman Empire (c. 1560-1830)," *Wiener Zeitschrift für die Kunde des Morgenlandes*, no. 71 (1979): p. 154.
8. Heyd, *Yakin Doğu Ticaret Tarihi*, p. 605; F. B. Pegolotti, *Pratica della Mercatura*, edited by A. Evans (Cambridge, Mass., 1936), pp. 55-57; F. Thiriet, "Les relations entre la Crète et les émirats turcs d'Asie Mineure au XIVe siècle (c. 1348-1360)," *Actes du XIIe Congrès International d'Études Byzantines*, vol. 2 (Belgrade), pp. 213-21; E.A. Zachariadou, *Trade and Crusade: Venetian Crete and the Emirates of Menteshe and Aydin (1300-1415)* (Venice, 1983).
9. L. de Mas Latrie "Commerce d'Ephèse et de Milet au Moyen age," *Bibliothèque de l'École des Chartres*, vol. 25 (1864), p. 225.
10. C. Orhonlu, *Osmanli Imparatorluğu'nda Derbend Teşkilati* (Istanbul, 1967).
11. Ö.L. Barkan, "Quelques observations sur l'organisation économique et sociale des villes ottomanes des XVIe et XVIIe siècles," *Recueil de la Société Jean Bodin VII* (Brussels, 1955), pp. 289-311; S. Faroqhi, *Towns and Townsmen of Ottoman Anatolia. Trade, Crafts and Food Production in an Urban Setting, 1520-1650* (Cambridge University Press, 1984).
12. N. Beldiceanu, *Les Actes des premiers Sultans*, vol. 1 (Paris and The Hague, 1960), pp. 116-18.
13. R. Mantran, *L'Empire Ottoman du XVIe au XVIIIe siècle*, vol. 10 (London: Variorum Reprints, 1984), p. 169.
14. T. Gökbilgin, "Rüstem Paşa ve hakkindaki ithamlar," *Tarih Dergisi*, vols. 11-12 (1955), pp. 11-50.

15. F. Braudel, *La Méditerranée et le monde méditerranéen à l'époque de Philippe II* (Paris, 1966), p. 423; V. Magalhaes-Godinho, *L'Économie de l'Empire Portugais aux XVe et XVIe siècles* (Paris, 1969); S. Özbaran, "The Ottoman Turks and the Portuguese in the Persian Gulf, 1534-1581," *Journal of Asian History*, vol. 6 (1972): pp. 45-87; F. Lane, "The Mediterranean Spice Trade: Further Evidence of its Revival in the Sixteenth Century," in *Crisis and Change in the Venetian Economy in the 16th and 17th Centuries*, edited by in B. Pullan (London, 1968), pp. 47-59.

16. Mantran, *L'Empire Ottoman*, vol. 11, p. 221.

17. Mantran, *L'Empire Ottoman*, vol. 12, pp. 224-77.

18. Braudel, *Le Méditterranée et la monde méditerranéen*, p. 510.

19. D. Goffman, *Izmir and the Levantine World, 1550-1650* (University of Washington Press, 1990), pp. 10 and 20.

20. H. Inalcik, Imtiyazat, *Encyclopedia of Islam* (ii).

21. P. Masson, *Histoire du commerce français dans le Levant*, 2 vols (Paris, 1896-1911).

22. A.C. Wood, *A History of the Levant Company* (London, 1964); M.S. Kütükoğlu, *Osmanli - Ingiliz ticari münasebetleri* (Ankara, 1964).

23. N. Steengard, "Consuls and Nations in the Levant from 1570 to 1650," *Scandinavian Economic History Review*, vol. 15 (1967): pp. 13-55.

24. M. Devèze, *L'Europe et le monde à la fin du XVIIIe siècle* (Paris, 1970), pp. 64-65.

25. R. Mantran, ed., *Histoire de l'Empire Ottoman* (Paris), p. 222.

26. *Mühimme Defteri (MD)*. Başbakanlik Osmanli Arşivi, 66, p. 2. Küffara verilmesi memnu olan meta bunlardir: Tereke, barut, yarak, at, penbe, rişte-i penbe, kurşun, balmumu, sahtiyan, don yaği, gön, koyun derisi, zift.

27. L. Güçer, *Asirlarda Osmanli Imparatorlu—unda Hububat Meselesi ve Hububattan Alinan Vergiler, 16-17* (Istanbul, 1966); M. Aymard, *Maurice Aymard. Venise, Raguse et le commerce de blé pendant la seconde moitié du XVIe siècle* (Paris, 1966), p. 125.

28. Aymard, *Maurice Aymard*, p. 126.

29. H. Inalcik, "Osmanli Imparatorluğunun Kuruluş ve inkişafi, Devrinde Türkiye'nin Iktisadi Vaziyeti," *Belleten* 60 (1950): pp. 629-84.

30. H. Inalcik, *The Ottoman Empire. The Classical Age 1300-1600* (London, 1973), p. 134.

31. Braudel, *Le Méditerranée et la monde méditerranéen*, p. 361.

32. Aymard, *Maurice Aymard*, p. 50.

33. Braudel, Ibid.

34. R. Mantran, *Istanbul dans la seconde moitié du XVII siècle* (Paris, 1962), p. 487.

35. Mantran, *Istanbul dans la seconde moité*, p. 47.

36. Ibid.

37. Mantran, *Istanbul dans la seconde moité*, p. 403.

38. Aymard, *Maurice Aymard*, p. 50.

39. Braudel, *Le Méditerranée et la monde méditerranéen*, p. 535.

40. Aymard, *Venise*, p. 127; Goffman, *Izmir*, p. 37.

41. Braudel, *Le Méditerranée et la monde méditerranéen*, p. 536; Aymard, *Maurice Aymard*, p. 134.

42. Braudel, ibid.; Aymard, ibid.

43. Manisa Şer'iyye Sicilleri, *Manisa Müzesi*, vol. 1, p. 58.

44. Ibid.

45. Braudel, *Le Méditerranée et la monde méditerranéen*, p. 536.

46. A. Refik, *Onuncu Asr-i Hicride Istanbul Hayati (1495-1591)* (Istanbul, 1935); M.A. Cook, *Population Pressure in Rural Anatolia (1490-1600)* (London, 1972), pp. 1-5.

47. B.O. Arşivi, *MD-3*, pp. 4, 68, 135, 156, 161, and 175ff.

48. Braudel, *Le Méditerranée et la monde méditerranéen*, p. 536.

49. Aymard, *Maurice Aymard*, pp. 51-52.
50. Aymard, ibid.; 51; Gökbilgin, "*Rüstem Paşa.*"
51. Imdi emr-i şerifime muhalif küffar-i haksara tereke satan eğer sancakbeyleri ve eğer kadilar ve eğer zuama ve erbab-i timar ve gayrilardir her kim olursa olsun salb ü siyaset olunmak fermanim olub (B. Arşivi, *Ahkâm Defteri,* vol. 70, p. 645, quoted by Cook, *Population*, p. 5).
52. Mantran, *Istanbul dans la seconde moité*, p. 395.
53. Mantran, *Istanbul dans la seconde moité*, p. 408.
54. B. Cvetkova, *Vie économique de villes et ports balkaniques aux XVe et XVIe siècle* (Paris, 1970), p. 72.
55. B.O. Arşivi, *MD 10*, p. 223.
56. B.O. Arşivi, ibid.; p. 233; *MD 24*, p. 326.
57. B.O. Arşivi, *MD 3*, p. 448.
58. B.O. Arşivi, *MD 6*, p. 159.
59. R. Mantran, ed., *Histoire de L'Empire Ottoman* (Paris, 1989), p. 222.

Chapter 12

THE IMPACT OF THE MACAO-MANILA SILK TRADE FROM THE BEGINNINGS TO 1640

Rui D'Ávila Lourido

"Above there is heaven, on earth, Suzhou and Hangzhou." [1]

The Macao Maritime Trade Network

Between the fifteenth and the sixteenth centuries the Portuguese made contact with lands and peoples previously unknown to the Western World—areas which stretched from the Eastern coast of Africa, Arabia, India and China up to Japan and Korea, throughout the whole of Southeast Asia, from Malaysia to the Philippine Islands. The Portuguese empire attempted to control local oceanic space economically and politically from the Atlantic through the Indian Ocean to the Pacific Ocean.

China[2] was very important for Portuguese trade due to the various kinds of merchandise produced and the large quantities of silver consumed. The regions best known to the Portuguese were the flourishing mercantile regions of Liampó (Ningbo in the province of Zhejiang), Chincheo (this name was used by the Portuguese to designate the traders of Zhangzhou and the Quanzhou region of Amoy, in the province of Fujian[3]), and particularly Macao (Aomen in the district of Xiang Shan) in the province of Canton.

During the Spanish occupation of Portugal, conflicts arose among the Portuguese, Spaniards, and Chinese over the sharing of interests; at the same time the Dutch were fighting for control of the China Sea.

It is widely acknowledged that one of the factors which enhanced contact between European and Asian peoples, particularly the Chinese, was the exchange not only of goods but of knowledge, technology, and culture.

Main commodities

Chinese silk and Japanese and American silver were the main goods traded in Macao. A regional or long-distance circuit was used for their import and export to Japan (via Nagasaki), the Philippines (via Manila and then to Spanish America and Southeast Asia), India, and Europe (via Malacca-Goa). The Portuguese silk and silver trade was not isolated, but an integrated part of South China trade (ceramics and other precious goods), more specifically the trade of Canton and Macao. Goods arrived in Macao from the complex network of the trade routes of the Cape of Good Hope, the Red Sea, the Persian Gulf, and the Indian Ocean as well as those of Southeast Asia and America (via the Philippines).[4]

In general, the Asian trade was the main source of profit for Macao as well as for the Far East Portuguese trade network (Estado da Índia) when compared with the trade to Europe via the Cape of the Good Hope.[5] Macao's maritime trade was in competition with other European powers such as the Spanish in the Philippines, the Dutch in Formosa or in Batavia, and also with Asian powers such as the Chinese and the Japanese.[6]

The Macao and Estado da Índia trade network was in general terms a continuation of the earlier Muslim, Indian, Southeast Asia, Chinese, and Japanese trading network.[7] In the sixteenth and seventeenth centuries, the Portuguese maritime trading system was original in that it led to the creation of permanent settlements (populated with citizens of Portuguese origin, usually under military protection) throughout the vast area covered by their trade from Western Europe to Japan.[8] Macao was a crucial point of support for the Estado da Índia. It sought to be the exclusive intermediary for import and export trade between all Europe and China. The Macao-Manila-New Spain trade was one of the new maritime trade routes that connected European markets directly with Asian ones.[9]

Routes

There were four main trading routes from Manila: the most important of these connected the Philippines to New Spain; the second linked the Philippines to the Japanese market; the third the Malocan route linked Manila and Malacca; the last one led from the Philippines to Borneo, Siam, and Cambodia. Macao, on the other hand, was the center of three fundamental routes of Portuguese trade in the Far East. The Macao trade routes will now be described briefly.

The Macao-Japan Route

On 15 August 1549 the first formal Portuguese mission to Japan arrived in Kagoshima. This is considered to be the beginning of formal relations between the Estado da Índia and Japan.[10] The Portuguese royal monopoly on trade with Japan was established in 1550. The usual route from Estado da Índia for Japanese trade via Goa, Malacca, and China (Macao only after 1557) to Nagasaki. Until the Portuguese were expelled from Japan, the Macao-Japan route was the central and the most profitable part of their trade network. The historian António Bocarro wrote: "The voyages from the City of the Name of God [Macao] to Japan were the most important as we well know."[11]

The voyage from Macao to Japan was usually undertaken by four *pataxos*, which took about twelve days outward to Japan and ten days on the return trip. The bulk of the merchandise carried was pure Chinese silk, although Chinaware, wood, and other goods were also traded, mainly in exchange for silver, but also for copper and gold. In the 1630s, these voyages would bring in 65,000 taels to the royal treasury, excluding the copper profits, and one particular voyage brought in 10,000 taels.[12] In the period between 1585 and 1630, it is estimated that some 14,899 thousand taels of silver entered Macao, most of which was probably invested in Chinese goods which, in turn, were sold in Japan.[13]

In 1639, Japan issued a decree of expulsion, effectively limiting trade. Although traders from Macao continued to trade with Japan using Chinese agents and ships as intermediaries, the quantities were insignificant compared to previous volumes—one of the most profitable Macao trade routes was effectively closed.

The reaction of this enterprising community to such a dramatic situation, which was to be aggravated by the Dutch takeover of Malacca in 1641, was the intensification of the routes already connecting Macao to Southeast Asia: "Annually, in the city of Macao, navettas, junks, fragatas and small ships are sent to Tonquim, Quinam, Chiampa, Cambodia, Macassar, Solar, Timor and other places where trading is prosperous."[14]

The Macao-Malacca / Goa-Lisbon Route

The Macao-Malacca/Goa-Lisbon route was the one the Portuguese used to supply oriental products to Europe via the Cape of Good Hope. It was the official route between the Estado da Índia, with its headquarters in Goa, and Lisbon. It was used to transport the administrative, political, and military staff of Estado da Índia to the Orient. Traders, merchandise, and mail from Europe, Africa, and Japan circulated along the Macao-Goa-Lisbon route. The political feature of this route was underlined by the persistence of royal support even when it was no longer profitable in economic terms. It suffered devastating attacks by European powers competing in the Eastern and Far Eastern markets. Thus, the conquest of Malacca by the Dutch in 1641 dealt an irreparable blow to the safety of the Macao and Goa links, as it meant that the Dutch had replaced Portuguese authority along the sea routes between the Indian and Pacific Oceans.

Raw silk was the preferred merchandise exported from Macao to Goa. Between 1580 and 1590 alone, some 15 tons, worth 240,000 taels, were transported. The major import to Macao was silver; between 1585 and 1591 some 900,000 taels of American silver arrived in the city via the Cape of Good Hope. Other goods were also imported, including spices (mainly pepper), ebony, ivory, and sandalwood.

The Macao-Manila Route

In the context of the Macao-Manila route, we shall describe the frequency, fares and agents, kinds of sales contracts, rules governing the shipment of goods, and sailing regulations. Another important element is the smuggling trade which was carried on along this route, mostly by Portuguese and Chinese traders.

When analyzing the sea traffic between Macao and Manila, which totaled about eighty ships (seventy-seven ships have been documented between 1580 and 1642) from Macao, the first point to note is its irregularity (bearing in mind economic and political military constraints). The traffic can be subdivided into three distinct periods, each of some twenty years.[15]

A feature of the first period, between 1580 and 1600, is the spasmodic nature of the arrivals, i.e., one or two ships per year. During this period, only eight ships made the journey from Macao to Manila: there were two ships in 1580, one in 1582, one in 1583, and once again two ships in 1584 and 1588.[16] These twenty years can therefore be defined as a preliminary period.

In the second period, from 1601 to 1621, there were twenty-three ships—almost a threefold increase in relation to the previous period. Most of this increase came towards the end of the period, but nevertheless this can be considered to have been the period of growth and development. In 1601 there was one vessel, followed by a period of two years without any arrivals from Macao. From 1604 to 1606, respectively five, two, and one vessel entered Manila. Following a three-year gap, one vessel arrived in 1609 and another in 1610. In 1612, it is difficult to determine the origin of the seven Portuguese ships recorded by the Manila customs; however, it would seem that six came from Macao and one from Goa. In 1620, another five ships from Macao were recorded, but only one vessel sailed from Macao to Manila in 1621.

The third period from 1622 to 1642 presents a certain homogeneity and continuity, as in the fifteen years from 1627 to 1642 there was an average of three boats per year, although no arrival was recorded in 1634. The total number of forty-six boats represents a 50 percent increase in comparison with the 1601-1621 period. This period can therefore be regarded as one of expansion and the peak of the trade route between Macao and Manila (in terms of the traffic between the sixteenth and eighteenth centuries), ending suddenly with the official recognition of the new Portuguese King—João VI—in 1642 in Macao.

1627 and 1630 were the years that saw the greatest number of ships (six) sailing from Macao to Manila.[17] In 1628, 1629, and 1641, two ships came to Manila each year. The number of ships increased once again to three in 1631, 1633, and from 1637 to 1640 respectively. It rose to four in 1632 and 1635. The last ship in this period arrived in 1642. A full thirty years would pass before the arrival of a boat (pataxo) from Macao recorded once again in Manila, in 1672.

Periodicity

Before the invention of the steamship, navigation between China and Manila depended on the monsoons. There was therefore a period which was considered to be more favorable for the trip to Manila and back. The best period to leave the coast of China was at the time of the new moon in March; the ships returned from Manila at the end of May or June, before the typhoons season.[18]

According to António Morga and official Portuguese documents, for example, a certain Lopo de Carvalho requested reduction of his debt after one of his ships sank on a journey to Manila; the request was refused, although he said "that the voyage will be sold only to whom will navigate in the ordinary monsoons."[19] In this document it is stated that a license for a trip to Manila corresponded to each of the monsoons, but the owner of the license could send as many ships as he liked.

The intensity of the maritime traffic originating from the coasts of China can be classified by comparing a large number of documents.[20] The month when the largest number of ships arrived in Manila from China varied according to the period under observation. Between 1577 and 1644, some 1088 ships arrived, mostly in the months of May and June. Nevertheless ships continued to arrive throughout the rest of the year. From 1607 to 1645, January was the first month when ships arrived in Manila. Most of the ships arrived before July, but there were also one or two arrivals in November and even December.

From 1607 to 1610, of the 160 ships which called at Manila, the majority arrived in June, followed by May (with an average of 40 percent fewer ships) and March. In the years 1611-1612 and 1620, ninety-five ships were recorded; February registered the greatest number of arrivals each year. From 1627 to 1630, there were more arrivals in June, with more than twenty ships compared to an annual total of seventy-three. Between 1627 and 1635, 171 ships were counted, and June registered the greatest number of arrivals (around twenty), while January was the second busiest month. Between 1636 and 1640, May, followed by June, was the busiest month, with 154 ships entering the port of Manila each year. Between 1641 and 1644, eighty-six ships were registered; most of these entered the port of Manila between January and March, but they continued to arrive with a certain frequency during the following months up to July.

We may thus conclude that trade between Macao-Manila was conducted on an annual basis, though intermittently. Often the link was not officially established—illicit trade also took place more or less intensively, but did not always observe the cycle of the monsoons. When the Macao-Manila trade was officially authorized, the authorities of the Portuguese State of India laid down regulations specifying the need to observe the favorable period of the monsoons, "because the success of the voyages from Japan and Manila normally involves the ships with which they sailed from China to those parts at the beginning of the monsoons."[21]

Regulations Governing the Macao-Manila Voyage

The opening of China to overseas trade placed the trading community of Macao in an unfavorable position by reducing its importance as an intermediary between China, Japan, Manila, and the rest of Southeast Asia. The merchants reacted to this challenge in two ways: first, they continued their clandestine voyages to Manila, either using ships and Chinese contacts that sailed directly to the archipelago, also known as Luções,[22] or via indirect routes (Japan or regions in Southeast Asia); second, they intensified the pressure to have the Macao-Manila route reopened and regulated.

The intensification of trade along the routes from Macao to "Solor, Timor, Macassar, Cochinchina and other parts of that coast"[23] reduced the revenue of Malacca as the profits that traditionally went to it were then absorbed by Macao.[24] The clandestine trade that linked Macao to Manila damaged the interests of merchants and of the Spanish pressure group connected to the Seville-New Spain route.[25] When the Macao traders supplied silk to the American market via the Philippines, the Spain silk trade from Seville to America and to the Philippines declined. Thanks to that trade, Macao increased the amount of American silver sent to China via the Philippines. This also increased the price of silk sold by the Portuguese in Manila. Goa revenues also decreased with the reduction of the quantity of silk sent to Europe via the Philippines. All of these factors contributed to making the Indian regional authorities decide to legalize the Macao-Manila route and make it official as the only way of supervising it and regulating its trade by making of it a royal monopoly. Thus the Viceroy Count of Linhares, after referring to these facts, adds that this legalization, according to his understanding, eliminates the rivalry between Macao and Malacca along the Southeast Asian routes with the aim of reaching Manila.[26] In a letter dated 4 May 1523, Viceroy Count Admiral D. Fernando da Gama ordered that all profits from the Macao-Manila route be directed to the royal treasury.[27] Thus emerged new laws and judicial rights, such as contracts and regulations governing navigation between Macao and Manila. The Treasury Council defined regulations concerning voyages and supervised their implementation (either through a Royal Treasury monopoly or under a private regime) according to the general principles set out in the royal letters. When, on 16 November 1629 the Council decided to move for a concession system to private merchants, it justified its decision by stating "that it would be more profitable to sell the voyage with this system, than to do so at the expense of the Crown."[28]

The Treasury Council (consisting of the Viceroy, various ministers, and deputies of the Estado da Índia), after publicly announcing the sale and having respected the legal period of time stipulated by the regime (for the conditions of purchase), could sell the Macao-Manila voyage, either singly, or for one or three successive years (for a sum of 30,000 xerafins per annum in the 1620s and 1630s), or together with the voyage Macao-Japan (for 70,000 xerafins).

The obligations stipulated by the regime required that a minimum number of ships and voyages should be made during the period of concession. The reason for this was that the profits from this voyage allowed the Royal Treasury and the private merchants to finance their projects. Thus the 1629 contract stipulated, for the owner for three years of voyages between Macao and Manila and between Macao and Japan, a minimum of nine ships to Manila (three per year) and thirteen to Japan. The other obligations under the contract were that, on each voyage from Japan, 1200 picks of copper should be transported (the royal monopoly); that 50,000 xerafins in cash should be paid in advance to the treasurer of Goa; that the warrantors should be wholly responsible; that 30,000 patacas should be paid to reimburse the providos;[29] that the registers and accounting books should be submitted to the Provedor Mor;[30] and that goods should be identified and kept in storehouses reserved for the purpose.

Under the regime, the main benefit for the owner of Macao-Manila and Macao-Japan navigation rights was a monopoly of these routes: "No one may send goods to or go to Japan or Manila during the period of this contract without a licence from Lopo Sarmento de Carvalho."[31] The owner could thus handle freight for other traders also wishing to send goods to Manila or Japan. He enjoyed the right of compensation in case of shipwreck; the possibility of undertaking these voyages personally or through his administrators; and finally, the possibility of keeping and taking advantage of all profits derived from the voyages and the number of ships that he intended to put to sea (under the obligation of payment established in the contract). These conditions usually made it possible for the owner to become wealthy following a single voyage. Manoel Ramos, on behalf of the Estado da Índia treasury, was appointed administrator of the voyages to Japan and Manila. In 1629 he received 500 taels less than the Capitão Mor (who received 2,000 silver taels of reales).[32]

In 1637 the royal monopoly on the Macao-Manila route was established by a new regime. Direct private trade with Manila was forbidden; private traders were allowed to carry their goods only in a small royal ship, to avoid rivalry with the Seville route trade. Lourenço Liz Velho, a Macao citizen, was appointed Capitão Mor of the Macao-Manila route, and also given the functions of *feitor* (factor). It was laid down that he should not be involved in any trade but would receive a salary of a thousand patacas and two patacas per day as living expenses; the clerk or secretary would receive 400 patacas.[33]

The rules also determined what was to be done with the profits from the voyages, which were usually addressed to the Royal Treasury and were now reserved for the building of new ships and financing the Goa shipyard.[34] According to the diary of the Third Count of Linhares,[35] the Treasury Council, at its meeting in 1629 to sell the rights to the voyages to Japan and Manila, gave first preference to Macao, whose representative, however, refused to buy the rights as he did not agree with the terms. The rights were then sold to a wealthy shipowner and nobleman living in Macao, Lopo Sarmento Carvalho.

The laws and regulations with regard to the Macao and other Estado da Índia routes reflected the Portuguese administration's conservative view regarding mercantile innovation. In contrast, Holland and England had, by this time, already laid the foundations for a precapitalist economic system, which then overtook the debilitated Portuguese and Spanish economic and colonial system.

Each merchant was considered to be one soldier fewer by the central and local Portuguese administration of Estado da Índia and Crown staff. Official Crown policy preferred soldiers to merchants and therefore sought to prevent public officers and soldiers from participating in private trade. The documentation reflects these conflicts and the negative effect of these orientations. The maritime trade to Manila was so profitable that the Portuguese (traders, officers, soldiers, clergymen, and sailors) continued to trade, even when it was forbidden; they used clandestine Chinese ships and other ports of departure. In 1592 the Portuguese authorities ruled that any person sailing from China to India (merchants included) should not disembark before arriving at the port of Goa in order to ensure that there were enough men on board to defend the vessels in case of danger.[36]

Another aspect of the anti-trade mentality of the Portuguese administration, was the discrimination against wealthy traders (possessing more than 50,000 xerafins) who were mainly New Christians (meaning Jews). Bocarro, the official chronicler, mentions that the wealthy Portuguese traders did not feel free to trade in Goa, fearing that they (or their money) might be called on to serve the King or that the Inquisition might interfere with their business and habits.[37] The Spaniards in Manila were in a similar situation; all Spanish soldiers were strictly forbidden to trade with America (mainly with Acapulco).[38]

Regulations Regarding the Shipment of Goods

On 4 May 1635 the Viceroy Count de Linhares wrote to Goa to the administrator of the voyages from Japan to Manila, instructing that sailors should be hired in sufficient numbers and that nothing be transported on deck or in the cabins, other than clothes, and everything should be in the right place, because carrying goods on deck was the cause of many shipwrecks.[39]

These measures were meant to rectify common profit-driven, but unsafe, practices such as the overloading of ships and the use of areas not intended for transport as well as the reduction of the number of crewmen to increase profits by transporting more goods in empty cabins—this obviously made sailing the ship more difficult and increased the risk of shipwreck in case of bad atmospheric or maritime conditions. Further regulations (Regimento) were laid down in 1637 concerning the Macao-Manila route. Romão de Lemos was ordered to ensure that crews did not transport larger quantities of goods than allowed by the regulations and that goods were not transported in the wrong places.[40] The Regimento also stipulated a monetary compensation of 50 patacas[41] for officers who did not break the rules by loading goods in the cabins.[42]

From these instructions it can be deduced that on journeys from Macao to Manila, over which the Royal *fazenda* ruled, the same abuses as on the other maritime routes were being committed. Some owners even modified the interior compartments of their ships and also filled the deck with goods, thus threatening the stability of the ship and restricting the crew's mobility.[43] The penalty for transgressing the regulations regarding the season was the loss of the right to any compensation in case of damage or loss.[44]

Taxes

The Macao-Manila route and its silk trade was a source of profit not only for the traders themselves, but also for the Macao and Manila customs in the form of taxes. The Chinese authorities also imposed various types of taxes on the Portuguese and other foreign vessels whether they arrived in Macao or in Guangzhou. Two kinds of taxes were levied on the Portuguese, a trade tax on ships, and rent for the right to live in the territory of Macao.

Foreign and private trade with South China, particularly with the Fujian province, was officially allowed in 1567 following lengthy negotiations between the Chinese authorities (imperial and regional). Until 1567 only official tribute trade was allowed in China, Macao being the only exception. The Chinese demand for silver was clearly, as mentioned earlier, the reason for Chinese acceptance of Portuguese trade along the South China Coast in a report of 1535 from the Cantonese Governor, Bu zheng shi, called Lin Fu.[45]

Customs duties were the responsibility of the Department of Foreign Commercial Ships, or Shi Bo Si, which the Chinese authorities transferred to Macao in 1535. The method of calculating these taxes changed over this period. Between 1535 and 1571, the Chou Fen method was used (taxes being worked out on a percentage basis, 20 percent over the value of the goods), then in 1571 the Zhang Chou method was adopted (taxes were worked out according to the tonnage of the ships). The reason for this change was that there was some difficulty in calculating the specific value of each of the goods.[46]

These customs duties were not applied equally to all foreign ships; the Portuguese in fact received privileged treatment in relation to other European and even other Asian ships. Portuguese ships, up to 200 tons, were classified in two categories depending on whether it was their first voyage to China or not. The tax on the first voyage was 1,800 taels of silver. For all subsequent voyages, Portuguese ships had to pay only 600 taels of silver. Other foreign ships, independent of the number of trips made to China, had to pay a tax of 5,400 taels of silver. Portuguese ships thus (except for their first voyage) paid one-ninth of what other foreign ships paid.

Various Chinese sources mention the customs duties charged in Macao and the manner in which they were charged.[47] On the arrival of foreign ships in Macao, the Mandarin in charge would inform the district of Xiang shan in order to receive instructions from Bu zheng shi and from Hai Dao Fu shi (Admiral of the Command Station of Guandong Province). The Shi Bo Si and the Chief of the District would send officials to the ship in order to measure it and thus establish the tax according to the regulations. The ship would then be registered and the money handed over to the Chinese authorities.

There were two other ways in which Portuguese ships were privileged: first, the military ships which escorted Portuguese vessels paid no taxes; and second, a Portuguese ship involved in an accident would be rescued by the Chinese without payment being asked, whereas other foreign ships in such situations would be charged by the rescue service. Commerce with Portugal was therefore clearly favored—there were considerable advantages for the transport of goods in Portuguese ships.

Zhang Ru Lin and Yin Guang Ren (the authors of *Monograph of Macao Ao Men Ji Lue*) tell us that the *fan bo* (smaller than ocean-going ships) were authorized to sail in Chinese waters, classified as *xiang*. Twenty of these ships were granted licenses by the Chinese maritime authorities. These authors also mention that over the next twenty years, disasters at sea reduced the number of ships by half.[48]

Other Macao Taxes

The City of Macao, through its Council, charged half a percent on the goods entering the city. In 1606 the Portuguese Viceroy, Bishop D. Pedro de Castilho, wrote to his king about the tax of half a percent requested by the inhabitants of the city of Macao in China in order to strengthen the walls of the city and pay for a captain.[49] On 10 January 1607 the king gave his assent.[50]

In response to attacks from the Dutch and English navies, the Senate of Macao raised the taxes on goods aboard foreign ships, according to their quality, from 1 percent on lower quality goods, 1.5 percent on those of medium quality, and 2 percent on high quality goods.[51] In 1623 Macao customs duties rose to 10 percent for the fortification of the city.[52]

According to the representatives of Macao in Goa,[53] in 1623, the Macao City Council's expenses were as follows: 10 percent for payment of taxes to the Chinese customs, another 10 percent to pay the Capitão Mor of the Macao-Japan voyage, and 6 to 7 percent for ordinary expenses.[54]

Manila Taxes

The Manila customs also levied different types of duties in the form of the *almojarifazgo* (maritime trade taxes) which generally can be divided into a relatively low tax and another relatively high one. From 1610 onwards there was a tax of 3 percent on all commerce originating from the Indian Ocean and Japan and a tax of 6 percent on Chinese commerce.[55] These various taxes, however, were not very significant in relation to the revenues. On a long-term basis, they reflected essentially a political will to support and favor trade with certain regions, and to make trade more difficult or even discourage it with others; in other words, it was an attempt to control the predominance of the Chinese in the economic activities of Manila. In Manila, between 1630 and 1640, ships arriving from Macao would pay different taxes: if private, they paid 6 percent; if royal, they paid 14 percent, including transport charges.[56]

The *pancada*[57] was the common contract used in the city of Manila. This consisted of a system of evaluation of cargo in global terms, of its sale and purchase in bulk by the Spanish merchants, and of silk and other goods transported by junks from the various ports of South China. The price of Chinese merchandise varied annually, depending on the quantity and quality and on variations in the flow of silver to China. In fact, the merchants from Macao protested at the inflation of the price of silk in Canton and Macao, due to the vast amount of silver that reached China with Chinese merchants (from Fujian Province). The Portuguese could only react by accepting the purchase at the market price and selling the goods, or refusing it and returning it to Macao, a very expensive alternative. However, the Macao merchants managed to carry on a very profitable trade with Manila. The *pancada* system was not new to Portuguese merchants; it was also applied by the leaders of the local merchants in Japan when the silk was bought from the Portuguese merchants, after which the Japanese would redistribute it for resale.[58]

The profits derived from Portuguese commerce along the Macao-Manila route can be estimated by examining the *almojarifazgo* taxes in

Table 12.1   Annual average value, in pesos, charged by the customs of Manila and the percentage of the total amount of income obtained.

Date	MACAO		China		Japan		India		Other		Total	
	Avg	%	Avg	%	Avg	%	Avg	%	Avg	%	Avg	%
1586 / 1590	1,159.0	8.66	3,750.0	28.02					8,474.0	63.32	13,383.0	100
1591 / 1595			22,065.0	61.00	295.0	0.80			13,795.5	38.20	36,155.5	100
1596 / 1600			24,155.5	56.04	258.5	0.60	861.0	1.99	17,829.5	41.37	43,104.5	100
1601 / 1605	200.0	0.50	30,104.2	70.03	572.2	1.33			12,106.5	28.14	42,982.9	100
1606 / 1610	8.6	0.01	46,382.6	78.52	46.0	0.08			12,629.0	21.39	59,066.0	100
1611 / 1615	50.0	0.10	64,432.0	91.40			396.5	0.50	5,476.5	8.00	70,355.0	100
1616 / 1620	6,798.0	13.20	31,045.0	60.30	353.0	0.60	2,463.0	4.79	10,678.0	21.11	51,337.0	100
1626 / 1630	7,110.5	27.65	11,513.0	44.76	31.0	0.11	1,813.2	7.10	5,252.2	20.40	25,720.0	100
1631 / 1635	9,327.6	22.10	24,951.2	59.00	17.4	0.04	1,281.0	3.04	6,611.8	15.82	42,194.0	100
1636 / 1640	3,556.8	11.46	23,927.0	77.10			898.4	2.90	2,654.8	8.54	31,037.0	100
1641 / 1642	15,735.5	50.80	13,194.5	41.98					2,495.5	7.94	31,425.0	100
1643 / 1645	6,294.0	28.50	12,305.4	55.40			677.8	3.10	2,797.8	13.00	22,075.0	100

Source: P. Chaunu, *Les Philippines et le Pacifique des Ibériques* (XVIe, XVIIe, XVIIIe siècles), Introduction méthodologique et indices d' activité, pp. 200-6.

Manila and the arrival of ships from Macao, China, India, and Japan. In order to obtain a fairly homogenous unity, the annual average values of five countries in five years (starting from the global values of the *almojarifazgo*) are used (see Table 12.1).

By comparing the information in Table 12.1 with data referring to the number of ships reaching the port of Manila from Macao in the same period (see Table 12.2 and Figures 12.1-12.6), the main features of the three periods suggested can be verified.

Table 12.2   Number of ships traveling from Macao to Manila between 1580 and 1642.

YEARS	SHIPS	YEARS	SHIPS	YEARS	SHIPS
1580	2	1601	1	1622	0
1581	0	1602	0	1623	0
1582	1	1603	0	1624	0
1583	1	1604	5	1625	0
1584	2	1605	2	1626	0
1585	0	1606	1	1627	6
1586	0	1607	0	1628	2
1587	0	1608	0	1629	2
1588	2	1609	1	1630	6
1589	0	1610	1	1631	3
1590	0	1611	0	1632	4
1591	0	1612	6-7	1633	3
1592	0	1613	0	1634	0
1593	0	1614	0	1635	4
1594	0	1615	0	1636	1
1595	0	1616	0	1637	3
1596	0	1617	0	1638	3
1597	0	1618	0	1639	3
1598	0	1619	0	1640	3
1599	0	1620	5	1641	2
1600	0	1621	1	1642	1

Figure 12.1   Origin and number of ships arriving at the port of Manila.

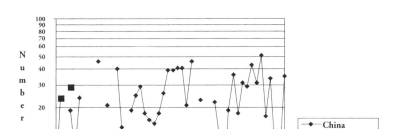

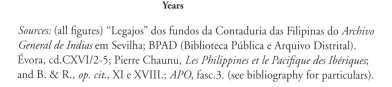

Sources: (all figures) "Legajos" dos fundos da Contaduria das Filipinas do *Archivo General de Indias* em Sevilha; BPAD (Biblioteca Pública e Arquivo Distrital). Évora, cd.CXVI/2-5; Pierre Chaunu, *Les Philippines et le Pacifique des Ibériques*, and B. & R., *op. cit.*, XI e XVIII.; *APO*, fasc.3. (see bibliography for particulars).

Figure 12.2   Number of ships arriving in Manila from China
(apart from Macao).

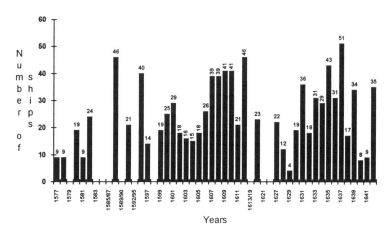

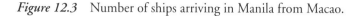

Figure 12.3 Number of ships arriving in Manila from Macao.

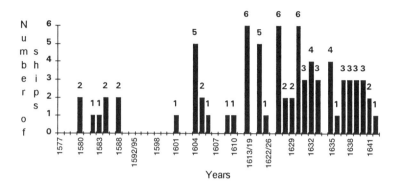

Figure 12.4 Number of ships arriving in Manila from Japan.

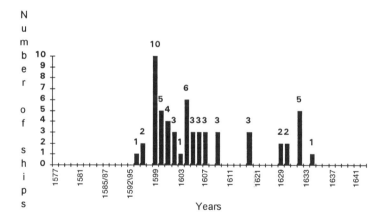

Figure 12.5 Number of ships arriving in Manila from India.

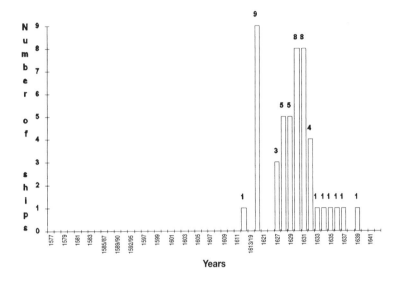

Figure 12.6 Number of ships arriving in Manila from other ports of the Philippines and unidentified places.

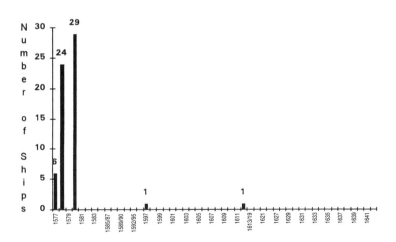

The initial period (1580-1600) recorded not only the lowest number of ships (eight), but compared with the other periods, cargo also reveals an inferior global value. The periods in which the total amount of cargo transported from Macao was the least valuable were the years 1606-1610, 1611-1615, and 1601-1605, in which they paid an annual average of 8.6 pesos, 50 pesos, and 200 pesos respectively. During the period of development (1601-1621), there was a 255 percent increase in the number of ships (twenty-three), and a significant increase in the global value of transported goods (increasing from an annual average of 8.6 pesos charged by the *almojarifazgo* in 1606-1610 to 6,798 pesos during the period 1616-1620). The period of expansion (1622-1642), with an increase of 501 percent in the number of ships (forty-six), also reached a peak in the global value of the cargo transported in boats from Macao which were taxed in Manila. The annual average in 1641-1642 is the highest with a value of 15,735.5 pesos or 50 percent of the total charged by the customs of all the ships that entered Manila. A rather curious point (also based on the accounts of the *almojarifazgo*) is that in those two years, only three ships arrived, while in 1627 and 1630, six ships arrived from Macao, the highest number of ships until the end of the eighteenth century.

Trade in China, Macao and Manila, Japan and India

Data has been gathered on Chinese, Japanese, and Indian trade with the aim of identifying other alternative routes used by the Portuguese merchants of Macao to ensure the continuity of their trade (frequently in a clandestine manner).

Trade with China and the Philippines gradually developed as the Ming dynasty adopted a more open approach to maritime commerce with foreigners. During the reigns of Jia Jing (1522-1567) and Mu Zong (1567), Japanese pirates plagued the Chinese coasts, making maritime trade difficult. Thus, the mandarin in charge of the province of Fujian (Du Ze-Min) requested that his region be opened to maritime trade with eastern and western countries. At this time Chinese traders could travel freely overseas if they were issued a proper license.[59] In 1589, eighty-eight licenses and later 110 licenses were granted. In 1597, 137 licenses were requested for ships from the Zhangzhou (Fujian, Chincheo) region. Half of the licenses were given for trade in the Eastern Ocean and the other half for trade in the Western Ocean, with a different tax being charged for each region for the registration of the licenses.[60] The clandestine trade flourished with its new-found freedom. The port of Moon in Zhangzhou began to trade directly with the island of Luzon, thereby replacing the much longer Guangzhou to Luzon route, via Champa (Viet Nam) and Borneo. Although the Portuguese tried to monopolize and secure exclusive commercial relations with Macao and Manila, direct trade between the Chinese and the Philippines continued and gained in importance while Portuguese trade with Manila declined.

The enormous Chinese market, with which the Portuguese were in contact through the flourishing mercantile life of the Canton (Guangdong), Chincheo (Fujian), and Liampó region (Ningpo-Zhejiang), impressed them so much that many authors in those times were convinced that, with free access to Chinese commerce, Portugal could renounce all its other markets. Here are two illustrations: "If Chinese trade is open to us, Portugal could renounce all other markets because Chinese goods are highly appreciated in all Asia and all over the world;"[61] "If the Portuguese could have free access to Chinese trade, Macao could survive and grow without any other voyages to Japan and Manila, because the Chinese Kingdom is such that their vassals may survive without foreign trade, and the Macao inhabitants are considered by the Chinese authorities as Chinese vassals (dependents)."[62]

A similar view, believing that trade with Asia was strategically more important than trade with America, is illustrated by a document entitled "Dissertation to prove that the East Indies were more important than the West Indies, because of its commerce, and connected with this we unveil the origin of the contemporary decadence of Eastern trade, and the Spanish state of poverty."[63]

Due to its geographical position, Macao was forced to buy its goods in Canton: "Within the limits of the city no products or textiles are produced and all that is necessary for these voyages [of trade with Southeast Asia, Japan, and India] has to be brought from Canton in junks and other ships;" the food supply also depended on the goodwill of the Chinese.[64]

The Macao merchants would choose their own representatives to negotiate and establish contacts in Canton. The presence of Portuguese traders in Canton was occasionally used by the Chinese authorities, in the event of a dispute between the two nationalities, to force Macao to obey and execute their instructions. In 1621, for example, the Chinese mandarins threatened to capture the Portuguese who were in Canton and to keep their silver in order to make them destroy the houses built by the Jesuits in the "Ilha Verde."[65]

Fairs and Merchants

The most prestigious silk came from Central China, especially from Jiangsu and Zhejiang. External demand (particularly from Europeans) for Chinese silk led to the rapid economic development of the Chinese regions where silk was produced and marketed (Canton and Fujian Provinces). The Chinese proverb quoted on the title page of the present text: "Above there is heaven, on earth, Suzhou and Hangzhou," reflects this prosperity. Chuan Hansheng mentioned the important part played by American demand for silk in later Ming and Qing times in the development of the cities (in the Jiangsu and Zhejiang Provinces) mentioned in the proverb above.[66] The biennial fairs in Canton (December/January and May/June) could last several weeks or months. Various textiles, Chinaware, and other products were also bought by Portuguese traders at these fairs.[67]

How were the merchant ships received in Manila? The Chinese ships would arrive in the Bay of Manila, whereupon a Spanish ship on guard would go out to meet them; three soldiers would then accompany them into the port of Manila. The officers from the Royal Treasury of Manila would board the ships to evaluate and register the cargo and would then charge 3 percent of their global value. The goods were transferred in sampans to the Parián (Chinese market place)[68] or to other warehouses where they could be sold. The main cargo, as already mentioned, consisted of raw silk and textiles which could be sold freely without interference from the Spanish authorities; silver and reales were the only currency used for trade.[69]

In Manila these goods, which arrived from the south during the monsoon season (March and April), were transported in the galleons which in June would sail to Nueva España. The most powerful merchants, however, the *sangleys*[70] (Chinese) and the Spanish, would remain in Manila to sell the rest of their goods to the highest bidder.[71] Some six to seven thousand *sangleys* lived permanently in Manila, three or four thousand of them in the vicinity of the Chinese marketplace. The number of Chinese who sailed on this route was estimated to be "more than two thousand."[72]

By the end of the sixteenth century, an average of forty junks from Guangzhou, Quanzhou, and Fuzhou, which mainly transported silk, but also other Chinese goods, traveled to Manila. Sebastião Soares Paes states that in 1633, with the beginning of the Royal monopoly of the Macao-Manila route, direct trade between China and Manila was intensified: "Forty ships called somas left the province of Chincheo (Fujian, mainly from the bay of Amoy) for Manila overloaded with merchandise."[73] Pedro de Baeza refers to an annual average of arrivals (by the end of the first decade of the seventeenth century) of thirty to forty junks from the province of Fujian, which would come and sell embroidered or plain silk in exchange for the much desired silver. Possibly exaggerating a little, Baeza estimated it to be 2.5 to 3 million reais of silver annually.[74] A rather more realistic statement is the one which, in 1591, estimated it at about 300 thousand pesos annually. The currency normally used was the silver peso of eight reais.[75]

The volume of goods transported by Chinese traders provided the Manila customs with 40,000 pesos annually in customs duties calculated at a rate of 3 percent. The sale of this merchandise gave China an annual income of one and a half million pesos in gold.[76]

In the last quarter of the sixteenth century, Chinese traders from Fujian Province played a leading role on the China-Manila route. This is clear from the level of tax they paid, which frequently exceeded 50 percent of the revenues from customs duties in Manila. The Chinese goods into Manila continued to increase; from 80 percent, at the beginning of the seventeenth century, it accounted in 1641-1642 for more than 90 percent of taxes paid in Manila (in relation to total tax revenue).[77]

The origin of this Chinese influence was both internal and external. The economic and social development of the late Ming Dynasty was an internal factor, while external factors included Chinese control of the silk trade, the war between the European nations in the Indian and Atlantic Oceans, long-standing experience of trade in the Indian Ocean, and the shrinking of Japanese trade in the Philippines.

However, those who suffered most from this increase (commerce established directly with Manila by the Chinese from the provinces of Fujian and Guangdong) were the Portuguese from Macao. They felt that their position as intermediaries between the Chinese consumer and producer markets and the Philippines was weakening. Another factor of concern to the merchants from Macao was the direct commerce which existed between Manila and Japan, in spite of official bans. There were numerous rulings by the Portuguese authorities, especially by the Capitão geral of Macao, aimed at impeding and even forbidding trading by "Chinese merchants with Manila and Japan." Fines and punishments were prescribed for those who did not obey the law: five hundred *pardaus* of reales and confiscation of the goods in favor of the Royal Treasury. Those who denounced this type of trade would be rewarded with a sum of 100 *pardaus*, to be paid by the guilty party. These regulations were published in the usual places [on the city walls of Macao] with a translation in Chinese.[78]

Maritime commerce opened up during the Ming dynasty (at the end of the sixteenth century) and stimulated Chinese trade with Southeast Asia, as testified to by both Chinese and Portuguese documentation of that period. The letters from King Philip, for example, illustrate the way in which the authorities tried to protect the interests of the Iberian Empire in Southeast Asia. The aim of such legislation was to prevent Chinese merchants (*chincheos*) from sailing directly to the regions of the "Sunda, Patane, Andregir, Jambix and Solor" and buying pepper and sandalwood directly, thus protecting the routes and markets connected with Portuguese Malacca.[79] The opening up of the Middle Empire to external trade made it easier for Spaniards from the Philippines to trade directly with China. The merchants from Macao, however, protested strongly. An example of this is the letter from the Viceroy and Bishop D. Pedro de Castilho to the king, in which the former spoke of the interests of Macao's inhabitants, forbidding "the Spanish from the Philippines trading directly with China."[80]

Data included in the chart, such as the "Annual average value, in pesos, charged by the customs of Manila and the percentage of the total amount of income obtained," lead us to the following conclusion:

The peak period of trade on the Macao-Manila route does not coincide with the period of peak trade on the China-Manila route. Between 1580 and 1645, Chinese maritime trade with Manila accounted for most of the money collected in taxes by the *almojarifazgo* (with the exception of the period from 1586 to 1590, the only time when commerce in Nueva España was over 40 percent, reaching 61 percent of the customs revenues).

The initial period (1580-1600) was also the "take-off" of trade between China and Manila, which increased from 28.02 percent (corresponding to 3,750 pesos as an annual average in 1586-1590) to 56.4 percent (corresponding to 24,155.5 pesos as an annual average in 1596-1600). During this period no ships from Macao were registered by the Manila customs; goods from Macao were probably carried on Chinese ships).

During the following period (1601-1620), there was little commerce from Macao whereas Chinese commerce with Manila expanded and indeed peaked. There was a sudden rise of 70.03 percent (30,104.2 pesos) in the annual average of the *almojarifazgo* in 1601-1605, reaching 91.4 percent (64,432 pesos) in 1611-1615, after overtaking 78.5 percent in 1606-1610. It is interesting to note that this peak in Chinese commerce corresponds to shrinking Portuguese trade between Macao and Manila (with lower annual averages: 1606-1610 with 8.6 pesos, which represented 0.01 percent of the customs duties levied in Manila, and in 1611-1615 with 50 pesos representing 0.1 percent of the *almojarifazgo*). From 1515 onwards Chinese trade in Manila began to decline.

The period of recession lasted from 1620 to 1645 (lasting until 1670-1680, which was the beginning of another long period of expansion); Portuguese trade with Manila peaked at that time.

Trade between Japan and Manila, however, was on a much smaller scale. It began between 1591-1595 (295 pesos corresponding to 0.8 percent of the *almojarifazgo*) and 1596-1600 (258.5 pesos corresponding to 0.6 percent of the *almojarifazgo*). It should be noted that no ships from Macao arrived in Manila during these ten years. Thus, some merchants from Macao may have used certain Chinese ships. In the following period (1601-1605), there was a rise to 572.20 pesos as an annual average, corresponding to 1.33 percent of the global value of the *almojarifazgo*. The final period (1606-1635) was one of recession with 46 pesos in 1606-1610, then a small recovery in 1616-1620 with 353 pesos, but then with the lowest point in 1631-1635 for an annual average of 17.4 pesos.

As for trade originating from India, the years 1626-1630 were, in terms of percentages, those which contributed most (7.05 percent, corresponding to 1,813.25 pesos) to the *almojarifazgo* of Manila; although, 1620 was the year in which the cargo of the nine Portuguese ships which sailed from India to Manila was most valuable. Therefore, although no ships were registered between 1616 and 1620, the value of the customs duties paid in 1620, divided by the respective fifth (1616-1620), still corresponds to the highest annual average with a value of 2,463 pesos. The years in which registered cargo was least valuable were 1611-1615 and 1641-1645, when an annual average of 396.5 and 507.2 pesos were levied respectively.

It is interesting to note that in the periods during which the merchants of Macao were not able to send their ships directly from Macao to Manila, Portuguese commerce with Manila used other intermediary ports in Southeast Asia to trade with Manila such as Macassar, Cambodia, and Cochinchine. Malacca sent at least one ship in 1597;[81] its cargo was evaluated and registered in the accounts of the *almojarifazgo* at a rate of 1.99 percent, with 861 pesos as an annual average from 1596 to 1600.

Caution is required, however, when interpreting the above data because they do not provide all the facts about maritime traffic along the Macao-Manila trade route. What must be taken into account is the fact that since trade was often officially forbidden, its continuity was ensured through smuggling. Other routes, depending on the period and political circumstances, permitting communication with Manila, would thus be used, namely via Southeast Asia, India (especially from Goa), or from Japan. From the Indian ports of Goa, Malabar, and Coromandel and from Malacca, some fifty Portuguese ships arrived in Manila between 1577 and 1644. Another way of getting around official restrictions was by using ships from other countries—such as Japanese vessels in 1591, 1599, 1600, and 1601—to carry Portuguese goods. It is probable, however, that Chinese ships were used for most of the clandestine commerce between Macao and Manila, with independent merchants from Macao traveling in ships originating from Canton, or through *respondentes* (Chinese agents).[82] Further documentation supporting this can be found in the *legajos* (codex) of the *Contadoria* which refer to the presence of Chinese Christians in 1633 and 1634, and also mention that the Chinese captain of one of the thirty-nine ships in 1608 was Christian. They also say that of five of the thirty-three Chinese ships in 1631 were owned by a Chinese Christian. The Portuguese could therefore use some of these ships which were registered in customs without mentioning the place of origin, as well as some of the registered coastal trade ships.

Chinese Merchants in Manila

The large quantities of silver transported by the Spaniards from America to Manila gradually attracted more merchants, especially from China. The Chinese community in Manila quickly grew and prospered. Many (about 2000) of those involved in trade with Manila came from the city of Zhangzhou in Fujian Province, and sometimes stayed for a long period of time (the term used for such a period in Manila was "spend the winter") in order to sell their goods at a more advantageous price.

Many of the Chinese who came to Manila settled there permanently, but there was also a Chinese community living there temporarily. The Chinese were all required to live in a quarter under the Spanish name of Alcaiceria, and known in Chinese as Jia Nei. However, it was referred to locally as *parián* (meaning the silk market), which clearly reveals that their main activity was the silk trade. This Chinese group comprised the most important traders in Manila. The Chinese community included a large number of non-differentiated workers, but also a highly-specialized group, featuring a large variety of artisans who, according to contemporary sources, were extraordinarily versatile. They were considered essential ("without Chinese people, Manila would be a miserable place; thanks to them, Spain becomes wealthy"[83]) to daily life in Manila and in the Philippines, for they were generally recognized as able and conscientious workers.

Chinese migrants settling in Manila belonged to the lower social classes. Friar Juan Colbo refers to their humble origins, saying they were "the scum of the Earth," but among them there were also merchants who grew rich from the Macao-Manila trade. While trade was dominated directly or indirectly by rich merchants, some less prosperous men competed with them. Such trade was authorized (after 1567) by the Chinese authorities. Some of the traders used novel methods such as granting credit.[84]

Such Chinese predominance can be traced to internal and external factors. The most important were, internally, Chinese economic and social development at the end of the late Ming dynasty and, externally, control of the silk trade from China by the large Chinese community living in Southeast Asia. Chinese traders profited from the rivalry and war between the European nations in the Indian and Atlantic Oceans. They also had considerable trading experience with Southeast Asia and a large merchant fleet, and benefited from the reduction in Japanese trade in the Philippines.

Conclusion

During the late sixteenth and the seventeenth centuries, Macao, Japan, and Manila were powerful commercial centers for trading in silk, silver, and other Chinese goods (such as porcelain). This activity must be analyzed in the historical context of trade between East and West. The Europeans in the sixteenth and seventeenth centuries established direct contact with the Asian sources of production and endeavored to control them.

During this period, silk, silver, and porcelain assumed a predominant role on the Macao-Manila route and throughout the Macao trade network. Portuguese commerce rapidly expanded into a unique global trade network. The dynamic network that connected China with Pacific and Atlantic markets has been studied by Pierre Chaunu, who pointed out the correlation between overall European price levels (particularly in Holland and Spain) and the overall situation of Pacific trade.[85]

Manila and Macao became important trade centers in the Far East for two main reasons: the first was the geographical and political situation of the two Iberian colonies. Macao acted as the gateway to China, and, with Manila, served as intermediary for Chinese trade to Japan, America, and India. The second reason was economic and technological, and relates to the seafaring capacity of Portugal and Spain which allowed a direct connection between the Far East and the European worldwide economic system. Macao and Manila became the most important intermediaries for silver from both Nueva España and Japan to China (which absorbed most of the silver available in the sixteenth and seventeenth centuries).

According to recent research on China,[86] from the last quarter of sixteenth century until the fall of the Ming Dynasty (1644), most of the silver imported by China came from Japan. However, American silver was also relatively important in the global amount of silver (10 million taels) in the Ming treasury (Taicang). Silver imports during the late Ming Dynasty rose to unprecedented levels and exceeded the scale of the pepper trade. From 1570 to 1642, the Chinese treasury recorded a gradual increase in silver from 2.3 million to 23 million taels.[87] Silver exported by the Portuguese to China until 1639, amounted to a little more than 2 millions kg: 1.65 million kg from Japan and 500,000 kg from Manila and via the Cape of Good Hope.[88] In the course of the sixteenth and seventeenth centuries, the silver trade made a significant contribution to the progressive circulation of money in Asiatic trade.

Considerable external demand (both European and Asian) for Chinese silk as well as Chinese demand for silver motivated the economic and social development of the Chinese silk production and trade centers.[89] According to W.S. Atwell, the Ming economy benefited from the silver trade in various ways: the development of agriculture, with particular regard to its specialization and its trading system; the rapid development of the artisan industries; the enlargement of the interregional trade in volume and new markets, and a general modification of the tributary system.[90]

The silk trade within Asia and to Europe, via Portuguese routes to Japan, India, and the Cape of Good Hope or Spanish routes via America, contributed greatly to the development of the American, European, Indian, and Japanese silk industries. Paul Mantoux states, with regard to the repercussions of the Eastern textile trade on Europe, that "la nouvelle industrie est fille du commerce des Indes."[91] Finally, East-West trade and the Macao-Manila route in the sixteenth and seventeenth centuries gave rise to contemporaneous European debates on mercantile theories.[92] F. Mauro says that the long maritime voyages were one of the most innovating and progressive factors, although the European economic system was still "commercial capitalism of a mixed nature" because it coexisted with a manorial system where archaic agriculture was predominant.[93]

The Chinese maritime trade may be classified into two main types: first, the governmental or official tribute trade, known in Chinese as *Gong Mao*; and second, the private trade, called *Si Mao*, which might be legal or clandestine, even including piracy. Private trade was regarded as smuggling by the Chinese imperial authorities until 1567 when it was legalized in Fujian Province.[94]

Thus, according to official Chinese regulations, the only way to trade with China was within the framework of the official tribute trade. The imperial administration only accepted those foreign countries traditionally registered on the list of the countries that paid tribute to the Chinese emperor. Thus, the Europeans were excluded from the official tribute trade, but the profits of the trade were so large that the Portuguese, and subsequently other Europeans, were stimulated to try hard to find a means of trading with China.

At the beginning of the seventeenth century, increasingly frequent Dutch and English attacks on the large Portuguese *naos* (ocean-going ships) and on Portuguese territories in Asia became a determining factor in weakening the Portuguese Estado da Índia (demographically, politically, and financially). These attacks had some significant consequences: in 1639, Dutch diplomacy succeeded in having the Portuguese banished from Japan; Malacca fell to the Dutch in 1641; navigation technology improved and this new technology was incorporated in smaller Portuguese ships, in order to make them faster and better able to escape from attacks at sea; Portuguese diplomacy made new agreements with its old enemies (an armistice with England in 1635 and with Holland in

1644) in order to break the blockade on Portuguese settlements in the Indian Ocean and Macao. From 1635 to 1644, according to A.R. Disney, the freight of the East India Company ships and of the Courteen Company was an effective way of breaking the Dutch blockade in the Indian Ocean.[95]

Under the terms of the Spanish agreement on sovereignty over Portugal, trade between the Portuguese and Spanish colonies was forbidden in order to preserve the specific economic interests of both societies. Thus, the Macao-Manila route was banished by the Spanish-Portuguese administration because it competed with the routes of Seville-America-Philippines and Lisbon-Goa-Macao via the Cape of Good Hope. The cause of this rivalry was the fact that Mexican and Peruvian markets were better supplied with silks and other Chinese products from the Philippines, thereby importing fewer worked silks from Spain. The Portuguese central power and traders associated with the Lisbon-Goa route also saw their usual profits reduced when the Macao and Malacca traders sold the silk directly in the Philippines. The profits from customs duties in Goa and Lisbon fell as goods transported on their routes were reduced.[96]

During the late sixteenth century and the first half of the seventeenth century, in spite of successive orders reaffirming the bans, the Macao-Manila route was frequently plied by private and clandestine Portuguese and Spanish traders. However, in response to pressure from the Portuguese in Macao and the Spaniards in the Philippines, the authorities in Manila and Goa, on behalf of the central authority in Madrid, legalized the Macao-Manila route during certain periods. The tolerance and subsequent regulation of clandestine Macao-Manila trade by the Portuguese Goa authorities must be related to the economic difficulties of the Estado da Índia. Some of the profits from Macao-Manila trade (such as the royal monopoly or concessions) were channeled into the royal treasuries of Manila and Macao, while others went to supply the Estado da Índia in its war against its European and Asian enemies.[97]

As usual economic interests drew the line between solidarity and conflicts. The Portuguese Macao traders protested against the admittance of the Portuguese Goa traders to the Canton fairs. In 1622, the viceroy protected the Goa traders against the Macao protest, by giving written authorization for their participation in one of the two annual fairs in Canton, and tried to exclude the Macao traders from that fair (September). The Macao *casados*[98] accused the Goa traders of being a threat to the stability of Portuguese-Chinese relations. They accused the Goa traders of not observing Chinese traditions and law and of merely seeking a quicker means of making money, as when they bought slaves to take to India in contravention of Chinese law and Macao-China oral agreements.[99]

In the years 1580-1642, three different phases in Macao-Manila trade may be distinguished according to the number of ships and customs duties paid in Manila. First, the "start-off" period (1580-1600); second, the development period (1601-1621); and finally, the expansion period (1622-1642), which was interrupted when Macao-Manila relations were officially severed as a consequence of Macao's support of the new Portuguese King, João IV, ending sixty years of Spanish sovereignty over Portugal.

The development of maritime trade during the Ming dynasty after the mid-sixteenth century is recorded not only in Chinese documents, but also in those of the Portuguese and Spaniards. Chinese merchants, especially financiers, played an important role in Macao trade as well as in the economic life of Manila. This was recognized by the Spanish writers of the time who refer to their presence as indispensable.

During the sixteenth and seventeenth centuries, Macao traders faced competition from Chinese traders, especially from Fujian, Zhejiang, and Canton (Guangdong). Between 1580 and 1645, Chinese trade with Manila reached a peak both in terms of the number of ships and the amount of duties paid to the Manila customs—except in 1586-1590 when the Nueva España provided 61 percent of the total tax revenue collected by the *almojarifazgo*.

The peak period in the Macao-Manila trade (1621-1642) does not coincide with the peak period of trade between other Chinese ports and Manila, but was complementary. The years 1611-1615 marked a peak in China-Manila trade (excluding Macao) with 64,432 pesos (annual average) corresponding to 91.4 percent of all duties paid in Manila. In that period, Macao only represented 0.1 percent of Manila customs duties. The intricate correlation between Chinese and Manila trade meant that when trade declined in China, it did so too in Manila. The years 1671-1675 saw the lowest level of Chinese trade recorded in Manila with 19.05 percent of the Manila *almojarifazgo*.[180]

Japan-Manila trade was generally on a smaller scale. The period 1601-1605 was its peak period with 1.33 percent of the Manila *almojarifazgo*. When Macao traders had difficulty in sailing directly to Manila, they would sail there from other ports. They probably did this from Japan in 1591-1600. India-Manila trade reached its peak in 1626-1630 with 7 percent of the Manila *almojarifazgo*. However, in 1620, nine Portuguese ships arrived from India with the most valuable cargo recorded during the 1586-1642 period.

A practical capacity to overcome obstacles by finding alternative trade routes was an example of Macao's ability to survive the interruption and loss of trade with Japan, Manila, and Malacca. Macao traders resorted to clandestine traffic through Chinese agents or by shipping goods along alternative routes from Siam, Cambodia, Cochinchina, Tonkin, Timor, and Macassar.[181] From some of these ports, Macao merchants were able to trade with Manila when Macao ships were banned from that port. According to Claude Guillot, the best period for Macassar and Banten trade (until the late seventeenth century) was when they traded with Manila.[182] During the second half of the seventeenth century, Macao traders were particularly active in the Macassar-Manila trade.[183] Ships from other European countries were also used by Macao traders. The English ship of Francis Breton, President of the East India Company in Surate, is an example of the ships sent to Manila in 1644-1645.[184]

The Portuguese community of Macao mixed with the Chinese community and adapted to Chinese customs. By the late sixteenth and early seventeenth centuries, Macao had become a cosmopolitan city with strong financial roots, which was defended militarily by a network of fortifications against its numerous maritime enemies such as the Dutch and English.

The Portuguese model of expansion established in the Indian Ocean was reproduced in Macao for several reasons: its preference for luxury goods such as silk, porcelain, and silver; the great mobility of the Portuguese; and the centralized system of administration (in spite of the original dual form of power, in which the city council played a fundamental role in Macao trade).

Macao was in fact an exception in the Portuguese Estado da Índia, due to its particular geopolitical and economic situation. Its fragility stemmed from its vulnerability to Chinese attacks, as the Chinese could simply close the Macao gate—Porta da Barreira—thereby preventing trading activities and submitting the city to famine. On the other hand, Macao's strength lay in the fact that it played a key role in the dissemination of the abundant and precious Chinese merchandise, and also in the silver trade, of strategic importance to China and, in particular, for the superiority of the Guangdong authorities over those of Fujian.

Macao was dependent on Chinese trade and the traders played a key role in Macao policy. Thus, when the Portuguese aristocratic officials were strong enough to impose a utopian expansionist policy in Macao, the city clashed with the Chinese authorities, became unstable and trade diminished. The pragmatism and realism of Macao's people and their collaboration with the Chinese authorities were decisive for the acceptance of the Portuguese in China, as well as for the stability of Macao over the centuries. Macao was a Portuguese city, but nevertheless accepted that sovereignty over its territories be shared between Portugal and China. This was what made Macao a unique city and society.

Thus, the Macao maritime routes, as mentioned earlier, were not only commercial in nature. Founded on mutually profitable trade, they naturally developed as a point of convergence between the different communities which shared and exchanged customs, cultures, and religions.

Notes

1. Chinese adage, from the Ming-Qing Dinasty, expressing the prosperity of the meridional Chinese cities of Suzhou and Hangzhou due to the increase in the demand for silk from foreign markets. Chuan Hansheng mentioned the important role of the American market in the development of Chinese meridional provinces. Chuan Hansheng, "The Chinese Silk Trade with Spanish America from the late Ming to the mid Qing Period," in *Chine Ancienne, Actes du XXIX Congrès International des Orientalistes,* Section organisée par Michel Soymié (Paris: L'Asiathèque, 1977), p. 86.
2. Also called *The Middle Kingdom* or *The Great Middle Empire.*
3. See Claudine Salmon and Denys Lombard, "Un vaisseau du XIIIe s. retrouvé avec sa cargaison dans la rade de Zaitun," in *Archipel,* vol. 18 (1979): pp. 57-67; Cheng Dasheng and Denys Lombard, "Le rôle des étrangers dans le commerce maritime de Quanzhou ('Zaitun') aux 13e et 14e siècles," in *Marchands et hommes d'affaires asiatiques dans l'océan Indien et la mer de Chine, 13e-20e siècles* (Paris: Denys Lombard and Jean Aubin, 1988), pp. 21-29.
4. For a global view of the Portuguese expansion and economy see Vitorino Magalhães Godinho, *Os Descobrimentos e a Economia Mundial,* 2 vols. (Lisbon, 1963-1965), or 4 vols. (Lisbon, 1983-1984). For a global view of the Malacca trade routes see Luis Filipe Ferreira Reis Thomaz, "Os Portugueses em Malaca, 1511-1580," 2 vols. (Graduate thesis, Biblioteca da Faculdade de Letras da Universidade de Lisboa, Lisbon, 1964); on Southeast Asia and the Malasian and Indonesian archipelago, see Luis F.R. Thomaz, "Les Portugais dans les mers de l'Archipel au XVI siècle," *Archipel,* vol. 18 (1979): pp. 105-25; and Manuel Lobato, "Política e Comércio dos portugueses...."
5. See J.E. Willis, Jr., "Maritime China from Wang Chih to Shih Lang: Themes in Peripheral History," in *From Ming to Ch'ing: Conquest, Region and Continuity in the Seventeenth Century,* eds., J.D. Spence and J.E. Willis, Jr. (New Haven, 1979), pp. 210-13.
6. See the letter from Felipe I of January 1595, asking the viceroy Matias de Albuquerque for his opinion on how to limit the Chinese pepper trade to Malacca: "impedir os chineses [Chinchéus] de ir buscar pimenta a Sunda, patane, paru [sic], Jambiz [sic], Andrigim, e outros locais [not mentioned], e unicamente autorizá-los a negociar em Malaca para bem da Fazenda Real" in *APO.,* fasc. 3º, par. 1ª, doc. 78, pp. 286-99; also in *Boletim da Filmoteca Ultramarina Portuguesa (Bol.FUP).,* no. 2, pp. 309-12. The original is in the Historical Archive of Goa (HAG), *Livros das Monções,* No. 3-b (fls. 430-37). Another letter from D. Felipe I of 28 February 1595, from Lisbon, giving details of the same order to Viceroy Matias de Albuquerque, to forbid "por todos os meios (manda enviar duas fustas com 60 soldados),

os Chineses (Chinchéus) de ir buscar sândalo às ilhas de Solor, não só pelo prejuizo para a fazenda Real, mas também pela desordem que causam. O Bispo de Malaca já escrevera ao rei a denunciar igualmente esta grave situação, visto ser necessário favorecer a comunidade cristã de Solor, que vinha aumentando," in *Filmoteca Ultramarina Portuguesa*, ficheiro 2, gaveta 1, divisão 6 e 7, fichas 70-1, exposição 5/3, documento 44; *Bol.FUP.*, no. 2, pp. 332-33; HAG., *Livros das Monções*, no. 3-b (fls. 589-90r.)

7. Luís F.R. Thomaz, "Les Portugais dans les mers de l'archipel au XVIe siècle."

8. According to K.N. Chaudhuri, the easternmost limit of the Indian Ocean, the Pacific, "remained unnavigable to Asian sailing-ships," in "Portuguese Maritime Empire, Trade and Society in the Indian Ocean during the Sixteenth Century," in *Portuguese Studies*, vol. 9 (1992): p. 63.

9. Another very profitable route was the Macao-Japan route started in the 1540s and monopolized by Portuguese traders during the forbidden period of trade between China and Japan (1557-1567). However, this monopoly was gradually broken by the Chinese smuggling trade and afterwards by other European powers, particularly the Dutch.

10. In 1543 a private Portuguese ship arrived on Tanegashima Island and was considered to be the beginning of the European private trade to Japan. See G. Schurhammer, "O descobrimento do Japão pelos Portugueses no ano de 1543," *Anais da Academia Portuguesa de História,* 2d series, no. 1 (1946); João Paulo Oliveira e Costa, "Oda Nobunaga e a expansão portuguesa," in *Revista de Cultura*, no 13/14 (Macao, 1991): pp. 258-72.

11. Original quotation: "As viagens que se fazem desta cidade do Nome de Deos bem se vê que a principal e de mais consideração he a de Japão," in "Descrição da Cidade do Nome de Deus da China" in C.R. Boxer, *Great Ship From Amacon,* p. 40.

12. Bocarro, in the above-mentioned description, p. 41.

13. Boxer, *The Great Ship,* p. 157.

14. Marco d'Avalo, "Descrição de Macau, em 1638," in Boxer, *The Great Ship,* p. 86.

15. See in the bibliography the list of the "legajos of Fundos da Contaduria of Arquivo das Indias de Seville" (from 1577 to 1645), which was used for this work. The *almojarifazgo* is the designation used in the Spanish Empire for a series of taxes levied on maritime commerce (roughly calculated according to the value of the merchandise—*ad valorem*). From an examination of the documents (mainly, the *Extracto historial del expediente que pende en el Consejo de Indias a instancia de la ciudad de Manila* ... [Madrid, 1736], fs. 324, gr. in 4º.), it can be said that there is a direct link between the degree of mercantile development (of the maritime trade) and the total tax revenue (of the *almojarifazgo*) of Manila. See Pierre Chaunu, *Les Philippines et le Pacifique des Ibériques XVIe-XVIIIe siècles, Introduction méthodologique et indices d'activité* (Paris, 1960).

16. The *lejado* (c. 1200) does not define the origin of numerous vessels, and it is therefore impossible to give accurate data for 1578 and 1579.

17. At least until 1787, according to data compiled by Pierre Chaunu, *Les Philippines.*

18. "Treslado do assento que se tomou em conselho da fazenda sobre a composição que se faz com Lopo Sarmento de Carvalho, por via da transação," Codex CXVI//2-5, fl. 99, of the Biblioteca Publica e Arquivo Distrital de Évora published in the *Diário do 3º Conde de Linhares*, pp. 87-91, and in the work of C.R. Boxer, *The Great Ship*, pp. 253-56. Note that both Marco d'Avalo and António Bocarro, in their descriptions of Macao, give an inaccurate account of the Macao-Manila voyage in those times. The former states (p. 85) that the vessels left Macao in April and generally returned in October, while the latter says that it was possible to navigate "the whole

year to Manila" (p. 47) which, as we have observed, was not recommended. This contradiction is probably based on the stories which were told in Goa about illicit trade, which possibly did not strictly conform to the normal calendar.

19. Documentation referring to the *almojarifazo* of Manila (*legajos* dos Fundos de la *Contaduria* de los Arquivos das Índias de Sevilha), see Pierre Chaunu, *Les Philippines et le Pacifique des Iberiques XVIe - XVIIIe siècles, Construction Graphique*, pp. 66-67.

20. "Regimento que se deu a Romão de Lemos que vay por administrador das viagens de Japão e das mais anexas a ellas que se fazem por conta da fazenda de sua magestade (24 de Abril de 1637)" in HAG, "Livro do regimento e instruções," III, fls. 38-51; and published in full in Boxer, *The Great Ship*, pp. 286-306.

21. Generalizing the use of the name of the island of Luçon (Luzon), where the city of Manila is situated.

22. See Boxer, *The Great Ship*.

23. "o que hé em grande perjuiso do rendimento da dita alfandega, a que convem acodir pella grande despeza que de ordinário faz a fazenda real com as armadas que tras naquelles mares [which represent a great loss for the royal treasury, that needs to increase its profits because the royal treasury expended a lot of money supporting the navy in the Indian Ocean]," Boxer, *The Great Ship*, p. 290.

24. HAG, "Livro," p. 293.

25. In this letter, the Viceroy says "The *chós* [a ship] that sailed in secret from China to Manila as you wrote in the last letter is why I ordered the voyage Macao-Manila to be made in a small *pataxo*. The ships found in Manila from the Macao islands will be captured with their textiles because the voyage is a crown monopoly." Letter from the Count of Linhares to Manoel Ramos, administrator of the voyages from Japan, Manila, and Goa, 4 May 1635, in ANTT (Arquivos Nacionais – Torre do Tombo), Lisboa, *Livros das Monções ou documentos remetidos da India*, vol. 34. fls. 63-66, published in full in Boxer, *The Great Ship*, p. 273.

26. In the Codex CXVI//2-5, this letter occupies folio no. 44, and is found among the papers of the Capitão Geral [Captain General] of Macao, D. Francisco de Mascaranhas of the Fundo Geral de Manuscritos da Biblioteca Arquivo Distrital de Évora.

27. In ANTT, *Livros das Monções*, vol. 38, fls. 349- 55. On this subject, see: "Carta do Vice Rei D. Fernando da Gama, who in the name of the king ordered the Macao-Manila voyage for the royal treasure," in Fundo Geral de Manuscritos da Biblioteca e Arquivo do Distrito de Évora, Codex CXVI//2-5, f. 44.—Papers on the controversy between the Capitão Geral of Macao, D. Francisco Mascarenhas, and the city, about the justice and convenience of the voyage from Manila, ibid., fls. 78-165. The "Treslado de assento que se tomou en Conselho da fazenda sobre a composição que se fez com Lopo Sarmento de Carvalho, por via da transacção..." ibid., fl. 99, appears in Boxer, *The Great Ship*, pp. 253-56, and the remaining documentation in pp. 245-306. Documents on the Macao-Manila trade, ibid., Codex CXVI//2-5, fl. 253. Order from the Capitão Geral D. Francisco Mascarenhas on the Manila and Japan trade, ibid., Codex CXVI//2-5; fl. 270.

28. The person who received a specific voyage attributed by the Portuguese authorities as a reward for the work that he had done for the Portuguese crown.

29. An important officer of the Portuguese financial department of Estado da Índia.

30. ANTT, *Livros das Monções*, vol. 38, fl. 352.

31. "Carta do Desembargador Sebastião Soares Paes para a Princesa Margarida, Duquesa de Mantua," January 1637, ANTT, *Livros das Monções*, vol. 38, fl. 468, in Boxer, *The Great Ship*, pp. 280.

32. HAG, "Livro," 3, fls. 38v.-51; in Boxer, *The Great Ship*, pp. 286-306.

33. In the original: "Aplicando tudo o que ellas montare aos gastos da riveira de Goa apresto das Armadas e fabrica dos navios," ANTT, *Livro das Monções*, vol. 38, fl. 353.
34. *Diário do Terceiro Conde de Linhares*, Vice-Rei da India, I, Lisbon, 1937, p. 52. This period extends from 6 February 1634 to 16 February 1635.
35. By order of Felipe I, written in Goa on 7 April 1592, in HAG, "Livro" 1º de Alvarás fl. 12 v. and in *Archivo Português Oriental*, Fascicle 3, pt. 1, doc. 109, pp. 353-54.
36. Bocarro states "que por nenhum modo querem (os grandes mercadores, cazados) passar a Goa por näo lançarem mäo delles ou as justiças por algum crime, ou os V. Rey para serviço de sua Magestade e assy tambem muitos mercadores solteiros muito ricos em que melitam as mesmas rezös." in Bocarro, "Descrição da cidade de Macao," edited by Boxer in *Macao na Época da Restauração*, pp. 28-29.
37. Morga, *Sucesos*, p. 349, "Su Magestade prohibe à los que tiram su sueldade de la guerra en las islas, el ser mercadores, y ordena al gobernador, no se lo consienta, mi cargar para la Nueva España."
38. "The disasters on the Portuguese ships [sailing in the China Sea] were due to the overloading of the deck." ANTT, *Livro das Monções*, vol. 34, fls. 71-73; also in C.R. Boxer, *The Great Ship*. See note 26.
39. "Nos contratos dos fretamentos que se fizeram com os donos e senhorios dos navios que ouverem hir assy a Jappão como a Manila, se lhes não darão arcas de bomba nem payões nem outros gasalhos libertos para nelles levarem fazendas, nem nos que se lhes derem para as velas e sobresçelentes nos mesmos navios poderão embarcar nen-huma sorte de fazenda, assy elles como os mestres pilotos e maes officiaes, excepto os caixões de liberdade que lhes custuma dar que não excederão da medida que sempre foi costume," in "Regimento que se deu a Romäo de Lemos qe vay por admin-istrador das viagens de Japão e das mais anexas a ellas que se fazem por conta da fazenda de sua Magestade (24 de Abril de 1637)," in A.C. da Silva Correia, *História da colonização Portuguesa na Índia*, vol. 3, (1951), pp. 66-90, idem, vol. 4, (1952), pp. 98 ff., and published in full in C.R. Boxer, *The Great Ship*, pp. 286-306.
40. *Pataca* (*patacão*), money of account, with a value of 360 *reis*. Usually equated with the *cruzado*, with the *S. Tomé* or the rial-of-eight, see Boxer, *The Great Ship*, p. 336. W. Barret refers to silver *patachines* at Goa in 1584, worth 6 *tangas* of good money or 360 *reis* (according to Boxer quotation). See António Nunes, "Livro dos Pesos da Índia, e assy Medidas e Moedas" (1554), pp.1-64.
41. "Em lugar dos camarotes que se davão nos altos aos ditos officiaies, se lhes darão maes a cada hum sincoenta patacas; e levando algumas fazendas fora da dita liber-dade fareis que com effeito paguem os fretes della a fazenda real como se fora debaixo da cuberta sem lhes admitir resão em contrario;" in "Regimento que se deu a Romão de Lemos..." (24 April 1637), in A.C. da Silva Correia, *Historia* in C.R. Boxer, *The Great Ship*, pp. 286-306, and particularly p. 291.
42. "Regimento que se deu a Romão de Lemos...," in HAG, "Livro," vol. 3, fls. 38v.-51; C.R. Boxer, *The Great Ship*, pp. 286-306.
43. "As embarcações que assy partirem de Macao fora dito tempo posto que se perçäo, ou aribem näo entrarão no numero das de que se lhe ade fazer o abatimento por rota porquanto o dito abatimento se lhe faz mais que aquellas que partirem dentro do dito mez.de julho." In "Treslado da arrematação e venda de tres viagens, da China pera Jappão juntamente outra tres da China pera Manilla, o Lopo Sarmento de Car-valho p. preço e contia de trezentos e seis mil cruzados p. lla. manra. Abaixo," ANTT, *Livros das Monções*, vol. 38, fls. 349-55. Published in full inC.R. Boxer, *The Great Ship*, pp. 248-49.
44. Chang Pin-Tsun, "Chinese Maritime Trade: the Case of Sixteenth Century Fuchien (Fukien)" (Ph.D. diss., Princeton, New Jersey, 1983), p.165; K.C. Fok, "The Macao

Formula: A Study of Chinese Management of Westerners from the Mid-sixteenth Century to the Opium War Period" (Ph.D. diss., Hawaii University, 1978), pp. 33-64, and an abridged version in Portuguese—"O debate Ming acerca da acomodação dos Portugueses e o aparecimento da 'Fórmula de Macao,' a colónia portuguesa e as primeiras reacções Chinesas," in *Revista de Cultura*, vol. 16, (Macao: Instituto Cultural de Macao, 1991), pp.13-30; Luís G. Gomes, *Ou-Mun Kei-Leok, Monografia de Macao* (Macao: Quinzena de Macau [October 1979 – Lisbon]), p. 103.

45. Huang Hongjian, *História de Macao* (Nanjing, 1986). I wish to thank Dr. Lu Yanbin and Dr. Wang Suo Ying for their translation of the 6th chapter, "External Trade in the Ming Dynasty;" Luís G. Gomes, *Ou-Mun Kei-Leok*, has published several reports on foreign trade, including "Memorial de Uóng-Hei-Mân acerca do facto de se dever prestar grande importância às fronteiras ser o mesmo que fazer ressuscitar o povo," pp. 100-4, and "Memorial de P'óng-Sèong-P'áng acerca da forma como deve ser dividida Macao e como se deverá proceder para manter a tranquilidade em todas as reintrâncias do litoral," pp. 104-9.

46. For an analysis of Chinese customs, see also *Yue Hai Guan Zhi* (Reports of the Guangdong Aduana), and *Guangdong Fu Yi Quan Shu* (Global Report of the Tax and Corvée of the Guangdong Province). See also *Xinxiu Xiangshan Xianzhi*, edited by Zhu Huai (1927), ch. 6, p. 27a.

47. "From the time when Kuóng-Iâm was mayor of Hèong-Sán..." to the period when "the mayor was U-Lâm...", in Luís G. Gomes, *Ou-Mon Koi-Leok*, p. 227.

48. "Pretendem que S.M. lhes conceda nas fazendas que nella entrarem, pera com esse dinheiro cercarem a cidade e sobre se por nella hum capitão assistente que entenda nesta obra e tenha a seu cargo a guarda da dita cidade...," in BA (Biblioteca da Ajuda), Codex 51-VIII-18, nº. 199, 17 December 1606.

49. BA, Codex 51-VIII-6, nº. 620, royal letter to Bishop D. Pedro de Castilho "sobre o direito por sento que pedem os moradores de Macao...."

50. Luís G. Gomes, *Ou-Mon Koi-Leok*, p. 227.

51. "Treslado dos Apontamentos de Lopo Sarmento de Carvalho" (1-3 May 1623), "Treslado da Resposta dos Procuradores da Cidade de Macao," in C.R. Boxer, *The Great Ship*, pp. 241-44.

52. Manuel Pereira, João Simões de Carvalho and Lourenço de Carvalho were the representantes of Macao in Goa. On 3 May 1623, they signed the document entitled "Treslado da resposta aos appontamentos de lopo sarmento depois de serem tratadas no conselho do estado" (Transcript of the reply of the representatives of the City of Macao) in C.R. Boxer, *The Great Ship*, pp. 243-44.

53. "Treslado da Resposta."

54. Codex 1209: the *almojarifazgo* on Chinese trade before and after the tax increase from 3 to 6 percent in 1610 reveals, after a short initial period, an increase in the global amount of income subject to the former tax of 3 percent, in part due to the systematic under-evaluation of goods in the Manila customs. See Pierre Chaunu, *Les Philippines*, pp. 34-35. In 1607 and 1608, 78 Chinese boats paid 70,093 1/2 pesos, at the rate of 3 percent (cd. 1207); in 1609-1610, the application of the new tax of 6 percent to 82 Chinese ships increased the income to 128,338 pesos. The unitary payment increased from 900 pesos to about 1,500 pesos between 1607-1608 and 1609-1610. In 1611, 31,683 pesos were charged for 23 ships, which means a tax of about 1,400 pesos per ship. In 1612 with the payment of 97,180 pesos for 46 ships, the unitary payment was of about 2,100 pesos; and in 1620 the level of 1,200 pesos was maintained. On the other hand, in 1627, the payment for each ship decreased to about 830 pesos, corresponding to about 17,450 pesos paid to the customs.

55. Pierre Chaunu, *Les Philippines*, pp. 200-6; S. J. Pires and Benjamim Videira, *Viagem do comércio Macao-Manila*, p. 24.

56. The explanation of the name of the "Pancada" system is not clear. José Caetano Soares gives us two possibilities: the name originates either from the "The customs of the auctioners to close the bidding by knocking on the table in the markets, or the regional term used in the North of Portugal;" "viagar de pancada" which means to follow in a group (in *Macao e a assistência*, p. 120). C.R. Boxer, *The Great Ship*, p. 66.

57. Directive of 'Conde Vice Rey da Índia,' Dom Francisco Mascarenhas, 1584, in Codex 49 IV- 57, fls. 170 verso and following; 'Jesuitas na Ásia' of BA, First published (according to C.R. Boxer) by Y. Okamoto in *Nichi - po Kotsu*, 2 (Tokyo, 1943), and by Boxer in *The Great Ship*, pp. 197-200.

58. Chang T'ient-Tse, *Sino-Portuguese Trade from 1514 to 1644: A Synthesis of Portuguese and Chinese Sources* (Leiden, 1934).

59. Stephen Chang Tseng-Hsin, "Commodities Imported into the Zhang-Zhou Region of Fujian, China, during the Late Ming Period—A Comparative and Analytical Study" (Paper presented at a symposium, 31 August 1989, University of Heidelberg, 1989), p. 3.

60. This quotation in Portuguese: "se possuirmos livre só o comércio da China bastava sem nenhum outro porque pera todo este Oriente serve o que nelle ha e pera todo o mundo...." was justified according to Bocarro, by: "de tudo o que a natureza produzu em muitos Reinos ha neste só muita cópia que parece que só nelle se dá, e nunca houve tanto cabedal de mercadores que lhes faltace em Quantão senão duma sorte, doutras muitas de fazendas e todas que servem." The quotations are from the historian, António Bocarro, in *Descrição da cidade do nome de D.s da China*, a voluminous work of 300 pages with the plans of 48 forts or Portuguese possessions in Asia. The full title is *Livro das Plantas de todas as Fortalezas, Cidades e Povoaçöens do Estado da ïndia Oriental com as descripçoens da altura em que estäo, e de tudo que há nellas, Artilharia, Presidio, gente de Armas, e Vassalos, rendimento, e despeza, fundos e baxos das Barras, Reys da Terra dentro, o poder que tem, e a paz, e a guerra, que guardäo, e tudo que está debaxo da Coroa de Espanha. Dedicado à Serenissima Magestade del Rey Felipe o IV das Espanhas, e III de Portugal Rey, e Senhor nosso* (Goa, 1634). The description of Macao used here was published in C.R. Boxer, *Macao na Época da Restauração (Macao three hundred years ago)* (Macao Imprensa Nacional, 1942), p. 37.

61. The original quotation: "Sendo que se lhes tivessem liberdade pera entrar e mercanciar pello Reino poderão conservarse, e crescer sem mais viagens para Japão, nem pera Manila, por resão de ser tal a monarchia da China que não necessita de comercios estranhos pera sustento dos Vassalos, e os de Machao estão lá tidos por vassalos...." BA, 54-XI-219, J.P. de Azevedo, *Advertencias*, f. 20v.

62. Original title: *Discurso en que se muetra ser da mas importancia, las Índias orientales, que las occidentales en racon, do comércio y al preposito se discubren las cauzas de estar perdido el comércio delas orientales y espana reducida a la ultima pobreça que vemos*, BA, Codex 51-VII-27, doc. no. 21, fls. 196-210 (sem data), anonymous, in Spanish (Lisboa, 1626).

63. "Relação do principio que teve a Cidade de Macao e como se sustenta ate o presente," BPAD, Évora, Codex CV/2-7, fol. 65, published by Fr. Manuel Teixeira, *Macau e a sua Diocese: O Culto de Maria em Macau* (Macau, 1969), p. 423.

64. "Noticias verdadeiras das contendas que houve em Macao sobre a Ilha Verde no anno de 1621 São tiradas dos papeis que se conservão na secretaria da Provincia de Japão do Collégio da Madre de Deus da companhia de JHS em Macao." Written in January 1747 by João Alvares, pages 24-24v. contain an extract from the annual let-

ter of 30 December 1621 by Father António Leite which puts pressure on the Portuguese and is referred to as "os portugueses com sua prata fazendo seus empregos, tratos e mercancias" em Cantão. Codex 49-V-4 consists of 26 folios which belong to the Jesuit collection in Ásia, J.M. Braga published the fl. 10v.

65. Chuan Hansheng, "The Chinese Silk Trade with Spanish America from the late Ming to the Mid Qing Period," in *Chine Ancienne, Actes du XXIX Congrès International des Orientalistes,* section organized by Michel Soymié (Paris: L'Asiathèque, 1977), p. 86. See also Vitorino Magalhães Godinho, *Os Descobrimentos e a Economia Mundial,* 2d ed., vol. 4, pp. 217-18.

66. When, in 1574, the Chinese Government built the gate called "Porta da Barreira" or "Porta do cerco" in the extreme north of the peninsula of Macao and put it under military observation, it implicitly recognized Macao as a special zone. The door was only opened six times a month for the Portuguese in Macao to get supplies. From 1578 on, the Portuguese were authorized to negotiate with Guangzhou. On Canton fairs, see Jorge Manuel Flores "'A mão direita de Cantão:' Macau e o comércio do rio das pérolas, (séculos XVI-XVII)," in *As relações entre a Índia Portuguesa, a Ásia do Sueste e o Extremo Oriente, Actas do VI Seminário Internacional de História Indo-Portuguesa,* (Macao 22-26 October 1991), edited by Arthur Teodoro de Matos and Luís Felipe F.R. Thomaz (Macao and Lisbon, 1993).

67. For a description of Parian, see the first detailed account by the first Bishop of Manila, "Relacion de las cosas de la China del Parian de Manila," of 24 June 1590, pp. 309-26; and see "El Parian de les Sangleyes," pp. 151-74; both texts in Carlos Sang, *Primitivas relaciones de España com Asia y Oceania* (Madrid, 1958).

68. "Es plata y *reales,* que no quierem oro, ni otras algunos rescated, ni los llevan á la China," in António Morga, *Sucesos de las Islas Filipinas,* p. 353.

69. Originally the Chinese in the Philippines were all known by this term; in the seventeenth century it began to be used exclusively to designate the Chinese residents of the Philippines; see P. Juan Cobo, first Bishop of Manila; Carlos Sanz's work, *Primitivas relaciones,* pp. 151-74, 309-26, and Boxer; *South China in the Sixteenth Century* (London, 1953), p. 260.

70. António Morga, *Sucesos de las Islas Filipines,* p. 354.

71. Carlos Sanz, *Primitivas relaciones,* p. 321.

72. "Carta de desembargador Sebastião Soares Paes para a Princesa Margarida, Duquesa de Mantua," Goa, 19 de Janeiro 1637, ANTT in *Livros das Monções,* 38, fls. 468 ff., and in C.R. Boxer, *The Great Ship,* pp. 278-86. This letter is an answer to a letter from the Duchess of Mantua (Regente do Reino de Portugal) of 7 March 1636.

73. Pedro de Baeza, "Esta relación y discurso, me mando V. Excelência que hiziesse... para que en el satisfizesse las dudas que me puseron cerca de la grande costa que la armada habia de hacer" (Madrid, 1608), fls. 11v., 13. In C.R. Boxer, *The Great Ship,* p. 74.

74. Rial-of-eight (*peso de ocho reales; peso de plata; el duro*). The most common and most popular European coin in the Far East after the establishment of the Spaniards in the Philippines (C.R. Boxer). In Goa in 1584 it was officially valued at one cruzado (400 *reis*) or 6 2/3 *tangas*; in Peter Mundy's day, worth about 10 *tangas*. The peso in gold coin or the *peso de oro* was in circulation and was worth 16 Spanish *reais*. For more detailed information about gold currency, see C.R. Boxer, *The Great Ship,* pp. 336-37.

75. *Guang Dong Hai Fang Hui Lan* (Collection on the Maritime Defense of Guangdong), rolo 37, made by Lu-Kun. Translated by Dr. Lu Yan Bin. António Morga in his work *Sucesos de las Islas Filipinas* wrote: "Los derechos del tres por ciento de las

mercadorías que traen de la China los navíos sangleyes, valen un año con otro, cuarenta mil pesos" (p. 360). In this work he refers to "Relação escrita pelo Almirante D. Jerónimo de Bānueles y Camillo" in which he informed the king "that one and a half million in gold enter China each year" (p. 350).

76. Pierre Chaunu, *Les Philippines*, pp. 199-219.
77. "Fundo Geral de Manuscritos" in BPAD of Évora, Codex CXVI//2-5, fl. 270, "Mandado do capitão Geral D. Francisco de Mascarenhas, acerca do comércio com Manilla e Japão."
78. See the letter from Felipe I in January 1591 to Viceroy Martins de Albuquerque in HAG, *Livro das Monções*, no. 3, fl. 430 (2ª via) and fl. 438 (4ª via), also published in the Archivo Português Oriental, Fasc. 3, pt. 1, doc. 78, pp. 286- 99, or *Boletim da Filmoteca Ultramarina Portuguesa*, no. 2, pp. 309-12, ref.: 13, 20-23//4-4; or another royal letter, four years later (28.2.1595) in which the Viceroy was instructed to prevent, where possible, the *chincheos* from going to the islands of Solor to obtain sandalwood, not only because of the damage suffered by the Royal treasury, but also because of the disruptions which they caused. In *Boletim da Filmoteca Ultramarina Portuguesa*, no. 2, pp. 332-33, ref. 44, 70-71//5-3, or in *Livro das Monções*, no. 3-B, pp. 589-90.
79. BA, Codex 51-VIII-18, no. 243, fs.112-3v.
80. AGI, *Filipinas*, cd. 1204.
81. See the titles of *respondência* of Tristão Tavares (1637) and Pero Fernandes de Carvalho (1638), published in C.R. Boxer, *The Great Ship*, pp. 284-87. Among the various documents confirming the existence of smuggling, two examples should be mentioned: the letter from Sebastião Soares Paes to Princess Margarida, Duches de Mantua, on 19 January 1637, in ANTT, *Livros das Monções*, vol. 38, fls. 468 et seq. This is the reply to a letter from Princess Margarida written on 7 March 1636. Boxer published a résumé of this letter in English in the article "Portuguese Commercial Voyages to Japan 300 years ago," in *TJS* vol. 31 (1933-1934): pp. 65-75; this author also published the complete text of the letter in Portuguese in *The Great Ship*, pp. 278-86); see the *Mandado do Capitão Geral D. Francisco de Mascarenhas* on Macao-Manila-Japan trade. The original is in the BPAD of Évora, Codex CXVI//2-5, f. 270.
82. The original of this quotation is: "si no hubiera chinos en estas Islas era Manila una miséria, porque con los chinos ganan los castillas." This idea is commonly found in Spanish documentation of the time, mainly written by Frade Juan Cabo or the first Bishop of Manila, published by Carlos de Sanz, *Primitivas relaciones.*, pp. 281, 283, 277-78, 315.
83. "Es gente muy prática, é inteligente en la mercancía... y saben fiar, y hacer comodidad liberalmente à quien saben les trata verdad, y no les ha de hacer falta en la paga," in António Morga, *Sucesos*, p. 354. The activity of these usury merchants is also mentioned in a document stating that three-quarters of the total amount of the goods of Manila's neighbors were sold in Mexico "fiadas por los Sangelyes," in C.R. Boxer, *Azia Sinica e Japonica,* I, pp. 225-27.
84. Pierre Chaunu, *Les Philippines*, p. 265.
85. Brian Moloughney and Xia Weizhong, "Silver and the Fall of the Ming: a Reassessment" in *Papers on Far Eastern History* (Canberra: Australian National University, 1989), pp. 51-78.
86. Moloughney and Xia, "Silver," p. 68.
87. Moloughney and Xia, "Silver," p. 59; George Bryan Souza (*Survival of Empire*, pp. 56-57) suggests that, between 1546 and 1638, 36.6 million to 41.1 million taes were imported from Japan; Kozo Yamamura and Tetsuo Kamiki, "Silver Mines and

Sung Coins—A Monetary History of Medieval and Modern Japan in International Perspective" in *Precious Metals*, p. 351, make a different calculation for a period of 40 years ending in 1600. They suggest 900,000 to 1.5 million kg.

88. In Zhejiang, Jiangsu, Fujian and Canton provinces. Chuan Hansheng, "The Chinese Silk Trade," p. 86, points out the importance of the American demand for silks for the development of the above-mentioned Chinese centers.

89. W.S. Atwell, "Notes on Silver, Foreign Trade, and the Late Ming Economy," *Ch'ing-shi Wen-t'i*, vol. 3, no. 8 (1977). See also R. Huang, *Taxation and Government Finance in Sixteenth Century Ming China* (Cambridge, 1974), p. 243.

90. Quotation in Paul Leuilliot, "Influence du commerce oriental sur l'économie occidentale," in *Sociétés et compagnies de commerce en Orient et dans l'Océan Indien, Actes du huitième colloque international d'histoire maritime* (Beyrouth, 5-10 September 1966) (Paris, 1970), p. 620.

91. Duarte Gomes de Solis, *Discursos sobre los comercios de las dos Indias donde se tratam materiais importantes de Estado y Guerra* (Madrid, 1622). Published by Móses Amzalak (Lisbon, 1943). Solis was one of the first Portuguese economists whose work was significant for his time. See by the same author, *Alegacion en favor de la Compañia de la India Oriental, y commercios Ultramarinos que de nuevo se instituyo en el Reino de Portugal* (1628; reissued by Móses Amzalak, Lisbon, 1955). Also *Mémoires inédits de Duarte Gomes de Solis* (December 1621), edited by Léon Bourdon (Lisbon, 1955). This edition includes his work *Arbitrio sobre la plata*. See Solis, "Discurso en razon de la Compañia Oriental que tiene los rebeldes de Olanda y Ingleses" (c. 1618), published by Gentil da Silva in *Alguns Elementos para a História do Comércio da India de Portugal* (1951).

92. F. Mauro, "Concepts économiques et économie coloniale à l'époque du capitalisme…." was justified according to Bocarro, by: "de tudo o que a natureza produz económique, Aix-en- Provence, 1962," vol. 2 (1965), p. 715.

93. Chang Pin-Tsun, "Chinese Maritime Trade, p.165.

94. A.R. Disney, *Twilight of the Pepper Empire: Portuguese Trade in Southwest India in the Early Seventeenth Century* (Cambridge, Mass., 1978), pp. 148-54; see also H.B. Morse, *The Chronicles of the East India Company Trading to China, 1635-1834,* 5 vols. (Oxford, 1926-1929), (new edition, Taiwan, 1975), vol. 1, pp. 14-30.

95. This is the argument also expressed by the then Spanish *feitor* in the Philippines, Antonio Morga: "Por haberse engrosado tanto este trato, que hacia daño y perjuicio à las mercaderias de España, que se cargaban al Perú y a la Nueva España, y a los derechos reales, que por razon dellas se cobran, y haberse acodiciado los hombres de negocios de Méjico y el Perú, à tratar y contratar en las Filipinas, por mano de sus encomenderas y factores; de suerte, que cesaba en la mayor parte el trato de España," in Antonio Morga, *Sucesos*, p. 350.

96. In April 1629, a secret order from King Felipe IV, authorizing Macao-Manila trade was personally conveyed by the Viceroy Miguel de Noronha on his voyage to India, and appears in ANTT, *Livros das Monções*, vol. 38, fl. 351; *Diário do 3º Conde de Linhares*, I, pp. 51-52; C.R. Boxer, *The Great Ship*, p. 250.

97. *Casado* means a Portuguese man married and settled in a city under Portuguese control. Being a *casado* gave a man a number of privileges and obligations to the Portuguese administration. It corresponded to a social status of privilege and honor.

98. "Arezoado, em que se apontão alguas rezois por onde não convêm ao bem desta cidade erem os Portugueses a Cantão a feira" (1622), in Luís Gonzaga Gomes, "Documentos Setecentistas Portugueses no Arquivo Colonial da Holanda," *Boletim do Instituto Luís de Camões* (1975): pp. 40-60.

99. According to data given in Pierre Chaunu, *Les Philippines*, pp. 202-3.

100. "Termo de fretamento que se fez para o Macassar, Cambodja, Cochinchina, Ton-
     quim e mais partes conforme o consentimento dos senhorios das embarcações de 12
     de Novembro de 1640," in *AM*, vol. 3, no. 2 (August 1930): pp. 61-63.
101. Claude Guillot, "Les Portuguais et Banten (1511-1682)," in *Revista de Cultura, Os
     mares da Ásia, 1500-1800, Sociedades Locais, Portugueses e Expansão Europeia,
     Macao*, nos.13-14 (1991), pp. 80-95; see also Chaunu, *Les Philippines*, pp. 160-61;
     between 1641 and 1646, eight ships sailed from Macassar to Manila.
102. Claude Guillot, "Les Portuguais et Banten," p. 93.
103. "The man who spurred that inspiration was an enterprising Portuguese merchant in
     Surat, Joseph de Brito, who pointed out to Francis Breton the considerable benefits
     that would be gained from trade in Manilla," in Serafin Quiazon, *English 'Country
     Trade' with the Philippines, 1644-1765* (Quezon City: University of the Philippines
     Press, 1966), p. 5. More information on José de Brito can be found in W. Foster,
     The English Factories in India, 1642-1645 (Oxford, 1927), p. 219.

Chapter 13

Inner Asian Muslim Merchants at the Closure of the Silk Routes in the Seventeenth Century

Isenbike Togan

The decline of the overland Silk Routes is in general associated with developments that shifted the greater part of the transcontinental trade to the sea routes.[1] While this shift indeed involved an increase in the volume of trade between East and West, trade along the old routes continued nevertheless in a different form. It is this change in the nature of the organization of such trade and traders that we mostly perceive as the decline of the Silk Routes. The aim of this chapter is to bring a further qualification to the decline of the Routes by demonstrating that the trade and traders did not cease to function, and that instead, state formations that were playing the role of intermediaries along the Routes were eliminated. That elimination was due to the expansion of sedentary empires of the early modern age. It was at the moment when two of those empires, the Chinese and the Russian, came into direct contact with each other, starting with the treaties of Nerchinsk (1698), that the "intermediaries" were curbed in their activities and lost their function.[2] As a result the merchants—in this case the Muslim merchants of the Silk Routes—became merchants of the empires who were involved much more with intracontinental than with transcontinental trade, as had formerly been the case.

Intermediary political structures had existed in Inner Asia since ancient times and had been of nomadic or sedentary origin. Their main characteristic was the fact that they relied heavily on trading activities along the transcontinental trade routes. Such formations were not indigenous to Inner Asia. But in the Inner Asian context they should be regarded as quite distinct from the so-called conquest dynasties.[3] States that played the role of intermediaries were not conquest dynasties; instead they thrived by making the best of their own strategic location within trade routes. The Wusun in the Han times, the Kushan or the later Uighur Kingdoms of Kocho and Gansu, as well as the Tangut State in East Asia, and the Ghaznevids and Khwarezmshahs in West Asia, are examples of such states thriving especially on the overland trade between West and East Asia. The Persian epic *Shahnama*[4] provides us with an episode of the historical dilemmas faced by such political formations playing the role of "intermediaries." When news reached the Hephthalite Kingdom that the ruler of Northern China was sending an envoy to the Persian ruler because he "desired to win the friendship of the King," the reaction was as follows

> Ill has befallen us from the stars. If now
> the monarch of Iran and Khan of Chin
> negotiate and thus become good friends,
> that friendship will hold menace for ourselves.
> And this our state be wasted on two sides,
> we must make a foray and deprive
> the envoy of his life.[5]

The envoy was accordingly killed and the Khwarezmshahs of Transoxania acted in like fashion when the Mongols sent their first merchant caravan.[6] In these polities, thriving as they did on merchant activities, political and merchant power were interdependent. This interdependence found in the Islamic age an ideological framework in the form of the Islamic law (*shari'a*) that was everywhere in force for Muslim merchants. From the eighth century on, Muslim merchants gradually extended their sphere of influence eastward towards China. By the thirteenth century Muslim merchants had become the masters of the Silk Routes of Inner Asia, especially as members of Muslim Merchant Companies called *ortak* (partner).[7]

From the early days of Islam, this spirit of interdependence between political and merchant power contributed in some measure to development—Muslim merchants would either precede or accompany new "Islamic" governments along the trade routes. As a rule they acted as "intermediaries" along the overland trade routes, i.e., the Silk Routes. Muslim merchants, however, did not penetrate the China trade. Their eventual infiltration of the China trade did not lead to the establishment of an Islamic government, on the contrary, it was in cooperation with the Mongols in the Mongolian World Empire. This took the form of a partnership between Muslim merchants and the Mongols.[8] This translation for Muslim merchants and political formations from interdependence to partnership did not develop to the advantage of the Muslim merchants operating in the overland trade.[9] Under the Mongolian Empire, this partnership evolved within half a century to take the form of patronage of the merchants. Muslim merchants who were partners in the state became merchants with privileges in the service of the state. Those who were not privileged were stripped of their special rights and were compelled to pay taxes.[10]

From then on, the majority of the Muslim merchants operating in the overland trade mostly held a subordinate position described by Hodgson as being "under the military patronage state."[11] By the fifteenth or sixteenth centuries these military patronage states had become regional empires, such as those of the Ottomans, Safawids, and Timurids in India (the Mughals). This regionalization of Asia under major empires meant that Muslim merchants had to face political formations that could not be manipulated by Muslim merchant associations.

Concomitant with these changes, a new phenomenon appeared in Inner Asia, i.e., a tendency among Muslim merchant groups to wrest their autonomy from political formations by associating themselves with Islamic Sufi orders (*tarikahs*), among which the Nakshbandiyya were to take the lead. From the fifteenth century onwards, we observe in Inner Asia not so much the formation of regional empires as the expansion of Nakshbandi networks in which traders played a major role. It was also during this time that the Muslim merchants in Inner Asia became known generally as "Bukharans." Most of these Bukharan merchants were associated with various *khankahs* or *takiyas* (hostels) that were known as "Bukhari" or "Bukharliyya." For the most part these Bukhari strongholds were of Nakshbandi denomination, although some of them belonged to the Kadiriyya.[12] The merchants and Sufis associated with these hostels were not all from Bukhara. Khokandis in the eighteenth and nineteenth centuries for instance were called Bukharans because they were associated with Bukhari *meshayikh* (spiritual leaders). Likewise a merchant from Turfan (in present Xinjiang, People's Republic of China) was also known as the "Bukharan from Turfan." It would seem that this appellation was influenced by the role Bukhara played as a pilgrimage site where the tomb of the founder of the Nakshbandiyya *tarikah* was located.[13] It would also appear that, because of the importance of the khojas from Kashgar and within the Nakshbandiyya networks, Tarim Basin—where these cities are located—was called "Little Bukhara" even in the nineteenth century. In other words this appellation concerns the cities south of the Tianshan in present Xinjiang, also known as Eastern Turkestan. In fact, a German observer taking issue with the term "Little Bukhara" says the following in 1863:

Little Bukhara. The plateau between Thian schan and Kuen Iuen is so-called. It is also known as Upper Tatarei or Eastern Turkestan. However, the term 'Little Bukara' as A. Erman points out, is meaningless and should no longer be used. In fact Eastern Turkestan is not small, nor has it any links with the State of Bukhara—which is part of (independent) Turkestan—other than the fact that its caravans passed that way.[14]

The survival of this appellation into the nineteenth century indicates the intensity of Nakshbandi networks in the seventeenth century. Thus, in the regions where these networks functioned—especially in the Tarim Basin where neither the Mongols nor Temür had been able to patronize the merchants of the oasis cities—the interdependence between merchants and political formations of the earlier Islamic age continued.

In the seventeenth century, as the relationship between Muslim merchants, intermediary governments, empires, and Sufi orders crystallized, the formation of modern empires and their subsequent domination over Asian affairs left little room either for "intermediary governments" or for Muslim merchants functioning in interdependence with them. As a result, Muslim merchants became localized under the cloak of Sufi orders and at the same time transformed themselves into dependent elements of the empires. It is in the context of this transformation that seventeenth century "Uighur"[15] merchants will be examined below. To illustrate the situation I will focus on the second half of the seventeenth century when the Uighur merchants had to operate under the Western Mongol Zunghar banner. At the same time, as a result of their Nakshbandi affiliations, they also experimented with an Islamic State, leading to the formation of the Khoja Rule in 1679 under Appak Khoja. But both the Zunghars and Appak Khoja's Islamic State were only intermediaries. However, the days of "intermediary" formations were gone for both nomadic and sedentary polities. The seventeenth century saw the rise of early modern empires.

The first quarter of the seventeenth century witnessed the rise of the Manchu State which, in the second quarter, allied itself to the eastern Mongols as subordinate partners, conquered China and established the Qing Dynasty (1644-1911). On the other hand the Russian Empire was expanding rapidly towards the Pacific. In India the Timurids under Babur had established their territorial empire that came to be known as the Mughal Empire (1526-1707). With the Ottomans in the west (1290-1920) and the Safawids (1503-1722) in Iran, the peripheries of Asia had accordingly been marked out.

In Inner Asia on the other hand, both the Özbeg Khanate in Transoxania and the Sa'idiyya State in the Tarim Basin were political formations that depended on precarious power balances.[16] Unlike the regionalization of empires, here in Inner Asia we witness a tendency towards a dissolution of centralized regimes and a development of many smaller nodal points. It is a process that developed as the Ozbeg Khanate and the Sa'idiyya State converted from being political structures based on nomadic and sedentary constituents to states with more purely sedentary interests. The political and economic vacuum that resulted from this shift both in the north of Transoxania and north of the Tarim Basin was then utilized by nomadic groups, i.e., the Lamaistic Buddhist Western Mongols known as the Zunghars in the seventeenth century and the Muslim Turkic-speaking Kazakhs or Mongols later on in the eighteenth century.

The Western Mongols, on the one hand, were descendants of the Oyirad (Oirat) Mongols and, on the other, owed their political existence to the population movements of the beginning of the seventeenth century following the formation of the Manchu State. Thus, as a result of population shifts and the ensuing warfare in Mongolia, the Western Mongols had moved westward by 1616: some into Tarbaghatai, some towards the Irtysh and the Volga region, and others to Eastern Tibet, the Qinghai province of the People's Republic of China. Meanwhile an independent extension of the Kökenor (Qinghai) branch was nomadizing between Lakes Balkash and Zaysan, and gradually extending its presence to the summer pasture grounds in the north of Turfan. In central Tianshan and to the east of it, the Khoyid under their leaders Yeldeng Taishi, his brother Sumur, and their sons, Chuchkin and Yalpu, began to exert their influence in the Tarim Basin from the late 1640s on. Their activities concentrated mainly around Karashahr or Chalish, the passway to the Tarim Basin from the north near present Korla. Some of these Khoyid leaders bore Muslim names, such as Ebu Shah or Sultan Taishi, indicating that the Mongolian- and Turkic-speaking populations were not as divided by religious fervor as was destined to be the case in the nineteenth century. Sultan Taishi is known in Russian records for the envoys he sent to Russia in 1657.[17] By 1655 the Tarim Basin was practically encircled by different Western Mongol groups, whether by the Zunghars in the north or the Kökenor branch in the south and southeast.

In these circumstances, envoys or tribute missions sent from Sa'idiyya State to China (see below) were under threat from Western Mongols. In one such case, an envoy from Yarkand was threatened on his return trip by a Mongol prince who was nomadizing between Hami and the Jiayuguan.[18] It is also no wonder that the Western Mongol princes were not alone in being interested in the affairs of the Tarim Basin; the Chinggisid princes of the Tarim Basin would try to use Mongol power for their own ends, allying themselves from time to time with the Zunghars in particular.

The rulers of the Tarim Basin were descendants of Chinggis Khan and of the leaders of the Dughlat, a Mongolian tribe. Earlier they were known as the Later or Eastern Chaghataids (c. 1347-1570)[19] as they were established on the remnants of the Chaghatai Ulus, the patrimony of Chinggis Khan's second son. As Later Chaghataids, under the leadership of Tughluk Temür (1347-1363), a descendant of Chinggis Khan from a minor line, they had also adopted Islam. Their Muslim identity became so important that the sixteenth century author Mirza Mehemmed Haidar Dughlat finds it appropriate to speak of them only as Muslim Mongols, who in Western scholarship have generally been known as Moghuls. The relationship of these later Chaghataids or the Muslim Mongols (Moghuls) to the earlier Chaghataids is also recognized by the early Qing authorities. A decree dated 19 July 1646 and addressed to the Khan of Turfan reads: "According to my recollections, your country, the Turfan region, is the land that was previously granted to Chaghadai, the second son of the Yuan ruler Chinggis Khan."[20] The Muslim identity of the inhabitants of the Tarim Basin also finds expression in another early Qing entry from 16 August 1645 where the Khanate is referred to as *Huihui guo*, meaning literally "the Muslim country,"[21] probably because it was the Muslim country closest to China.

The Later Chaghatai Khanate was a political structure in which the Islamic, Mongolian, and Turkish traditions had merged—as such it was rooted both in nomadic and in sedentary interests. Already by the beginning of the sixteenth century, however, its rulers became more firmly established in the agricultural domains to the south of the Tianshan and slowly lost the support of the nomadic populations.[22] It was also during this time that the Islamic Sufi orders began to penetrate Tarim Basin politics.[23] Since both trends—sedentarization and affiliation with Sufi orders—started with the reign of Sultan Sa'id Khan (1514-1533), the rule of Chinggisid princes from 1514 until their elimination from rule by Appak Khoja in 1679 was referred to by present Uighur scholars either as the Sa'idiyya State or, from their capital in Yarkand, as the Yarkand Khanate.[24] The Sa'idiyya State presented a curious picture. Population-wise it had a sedentary basis, yet its political ideology was still very much influenced by steppe traditions and as such lacked a centralized rule. The state was based on the principles of power-sharing, mostly among brothers. Power was not always shared on peaceful terms, it allowed for military as well as political maneuvering depending upon the circumstances. Thus we see Chinggisid princes ruling in the different cities of Tarim Basin, generally regarding one or two of their number as "seniors." At first the rulers of Yarkand and Turfan played the role of seniors. By the middle of the seventeenth century, 'Abdullah Khan (1636-1668) had been successful in getting his own rule recognized as "primus inter pares."[25]

In the year 1655 the situation was such that according to all appearances there was only one ruler, i.e., 'Abdullah Khan governing in Yarkand. However, his envoy to the Qing court, a certain Kebeg, was at pains to convince the authorities that the Tarim Basin was not governed by one person but by seven brothers each ruling from a city under his jurisdiction and recognizing the ruler of Yarkand as senior. He says:

> The rulers of Hami, Turfan and Yarkand are all brothers. Their father's name was Abdurrahim. He ruled in Yarkand. He died a long time ago. He had nine sons. The eldest is 'Abdullah Khan and he rules in Yarkand. The second son is Ebul Mehemmed Khan. He used to rule in Turfan, but died two years ago. He was succeeded by the next son in order, Sultan Sa'id Khan. The next son in order was Babai Khan; he used to rule in Hami. Because he was found guilty by the 'Heavenly Court' [i.e., China], the ruler of Yarkand arrested him and had Ebul Mehemmed Khan's son succeed him. The next son in order is Mehemmed Sultan and he rules in Pali. The next son, Shah Khan, rules in Kucha [Kuqa]. The next one died quite young. The next one, Ismail, rules in Aksu. The next one rules in Khotan [Yutian]. Previously, whenever the ruler of Yarkand asked his brother to send a tribute mission from Turfan, the mission documents carried the name of the Khan of Turfan. At present the ruler of Yarkand is recognized as senior by his brothers, so that the documents carry the name of the Khan of Yarkand.[26]

As if to substantiate his picture of harmony and account for the fact that circumstances in his homeland were different, Kebeg adds: "We little countries do not know the Great Rites and Decorum (*dali*)." When the Qing authorities inquired as to why different names were used in different documents, it seems that the simplest solution was for Kebeg to assume a condescending attitude, thereby indicating the existence of many rulers in his country.[27] The above words were expressed in relation to these facts which would explain why different tribute caravans appeared to be commissioned by different rulers. If it were not in the interest of the Sa'idiyya rulers and princes to send different tribute caravans, the envoy Kebeg could content himself with speaking of the rule of 'Abdullah Khan alone, as contemporaneous local historical sources do.[28] Accordingly his attempt to paint a rosy picture of seven brothers ruling in harmony should be presented with some reservations.[29]

In fact, the "little countries" mentioned by Kebeg were facing severe problems at this juncture. They were situated in the oasis cities which were both centers of agricultural production and halting places in the overland trade. All the rulers and princes were eager therefore to retain their position as intermediaries between China and the West. This enabled them to establish quite effective networks with which to squeeze profits out of the caravan merchants. The fact that there were seven rulers meant repeated pressure on the caravan merchants. By the turn of the seventeenth century the Chinggisids ruling in the Tarim Basin had lost control of the north of Tianshan.[30] Loss of control of the north also meant loss of military power;[31] thus, the ruling Chinggisids found themselves ruling the old cities in the Tarim Basin in much the same way as the earlier city states played the role of intermediaries in the overland trade. However, they found the situation extremely difficult as they were surrounded on almost every side by different Western Mongol groups. The rulers attempted to collect transit fees besides initiating caravans of their own.

Benedict de Goes' account gives us detailed information on the circumstances prevailing in Yarkand at the start of the seventeenth century. He arrived in Yarkand in 1603 on his way to China; the caravan of merchants he had accompanied there from Kabul dispersed so that he had to wait for another one to form. Mehemmed Khan, the ruler of the western domains, sold the right to put together a caravan in his name for 200 sacks of musk. The caravan leader thus acquired the right to act as the leader of a diplomatic mission. This was common practice. The sixteenth century Ottoman traveler, 'Ali Akbar, mentions this too, saying: "Merchants coming from Islamic countries use the overland caravan route. They have to use the title 'envoy.'"[32] Goes then tells us that the ruler also confirmed that all the people joining the caravan were under the command of the caravan leader. The latter in addition secured the right to act as "envoys" for four more persons. For this he had to pay a lot of money and present valuable gifts. The members of the caravan had all purchased their "seats" in the caravan. Here we see in great detail how a caravan heading towards China took on the role of a diplomatic mission, which in Chinese parlance would be referred to as a tribute mission. "There was no other way for them to enter that country," says 'Ali Akbar.[33] Once the caravan had started out, the documents were examined at a place called "Yolchi,"[34] meaning a checkpoint for caravans. This is where exit dues were paid. Goes further tells us that the merchants would be informed as to when they could leave, since their arrival time was determined by the Ming Court. They could not go there every year, and were obliged to arrive at determined intervals.[35] Such circumstances explain why each city would try to send a caravan in the name of its ruler. In the case of Kebeg's 1655 mission, we even see that a separate mission from the small town of Bai near Kucha also arrived in China.[36] Although these city caravans would be profitable for the merchants involved, it seems that the costs involved were too high so that we see merchants gradually turning for protection elsewhere. This was facilitated by the changing balance of power among new actors on the Inner Asian scene. With the turn of events and competing nodes of power, they were going to associate themselves with the Zunghar Mongols who were establishing their empire in Inner Asia (1640-1759). It was the emergence of the Zunghars that led to the weakening of the Sa'idiyya Khans.

As a consequence, notwithstanding Kebeg's reassurances about the "harmonious alliance" that ruled his country, there occurred a good deal of internal strife among the cities of the Tarim Basin as well as between the Western Mongols and the Chinggisid princes, who were the rulers of the Tarim Basin. The "security" of the trade routes leading through the cities of the Tarim Basin came under threat. The local historian Shah Mahmud ibn Mirza Fazil Choras reported in 1633 that the stretch of the road connecting Kucha to the Turfan road was no longer safe.[37] As this stretch covers the central portion of the northern edges of the Tarim Basin, the information indicates that Yarkand was cut off from trade with China. We see 'Abdullah Khan conducting various campaigns into the Ferghane area in an effort to increase his sphere of influence and bargaining power in relation to outlets. But he was defeated most of the time by the Kirghiz or by the Zunghars whose forces were better disciplined than his.[38] The eastern part of the domains came entirely under Zunghar domination after 1659.[39]

The problems of the Tarim Basin routes had certain repercussions in the western provinces of China. It appears that many people were moving into Western China so that they could carry on private trading with Tarim Basin cities and Hami. In this way, apparently, the merchants tried to overcome the squeeze of the so-called official "tributary" missions. The volume of this official trade, however, was not insignificant; Ming quotas established the minimum "official" quantities for such trade and give some idea of its volume. Those quotas remained operative even after the downfall of the dynasty and were in fact adopted by the Qing later in 1646:

> We have examined the old regulations. When Turfan came to present tribute, what they could purchase in the capital is shown below on a per capita basis: 15 *jin* [7.5 kg] of tea, 50 sets of chinaware; 5 copper jugs, 15 bolts of *sha*, *lo* silk and satin of diverse colours, 30 bolts of *juan,* 30 bolts of grey-blue striped cotton, 30 bolts of white linen, 30 *jin* of quilting cotton, 2 rugs with flower designs, 300 sheets of paper for ritual purposes, 5 *jin* of paint of diverse colours, 30 *jin* each of sweetmeats, dried fruits and ginger, 30 *jin* of medicine, 30 *jin* of black prunes and 10 *jin* of white and black alum.

After departure from the capital, when they arrive at Lintaofu and Lanzhou, they can acquire oxen, sheep, ploughs, shovels and iron pots from the members of the garrison troops stationed there … But it is forbidden for them to purchase iron or military weapons.[40]

In addition to this official trade, there was a great deal of private trade going on, which was always a cause of concern to Chinese bureaucracy. By 1656 an immigrant population of Muslim Uighurs had joined the already large Muslim population (the present Hui) in the area of Suzhou (the present Jiuquan) and Ganzhou (the present Zhangye) area. Speaking of the Muslim population in Suzhou, Matteo Ricci says that they resided here in large numbers because of the trade with Kashgar and other places in the west. In fact the Muslims were so numerous that they lived in a separate part of the city.[41]

The Governor-General of Sichuan Shaanxi also submitted a memorial in 1656 in relation to these issues:

> While the earlier Ming Dynasty was using the loose-rein (*jimi*) policy against the people in the outer frontiers, these people had acquired some very bad habits. Because the people of Turfan are avaricious, they used to bring along four or five hundred people when they came to present tribute. They called them 'hostages' and, instead of taking them back with them when they returned, they left them in Inland [i.e., China] in order to pursue their profit-making. These people in turn then carried on their [commercial] relations secretly with Hami. Therefore in the five counties of Ganzhou (present Zhangye) the number of Muslims is increasing every day. It was such people who contributed to the earlier rebellion. Now they have repented and are presenting tribute. But they begin by bringing along men and women and then request food and similar items. If we permit them to stay in the Interior [China], they will shortly cause a calamity.[42]

The above-mentioned revolt had taken place in conjunction with the establishment of the Qing Dynasty. Different groups of Muslims established an administration within the city of Suzhou and acknowledged the leadership of a Chinggisid prince, Torumtai, son of Sultan Sa'id Babai Khan from Turfan. The issues in this revolt appear to have been quite complex.[43] On the one hand Chinggisid princes were involved, on the other, the Turfan ruler abducted about 150 people from this region. If he had come in support of the rebels, he need not have abducted people from the same place. Later when the Qing authorities asked for these people to be returned, the request was not granted on the pretext that they had been taken away by the Zunghars.[44]

This problem was still not solved in 1686 when the ruler of Turfan once again requested the return of these people:

Now I am specially sending our local products as a present. Many of the people who were taken along by the chieftains in their tribute missions remained in the Gansu area. Later on they gradually started to live in the Xining area. Please see to it that they return in order to assist our tribute envoys in their journeys back and forth.[45]

I am inclined to interpret these repeated requests about people who had made their homes in China as so many attempts by the Tarim Basin princes to regain control of merchants who were slipping away from their sphere of influence.

Two independent developments seem to have been at the root of this disenchantment with the Tarim Basin princes. In the first place, the seventeenth century marked the start of the influence of the *khojas* of the Nakshbandi order in the politics of the Tarim Basin and also among merchant groups. And secondly, we also know that during this century the *khojas* were active in the Gansu region.[46] These *khoja* networks were also quite effective in establishing alliances with the Zunghars. As a result, Muslim caravan traders became increasingly closely affiliated with the Nakshbandi order and trade network, on the one hand, and made use of the larger networks of the Zunghars by serving as their traders and envoys on the other. This accounts for the fact that there were fewer and fewer tribute missions from the Tarim Basin to China.[47] Muslim caravan leaders were making use of three centers in particular outside the Tarim Basin. The first of such centers operated in the Gansu region within the Nakshbandi networks, the second in Bukhara in Transoxania, while the third operated in Ili as part of the Zunghar networks. Mention has already been made of the fact that these merchants were known universally as Bukharans, probably because of their connections with the Nakshbandi groups center in Bukhara.

The center in the Gansu region was connected not only to the China trade but also to Russia and Tibet. Cities such as Ganzhou (Zhangye), Lanzhou, Suzhou (Jiuquan), Tankar, and Xining were all situated in this region. At this time they were all under the jurisdiction of the Governor-General in Shaanxi. Ysbrands Ides, a Danish merchant who traveled as an envoy from Russia to Beijing in 1693, speaks of this trade as follows:

This Province [Shaanxi] also borders on the Upper Principality of Tibet which extends to the Territories of the great Mongol, from whose Dominions great numbers of Merchants come to the vast trading city of Zunning, in the Kingdom of Xiensi [Shaanxi]: and the door of commerce being for some time opened here and liberty granted to them as well as Muscovites and Tartars to trade here; they have with their wares and trade introduced the Mahometan Religion which, as weeds grow apace, is spread all over

China, to that degree that there appears more of that accursed seed than the true Doctrine of Jesus Christ.[48]

The Transoxanian centre was also connected to the Indian, Near Eastern, and Russian trades. In the Near East we know of Bukharan traders in Aleppo.[49] These connections were later cultivated by the Khokand Khanate. We also know that Kashgari merchants had strong connections with Mecca, a connection used both for pilgrimage and trade. Both merchants and rulers who encountered political problems would customarily take the route which led through Badakhshan, Kashmir, and India. The Indian trade was also connected to the Khotan-Kashmir route in the Tarim Basin, mostly frequented by Uighur merchants, the so-called Bukharans. But the Transoxanian route was also inhabited by Indian trading colonies, involved principally in usury and banking rather than in carrying goods.[50]

The third center developed in the seventeenth century as a result of the rise of the Zunghars. Camping grounds and tiny "towns" consisting of a few mud-brick houses grouped around a lamasery as in the region of Qobogh Sari and Ili are frequently mentioned by Russian envoys on their way to China.[51] The records of yet another embassy (Sparthary Milescu) mention that by 1676 the trade routes through the Tarim Basin had been replaced by new routes through Zunghar territory:

> The 5th July [1676], a Bukharan, a citizen of Turfan came to see the Ambassador [i.e., Sparthary Milescu] who had been last year to China; but had not gone back to Tobolsk on account of the war. He said there were seventy-two of them, and they arrived with the Tarkhan Lama, who was sent by the Kalmuk Khan Ochirtu, to trade, having with him horses, and slaves, and a few ermines, which they had sold cheap - 25 *lans* per hundred; and good horses at 70 and 80 *lans*, poor ones at 30 and even 20; good slaves went for 100 *lans*, others for 70 or less. As to the war, he said that there was fighting still going on between Galdan and Ochirtu, so that they knew not whether the caravan could get through to Tobolsk or not. He was questioned closely as to the road from China to Asterkhan, how one could go. He answered that from the last Chinese town, from Kokotana [the present Hohhot], to the Bukharan town of Trufan [i.e., Turfan], where Baba Khan lives, who has often sent his envoys to the Great Tsar, it is a 40 days' journey with pack animals as the caravans go, and from Trufan they go to the Bukharan town Samarcand, also by caravan, in 60 days. And from Samarcand to Asterkhan by caravan is 20 days or less, according to the pace, with a certain small danger from the Kalmuks and their natives up to Trufan, *but none from Trufan to Asterkhan* and the way lay through Ochirtu's Kalmuks.[52]

The activities of the Bukharan merchants (among whom the Uighur merchants played an important role) are described in Russian sources.[53] These merchants brought Chinese, Central Asian, and other goods to the autumn fairs at Lake Yamush on the right bank of the Irtish River. Here they did business with Mongolian, Russian, and Siberian merchants. The salt deposits around Lake Yamush had come under Zunghar control so that salt supplies for Tobolsk were dependent on the whims of Zunghar princes.[54] The Zunghars in fact used every possible means to establish themselves as an indispensable element of the Inner Asian trade routes. They were not in a position to conquer China, neither did they entertain any such objective. Their objective was to become the indispensable intermediary in the Sino-Russian trade. To this end they spread rumours in the manner of many other intermediaries in the past. In one of their early encounters with the Russians they tried to create the impression that China was at a distance of three years.

The Uighur merchants, whom local sources call after the cities of their origin and non-local ones call either Bukharans or Muslims,[55] associated themselves with the Zunghars as a means of getting away from the strife and pressures of the Tarim Basin, but also because the Zunghars in all probability did not tax them. The Zunghars taxed the local population of Tarim Basin after 1679 when they began to intervene in Tarim Basin politics on behalf of Appak Khoja whom they installed as the ruler of the country in their name. From that time on, the names of Uighur merchants occur frequently in the Zunghar embassies to the Qing court. The Uighur (Bukharan) merchants whom Sparthary quotes had also come in a Zunghar caravan. Such caravans, which the Qing court sought to limit to approximately 200 persons,[56] expanded to contain as many as 2,000 or 3,000 people at a time. Erke Beg, Ibrahim, Kör Mahmud, Kurban, Kurbanbay, Mahmud, Noyan Khoja, Pulad Khoja, Said, Seyfeddin, Shah Huseyin, Shah Khoja, and Tashlan Khoja are some of the mission leaders mentioned in the sources. Their names tell us that they were Muslims. Disconcerted by the fact that there were large numbers of Muslims among the Zunghar envoys, the Qing court raised certain objections but were assured that the envoys of the *tayishis* (Zunghar princes) had always been Muslims.[57] This kind of large tribute mission consisting of at least 2,000 people continued at least up to 1694.[58] It should be noted, however, that the Turfani merchant whom Sparthary met in 1676 spoke of their participation in the Zunghar trade before the Zunghar occupation of the Tarim Basin.

By joining the ranks of Zunghar tribute missions, the Uighur merchants of the Tarim Basin confined their movements mainly to routes north of the Tianshan. The Zunghars had rendered the major routes leading south of the Tianshan inhospitable, thereby diverting them to pass through their own territory. The new routes extended from Turfan to Samarkand over the Tianshan (sixty days) and led to Astrakhan (twenty days). The Samarkand route was also connected to the routes connecting Kabul to Iran and Kashmir to India. Further the Tobolsk-Tara-Yamush Lake route led along the Irtish to Turfan and from there to Köke Khota in twenty days (present Hohhot). From Turfan they also extended to Suzhou (present Jiuquan) and from there to Xining and Tibet.

It is also noteworthy that the so-called White Mountain or, to be more exact, the "White Cap" faction of Appak Khoja's followers were located in such cities as Kashgar, Aksu, and Kucha along the southern slopes of the Tianshan. Appak Khoja was instrumental in bringing Zunghar domination to the Tarim Basin in 1679. Yet the inhabitants of the oasis cities did not yield to this domination—more than 74,000 people were killed in the struggles against the Zunghars and Appak Khoja.[59] The sources make it clear, nevertheless, that Appak Khoja was assisted by the notables of these oasis cities, along with his followers who numbered 300,000. In the eighteenth century the notables of these cities decided that the days of the Zunghar were over. They were guided in this above all else by their White Cap (or Mountain) Nakshbandi affiliations.[60]

In conclusion I wish to emphasize that the general developments affecting the closure of the Silk Routes in the seventeenth and eighteenth centuries may be considered as part of the crisis of the seventeenth century as a whole. More specifically, however, it was caused by the fact that the rulers of the Tarim Basin were confronted with grave difficulties as intermediaries. Their merchants sought outlets in alliance with the Zunghars who were yet another intermediary formation. Developments on the Asian continent left no room for intermediaries, while merchants continued to trade as members of modern empires. Their affiliation with the Nakshbandi networks compensated for the weaknesses of the political structures of the Tarim Basin. The close spiritual ties among the merchants enabled them to carry on their commercial activities at a specific level without being too disturbed by political changes at a general level.

Notes

1. A.G. Frank, "The Centrality of Central Asia" (Urumqi Seminar Paper, 1990).
2. Adopting a slightly different approach, Morris Rossabi sees here the exclusion of Muslim merchants from the tea trade of China (M. Rossabi, "Muslim and Central Asian Revolts," in *From Ming to Ch'ing*, edited by J.D. Spence and J.E. Wills, Jr. [New Haven and London: Yale University Press, 1979], p. 91) whereas my emphasis here is on the continuation of trade with different trading patterns. In a later study Rossabi states that short-distance caravan-trade did not diminish. In his opinion internal political disturbances around the Tarim Basin contributed to the decline of long-distance trade. He further maintains that commerce between pastoral and sedentary societies continued uninterrupted even after the sixteenth century (M. Rossabi, "The 'Decline' of the Central Asian Caravan Trade," in *Ecology and Empire*, edited by G. Seaman [Los Angeles: Ethnographics/USC, 1989], pp. 81-102). A recent study by Stephen Dale (S. Dale, *Indian Merchants and Eurasian Trade* [Cambridge: Cambridge University Press, 1994]) shows, on the other hand, that Central Asian trade was still an important factor in Asian commerce.
3. T. Barfield, *The Perilous Frontier: Nomadic Empires and China* (Cambridge, Mass.: Basil Blackwell, 1989), pp. 164-84.
4. Names and terms in Eastern Turki, Persian, Arabic, and Modern Uighur have been transcribed according to the system developed by Janos Eckmann in his Chaghatai Manual with the following changes: c is j, cis is ch, g is gh, h is kh, q is k (to differentiate it from the *pinyin* q), and s is sh.

   In phonetic reconstructions from Chinese texts I have not used diacritical marks because, in such cases, names were not necessarily written on the basis of texts. The oral tradition played an important role in most cases.
5. Firdawsi, *The Shah nama of Firdausi*, translated by A.G. Warner and E. Warner, vol. 7 (London: K. Paul, Trench, Trübner & Co, 1905-1915), p. 329.
6. Barthold,1968, p. 399.
7. I. Togan, "The Mongols' Trade Partners: A Study of Chinese Trade under Mongol Rule," in *Toplum ve Bilim* (in Turkish with an English Summary), vols. 25/26 (1984), pp. 71-90.
8. T. Allsen, "Mongolian Princes and their Merchant Partners, 1200-1600," in *Asia Major*, 3d series, vol 2, pt. 2 (1989).
9. In the sea trade the earlier trend continued well into the later Middle Ages and the early modern period up to European expansion into the Southern Seas. Marshall D. Hodgson states to this effect: "Trade in the Southern Seas was largely in the hands of numerous more or less independent Muslim trader cities, over which the inland powers had relatively little control in many cases. In an area like Malaysia, for instance, the chief figure in the town, the 'sultan,' was likely to be essentially a merchant, who might even monopolize the trade of a given port, and sometimes was also able to control other ports at a distance." (M.G.S. Hodgson, *The Venture of Islam*, vol. 3 [Chicago: Chicago University Press, 1974], p. 19).
10. Togan, "The Mongols' Trade Partner;" Endicott-West, 1989.
11. Hodgson, *The Venture of Islam*, vol. 2, pp. 400-10.
12. de Jong, 1978, pp. 78-81.
13. A. Vambery, *Travels in Central Asia* (New York: Arno Press, 1970), p. 211.
14. An anonymous note appearing in the German geographical journal, *Globus* vol. 4 (1863): p. 64.
15. The name Uighur has been in use in this region for more than a millennium, but with more restricted meanings than is the case today (D.C. Gladney, "The Ethno-

genesis of the Uighur," in *Central Asian Survey*, vol. 9, no. 1 [1990]: pp. 1-28; Geng Shimin, "On the Fusion of Nationalities in the Tarim Basin and the Formation of the Modern Uighur Nationality," in *Central Asian Survey*, vol. 3, no. 4 [1984]: pp. 1-14). I use it here to indicate the seventeenth-century ancestors of the present Uighurs in Xinjiang Uygur Autonomous Region, PRC.

16. *UKT. Uyghurlarning Kiskecha Tarikhi* (A Short History of the Uygurs), by 'Aziz Yusup and Tursun Palta. Urumchi, Shinjang Khalk Nashriyati (Title in Chinese: *Weiwur lishi*) (Xinjiang, PRC, 1990), pp. 304-38.

17. I. Ya Zlatkin, *Istoriya Zhunkarskogo Khanstva (1935-1758)* (Moscow, 1964), p. 207.

18. MHWB = Qinding waifan menggu huibu wanggong biaozhuan. 1802. Beijing, This Palace edition *of Wuyingdian* is available at Collège de France, Paris (no. 90-92), 4r. For the different edited versions of the work, see I. Togan, "On the Compilation of the Multilingual Ch'ing Work: The *Iledkel Sastir* or the *Piao Chuan*," in: Niguca Bicig. An Anniversary Volume in honor of Francis Woodman Cleaves, *Journal of Turkish Studies*, vol. 9 (1985): pp. 1-5; I. Togan, "Eastern Turkestan in the Seventeenth Century with an Emphasis on the Turfan Chapter of Ch'in-ting wai-fan meng-ku hui-pu wang-kung piao chüan" (completed manuscript in Turkish), in *Sources of Language: Oriental Ages and Literatures Series* (forthcoming), p. 98.

19. KT, pp. 302-3; Ho-dong Kim, "Succession Struggle and Tribal Politics in the former Moghul Khanate," in *Journal of Oriental History* (In Korean with an English summary) vol. 33 (1990): pp. 63-100.

20. QSL = *Daqing Lichao Shilu* (Veritable Records of the great Qing Dynasty) vol. 4 (Taibei, 1964): p. 312; *Shun* 26: 16v-17r.

21. QSL, vol. 4, p. 220; *Shun* 18: 24r; Togan, "Eastern Turkestan in the Seventeenth Century," p. 78-79.

22. I. Togan, "Islam as a State Power in a Changing Society: The Khojas of Eastern Turkestan," in *Identity in the Muslim Societies of Central Asia*, edited by J. Gross, (Durham, N.C.: Duke University Press, forthcoming).

23. I. Niyaz, *Tarikhtin Kiskecha Bayanlar* (Short Notes on History) (Kashkar: Kashkar Uyghur Nashriyati, 1988), pp. 269-75. Title in Chinese: *Jian ming lishi.*

24. Here I have adopted the terminology used by Uighur scholars in Xinjiang Uygur Autonomous Region, PRC. I have argued elsewhere that any wish to create a category of *Moghul* as distinct from Mongol is not realistic as our sources do not permit us to make such a distinction on the basis of the Arabic alphabet as used for Persian or Chaghatai Turkish. See Togan, "Islam as a State Power." I think therefore that the local terminology of Sa'idiyya State is quite useful.

25. Togan, "Islam as a State Power."

26. MHWB, 3r-3v

27. We do not have to take Kebeg's words literally as they appear in the QSL: such Chinese versions of his words were intended mainly for home consumption.

28. O.F. Akimushkin, *Shah Mahmud ibn Mirza Fadil Churas: Khronika*, translation with critical text, commentary and study (Moscow, 1976). (Pamiatniki pis'mennosti Vostoka, 45).

29. Kebeg's information about the nine sons and seven rulers contains certain inaccuracies, but this seems to have been deliberate. As he was trying to avoid mentioning any unpleasant personalities, he appears to have provided some additional fictitious information, i.e., in the references to Sultan Sa'id Baba Khan. Otherwise the account may be regarded as accurate.

30. Togan, "Islam as a State Power."

31. It seems that 'Abdullah Khan was alone in being able to muster armies of any size, but he was unable to keep them under control; in the western campaign to Ferghane Valley there was a lot of looting and the soldiers could not be restrained.

32. Yih-min Lin, *Ali Ekber'in Hitayname adli eserinin Çin kaynaklari ile mukayese ve tenkidi* (Tai-pei, 1967), p. 156.

33. Lin, *Ali Ekber'in*, p. 156.

34. A place still known today as being located at the junction of the mountain roads where they meet between Artush and Beshkerem. Personal communication by Memet Sabit, curator in the Office of Antiquities, Kashgar, Xinjiang.

35. M. Wessels, *Early Jesuit Travellers in Central Asia* (The Hague, 1924), p. 25.

36. MHWB, 3r; Togan, "Islam as a State Power."

37. Akimushkin, *Shah Mahmud*, p. 75a.

38. UKT, p. 318.

39. I. Niyaz, *Tarikhtin Kiskecha Bayanlar* (Short Notes on History) (Kashkar: Kashkar Uyghur Nashriyati, 1988), p. 224. Title in Chinese: *Jian ming lishi*.

40. QSL, 4: p. 310; *Shun* 26: 11r-12r.

41. L. Gallagher, *China in the Sixteenth Century: The Journals of Matthew Ricci, 1583-1610* (New York, 1953), p. 513-15.

42. MHWB, 4r-4v.

43. Rossabi, "Muslim and Central Asian Revolts," p. 192.

44. MHWB, 3r. Only fifteen of the captives were returned.

45. MHWB, 6v.

46. Fletcher, "Ch'ing Inner Asia."

47. Rossabi, "The 'Decline' of the Central Asian Caravan Trade."

48. E.Y. Ides, *Three Years Travels from Moscow Over-land to China: thro' Great Ustiga, Siriania, Permia, Sibiria, Daur, Great Tartary, etc. to Peking* (London, 1706), pp. 126-27.

49. I am indebted to Professor Bruce Masters for this personal communication.

50. Paper delivered by Professor Stephen Dale at Washington University in St Louis.

51. J.F. Baddeley, *Russia, Mongolia and China* vol. 2 (London: Macmillan and Co., 1919), pp. 123-26, 139.

52. Baddeley, *Russia*, vol.1, p. 379 [My emphasis]

53. J. Fletcher, "V.A. Alexandrov on Russo-Ch'ing Relations in the Seventeenth Century: Critique and Résumé," in *Kritika* vol. 7.3 (1971): pp. 138-70.

54. Baddeley, *Russia*, vol. 2, p. 90

55. This is a case where appellations from different sources fail to overlap. All of them have a subjective relativity. For local sources—i.e., Central Asian Muslim ones—the city of origin is important, as they primarily address a local audience; local sources therefore are precise in detail. Such precision does not necessarily indicate a lack of common identity. It is quite clear that the local Central Asian sources speak from the vantage point of a Muslim population whose primary language is Turki but among whom Persian also plays an important role. Non-local sources, on the other hand, are inclined to overgeneralize. Islamic sources from the Middle East and Russian sources speak of Bukharans or Bukhariots whereas Chinese ones speak of Muslims.

56. QSL, 9, pp. 1492-93; *Kang*, p. 116: 24r; SMFL 1, pp. 267-70; 2.33r-34v.

57. SMFL, 1, p. 196; 1: 34v.

58. SMFL, 3, pp. 1155-58; 14: 5r-6v.

59. Niyaz, *Tarikhtin Kiskecha Bayanlar*, p. 236.

60. Here I am using Ibrahim Niyaz's term, i.e., "White Cap" (*ak takiya*) in preference to White Mountain (*ak taghiya* or *ak taghlik*). See Niyaz, *Tarikhtin Kiskecha Bayanlar*, pp. 275-79.

Chapter 14

THE EXCHANGE OF MUSICAL INFLUENCES BETWEEN KOREA AND CENTRAL ASIA IN ANCIENT TIMES

Song Bang-Song

Introduction:
The Influence and Acceptance of Foreign Music

Korea has enjoyed a continual exchange of cultural influences with her neighbors throughout history, particularly in the realm of music. Present day Korean music originated in the Three Kingdoms period of Koguryo (37 B.C.-A.D. 668), Paekche (18 B.C.-A.D. 660), and Silla (57 B.C.-A.D. 935). Korean music was closely related to the musical culture of her immediate neighbor, China, as well as to that of Central Asia. It is the author's understanding that the major theme of the current UNESCO-sponsored international seminar on "Korean Culture and the Silk Road" is designed to explore, academically, various fields of Korean culture, each from its own angle.

The terms "influence" and "acceptance" are two academic terms of significant importance which are invariably used in any discussion on the mutual relationship in cultural exchanges with neighboring countries. Consequently, the two terms have to be clearly defined and differentiated, according to how the relationship with the foreign culture is viewed. We will use the term "influence" to describe the reception of one culture by that of another.

The influence and acceptance of foreign culture take place repeatedly in history. A particular cultural aspect of a nation may dominate another, or a culture of one nation may accept that of another of its own volition, while the two may interact with each other on equal terms. The issues of influence from and acceptance of foreign culture are so complex and diverse that they are quite difficult to grasp. However, the author will attempt to explore how music from Central Asia was accepted in the ancient history of Korean music, from the Three Kingdoms period until the Unified Silla period. We will cover four subjects in terms of acceptance of music from Central Asia: Buddhist chant (*pomp'ae*) of Unified Silla; Ch'oe Ch'i-won's *Hyangak chabyong osu* or "Five recited poems of *hyangak*;" the traverse flute (*hoengjok*) and five-stringed lute (*ohyon pip'a*) of Koguryo; and modal terms (*wolcho, pansopcho, hwanjongo*) of Tang music in the three bamboo instruments (*samjuk*) of Silla. On the basis of research in progress, an overview will be conducted in the following three sections.

Pomp'ae of Unified Silla and Ch'oe Ch'i-Won's Hyangak Chabyong Osu

Buddhist chant (*pomp'ae*) is an important musical genre which developed in close relation with Buddhist rites. Though it is said that the root of *pomp'ae* may be traced back to Brahmanism based upon Indian Vedic thought, the ancient *pomp'ae* is known to have been derived directly from the Chinese *fanbai* initiated by Cao Zhi (Cho Sik in Sino-Korean: 192-232) of the Wei Dynasty in the third century.[1] If Chinese *fanbai* was rooted in the Buddhism of India, then it may be reasonable to assert that Korean *pomp'ae* might have been historically related to the musical culture of Central Asia.

Buddhism was introduced into Koguryo in 372 (second year in the reign of King Sosurim), then into Paekche in 384 (first year in the reign of King Ch'imnyu), and then to Silla in 535 (twenty-second year in the reign of King Pophung). Thus *pomp'ae* seems to have been introduced into the Three Kingdoms along with the introduction of Buddhism, because religious rituals must have been indispensable in spreading Buddhism along with the three Buddhist treasures (priest, scripture, and statues). There is, however, no bibliographical data extant today to prove this except for two historical materials containing the record on Silla *pomp'ae* during the South-North Dynasties period in China: the monumental inscription for the Zen monk, Chin'gam, and Ennin's (Won In in Sino-Korean: 793-864) *Diary of Pilgrimage to Tang in Search for the*

Law (*Nitto guho junrei gyoki*). *Pomp'ae*, as practiced in Unified Silla, may be summarized as follows.[2]

Zen monk Chin'gam, a high Silla monk, (Hyeso: 774-850) went to Tang in 804 (fifteenth year in the reign of King Aejang), returned home in 830 (fifth year in the reign of King Hungdok), and taught *pomp'ae* at a famous Buddhist temple now known as Ssanggyesa. He introduced *pomp'ae* of the Tang style to Silla society in the early ninth century. At about the same time, a Japanese high monk, Ennin, toured Tang from 838 to 847, and recorded in his travelogue that three styles of *pomp'ae* were practiced at a Silla temple (Choksanwon) located in the Shantung peninsula of China. They comprised the first Silla style in practice in Silla society, the second Tang style then popular in Tang society, and the third Japanese style then in vogue in Japanese society.

As the Zen monk, Chin'gam, taught *pomp'ae* he had learnt in Tang, China; it must have been the Tang-style *fanbai* of the early ninth century as referred to in Ennin's travelogue. It may also be safely assumed that *pomp'ae* of either the Silla or Japanese style must have been played respectively in Silla or Japanese society prior to the ninth century. One of them must have been what the Silla accepted and developed into a more enriched Silla form.

The five poems of *hyangak* (*Hyangak chabyong osu*) in Chinese characters by Ch'oe Ch'i-won (born in 857) are important documents which depict an aspect of the performing arts in Silla society towards the end of the ninth century. Ch'oe Ch'i-won went to Tang in 869 (ninth year in the reign of King Kyongmun) at the age of twelve, passed the state civil service examination, served in a government post, and then returned home in 885 (fifth year in the reign of King Hon'gang). The five poems of *hyangak* category may be found in the court ballet performance of the *hyangak* and the *tangak* in his *Koryosa* (History of Koryo).[3] It may be construed that Ch'oe Ch'i-won labeled the five performing arts of Central Asia as *hyangak* (native music), because the masked dance plays had already been accepted in Silla society towards the end of the ninth century. The five mask plays, *Kumhwan, Wolchon, Taemyon, Soktok*, and *Sanye*, are said to be typical of Silla music *hyangak*, but in the field of Korean studies, evidence suggests that they were in fact derived from the performing arts of Central Asia.

Kumhwan was assumed to have been related to a play called *lung-wanxi*, a kind of ball game from Central Asia, while *Wolchon* was thought to have been a sort of masked dance play handed down in the Hetian region of Yutian, now Hotan in Central Asia. *Taemyon* was described as having been related to *Ta-mien-hsi* (lit. "big mask play") of Tang—deriving from the barbarian dance of Kuei-tsu, a kind of Shamanistic dance play from Central Asia.[4] *Soktok* was interpreted as a sort of dance play originating from Soghd, now the Tashkent and Samarkand regions of Central Asia. *Sanye* is thought to have derived from a lion's mask play belonging to the Gnizi tradition of Central Asia that is believed to have been related to the Chinese *Xiliang ji.*

The Transverse Flute and the Five-Stringed Lute of Koguryo

Koguryo, bordering on the Asian continent proper, was the first nation among the Three Kingdoms to develop Korea's ethnic musical culture in its continual cultural exchange with the continent, and thereby spread its prestige abroad. A number of research articles on the musical history of Koguryo and Central Asia have already been published in the field of Korean historical musicology.

The musical culture of Koguryo has been recorded as *Koryoak* (*Gaoli yue* in Chinese) or *Koryogi* (*Gaoli ji*) in the authentic histories of China, and as *Komangaku* in Japanese historical documents. Although the musical culture of Koguryo in the Three Kingdoms period has been highlighted in various ways by historical documents on music, its relationship with Central Asia will be surveyed in terms of two musical instruments in use at the time; that is to say, the transverse flute (*hoengjok*) and the five-stringed lute (*ohyon pip'a*), since those instruments were closely related to the *hyangak* instruments of Unified Silla (668-935).

The Koguryo flute, played in a horizontal position like the present-day bamboo flute, was recorded in three ways in authenticated Chinese histories: *hoengch'wi* (*hengchui* in Chinese), *chok* (*di*), and *hoenjok* (*hengdi*); and *yokobue* in the Japanese historical documents.[5] According to these literary documents, the transverse flute is assumed to have been played in Koguryo society up to the sixth century. The relevant archaeological source is a mural painting on Tomb No. 17 at Chiban (Qian), Manchuria, which is thought to have been built in the sixth and seventh centuries.[6] A mural painting of a musical performance on Tomb 1 at Changcho'on (Changchun), Manchuria, would suggest that the historical origin of the Koguryo flute can be traced to the following literary sources.

In view of the fact[7] that the transverse flute was played not only in *Koryogi* (*Gaoli ji*), but also in *Kanggukki* (*Gangkuo ji*), *An'gukki* (*Ankuo ji*), *Sorukki* (*Shuchi ji*), and *Kujagi* (*Guizi ji*) from among seven performing groups called *Ch'ilbugi* (*Qibu ji*) during the Ta-yeh period (605-616); the origin of the Koguryo flute and the Chinese transverse flute may both be traced to Central Asia. Such regions as Suchi (now Kashgar), Kangguo (Samarkand), Anguo (Bukhara), and Quizi (Kucha) had been historically linked to the caravan route between China and Central Asia, namely the Silk Road.

The five-stringed lute of Koguryo, related to musical instruments of Central Asia, was recorded as *ohyon* (*wuxian*) or *ohyon pip'a* (*wuxian pipa*) in the authenticated Chinese histories, but recorded as *hyang-pip'a* (lit. "native lute") in the *Samguk sagi* or *History of the Three Kingdoms*.[8] *Ohyon pip'a* was the name given to the lute because it had five strings. Since the lute had a straight neck, however, it was also called *chikkyong pip'a* ("lute with a straight neck"). The five-stringed lute with a straight neck (*ohyon pip'a*) differs structurally from *sahyon pip'a* or the four-stringed lute which was also known as *kokkyong pip'a* ("lute with a curved neck") or *tang pip'a* ("Chinese lute").

According to the seven or nine performing groups (*Qibu ji* or *Qiubu ji*) and the ten performing groups (*Shibu ji*) of Tang China,[9] the five-stringed lute was also played in *Koryogi* (*Gaoli ji*) and in such performing groups as *Anguo ji* (Bukhara), *Shuchi ji* (Kashgar), *Xiliang ji* (Hexi region upstreams on the Yellow River), *Guizi ji* (the Kucha center on the northern route along the Tienshan Mountains), and *Tienzhu ji* (India). Thus, the origin of the five-stringed lute may lie in Central Asia. Chinese historical documents and archaeological evidence have revealed that the five-stringed lute of Koguryo was played in the sixth century. The mural painting on Tomb No. 1 at Changchuan, Manchuria, however, suggested that the five-stringed lute was played in Koguryo society as early as the fifth century.[10]

As the transverse flute and five-stringed lute were used for *Guizi ji* and *Xiliang ji* music, which came to light after the conquest of Central Asia by Lu Guang in 382 (eighteenth year of Qianyuan), the two instruments must have been introduced into China towards the latter half of the fourth century. It may be safely assumed that the two natural instruments might have been available in Koguryo in the fifth century. In addition to the mural painting on Tomb No. 1 at Changchun, evidence to suggest that the transverse flute and the five-stringed lute must have been accepted in Koguryo society stems from the fact that Koguryo started active cultural exchanges with the earlier Qin State from around the end of the fourth century. Buddhism was introduced into Koguryo in 372 by the monk, Sundo (Sundao), from the earlier Qin State.

Wolcho, Pansopcho, and Hwangjongjo in the Three Bamboo Flutes (Samhyon) of Silla

The musical culture of Unified Silla (668-935) in the North-South Dynasties period of China can be viewed from two angles. Internally, the music of Unified Silla accepted the musical culture of Paekche and Koguryo, and developed them anew. Externally, Unified Silla accepted the mature musical culture of Tang China, thereby lending the musical culture of Silla a new dimension. After achieving unification of the Three Kingdoms, Silla accepted the transverse flute called *chok* of Paekche and the flute called *hoengjok* of Koguryo, and proceeded to develop the flutes into the three-bamboo flutes (*samjuk*) of Silla *hyangak*,[11] while the twelve-stringed zither (*kayagum*) of Kaya State, the six-stringed zither (*komun'go* or *hyon'gum*) and the five-stringed lute of Koguryo Kingdom were also accepted as the three-string instruments of Unified Silla *hyangak* in the North-South Dynasties period of China. The musical culture of Unified Silla was able to pursue further development in terms of native Korean music known as *hyangak*.

Cultural exchange with Tang was quite active in the North-South Dynasties period of China, and musical exchange between Unified Silla and Tang was no exception. The Buddhist chant (*pomp'ae*) of Zen monk, Chin'gam, and the Tang-style *pomp'ae* as referred to by the Japanese monk, Ennin, can serve as examples of musical exchange at the time. Another example is the musical features of the three modal systems of Tang music, *hawangjongjo* (*huangzhong*), *pansopcho* (*pan-she-t'iao*), and *wolcho* (*yueh-t'iao*), as referred to in the *Samguk sagi*.[12] These systems of Tang music were derived from the twenty-eight modal terms used in th secular music (*su-yueh*) of Tang. Musical features of the three modal systems follow.

Pancopcho is also known as *t'aejugyunjiujo* or *t'aejuu*, another modal term used in the form of Chinese *yayue*, which means *u*-mode (*yutiao*) in the *t'aeju* (*t'ai-t'su*) key. The modal term *wolcho* in *téaju* identical with *hwangjonggyunjisangjo* or *hwangjongshang* in the Chinese *yayue* form, i.e., *sang* mode (*shangtiao*) in the *hwangjong* (*huangzhong*) key. *Hwangjongjo* (*Huangzhongtiao*), also called *hwangjonggyunjiujo* or *hwangjongu* in the Chinese *yayue* form turned out to be a mode (*yutiao*) in the *hwangjong* key. Such modal terms in the fashion of Chinese *yayue* as *t'aejuu* (*pansopcho*), *hwangjongsang* (*wolcho*), and *hwangjongu* (*hwangjongjo*) are to be interpreted not in terms of *wijosik* (*weitaioshe*) but of *chijiosik* (*zhitiaoshe*).[13]

Pansopcho turned out to be related to *pandam* (*bandan*) from among seven modal systems of So Chi-p'a (Suizhipo), and the Chinese term *bandan* (*pantam* in Sino-Korean) was a Chinese transliteration of the original Sanskrit term, *pancama*. *Wolcho yuetiao*, otherwise called *irwol-cho* (*yiyuetiao*) derived from the *iwolcho* (*yiyuetiao*) was used in the ancient music of Piaoguo, now Burma, under the influence of Indian music at that time.

In the sum, since the three modal systems of Tang music for the three-bamboo flutes turned out to have been part of the twenty-eight modal systems of Tang secular music, which had been accepted in Silla society during the eighth century, it can be safely assumed that, from the standpoint of the overall context of Asian musical history, some Central Asian music was produced in Tang in the eighth century, and was reaccepted as musical culture for the three-bamboo flutes in the latter Silla period (780-935). In other words, the three modal systems of Tang music for the three-bamboo flutes constitute a clear proof that Silla society accepted Tang music as something new in its own musical culture. It may be assumed that the three modal systems were an outcome of cultural exchange undertaken through the Silk Road between Tang and Central Asia, and that outcome was accepted by Silla society in the ninth century.

Concluding Remarks:
The Ancient History of Korean Music and the Silk Road

In the historical development of Korean music, the Three Kingdoms and the Unified Silla periods were ages when the active acceptance of foreign music was pursued most vigorously. The transverse flute (*hoengjok*) and the five-stringed lute (*ohyon pip'a*) of Koguryo played an important role in developing the musical culture in the Three Kingdoms period towards a new direction. The Silla *pomp'ae*, five poems of *hyangak,* and the three modal systems of Tang music were actual examples of the acceptance of foreign culture and their development into outstanding performing arts in the Unified Silla.

Although part of the musical culture achieved in Koguryo and Silla societies was accepted by neighboring China, we have seen that the transverse flute and the five-stringed lute of Koguryo, *pomp'ae*, masked dance plays, and the modal systems of Tang music in Silla were closely related to the musical culture of Central Asia which China had accepted via the Silk Road. One can observe that ancient Korea, rather than having been predominantly influenced one-sidedly by foreign culture, accepted foreign music and remodeled it as her own.

In the case of Koguryo, if they had failed to accept such foreign musical instruments from Central Asia as the transverse flute or the five-stringed lute, and failed in making of them their own instruments, they would not have been able to export their music, *Koryoak* (*Komagaku*), to the ancient Japanese court.[14] The fact that Silla and Paekche as well as Koguryo influenced the ancient music of Japan is well known in the field of Korean and Japanese historical musicology. That is why more weight should be given to the term "acceptance" rather than "influence" in an account of the ancient history of Korean music and its relationship with foreign music.

While some of the Central Asian performing arts, accepted in China via the Silk Road, were accepted by the Korean people, the pattern of acceptance resembled various small streams in the overall flow of the ancient history of Korean music. The independent-minded Korean people have amply displayed their potential in the wide gamut of worldwide culture, including that of music, throughout the Three Kingdoms and North-South Dynasties periods. In a general survey of ancient Korean music, the important role played by Korean musicians in influencing the development of ancient Japanese court music has to be cited as an effect of the independent-minded capacity of the Korean people to accept foreign culture. This can be substantiated by the *Komagaku* tradition in present-day Japanese court music known as *Gagaku*.

Notes

1. Kim Tong-uk, *Han'guk kayo ui yon'gu* (Seoul: Uryu munhwasa, 1961), p. 10.
2. Lee Hye-ku (Yi Hye-gu), *Han'guk umak yon'gu* (Seoul: Kungmin umak yon'guhoe, 1957), pp. 252-59; Song Bang-Song (Song Pang-Song), *Han'guk umak t'ongsa* (Seoul: Ilchogak, 1984), pp. 126-30.
3. *Koryosa, juan* 71.1b1 (*Honsondo*), 4b8-6a9 (*Suyonjang*), 6a1-8b8 (*Oyangson*), 8b9-12a2 (*P'ogurak*), 12a3-13a8 (*Yonhwadae*); *Koryosa, juan* 71.31a3-31b6 (*Mugo*), 31b7-32a8 (*Tong-dong*), 32a9-33a1 (*Muae*), in which the court dance of Chinese origin (*Tangak chongjae*) and that of Korean origin (*Hyangak chongjae*)were listed as *tangak* and *sogak*.
4. Lee Du-hyun (Yi Tu-hyon), *Han'guk ui kamyon'guk* (Seoul: Ilchisa, 1979), pp. 58-66.
5. *Suishu, juan* 81.2a10-2b1; *Beishi, juan* 94.8a5-6; *Kujiruyen, juan* 30.905; and *juan* 34.11a15-16 *(Komagi), juan* 30.909 *(Komagaki)*; *juan* 30.908 (*Yokobueshi,* and *Yokobuesei)*.
6. Lee Hye-ku, *Han'guk umak yon'gu*, pp. 200-9.
7. Ibid, pp. 195-96; Kishibe Shigeo, *Kodai shiruku rodo no ongaku* (Tokyo: Kotansha, 1982), p. 105.
8. Song Bang-Song, *Han'gik umak t'ongsa*.
9. See Note 7.
10. Song Bang-Song, *Hankuk kodeumaksa Yeongu* (Iljisa, Seoul, 1985), pp. 22-36.
11. Ibid, pp. 77-109; Song Bang-Song, *Koryo umaksa yon'gu* (Seoul: Ilchisa, 1988), pp. 137-67.
12. Song Bang-Song, "Silla samjuk ui tangakcho yon'gu," *Han'guk hakpo*, vol. 56 (Seoul: Ilchisa, 1989): pp. 2-53.
13. Kishibe Shigeo, *Kodai siruku rodo no ongaku,* pp. 164-202; Song Bang-Song (trans.), "Tangsogak isipp'alcho wa kuja soyok ch'ilcho," *Han'guk umak sahakpo*, vol. 2 (Kyongsan: Han'guk umak sahakhoe, 1989), pp. 125-53.
14. Song Bang-Song, "Han'guk kodai umak ui Ilbon chonp'a," *Han'guk umak sahakpo* vol. 1 (1988): pp. 7-40; or *Kusagawan nonch'ong*, vol. 1 (Kwach'on: Kuksa p'yonch'an wiwonhoe, 1989): pp. 27-53.

Chapter 15

THE TRADE ROUTES AND THE DIFFUSION OF ARTISTIC TRADITIONS IN SOUTH AND SOUTHEAST ASIA

Nandana Chutiwongs

The cultural history of most countries in South and Southeast Asia appears to have been closely linked to trade and the trade routes. More and more evidence is being found to indicate that many communities in this part of the world formed a network of commercial activities since prehistoric times.[1] However, it was apparently the increased demand by Rome as well as by China for exotic and luxury goods that generated a great expansion of international trade around the beginning of the Christian era. While caravans were slowly plodding along the desolate land routes between India and China, ships taking advantage of knowledge of the monsoons plied regularly from many ports in the Indian subcontinent to Southeast Asia and even further east. Not only spices, but also aromatic roots, resins, and the other well-known natural products of Southeast Asia were conveyed along these routes. Surveys and excavations at Mantai,[2] Oc-éo,[3] U-Thong,[4] Ban Don Thaphet,[5] and many sites in peninsular Thailand[6] have brought to light a large variety of objects which originated from the Mediterranean world, from India and from China. These, together with the finds at Arikamedu[7] and the famous Begram hoard in Afghanistan,[8] bear witness to the diversity of the luxury products transported between Rome and China during the first centuries of the Christian era.

Many relay stations for caravans and ships, and trading centers for the acquisition and exchange of goods, grew up while the regions situated along the trade routes became partners in international trade. Trade generated material gain and wealth that laid the economic basis for the development of the communities involved, while the various centers of commerce flourished into centers of political power and culture. The caravans and trading ships from the Indian subcontinent brought with them to points further east many aspects of Indian culture—the benefits of which were realized by the élite of the new regions. The trade routes made possible the journeys of Buddhist monks and of Brahmins, motivated either by missionary zeal or by the quest for fame and power. These priestly travelers introduced Indian religions, rituals of worship, and concepts of divine kingship together with the mythologies that glorify the gods and the rulers; as well as the Indian system of state organization, of script and literature, and the use of Sanskrit as the sacred language. Under these influences of Indian culture, the internal structure of the new societies underwent a great change and Indianized settlements and states grew up along the trade routes. The traffic of monks and Brahmins from the Indian subcontinent then became counterbalanced and eventually overbalanced by that of pilgrims and envoys from overseas. Religious concepts and the artistic traditions that had been instrumental to religions found their way into Southeast Asia along the same route that had brought merchants and economic gain.[9] Buddhism and Hinduism became the strongest spiritual forces, and monuments and shrines were consequently erected in honor of the Buddha, the gods, and the divine rulers. Material wealth, largely acquired through trade, generated economic welfare which was further stabilized by agriculture. Trade and agricultural surplus supplied the necessary funding for the construction and maintenance of civil and religious edifices. Craftsmen, artists, and technicians were required by the courts, religious institutions, and other wealthy patrons. The community supplied manpower, paid or unpaid,[10] while the priests looked after the ritual procedures involved in the processes. These combined efforts created and maintained the monuments of faiths, and set forth the religious traditions which brought spiritual felicity and solace to the entire community.

Influences of artistic traditions from the Indian subcontinent flowed into Southeast Asia largely via the sea route which served as the most convenient channel of communication in those days. Although few written records from Southeast Asia provide relevant information as to the actual process of diffusion of such traditions, the existing monuments themselves bear indisputable testimony to the introduction and assimilation of those foreign elements which must have taken place at one time or another.

The process of transmission of cultural and artistic traditions evidently involved many types of agency and circumstance. Buddhism and Hinduism introduced their traditional architectural form and imagery.

Chinese accounts contain many references to Buddhist monks from the Indian subcontinent who erected temples, shrines or images in foreign countries,[11] presumably in their own native styles. The famous Gunavarman from Kashmir is also reputed to have painted figures of arhats and other Buddhist themes with his own hands in China.[12] Buddhanandi (Nan-té), a monk-sculptor and envoy from Sri Lanka, brought to the Chinese court a Buddha image of his own creation, which the Chinese described as an "incomparable" work, and must have established a stylistic model for the local craftsmen.[13] Durgasvamin, a Brahmin from South India who married a daughter of the king of Cambodia, erected a Sivalinga in a temple at Sambor Prei Kuk in the seventh century.[14] The Brahmin who assisted King Sanjaya in installing the royal Sivalinga on Gunung Wukir mountain in A.D. 732 may also have come from South India.[15] Guru Kumaraghosa from Gaudi (West Bengal), the preceptor of the Sailendra King of Java, who, according to the A.D. 782 Kelurak inscription, set up and consecrated an image of Manjusri,[16] would certainly have been involved in the foundation of the shrine which sheltered it.[17] There must have been more of such cases, recorded and unrecorded, through the centuries. It may well have been expected of learned Indian priests, both Buddhist and Hindu, that they should be capable of directing the construction of shrines and supervising the making of icons that were essential to their teaching and the ritual of worship. Besides Gunavarman and Buddhanandi, many other Buddhist monk-architects and monk-artists are mentioned in Chinese records.[18] Eminent Brahmins, too, were probably well-versed in art and architecture. According to Indian tradition, it was the *sthapaka* (architect-priest) who took the leading role in the planning and construction of religious structures.[19] Indian Brahmins and monks who are known from literary and epigraphical records to have held high functions at the many Southeast Asian courts,[20] must have contributed substantially to the diffusion of their own art traditions in the new countries.

Professional artists are also known to have traveled. Many were commissioned to work in foreign countries by kings, religious institutions, and other wealthy patrons. Some even stayed on in the new countries where their arts were highly appreciated. Dhiman and his son Bitpala, two famous artists from North India, are believed to have worked in Tibet during the eighth and ninth centuries when they established a school of sculptors trained in the North Indian style.[21] Artists and artisans from India and Central Asia were in great demand in Tibet and China.[22] Buddhanandi, the monk-sculptor from Sri Lanka, introduced the Sinhalese mode of making Buddha images to the enthusiastic Chinese court[23] and probably assisted court artisans to work in that style while he was in China during the fifth century. A-ni-ko from Nepal led a group of artisans to work for Kublai Khan in Tibet, and later on in China where he obtained a high function as controller of the imperial workshop and trained local artists in his own tradition.[24] Sinhalese craftsmen obviously took part in the restoration of Wat Mahathat at Sukhothai during the early fourteenth century.[25] The master-smith Suryya, whose name appears on a bronze image from Tapanuli in West Sumatra,[26] may have been an Indian from the Tamil country working in Indonesia during the fourteenth century. These instances record a practice which was apparently common in the old days. The transportation of artisans as prisoners of war from one country to another is also another fact recorded in historical documents.[27]

Works of art and religious objects were also transported along the routes used by merchants, missionaries, pilgrims, artisans, and envoys. Foreign works of art, distinguished for their beauty and aesthetic attractions, were among luxury objects greatly in demand by wealthy buyers. The pieces which had been highly estimated in the countries of destination were likely to be copied by local artisans, and may even have inspired new artistic modes. Icons and architectural models accompanied missionaries and pilgrims to and from their countries of origin,[28] and often formed part of the royal gifts presented by one court to another.[29] Many of these images and architectural models are recorded as having been copies of famous icons and edifices in the Indian subcontinent,[30] or replicas or even originals of sacred objects from elsewhere.[31] They were often received with high esteem in the new countries where more copies of them were produced. Making replicas of famous images, edifices, and sites has long been commonly practiced among Buddhists and Hindus.[32] The intention is to reproduce the efficacious powers of the originals and to translocate the sacred site in order to bring it within reach. The so-called Sandal Wood First Image, reputed to have been made during the lifetime of the Buddha, has been copied time and again in India and elsewhere, and replicas of the Mahābodhi Temple at Bodh Gaya exist in many countries. Allusions to the translocation of sacred Indian rivers occur in one of the earliest inscriptions of Java.[33]

Because making the principal replicas of sacred images or holy sites reproduced the sacredness and efficacious powers of the originals, copies had to be precise. The actual appearance of buildings and iconographic details of images had to be reproduced as precisely as possible. The artisans thus learned to depict the foreign styles which probably exerted a certain degree of influence on their later works. Attempts to copy foreign styles and to make faithful transcriptions of images and architectural models are well recorded in Chinese accounts, and are reflected in many artistic products of Southeast Asia. The earliest replicas usually bore a close resemblance to the imported models, although they inevitably betrayed certain traits of the local styles from which they had been produced.[34] A banner from Dunhuang[35] provides a good example of this kind of practice. It probably shows a series of famous Buddhist images worshipped in India, but the local artist, in copying the Indian style, expressed in each and every figure certain stylistic features characteristic of the local workshop. The products, on the other hand, heralded the emergence of a new style based on a mixture of Indian and indigenous traditions.

Besides models of sacred images and edifices, handbooks and treatises containing instructions for artisans must also have found their way into the far countries together with other types of Buddhist and Hindu literature. Sacred texts have always been much coveted by pilgrims and envoys on religious missions. An astonishing array of Buddhist texts circulated in China and references to Buddhist and Hindu treatises that could have provided guidelines for local architects and image-makers, frequently occur in Cambodian epigraphy.[36] A large bulk of such works, written in Sanskrit and in Pali, appear to have been known in Myanmar.[37] Several hundreds of Indian texts were taken by I-Tsing to China via Srivijaya.[38] The narrative reliefs at Borobudur in Java were evidently based on many important texts,[39] and a number of Buddhist and Hindu works on philosophy and ritual are still preserved in Bali.[40] Artisans, following textual instructions, were apparently able to produce iconographically-correct depictions of the religious themes even without having to study tangible models. New themes could thus be expressed in local idioms, and even new forms could have evolved as a result of the local interpretations of the imported texts.

There also exist records of images having been made after the descriptions supplied by missionaries or pilgrims who had seen the originals.[41] Besides tangible souvenirs collected at the sites, pilgrims and travelers undoubtedly carried home memories and impressions. Recollections of paintings, sculptures, buildings, and sites which had appealed to them spiritually or aesthetically could also serve as guidelines for reproductions in concrete form of what the travelers had seen on foreign soil.

Through various agencies and circumstances, many art styles based on the religious and artistic traditions of India and Sri Lanka grew up in Southeast Asia. Diverse streams of influences from abroad were received, absorbed, adapted to the environment, combined, and eventually harmonized with local elements. The imported religions and the arts they inspired became localized. Artisans, working for the new religions and depicting new themes, first imitated the imported styles but gradually modified these to suit local tastes and requirements. New styles then emerged, each showing juxtapositions and mixtures of many artistic traditions, variant in time and provenance, but harmoniously blended into a perfect unity. Each style displayed its own characteristic traits and its own course of development in accordance with its own historical, geographical, and cultural milieu. The trade route continued to function as a communication route and brought about more cultural contacts. New centers of religion and the arts arose, new groups of priests, pilgrims, envoys, and artisans traveled to and fro, carrying with them new philosophical ideas and artistic trends.

The network of trade and cultural exchange extended over the entire region of South and Southeast Asia, and the phenomena of borrowing and assimilating cultural elements continued down the centuries. India remained the principal fountainhead of Buddhist and Hindu culture until the end of the twelfth century when Buddhism suffered severe persecution. Hindu culture, nevertheless, retained its force in South India beyond that period. Sri Lanka, which was a stronghold of Buddhism, continued to be the most important center of that religion after it lost ground in India, and was the source of inspiration for Myanmar, Cambodia, and Thailand. When Buddhism in Sri Lanka suffered a setback as a result of foreign occupation, Myanmar in the eleventh century became an asylum for the scattered Sinhalese monks and assisted them in reestablishing the religion in the island.[42] Thailand in the eighteenth century sent ecclesiastical help for the same purpose,[43] and the religion of the Buddha prospers in Sri Lanka to the present day.

Indonesia from the seventh to the eleventh century was renowned for its Buddhist Mahayana learnings. In the tenth century, preeminent Buddhists from Campa went to Yavadvipapura (Java) for pilgrimage and for the acquisition of spiritual powers.[44] Cambodia in the same century could have obtained many sacred Buddhist texts from the same place.[45] Campa in the ninth century extended a cultural and religious influence as far as peninsular Thailand,[46] and possibly also Yunnan in South China.[47] Myanmar flourished as a great center of Buddhist studies and Buddhist art from the eleventh to the thirteenth century, and Thailand assumed a similar role from about the fourteenth century onward.

A few art forms have been selected to illustrate the consequences of the diffusion of artistic traditions in South and Southeast Asia and are described below.

The Stupa

The stupa, the most representative of all Buddhist monuments, has a wide distribution throughout Asia. Functionally, it is the monument built to contain the corporeal relics of the Buddha. Symbolically, it stands for Nirvana, the Buddhist Salvation, and may be regarded as the cosmic axis containing the nucleus of the eternal and all-redeeming powers of the Buddha. The monuments at Sanci in North Central India, dating from the second to the first centuries B.C., exemplify the earliest known shape of the Buddhist stupa. This consists of a simple and solid hemispherical body standing on a low base and crowned with a super-structure in the form of a balustrade raised around a pole that bears the parasols of honor.

Sri Lanka inclined in favor of a similarly simple form, but increased the dimension of the monument and placed it upon a spacious square platform supported by a row of elephant-caryatids. Four decorated altar-like structures were added around the body facing the four directions. The genesis of these structural and decorative elements goes back to India, but it was in Sri Lanka that they were combined into such a unity in response to the native Sinhalese sense of aesthetics and philosophical concepts. The Ruvavneli at Anurādhapura, which commenced in the second century B.C., is representative of the type which has been applied to the major stupas in Sri Lanka through the centuries. Such a combi-nation of stupa and terrace with elephant-caryatids inspired the design of a number of monuments from the fourteenth to the sixteenth century Thailand.[48] The distinctively ponderous hemispherical shape was also reproduced in Thailand in the fourteenth century,[49] and in Myanmar in the seventeenth and nineteenth centuries.[50] The phenomenon of stupa sheltered within a shrine, which existed in rock-cut forms in India, attained its zenith of development in Sri Lanka, as is represented by the Vatadage at Polonnaruva, dating from the twelfth century. Simplified versions continued to be built till the present day. The Vijayotpala at Gadaladeniya presents a fourteenth-century example of an architectural type which also occurred at Sukhothai[51] and probably also in Cambo-dia.[52] The stupa itself has a bell-shaped body, standing on a low base equipped with a triple moulding. This form is common to modest-sized stupas of Sri Lanka.

Borobudur in Central Java may be regarded as a highly developed and complex type of stupa. It consists of terraces, stupas, and sculptures systematically arranged into a diagram of the cosmos, centralized around a stupa which stands for the nucleus of the entire world-system. Verti-cally the monument evokes the image of the cosmic mountain, the axis of the world, around which clings the world of Name and Form con-sisting of different levels of existence, mundane and divine. Above these spheres of Name and Form, and crowning the entire world-structure, stands a stupa, the symbol of Salvation.[53] Building types which could have inspired the structural form of Borobudur are known from North India,[54] and parallels to it existed in Nepal,[55] Tibet,[56] and Myanmar; but nowhere else was the design as elaborate and as well conceived as at

Borobudur. According to some scholars, the structural plan of this monument may well have inspired the construction of the first temple-mountain of Cambodia.[57] Among the numerous examples at Borobudur, two major forms of stupa can be distinguished: one is pot-shaped and is frequently adorned with a garland or decorative band around the body; the other is bell-shaped, displaying an undecorated body and a low or lotus base, above which were carved two or three concentric lines suggesting mouldings. The first type was evidently based on Northern Indian prototypes, while the other recalls the most common form of the smaller types of Sri Lankan Stupas.

Myanmar in the classical Pagan period from the eleventh to the thirteenth century, also showed a pronounced tendency to erect important stupas on a stepped pyramidal base. The type is exemplified by the *hwehsandaw* of the eleventh century, the Shwezigon of the twelfth century, and the Mingalazedi of the thirteenth century. The Shwehsandaw consists of a single stupa standing on five receding square terraces, each with a flight of steps leading the way up to the top from four directions. No elaborately carved gateways or sculptured balustrades adorn these terraces. The basic plan is similar to that of Borobudur, but is almost entirely lacking in all the subsidiary elements and wealth of sculptures that embellish the Javanese edifice. The antecedents of this type of structure can be found in India,[58] but this particular design appears to have gone through an independent course of evolution in mainland Southeast Asia since the eighth century. The form of the stupa itself also shows a local adaptation based on more than one Indian prototype. The cylindrical shape of the body appears to have its origin in the style of the Andhra country in Southeast India, the influence of which became evident in the art of Myanmar after the sixth century. The decorated band around the stupa body is probably an element which Pagan itself borrowed from the medieval style of the Northeast India. The smoothly tapering superstructure represents the typically Burmese modification of the conventional forms known in India, Sri Lanka, and elsewhere. It is characteristic of Burmese stupas down to the present day. Recent examples, such as the Shwedagon at Rangoon, are remarkable for their heavily sloping shape which is formed by a broad base, attenuated body, and pointed pinnacle. The three components appear to be merging and receding into one another, giving the entire mass a smooth and sweeping profile.

Thailand has known many types of stupa, as is especially evidenced from the archaeological remains of the Dvāravatī period,[59] but was still experimenting with various forms until the fourteenth century when a completely new formula emerged. The so-called "lotus bud" stupa, an invention of the fourteenth century Sukhothai, appears to have been an amalgam of many types of monuments known to the architects at the time. It consists of a series of superimposed terraces and a tall body, being a solidified version of an image-shrine standing on its own plinth and crowned by a stupa-like element complete with tapering pinnacle. The main stupa of Wat Mahāthāt at Sukhothai belongs to this type. Standing on a tall, elevated base, it towers over all the subsidiary buildings which are evidence of the large variety of architectural forms constructed at Sukhothai between the thirteenth and fifteenth centuries. This new form went out of fashion after the Sukhothai period, and it was the simple bell-shaped type of stupa introduced from Sri Lanka that eventually became the favorite model of the Thais. The formula, however, had been gradually but steadily modified to suit Thai taste. The base became taller, showing multiple receding steps. The body assumed a slender and elongated form, while the superstructure soared up elegantly to end in a sharply pointed finial. Rich decorative patterns may cover the structure from top to base in the case of recent examples. In spite of the smoothly sloping silhouette of the entire form, each of its structural parts as a rule retains its individual identity. In comparison with Burmese stupas, the comparatively narrow base, elongated body and needle-like pinnacle of the Thai edifices invoke a higher degree of verticality, loftiness, and weightlessness.

The Temple

The chapel or hall of worship of the Buddhists and Hindus can take various forms. The type that was specially designed to be presided over by an image or images was originally conceived as a private chamber for the Buddha or the gods. The earliest image-shrine found in Sri Lanka displays a design which recalls one of the oldest types of free-standing temple known in India, datable to the earlier fifth century.[60] The plan, however, was soon modified in response to the Sinhalese mode of worship. The dimension increased probably to accommodate ritual gatherings typical of Theravāda Buddhism, and a side staircase appeared, possibly as an exit for worshippers.[61] The image-shrines of the earlier Anurādhapura period probably had a timber roof, resting on brick walls and stone columns. Image-shrines with a vaulted brick roof began to appear in the eighth century[62] and continued to be built into the Polonnaruva period. The major examples of the twelfth century, namely the Lankātilaka, Tivanka, and Thūpārāma at Polonnaruva, display in their ground plan, structural form and decorative themes a close resemblance to Hindu shrines of the Cola period of Southern India.

The earliest image-shrines of Southeast Asia show strong affinities to the Indian styles of the sixth and seventh centuries. Those found in ancient Cambodia are small structures of brick and sandstone, assignable to about the seventh century. None of them appears to have been a copy of any known building in India, though all display in general many stylistic elements common to the Indian Gupta style of the sixth century and the post-Gupta styles of the Indian peninsula of about the seventh century. The favorite form in Cambodia was that of a square cella crowned with a tower-roof, the decorative motives of which reflect the ancient Indian concept of the temple as replica of the cosmic mountain, the center of the universe. Such a form continued to develop locally, independent of Indian influence, and the profile of the roof gradually took on the shape of a pinecone or lotus-bud. Important temples were built on a terraced base, recalling all the more the image of the cosmic mountain, formed by diverse levels of existence and crowned with the residences of divinities and the supreme god. The local genius of Cambodia placed long halls and galleries upon the terraces, and eventually linked them to the towers to create a large and structurally harmonious unity. The twelfth century temple of Angkor Wat, dedicated to Visnu represents the culmination of this process and a unique achievement in the art of temple-building. Formed by an assemblage of towers, concentric galleries, porches, and staircases, positioned on different levels but systematically and ingeniously joined, the monument has acquired an impressive dimension and appearance that express in full the symbolical meaning of the Hindu temple. This masterpiece of architecture represents a local development of the fundamentally Indian form, expressing the originally Indian concept which had taken firm root in Cambodia and became part and parcel of Khmer culture. The complex of Bayon exhibits a remarkable feature in the form of gigantic faces looking down from each of the towers. These represent the all-seeing faces of the highest entity of the Mahāyāna Buddhist concept—a symbolic concept which originated in India but had never found expression in architectural form elsewhere. The Neak Pean of the twelfth and thirteenth centuries is a unique architectural transcription of the ancient Buddhist concept on the cosmic lake Anavatapta, which may have been introduced into Cambodia from Sri Lanka. A legend, telling of the pilgrimage of a foreign "Leper King" to the southern coast of Sri Lanka, still circulates on the island. It may record a historical fact dating back to the end of the twelfth century.[63]

The oldest temples in Indonesia are represented by the groups on the Dieng plateau, dedicated to Śiva and datable to around the eighth to ninth centuries. The architectural forms show close similarity to types occurring in sixth to seventh century India. Candi Arjuna and Puntadewa are strongly reminiscent of the Pallava style of the southern coast, while Candi Bima recalls the building tradition of post-Gupta North India. The type that became most current in Indonesia again consists of a square cella crowned with a multi-storied tower roof and recalls the concept of the cosmic mountain. The trend of development of this fundamentally Indian form appears to have been quite different from that of Cambodia. In the style of the eighth to tenth centuries, the temple body usually retained a box-like cubical form with both vertical and horizontal planes strongly emphasized, while the multi-storied roof showed an outline resembling that of a pyramid. More cella were sometimes added so that the ground plan assumed the form of a Greek Cross as is observed at Candi Kalasan and the central shrine of Candi Sewu. The Buddhist Candi Sari and Plaosan had a regular ground plan and two stories, thereby recalling a type of Sri Lankan image house of the Anurādhapura period.[64] These Indonesian shrines, however, were built entirely of stone, showing a roof structure that is common in South India, but digressing from the Indian prototypes through the use of miniature stupas as ornaments. Candi Lara Jonggrang, dedicated to the Hindu Trimūrti, carried on the process of local modification of important elements. The central shrine shelters a magnificent image of Śiva and depictions of his divine retinue. The building is tall and impressive, displaying a clear emphasis on the vertical planes which gives the structure an even more soaring appearance. Roof decoration consists largely of a curious motif which looks like a combination between a stupa and the so-called "āmalaka" typical of North Indian architecture.

The cella, together with its tower roof, tended to become more attenuated and taller in the thirteenth and fourteenth centuries. Candi Singasari had two stories, the lower one of which contained five cellas sheltering the images of Śiva and his divine retinue. The upper cella is now empty and only half of its roof remains intact. The form of the superstructure must have been close to that of a temple at Panataran dating from 1369 A.D. This has a similarly attenuated and cubical body and a tall, towering pyramidal roof crowned with a squarish finial. The accent is chiefly on the vertical lines, while the cubical form, sharp profile and extraordinary slenderness of the entire building recall the general outline of an obelisk. Candi Sukuh from the fifteenth century, dedicated to the worship of Śiva as mountain god, embodies a mixture of Indian and indigenous Indonesian elements. The main feature of the temple is a pyramid, the form of which brings to mind that of prehistoric terraces of Indonesia. Linga, the symbol of Śiva, was worshipped in this shrine, but the inner court also contained a number of obelisk-shaped stones reminiscent of prehistoric menhirs.

Additional foreign elements are noted at Candi Pari in east Java.[65] The monument, bearing the date 1371 A.D. on its lintel, displays in its massive appearance and decorative themes stylistic influences from Campā.

In Myanmar, the Burmese of the Pagan period combined two architectural types, namely stupa and image-shrine, and produced magnificent edifices such as the Nanda and the Thatbyinnu. The technique of the radiating arch enabled the Burmese to build spacious buildings required for Theravāda worship. The Nanda Ananda may be described both as a temple crowned with a stupa and as a stupa standing on layers of a tunneled base which contains cellas, images, and galleries for circumambulation. Buildings showing a similar amalgam of stupa and image-shrine existed in India,[66] but the ingenious process of developing the formula into such a schematic, well-balanced, and complex design was achieved locally. The cruciform ground plan may have been inspired by five-cella-type shrines known in India and Indonesia, although the closest parallel appears to exist in Paharpur in East Bengal.[67] The Thatbyinnu of the late twelfth century consists of a hollow image-shrine standing on two layers of tunneled bases and topped by a solid stupa. The crowning element of the Nanda displays a blend between a stupa and the multi-storied roof of Northeast Indian temples. In the case of the Thatbyinnu, the crowning element looks more like a stupa, having a smooth body albeit displaying, a squarish section typical of the tower roofs of Northeast India.

Thailand in the Sukhothai period was markedly in favor of spacious rectangular buildings with bricked walls and tiled timber roofs. Interiors consisted of a long nave often flanked by a pair of side aisles and two rows of columns that supported the roof. The Buddha image stood near the rear wall of this combination of shrine and assembly hall. The plan was not unlike that of the early Buddhist Caitya halls in India which were also designed for large gatherings. The Thais applied the same design and architectural form to their chapter-houses. A similar design appears in the chapter-houses of the two principal monasteries in present-day Sri Lanka. This formula may have been brought over from Thailand by the Sri Lankan or Thai monks who established the Syāma-Nikāya in Sri Lanka in the eighteenth century.

The Thai copy of the Mahābodhi temple, built in the fifteenth century at Chiengmai, presents an architectural form based on that sacred model at Bohd Gayā; however, the themes and stylistic details of the sculptural decorations on the wall betray influences of the Sinhalese tradition of the Polonnaruva period.

This is but a superficial and limited survey of the archaeological evidence for the diffusion of the artistic tradition and cultural exchange among countries linked geographically by trade, and spiritually by faith. Trade was one of the greatest sources of the economic welfare which laid the foundation for cultural development. Trade and trade routes were like important arteries feeding the body that is the material receptacle of the transcendental mind. In this world of Name and Form, spirit and body are closely correlated and interdependent. An episode from the life of Lord Buddha tells us that if the body does not function well, the spirit cannot find the peace or concentration that are essential if it is to progress towards a higher goal.

Notes

1. For further study, see I. C. Glover, *Early Trade between India and South-East Asia: A Link in the Development of a World Trading System* (Occasional Papers no. 16) (Hull: University of Hull, Centre for South-East Asian Studies, 1989).
2. M. Prickett, "Sri Lanka's Foreign Trade before A.D. 600: Archaeological Evidence," in *Asian Panorama, Essays in Asian History, Past and Present* (Colombo, 1988); J. Carswell, "The Excavation of Mantai." Paper submitted to the International Seminar: "Towards the Second Century of Archaeology in Sri Lanka," *Ancient Ceylone*, no. 7 (Colombo, 7-13 July, 1990), pp. 17-28; R. Silva, "Mantai-The Great Imporium of Cosmas Indicopleustes. Paper submitted at the Maritime Silk Route Seminar (Colombo, 12-14 December, 1990) (Sri Lanka: Department of Archaeology and Central Cultural Fund).
3. L. Malleret, *L'archéologie du delta du Mékong*, 4 vols. (Paris: EFEO, 1959-1963).
4. J. Boisselier, *Nouvelles connaissances archéologiques de la ville d'U-thong* (Bangkok: Fine Arts Department, 1968); J. Boisselier, "Travaux de la mission archéologique française en Thailande," in *Arts Asiatiques*, vol. 25 (July-November, 1966): pp. 28-37; H.H.E. Loofs, "Problems of Continuity between the pre-Buddhist and Buddhist Periods in Central Thailand, with Special Reference to U-thong," in *Early South Asia*, edited by R.B. Smith and W. Watson (Oxford: Oxford University Press, 1986), pp. 12-48.
5. I.C. Glover, *Early Trade*, pp. 12-48.
6. T. Srisuchart, "The Early Historic Sites and Archaeological Remains in Southern Thailand." Workshop on Archaeological and Environmental Studies on Srivijaya, *SPAFA Final Report* (Bangkok, 1985), pp. 113-30; M. Veraprasert, "Khlong Thom: an ancient bead-manufacturing location and an ancient entrepot." Seminar in Prehistory of South-East Asia, *SPAFA Final Report* (Bangkok, 1987), pp. 323-31.
7. R.E.M. Wheeler, A. Ghosh, and K. Deva, "Arikamedu: An Indo-Roman Trading-Station on the East Coast of India," in *Ancient India*, no. 2 (July, 1946): pp. 17-124.
8. J. Hankin, J.R. Hackin, J. Carl, and P. Hamelin, *Nouvelles recherches archéologiques à Begram (ancienne Kâpicî), 1939-1940*. Mémoires de la délégation archéologiques française en Afganistan (Paris, 1954).
9. For discussion on the 'Indianization' of Southeast Asia, see G. Coedès, *The Indianized States of Southeast Asia* (Honolulu: East/West Center, 1968); J.C. Van Leur, *Indonesian Trade and Society: Essays in Asian Social and Economic History* (The Hague/Bandung: Martinus Nijhoff, 1955); F.D.K. Bosch, *The Problem of the Hindu Colonisation of Indonesia: Selected Studies in Indonesian Archeology* (The Hague: Martinus Nijhoff, 1961); O.W. Wolters, *Early Indonesian Commerce, A Study on the Ori-*

gins of Srivijaya (Ithaca: Cornell University Press, 1967); P. Wheatley, *Nagara and Commandery: Origins of the South-East Asian Urban Traditions*, nos. 207-208 (Department of Geography Research Papers, University of Chicago, 1983).

10. For this subject, see also R. Silva, *Religious Architecture in Early and Medieval Sri Lanka* (Meppel: KripsRepro, 1988), pp. 2-3.

11. See A.C. Soper, "Literary evidence for Early Buddhist Art in China," in *Oriental Art*, vol. 2, no. 1 (1949): pp. 28-30, 34; A.C. Soper, "Literary Evidence for Early Buddhist Art in China," in *Artibus Asiae Supplementum* 19 (Ascona, 1959): pp. 5, 6, 43, 80-2, 85, 106, and 109.

12. A.C. Soper, "Literary Evidence," p. 43.

13. J.M. Senaviratna, "Some Notes on the Chinese References," in *JCBRAS*, vol. 24 (1917): p. 108; A.C. Soper, "Literary Evidence," p. 96; R. Silva, *Religious Architecture*, p. 226.

14. See G. Coedès, *Inscriptions du Cambodge* 8 vols. (Hanoi and Paris: École Française d'Extrême-Orient, 1937-1966), vol. 4, p. 27.

15. For different readings and interpretations of this inscription, see N.J. Krom, *Hindoe-Javaansche Geschiedenis*, 2d rev. ed. (The Hague: Martinus Nijhoff, 1931), pp. 123-26; G. Coedès, *The Indianized States*, pp. 87-88; H.B. Sarkar, *Corpus of the Inscriptions of Java*, vol. 1 (Calcutta: Mukhopadhyay, 1971), pp. 15-24.

16. See F.D.K. Bosch, "De Inscriptie van Keloerak," in *Tijdschrift Bataviaasch Genootschap*, vol. 69, nos. 1-2 (1929): pp. 1-56; Sarkar, *Corpus of the Inscriptions*, pp. 41-48.

17. This might have been Candi Lumbung as suggested by Prof. de Casparis; see J.G. de Casparis, *Inscripties uit de Cailendra-Tijd* (Bandung: Masa Baru, 1950), p. 105.

18. Soper, "Literary evidence," pp. 18, 28-29, 33-4, 43, 80-82, 85.

19. D.N. Shukla, "Vastu-Sastra," in *Hindu Science of Architecture* (with special reference to Bhoja's Samarangana-Sutradhara), vol. 1 (Lucknow: Vastu-Vanmaya-Prakasama-Sala, 1961), pp. 44-49.

20. Coedès, *The Indianized States*, pp. 52, 58, 60, and notes 15 and 16.

21. G. Tucci, *The Ancient Civilization of Transhimalaya*, in the Ancient Civilizations Series (London: Barrie and Jenkins, 1973), p. 139.

22. Soper, "Literary Evidence," pp. 81-82, 121, 170; Tucci, *Ancient Civilizations*, pp. 139-41; M. Bussagli, *Painting of Central Asia*, in the Treasures of Asia Series (Geneva: Skira, 1963), pp. 66-67.

23. See Note 13.

24. See U. Von Schroeder, *Indo-Tibetan Bronzes* (Hong Kong: Visual Dharma, 1981), pp. 504-5.

25. See A.B. Griswold, *Towards a History of Sukhodaya Art* (Bangkok, Fine Arts Department, 1967), p. 21. For this inscription see also *Inscriptions of the Sukhothai period* (1983), pp. 58-79.

26. See A.J. Bernet Kempers, *Ancient Indonesian Art* (Amsterdam: Van der Peet, 1959), p. 69, pl. 197.

27. For examples, see B. Rowland Jr., "Indian Images in Chinese Sculptures," in *Artibus Asiae*, vol. 10, no. 1 (1947): p. 5, note 2; Soper, "Literary Evidence," pp. 88-89; G.E. Harvey, *History of Burma* (London: Frank Cass, 1967), pp. 27-29, 168; N. Chutiwongs, *The Iconography of Avalokitesvara in Mainland South-East Asia* (Ph.D. diss., University of Leiden; Bangkok, 1984), p. 101.

28. See Soper, "Literary evidence," pp. 29, 31-32, 53; Rowland Jr, "Indian Images," p. 7; P.C. Bagchi, *India and China, a Thousand Years of Cultural Relations*, 2d. ed. (Bombay: Hindu Kitab Ltd., 1950), pp. 157-58; also H.W. Woodward Jr., "South-

East Asian Traces of the Buddhist Pilgrims," in *MUSE*, Annals of the Museum of Art and Archaeology, vol. 22 (University of Missouri-Columbia, 1988): pp. 75-91.

29. See Soper, "Literary Evidence," pp. 29, 40, 54, 70, 74-76, 86, 90.
30. Ibid., pp.1, 9-12, 22-24, 28, 30-32, 40, 47.
31. Ibid., pp. 47, 53-54, 58-59, 64, 74.
32. For examples, see G. Coedès, "Documents sur l'histoire politique religieuse du Laos occidental," in *BEFEO*, vol. 25 (1925): pp. 97-100; Soper, "Literary Evidence," pp. 88.
33. B. Ch. Chhabra, *Expansion of Indo-Aryan Culture during Pallava Rule* (as evidenced by inscriptions) (Delhi: Munshi Ram Manohar Lal, 1965), pp. 96-97.
34. See Rowland Jr., "Indian Images;" A.B. Griswold, *Essays offered to G.H. Luce*, vol. 2 (Ascona, 1966), pp. 37-73.
35. Rowland Jr, "Indian Images," pp. 8-18.
36. For examples, see K. Bhattacharya, *Les religions brahmaniques dans l'ancien Cambodge* (Paris: EFEO, 1961), pp. 46-50.
37. For examples, see N.R. Ray, *Sanskrit Buddhism in Burma* (Amsterdam: H.J. Paris, 1936), pp. 31-39
38. J. Takakusu (trans.), *I-Tsing. A Record of the Buddhist Religion as Practised in India and the Malay Archipelago (A.D. 671-695)*, 2d. Italian ed. (New Delhi: Munshiram Manoharlal, 1982), p. xxxiii.
39. A.J. Bernet Kempers, *Ageless Borobudur* (Wassenaar: Servire, 1976), pp. 87-136.
40. See F.D.K. Bosch, *Buddhist Data from Balinese Texts: Selected Studies in Indonesian Archeology* (The Hague: Martinus Nijhoff, 1961); H. Soebadio, *Jnanasiddhanta: Secret Lore of the Balinese Saiva-Priest* (The Hague: Martinus Nijhoff, 1971).
41. Soper, "Literary Evidence," pp. 18, 32.
42. See R.A.L.H. Gunawardana, *Robe and Plough* (Tucson: University of Arizona Press, 1979), pp. 271-74; W.M. Sirisena, *Sri Lanka and South-East Asia* (Leiden: E.J. Brill, 1978), pp. 59-64.
43. L.S. Derwaraja, *The Kandyan Kingdom of Sri Lanka, 1707-1782*, 2d. ed. (Colombo: Lake House, 1988), pp. 114-18.
44. E. Huber, "Études indochinoises," in *BEFEO*, vol. 11, nos. 3-4 (1911): pp. 303, 310; N. Chutiwongs, *Iconography of Avalokitesvara*, p. 429.
45. G. Coedès, *Inscriptions du Cambodge*, vol. 6, pp. 105-6; N. Chutiwongs, *Iconography of Avalokitesvara*, pp. 428-29.
46. S. Diskul, "Chedi at Wat Keo, Chaiya, Suratthani," in JMBRAS, vol. 53, pt. 2 (1980): pp. 1-4.
47. N. Chutiwongs, *Iconography of Avalokitesvara*, pp. 477-80.
48. For examples, see P. Charoenwongsa and S. Diskul, *Thailande: Archeologia Mundi* (Geneva: Nagel, 1976), pls. 168, 217.
49. See Ibid., pl. 191.
50. See Aung Thaw, *Historical Sites in Burma* (Rangoon: Ministry of Culture, 1972), pp. 131, 146.
51. See P. Charoenwongsa and S. Diskul, *Thailande*, pl. 182.
52. See J. Boisselier, *Le Cambodge* (Paris: A. et J. Picard & Co., 1966), p. 94; N. Chutiwongs, *Iconography of Avalokitesvara*, p. 312.
53. For the most recent synthesis and a critical survey of theories and hypotheses on the meaning of Borobudur, see J.G. De Casparis, "Recent Interpretations of the Borobudur." A critical paper submitted to the International Seminar: "Towards the Second Century of Archaeology in Sri Lanka," in *Ancient Ceylon*, no. 7 (Colombo, 7-13 July, 1990): pp. 17-28.

54. J.E. Van Lohuizen-de Leeuw, "South-East Asian Architecture and the Stupa of Nandangarh," in *Atribus Asiae*, vol. 19 (1956): pp. 279-90; A.K. Coomaraswamy, *History of Indian and Indonesian Art* (New York: Dover, 1968), p. 205.

55. U. Wiesner, "Nepalese Votive Stupas of the Licchavi Period: The Empty Niche," in *The Stupa, its Religious, Historical and Architectural Significance*, edited by A.L. Dallapiccola and S. Zingel-Avé Lallemant (Wiesbaden: Franz Steiner Verlag, 1980), pls. 3, 5, 7, 9.

56. G. Tucci, *Ancient Civilization*, pls. 75, 78-81, 83, 84, 89-98.

57. B. Ph. Groslier, *The Art of Indo-China*, in the Art of the World Series (New York: Crown Publishers Inc., 1972), pp. 99-101; H. Loofs-Wissova, "The True and the Corbel Arch in Mainland South-East Asian Monumental Architecture," in *South-East Asia in the 9th to 14th Centuries*, edited by D.G. Marr and A.C. Milner (Singapore: Institute of Southeast Asian Studies and the Research School of South-East Asian Studies, Australian National University, 1986), pp. 239-54.

58. See note 54.

59. See P. Charoenwongsa and S. Diskul, *Thailande*, pls. 15, 16, 36; A.B. Griswold, *The Arts of Thailand: Catalogue of the Exhibition in the United States, 1960-62* (Bloomington: Greenwood Press, 1960), fig. 1.

60. See R. Silva, *Religious Architecture in Early and Medieval Sri Lanka* (Meppel: KripsRepro, 1988), fig. 39 (7).

61. See S.B. Bandaranayake, *Sinhalese Monastic Architecture. Studies in South Asian Culture*, vol. 4 (Leiden: E.J. Brill, 1974), pp. 203-9, figs. 75-7; Silva, *Religious Architecture*, pp. 238-40, pls. 43 (1), 47, figs. 40 (1,4,5), 42, 43(2), 44(4).

62. See Note 61.

63. See N. Chutiwongs, *Iconography of Avalokitesvara* , pp. 81, 319-20.

65. See N.J. Krom, *Inleiding tot de Hindoe-Javaanshe Kunst*, 2 vols., The Hague, Marti-Hindoe-Javaansche Geschiedenis, 2d. rev. ed. (The Hague: Martinus Nijhoff, 1923), vol. 2, pp. 229-34.

66. D. Mitra, *Buddhist Monuments* (Calcutta: Sahitya Samsad, 1971), pls. 91, 92.

67. Mitra, *Buddhist Monuments*, pp. 241-42.

Chapter 16

THE DEVELOPMENT OF CHINA'S NAVIGATION TECHNOLOGY AND OF THE MARITIME SILK ROUTE

Sun Guangqi

Seen from the historical viewpoint of science and civilization, the Maritime Silk Route, the great passage linking East and West, was the fruit of human endeavors over the ages to understand, utilize, and ultimately conquer the seas. The development of the Maritime Silk Route was conditioned by many historical factors, one of the more important of which was, inevitably, navigation technology.

Without this practical skill, the Maritime Silk Route would have remained but a dream. The historical existence of a busy Maritime Silk Route, used not only for trade but also for official exchanges, testifies to the ancient Chinese development of navigation techniques, essential for ocean voyages.

This chapter examines the relation between navigation technology and the Maritime Silk Route at various stages in Chinese history, showing that the development of the former was a prerequisite for the evolution of the latter. Along the way, I should also like to offer some personal opinions on certain topics which are of interest to both Chinese and foreign researchers.

Establishment of Coastal Routes

Chinese sailors of the Han Dynasty (206 B.C.-A.D. 220), using the monsoons with the help of the sail and the rudder, opened up a coastal Maritime Silk Route based on southern Asia. Like all achievements of human civilization, the Maritime Silk Route must have been preceded by a long period of study and experimentation. In remote antiquity, when people living in the coastal regions of both East and West first put to sea, they could only sail short distances, keeping close to the coast because they had so little knowledge of and skill in sailing. After a very long time, those isolated sea routes began to draw closer and closer as they extended ever further. Then with the gradual improvement of navigation technology, and in order to meet the needs of their productive activities and daily life, the seafaring people of both East and West began cautiously to seek more distant shores, overcoming the obstacles posed by the sea. This must have been how the Maritime Silk Route began taking shape.

The Chinese living in eastern Asia on the west coast of the Pacific Ocean began to venture forth on primitive boats and rafts as long as 7000 years ago. After cruising close to the continent for some time, during the Shang dynasty, in about 1600 B.C., they began to turn their eyes outwards. Crossing the South China Sea, they established communications with the inhabitants of Southeast Asia. During the Western Han dynasty (third century B.C.), and particularly during the reign of Emperor Wudi (140-87 B.C.), following Zhang Qian's expedition to the west along the Land Silk Route, across Central Asia, Chinese sailors opened up the first route to the Indian Ocean, an indirect Maritime Silk Route following the coast of southern Asia.

In Ban Gu's *Chronicles of the Han Dynasty: Geographical Annals* we find the following description of a voyage along this route:

> Starting from Zhangsai, Rinan [now close to Hue in Viet Na], Xuwen and Hepu, the ship sailed for about five months before reaching Duyuanguo [on the southeast end of the Malay Peninsula close to the Singapore Straits]; after another four months sailing, the ship arrived at Yilumoguo [now Pegu in Myanmar]; and about twenty days later at Chenliguo [now close to Xili in Myanmar]; more than twenty days' marching brought the crew to Fuganduluguo [now Taigon Cheng in Myanmar]; from here, they sailed again more than two months to Huangzhiguo [now Kanchipuram near Madras in India] … to the south of Huangzhiguo, was Yichengbuguo [now Sri Lanka], and having reached this point, the envoy of the Han dynasty returned.

The Han envoy's round trip to Sri Lanka represented an outstanding navigational feat at that time. Another one was performed in A.D. 47 by Sipales, a seaman from Alexandria. Sailing across the Arabian Sea, he identified the pattern of monsoons over the northwest Indian Ocean and thus made the voyage between Western and Southern Asia considerably quicker and easier. An indirect Maritime Silk Route by way of Southern Asia was thus established as a result of the joint efforts of seamen of both East and West.

The crucial factor that enabled the Chinese people under the Han dynasty to play their part in establishing the Maritime Silk Route was the combination of their knowledge of the monsoons with their skill in using sail and rudder. As everybody knows, small rowing boats cannot be used for long voyages. Instead, use must be made of the winds—Nature's inexhaustible source of motive power—with the help of sails. In China, very simple and primitive sails were being used as far back as the Shang dynasty.[1] By the time of the Han dynasty, the sail had been quite well developed, and the so-called "cloud sails" were in use. Seagoing ships of that time also had rudders for more efficient steering. A clay model ship found in a grave of the Eastern Han dynasty in Guangzhou is clear proof of their existence.

The Chinese too began to study wind directions very early on. The fact that Bao Zhang Shi was able to "observe the weather by means of the twelve winds," as recorded in the *Book of Rites of the Zhou dynasty, Chun Guan*, makes it clear that by the Spring and Autumn period, or the Warring States period at the latest, the Chinese were already capable of drawing fine distinctions between the various wind directions and were aware of the sequence followed by clockwise-moving winds.[2] Under the Han dynasty, the periodic monsoons or trade winds favorable to navigation were called "Bo zhuo feng."[3] "Bo" means sea-going ships and "zhuo" means the oars that move the ship. "Bo zhuo feng" is, in fact, the equivalent of what are known in the West as the trade winds.

It was their use of sail and rudder, and their knowledge of the monsoons that enabled the ancient Chinese to sail as far as south Asia. Although Ban Gu did not actually use the term "monsoon navigation" in his writings, there is some indication of this skill in navigation journals of the Han dynasty. In the account in the *Chronicles of the Han Dynasty: Annals of Literature and Arts* of the Western Han dynasty's naval attacks on the Kingdom of Southern Yue in the fifth year of the reign of Yuan Ding (112 B.C.) and on the Kingdom of Eastern Yue in the following year, it is recorded that double-decker ships sailed south between autumn and winter when the northerly monsoon winds were blowing. We can therefore assume that the Chinese sailors set out on their journey along the Maritime Silk Route around November and arrived in Duyuanguo five months later, around April in the spring of the following year. In the next four months, they would navigate the Strait of Malacca and sail northward along the east coast of the Bay of Bengal, taking advantage of the southerly summer wind. Then all the way from Yilumoguo to Zanliguo, for the next twenty days and more, they would still have the benefit of a tail wind. As autumn and winter approached the ships would again take advantage of the northeast monsoon over the Indian Ocean, sailing southwest along the west coast of the Bay of Bengal, and reaching Huang Zhiguo in two months.

Although navigation under the Han dynasty was very dependent on landmarks along the shores, according to the *Chronicles of the Han Dynasty,* as many as 136 volumes had been written on nautical astronomy. Unfortunately, most of these have now been lost, so it is very difficult to make a precise evaluation of achievements in this field under the Han dynasty. The earliest reference to astronomical navigation now available in China is found in *Huai Nan Zi* where we read: "When a sailor has lost his way, he looks to the North Star for guidance."[4] But this is only one example of astronomical orientation, a useful skill, but still quite insufficient for ocean navigation which requires the ability to determine the exact position of the ship. Due to this limited knowledge of navigation technology, ships using this early Maritime Silk Route to southern Asia during the Han dynasty had to sail slowly along the coasts, taking a long time to reach their destinations by indirect routes. During the post-Han period of the Three Kingdoms and the Western and Eastern Jin Dynasties (A.D. 220-420), the Maritime Silk Route does not seem to have been developed much further, owing to the unstable domestic situation. However, with the increase of economic and cultural exchanges between the coastal regions of southeastern China and their off-shore neighbors, navigation skills continued to develop.

Establishment of High-Seas Routes

Thanks to their extensive knowledge of physiographical navigation and their skilful use of the monsoons, Chinese seamen from the Southern dynasties to the Tang dynasty (approximately fifth to tenth centuries A.D.) were able to establish two Maritime Silk Routes on the high seas, one making directly for the Persian Gulf and the other for East Africa.

In the use of sails, not only was effective use made of tail winds for forward movement, but winds from different directions were also used to sail sideways or to assist in maneuvering. According to Wan Zhen's *Chronicles of Foreign Matters*, ships sailing the South China Seas during the Three Kingdoms period (A.D. 220-280) already had "up to four staggered sails depending on the size of the ships. There was also a kind of tree with leaves in the shape of windows which were ten feet in length and could be woven together to make sails. The four sails did not face the same direction but were angled in a coordinated way to make the best use of the wind. The position of the sails could be adjusted depending on wind strength. This ingenious use of sails made it possible to keep up good speeds in strong winds and big waves without great risk."[5]

There was also a big improvement in the use made of the west Pacific and north Indian Ocean monsoons. According to the account given by Faxian (the Eastern Jin monk and traveler) in his autobiography *Faxian Zhuan*, of his voyage back from India, "It normally takes about fifty days to sail northeast to Guangzhou [Canton]" from Ye Po Ti Guo in southeast Sumatra and "sailing south-west" from the empire of Duo Mo Li at the mouth of the Ganges "with the early winter trade wind, it takes fourteen days and nights to get to Shi Zi Guo [now Sri Lanka]."[6] All this shows that the use of monsoons and trade winds and hence the speed of sailing had made great progress since the early days of the Maritime Silk Route.

The narrative journals kept during this period, which also served as navigation guides, gave much more detail than Ban Gu's records in the Han dynasty. Here are some examples from the Three Kingdoms period: "Setting off from Funan [now in Cambodia], and heading for Julikou [probably the eastern end of the Strait of Malacca] through the big Bay [Gulf of Thailand], then turning north-west for Liwan [Bay of Bengal], passing a number of countries, it took a little more than a year to get to Tian Zhujiang Kou [mouth of the Ganges]."[7] "Setting off on a large ship with seven sails from Jiana Diaozhou,[8] and sailing with a tail wind for more than a month we arrived in Taquinguo [an eastern outpost of the Roman empire]."[9] Another example comes from the Eastern Jin dynasty: "Setting off from Qinnanpu (Shou Lengpu) in Viet Nam and sailing southwards day and night with Mercury behind us and Sagittarius in front, we arrived in Funan in about ten days."[10] These journals mention specific ports, bays, rivers, and constellations giving the precise duration of voyages to areas west of southern Asia.

This improvement in navigation skills made it possible for the Chinese Maritime Silk Route to develop from coastal sailing to ocean navigation. This is clearly reflected in Faxian's autobiography, according to which it had become usual practice for sea-going vessels to cross the Bay of Bengal and head directly for Guangzhou from the Singapore Strait.

It was under such circumstances, starting from the Song dynasty, during the Southern dynasties period (A.D. 420-479), that Chinese seamen who had sailed twenty thousand *li* from Anxiguo (the mouth of the Persian Gulf) to Siketiao guo (now Sri Lanka),[11] opened up the coastal Maritime Silk Route, reaching the Persian Gulf. While "sailing west to Daqin, Tianzhu…the ships continued to explore new shipping lines and acted as envoys establishing various kinds of relations."[12] Some foreign scholars, including the German F. Hirth and the American W.W. Rockhill, consider that Chinese ships did not reach the Persian Gulf before the Tang dynasty.[13] This view is clearly mistaken, because in *Golden Grasslands and Precious Stones* written by Masudi, an ancient Arab traveler, we read "both Chinese and Indian ships sailed up to pay tribute to the king of al-Hirah." The al-Hirah kingdom was an ancient Arab State which existed from the third century to the beginning of the seventh century. Its capital, the city of al-Hirah, was three kilometers away from the ruins of ancient Babylon. The Lakhmid dynasty of al-Hirah was at the height of its prosperity at the turn of the sixth century. The Adee, a tributary of the Euphrates, ran through the city of al-Hira at the time. If Chinese ships could reach as far as the city of al-Hirah, there should be no question that they could reach the entrance to the Persian Gulf.

Under the Tang dynasty, the sailing skills of Chinese seamen were further improved thanks to increasing contacts and communication with foreign countries as well as progress made in science and technology. On the one hand, knowledge of both physiological navigation and the navigation journals, which served as sea-route guidebooks, was now much more detailed. For example: "Sailing south-east for two hundred *li* from Guangzhou to Tunmen Shan, then sailing west with a tail wind and coming up to Jiuzhoushi two days later;" "On Bulaoshan Hill, which stood on the coast two hundred li to the east of Huangguo;" "the people of Tiluoluheguo put up towers in the sea, and on these towers torches were lit during the night so that ships would not get lost."[14] On the other hand, they had a clearer understanding and could make more skilled use of monsoons. For example, Yi Jing sailed southwards with the northeast monsoon from Guangzhou in November of the second year of the reign of Xian Heng (A.D. 671): "It took them about twenty days to arrive in Feshi [now Palembang in Sumatra];" "He chose to cross the Strait of Malacca in May the next year with the south-westerly monsoon. Afterwards he headed for the mouth of the Ganges on the Indian subcontinent from Luoren Island [Nicobar Islands], setting off in winter. With the aid of the side wind of the north-east monsoon and the anticlockwise ocean current in the Bay of Bengal, he got to his destination only half a month later."[15] The use made of the monsoon in the northwestern part of the Indian Ocean can also be clearly seen in *Sea Routes from Guangzhou* by Jia Dan,[16] where we read: "They sailed on from Shiziguo [now Sri Lanka] along the north-east coast of the Arab Sea. It took only thirty-seven days to get to Wuciguo at the entrance to the Persian Gulf." This trip must have been made at the end of the winter or at the beginning of the spring as the mild northeast monsoon and counterclockwise ocean current prevailing at the time were both conducive to ocean travel.

The Chinese Maritime Silk Route entered a new era of overall prosperity in the Tang dynasty thanks to advances in navigation technology. Chinese seamen plied the vast area of the northern part of the Indian Ocean including the Arabian Sea, the Persian Gulf, and the Red Sea as well as the sea off East Africa. In his book *Sea Routes from Guangzhou*, Jia Dan gave a detailed account of this route which might be considered the longest one described. The sailing area it covered was also the largest at the time in the world and could be divided into three sections. The first section started from Guangzhou, went southward along the east coast of Indo-China, crossed the Gulf of Thailand, followed the east coast of the Malay Peninsula to Feshiguo on the island of Sumatra and then reached Dakelingguo (now the island of Java in Indonesia). The second section started from Jia close to Singapore, sailing west through the Strait of Malacca and past the Nicobar Islands, reached Shiziguo (now Sri Lanka) after crossing the Bay of Bengal, then sailed northwest along the west coast of India, and entered the Persian Gulf by the Strait of Hormuz, to reach Fodacheng (now Baghdad) on the Tigris. The third section started from Wuciguo (now Al-Basrah) at the head of the Persian Gulf, crossed the Strait of Hormuz again, sailed west along the south coast of the Arabian Peninsula to the entrance of the Red Sea, and finally, after crossing the Bab el Mandeb, sailed south to Sanlanguo close to the Zanzibar Channel.

This Maritime Silk Route of the Tang dynasty, linking Asia and Africa, showed China to be a pioneer of ocean navigation in terms of both the skills applied and the technology developed. In his book *Studies on Pu Shou Geng*, the Japanese scholar Kuwabara Jitsuzo wrote that during the Tang dynasty and the Five Dynasties period that followed, most Arabs and Persians preferred to take Chinese ships to sail to places east of southern Asia.[17] J. Sauvaget, who translated the famous Arabian travelogue *Travels in China and India* (also known as *Sulaiman's Travel Notes*) into French, notes that "The help given by the Chinese to the Arabs in the latter's attempts to sail the seas of the Near East should be duly acknowledged" and that "it was on Chinese ships that Persian merchants made their first voyages to the South China Sea."[18] The occasional voyages to China, like that of the Omani navigator Suhar, in the eighth century, were daring exploits made in single-mast sewn boats, and are not to be compared to the well-established Tang fleet cruising the high seas.

Nevertheless, scientific and technological knowledge at that time did not make it possible for this intercontinental sea route linking Asia and Africa during the Tang dynasty to do much more than hug the coastline. Only two sections of this route ventured further out to sea. One was the five-day voyage of about 340 nautical miles from Mount Juntunong (now Kunlun Island) to Xia (now the Singapore Strait) across the mouth of the Gulf of Thailand. The other was a four-day voyage of about 400 nautical miles from Pu Guo Ga Lan (now the Nicobar Islands) to Shizi Guo (now Sri-Lanka), crossing part of the Bay of Bengal. We can deduce that Tang dynasty ships were not built to sustain more than ten days' continuous sailing on the high seas because the skills necessary for all-weather navigation and astronomical orientation had not yet been mastered.

Maritime Silk Route under the Song and Yuan Dynasties

Under the Song and Yuan dynasties (from the tenth century to the middle of the fourteenth century), Chinese sailors opened up a Maritime Silk Route across the Indian Ocean, using all-weather magnetic compasses and rulers to measure the position of celestial bodies. The Song and Yuan dynasties were the golden age of ancient Chinese science and technology and also the heyday of the Chinese Maritime Silk Route. The sea route across the Indian Ocean opened up by Chinese seamen during this period further strengthened East-West exchanges.

Many historical factors played their part in this historic development, including the Chinese policy of actively promoting maritime trade by private agencies and the building of advanced sea-going vessels. But one of the key factors was the all-round improvement, including real breakthroughs, in nautical techniques. Joseph Needham described it as a transition from primitive navigation to accurately planned navigation, preceding this event in the West by two to three centuries.[19] Thus in the twelfth century, wherever the sailing boat could go, the technically sophisticated Chinese boat could go as well.[20]

Nautical techniques used under the Song and Yuan dynasties, which played a key role in opening up the Maritime Silk Route, covered a very broad range. They included wide-angle geographic vision in navigation, advanced techniques for pinpointing physiographical locations, the increased reliability of navigation guidebooks, the use of marine charts, detailed knowledge of oceanography, the practice of meteorological observation and skill in maneuvering a ship. But the most important thing was the use of all-weather magnetic compasses and rulers used to measure the position of celestial bodies as an aid to pinpointing locations. When striking out across the ocean it was absolutely necessary to be able to determine the ship's position. But the traditional way of determining the ship's position by landmarks was useless when the coast was no longer in sight. The technical means used to determine the ship's position exactly relied on the technique of track-plotting which involved ascertaining the ship's (unknown) position by reference to known positions, and the astronomical observation technique. The all-weather goniometer was used, and for celestial navigation an easily handled mariner's astronomical observation instrument was a must. The magnetic compass and the celestial body measuring ruler used by seamen of the Song dynasty thus met seamen's need to determine their position during ocean voyages.

It is well known that China was the first country in the world to construct the compass. According to historical documents, "sinan [the earliest Chinese compass] was invented to determine direction"[21] as early as the Spring and Autumn period (from the eighth century B.C. to the third century B.C.). But this spoon-plate-type magnetic goniometer was of little use on the rolling ocean waves. The primitive compass evolved over a long period of time and by the Song dynasty, China had produced the first constant-direction-pointing navigation instrument. This epoch-making event was based on all-round progress in science and technology, and especially on knowledge of the technique of artificial magnetization.

China's earliest magnetic navigation instruments were the *zhinanyu* (iron fish pointing to the south) and the *shuifuzhen* (floating needle). According to the historical documents, the *zhinanyu* was invented in the fourth year of Qing Qingli (1044) during the Northern Song dynasty.

The following instructions are given for its preparation: "Cut a slice of thin iron, 2 inches long, 0.5 inches wide, its head and tail as sharp as a fish, put it in a coal fire till it becomes red hot, then take it out by the head with the tail pointing to the first of the 12 Earthly Branches. Immerse the tail in a basin of water for a few minutes, then remove and keep in a hermetically sealed container." Instructions for use on board are: "Put a bowl of water on the lee side and float the iron fish in the water. Its head will always point to the south."[22] The *zhinanyu* could be used for navigation, but its weak magnetization by the geomagnetic field made it of limited practical value. In *Sketches and Notes at Mengxi*, a well-known book written by the scientist Shen Kuo in the eighth year of the Northern Song dynasty (1063), a method of flotation of the magnetized steel needle was introduced. "First, sharpen the steel needle with magnetite so as to make it point to the south," then "make it floatable,"[23] "by piercing a rush with the needle. When laid on water, it will point to the south, but always with a deviation in the position of the third of the ten Heavenly Stems."[24] In *Sketches at Pingzhou*, written in the first year of the reign of Xuanhe (1119) during the Northern Song dynasty, the author Zhu Huo says: "The seamen are well versed in geography. They take their bearings by observing the stars at night, observing the sun during the day, and observing the compass when the sky is cloudy or overcast." This is the earliest reference to the use of the compass as a guide for navigation in the history of Chinese and world literature. But to begin with, the compass was only a supplementary navigation instrument, to be used when the sky was overcast. As experience enabled the compass to give more accurate readings in all kinds of weather, it soon became the seamen's main instrument of navigation, and it was categorically stated that "ocean voyages should rely on the compass."[25] Meanwhile, the quantification of goniometry being urgently needed for track plotting, the simple "float needle"[26] was soon combined with the twenty-four positions (the 12 Heavenly Stems and the 12 Earthly Branches). This led to the development of "a needle disc"[27] (i.e., "wet compass"), which was "carefully monitored day and night" and "allowed not the slightest error." The "needle disc" used a single needle to give the direction or a combination of needle positions with a deviation of 7°30'. This development led to the plotting of "needle-position" charts, which told seamen which direction to steer in on a particular route. These so-called "needle-routes" were used for fixed-direction navigation.[28] A man called Zhou Daguan was sent as an envoy to Zhen La (present-day Cambodia) during the Yuan dynasty and his journey is described as follows: "He set off from Wanzhou and followed Dingweizhen [the 4th Heavenly Stem and the 4th Earthly Branch on the position chart, nautical direction 202°30'] ... to arrive at the city of Zhan."[29] The use of the compass and the "needle-position charts" enabled Chinese seamen to estimate the ship's position at a given time by track plotting, so that ships could sail out far from land. However, on the East-West crossing of the Indian Ocean, ships sometimes drifted off course with wind and current; so when Chinese seamen used the magnetic compass for navigation they always checked the ship's position (mainly the displacement of north and south) by observation of the celestial bodies (especially the height of the Dipper), so that critical errors in the determination of the ship's position by track plotting could be corrected.

Joseph Needham surmised that the instrument used by Chinese seamen of the Song and Yuan dynasties to measure the height of celestial bodies was "*Wang Dou*" (the Dipper-observer) and thus named it the "Dipper-and-seven-star-observer," saying that it might have looked like the Kamal or cross-staff used by Arab navigators.[30] *Wang Dou* was generally regarded as one of the many marine weapons and "was jointly used on ship." It may have looked like the blockhouse on the masthead of "Cook's Boat" used by the Hanseatic League in Northern Europe in the Middle Ages for watching the sea surface while cruising. In fact, judging by the remains found in the thirteenth cabin of the Song dynasty ship excavated in Houzhu, Quanzhou, Fujian Province, the ruler used by the seamen to measure the altitude of celestial bodies looked very like the bamboo straight-edge in everyday use on land.[31] It was graduated in *cun* and *chi*. The sailor held the ruler at arm's length with the lower end aligned on the horizon, then noted the graduation at the intersection of the celestial body with the ruler. This observation of the altitude of the celestial body could then be put to very good use. For example, the ship's latitude could be calculated on the basis of the altitude of the Dipper. Regarding the technique of astrolocation used in the Yuan dynasty, in *The Travels of Marco Polo* it states explicitly: "the Dipper can be seen only dimly from Gemali [now Cape Comorin]. If you want to see it clearly, you must sail out for at least 30 miles and the Dipper will then be one cubit above the horizon. The Dipper can be seen even more clearly from Malibaer [now Malabar in south-west India] at a height of 10 cubits." It has been shown that the term "cubit" is a European translation of the Chinese *chi* or *cun*. One cubit is about "1 *cun* or 25°25'."[32]

Using quantified readings of the magnetic compass and their celestial ruler, Chinese sailors greatly improved their navigation skills and opened up a new era in the history of the Maritime Silk Route. The Chinese "could not only travel deep into the hinterland,"[33] but also cut straight across the Indian Ocean. As Zhou Qufei of the Song dynasty writes in *Lingwai Daida Dasiquo*: "The seamen set off from Guangzhou in mid-winter, sailing down the north wind, and reached Lanli [now Banda-Huh, in Indonesia] in about 40 days. They stayed there until the following winter, then sailed with the North-East wind and reached Maliba [now Kamar on the Arabian Peninsula] in about 60 days." According to this account, this new route cutting straight across the Indian Ocean took sixty days and covered a distance of 2,500 nautical miles. Chinese seamen had thus moved from the stage of coasting along the shore to the advanced stage of ocean-going voyages. This historic achievement was a breakthrough both for Chinese navigation techniques and for the Maritime Silk Route.

Proliferation of Sea Routes in the Age of Zheng He

In the period of Zheng He's voyages to the Western oceans (1405-1433) at the beginning of the Ming dinasty, Chinese seamen, on the basis of the overall inheritance of the outstanding navigation techniques developed by China and foreign countries, opened up a Maritime Silk Route with a criss-cross networking pattern which was a historical achievement. At the beginning of the Ming dynasty, the Chinese Maritime Silk Route entered an unprecedentedly splendid historic period with the seven world-famous Western voyages of Zheng He's fleet. This great ocean-going event was the result of a number of factors, one of the most important of which was Zheng He's advanced navigation techniques. Zheng He's navigation techniques were many and various, and the voyages of his fleet were high-level demonstrations of world navigation skills in the first half of the fifteenth century. His main achievements were made in two areas instanced below.

First, sea chart and compass were widely used in physiographic navigation, and the "needle-trace" system introducing the practice of track plotting and correction was set up. Zheng He's Navigation Map (originally entitled "The Chart of Launching from Baochuan Shipyard and setting off from Long Jiang Guang to Various Foreign Countries") was the main navigation guide and indispensable for Western ocean voyages. It was both a sea chart as well as a nautical guidebook, not only marking in detail geographic positions of the various navigation zones in the western Pacific Ocean and the northern Indian Ocean and giving vivid descriptions, but also specifically indicating the positions of mountain peaks, islands, shoals, and reefs (to be passed or avoided), dangerous or narrow waterways, sea depth, sea bottom quality, and harbor signals, and describing accurate positioning and piloting methods. It is worth noticing that in this book there was a needle-trace system with a track-plotting and position-correcting function.

This kind of needle-trace system was not the simple one previously used for one-way voyages between two places but a more complicated one enabling a ship to change direction in mid-voyage or to sail on after reaching a first destination. The various natural phenomena along the route in the areas of physiography, meteorology, and astronomy were also recorded. This needle-trace technique used the magnetic compass to fix locations, calculate the voyage distance every two hours and predict displacement factors such as wind and hydrodynamic pressure difference in the navigation zone, so as to make the scheduled track tally with the actual track. This was typical of the techniques of traditional Chinese track plotting and correction. In the course of an ocean-going voyage, so long as the ship was steered strictly according to the chart "with accurate calculation of the distance every two hours," it could arrive safely at its destination.[34]

Second, in astro-navigation, Chinese seamen learnt and mastered the advanced techniques and means of navigation of Western countries, especially the Arab countries, and established the use of the astro-observation system for voyages in the Indian Ocean. As an important communication link between East and West, the Maritime Silk Route promoted interaction, synthesis, and the joint development of world civilization. The reason for Zheng He's outstanding navigational achievement was that the Chinese had learnt and mastered other countries' advanced navigation techniques. It was in the first year of the Yong Le period (1403) that Zheng He was "entrusted with a mission to the West." With his assistants Li Kai and Yang Min, he constantly corrected the errors of the needle-trace astro-observation charts, sea island positions and the flow of water, the height of mountains and the nautical charts,"[35] and he paid close attention to investigation and introduced the navigation techniques of Western countries to China.

In astronautical guidance, Zheng He incorporated the astro-observation techniques and the celestial rulers traditionally used by Chinese seamen, thus forming his own unique method. The four astro-observation charts for ocean-going voyages annexed to "Zheng He's Navigation Map" reflected the latest techniques of astro-navigation used by Zheng He's fleet when crossing the Indian Ocean. They were the Chart from Guli to Hulumos, the Chart from Ceylon Hill back to Sumatra, the Chart from Longxian Island to Ceylon Hill, and the Chart from Hulumos back to Guli. Armed with Zheng He's navigation technology, Chinese sailors made comprehensive progress in opening up the Maritime Silk Route, and operated fifty-eight major lines crossing different oceans, twenty-one of which crossed the Indian Ocean. A network of Maritime Silk Routes thus emerged extending the route used in the heyday of the Song and Yuan dynasties. From the technical and qualitative point of view, the navigational techniques of Zheng He's fleet vastly expanded Chinese naval capabilities.

To begin, it opened the longest ocean navigation line in the history of China's Maritime Silk Route. According to the document describing Zheng He's voyages, his fleet left the east coast of China and either went northwest to the Persian Gulf via the Arabian Sea or crossed the equator into the southern hemisphere, and arrived at *Ma Lin Di* at 8°55' (now Kilwa Kisiwani in Tanzania). It should be observed that Zheng He's navigation map shows the Maritime Silk Route in East Africa extending southward beyond *Ma Lin Di*. It is worth trying to establish what the final destination of the route was. Under the entry concerning Lin Shan (now Male Island in the Maldives) in *The History of the Ming Dynasty: The Volume of Foreign Kingdoms*, two other kingdoms called Bici and Sunic are mentioned, at which Zheng He called in order to present letters from the Chinese emperor. But China was so far away that the two kingdoms' envoys could not return the visit. Some researchers consider that Bici might be a version of Puciwa (now Brava in Somalia)[36] or an abriged version of Mozambique (15°4' S); Sunci could be a transliteration of Sofala (20°12' S) in Mozambique.[37]

Joseph Needham writes in his *Sciences and Civilization in China*,[38] that a European cartographer, Fra Mauro, produced a map in 1459, a footnote to which referred to a Chinese sailing boat "ZhenKe," stating that the boat had sailed from India, approached the coast of southern Africa and pushed on to Cape Agulhas on the Atlantic Ocean. In about A.D. 1420, a Chinese boat sailing from India crossed the Indian Ocean to Nannu Island off Cape Dibu, passed the Green Islands and the Dako Sea, and then held a west southwest course for forty days, finding nothing but water and sky. The shipping company estimated that the ship had sailed about 2,000 miles. After that, the situation became even worse, the ship turned about and after another seventy days came back to Cape Dibu. When the sailors disembarked to restock, they saw the egg of a giant bird called Da Peng. Needham's comment on this footnote was that this showed Chinese ocean-going sailing ships braving the stormy seas, rounding Cape Agulhas (the southern Cape of Africa), taking advantage of the southeast trade wind to sail until they were far from any land, then returning again to West Lokes in order to sail further south. The captain thus found himself back in the Indian Ocean and the voyage of discovery came to an end. Needham notes that we need be in no doubt that Chinese sailing boats in Zheng He's times (or even several centuries earlier) were capable of performing this miracle. If Fra Mauro's account proves true, this would be a landmark in the history of the Maritime Silk Route.

The second achievement of Zheng He's fleet was to establish a comprehensive network of navigation routes. The fleet frequently split up and recombined, establishing six central ports: Zhan Chang (now Qui Nhon and surrounding areas in central Viet Nam) with two incoming routes and six outgoing routes; Man ci Jia (now Malacca in Malaysia) with four incoming routes and four outgoing routes; Surnataci (now Samalanga on Sumatra) with one incoming route and six outgoing routes; Ceylon Hill (present Sri Lanka) with three incoming routes and seven outgoing routes; Lushuan (with nearby islands) with six incoming routes and seven outgoing routes; and Guli, with four incoming routes and six outgoing routes. The Maritime Silk Route had thus spread in all directions in the west Pacific and north Indian Ocean. Zheng He's fleet also sailed deep into the Indian Ocean, using Lushuan as its central port.

Its third achievement consisted in opening up routes across the Indian Ocean. As mentioned above, the first routes across the Indian Ocean (few in number and direction, without many alternatives) were opened up under the Song dynasty. Yet by the time Zheng He made his voyage to the Western Ocean, there were at least seven major routes across the Indian Ocean. These were Ceylon Hill-Bociwa (course 260°, 2,100 nautical miles); Guanyu-Mugudushu (course 262°30', 1,800 nautical miles); Xiaogelan-Mugudushu (course 258°, 2,000 nautical miles); Guli-Adan (course 267°30', 1,800 nautical miles); Guli-Cisa (course 270°, 2,000 nautical miles), Guli-Zuofar (course 300°, 1,400 nautical miles), and Guli-Hulumos (course 305°, 1,400 nautical miles). It took an average of twenty days' continuous sailing to cover up to 1,400 nautical miles or more on these routes, whether from north to south or east to west. At the beginning of the Ming Dynasty, the Maritime Silk Route thus reached the peak of its development.

In summary, a number of conclusions may be drawn. First, the Maritime Silk Routes linking East and West reflected the needs of the time and the historical necessity of developing civilization, in which navigation technology was to play its part. Second, navigation technology was a key to the development of the Maritime Silk Route and the expansion of the network. And, finally, the progress of navigation technology and of the Maritime Silk Routes was the result of two interacting systems complementing and benefiting one another.

Notes

1. See my article, "The possibility of the existence of sails in China before Christ and the Time of their Earliest Appearance," *Studies in the History of Ships*, no. 2.
2. *Jin Nizi*, "Taiping Yulan" (Peaceful Readings for the Emperor), vol. 10.
3. Cui Shi, *Peasants' Proverbs*.
4. *"Huai Nan Zi: Human Moral Teachings."*
5. Wan Zhen, *Chronicles of Foreign Matters*. See *Tai Ping Yulan* (Book of Ships).
6. See Zhang Xun, *Footnotes to Faxian's Autobiography* (Shanghai Classics Press, 1985).
7. Yao Shilian, *Chronicles of the Liang Dynasty*, vol. 54 (Zhong Tian Zhu Zhuan).
8. No consensus has been reached regarding the whereabouts of Jiana Diaozhou. Opinions differ widely, some placing it in Java and others in Myanmar, Sri Lanka, or the port of Asuli on the west coast of the Red Sea.
9. Kang Tai, "History of Foreign Countries Up to the Wu Kingdom," quoted from *Tai Ping Yulan*, vol. 359.
10. Ge Hong, *Classical Works on Miraculous Panacea of Grand Peace and Golden Juice*.
11. Zhu Zhi, *Funan Records*.
12. *Chronicles of the Song Dynasty. History of Border Tribes to the South*.
13. F. Hirth and W. W. Rockhill, *Annals of Foreign Lands—Works by Zhao Rushi on the Trade between China and the Arab States in the Twelfth and Thirteenth Centuries*.
14. Jia Dan, *Sea Routes from Guangzhou*. New edition of *Chronicles of the Tang Dynasty: Geography*.
15. Yi Jing, *Biography of Buddhist Monks of Great Repute of the Tang Dynasty who went to the Western Regions to seek Buddhist Doctrine*, vol. 2.
16. Jia Dan, *Sea Routes From Guangzhou*.
17. See Kuwabara Jitsuzo, *Studies on Pu Shou Geng*, p. 92.
18. See Introduction to *Relation de la Chine et de l'Inde*, written in 851. Text edited, translated and commented by Jean Sauvaget (Paris, 1948); and French edition of *Sights and Sounds of China and India* translated by Mu Genlai and others (Chin Press, 1983.)
19. Joseph Needham, *Science and Civilization in China*, vol. 4, chap. 29 (Cambridge University Press, 1971).
20. Davis, *The Rediscovery of Africa*.
21. Han Feizi, *Yudu*.

22. Ding Liang; Ding Du, *The Essentials of the Five Classics*, 1st series, vol. 15: "The Guide."

23. Shen Kuo, *The Sketches and Notes of Mengxi*, vol. 24.

24. Kou Zongshuang, *A Profound Story about Woods and Flowers.*

25. Zhao Rushi, *Zhu Fan Zhi* (A description of foreign lands).

26. Xu Jing, *A Mission to Gaoli (now Korea) in the years of Xuanhe, Sea Route.*

27. Wu Zhimu, *The Entry of Boats in Rivers and Oceans* (A Sketch of Mengliang).

28. *Great Encyclopaedia of the Yongle Reign*, vol. 15950: "A Body of Classical Writings. Ocean Shipping."

29. Zhou Daguan, *Local Conditions and Customs of Zhen La.*

30. Needham, *Science and Civilization in China*, vol. 4, chap. 29.

31. "A Newsletter on the Excavation of the Ships of the Song Dynasty at the Bay of Quanzhou," in *Cultural Relics*, vol. 10 (1975); Han Zhenhua, "A Celestial Ruler Used for China's Ancient Navigation," in *A Collection of Historical Relics* (September 1980).

32. Han Zhenhua, "A Celestial Ruler."

33. Wu Jian, *A Brief History of Foreign Islands* (preface), based on "Summaries of Ocean-going Voyages to over 100 Countries and Regions in Asia and Africa," by Wang Dayuan.

34. Gong Zhen, *Xiyang Fan Guo Zhi* (A description of Western countries).

35. See *The Current Tables of Ping Yang Shi Pond, Wenzhou Ningbo*, collected by Jimei Navigation School, Fujian.

36. Zhu Xie, *Zheng He* (San Lian Bookstores, 1956).

37. Shen Fuwei, *The Voyage of Zheng He's Fleet to East Africa*, vol. 1 (People's Communication Publishing House, 1985). The Collection of Zheng He's Voyage to the Western Ocean.

38. Needham, *Science and Civilization in China*, vol. 4.

Chapter 17

MONGOL NOMADIC PASTORALISM
A Tradition between Nature and History

Jacques Legrand

There is now a quarter of a century of unbroken study of Mongol realities, both historical and modern. Such long and sustained contact sometimes offers the illusion that one might oneself weigh upon the course of events. It means, in any case, that no episode can be shrugged off as some distant, alien incident and that familiarity with the events and the people carries an intense and ever present emotive charge. Even if curiosity had been lacking, my duty as an academic was to try to grasp events, occurrences, and developments in their broadest and most manifold implications. Beyond the trivial but so often acute perception of the inexhaustible vitality of ignorance, of the wily persistence of the object in eluding the grasp of intellect, a few ideas have taken shape that may be in place at this seminar. Although they are formulated in general terms and their scope may extend beyond the area of Mongol studies, these ideas and assumptions are not the "Mongol expression" of an imported vision. They arose from study of the Mongol area considered in and for itself, without the lure of hasty and lopsided comparisons and without any insistence that facts, to be confirmed as such, must fit particular moulds of explanation or justification. This in no way rules out interplay with the general trend of scientific knowledge, even if the disciplines concerned be sciences of matter as much as those of society.

Before coming more specifically to Mongol nomadism, I should like to stress an aspect pertaining both to knowledge and to practical forward-looking inquiry; pertaining also, I should add in this case, to the sense of responsibility that is an essential endowment of anyone advancing ideas, formulating projects or even—where the most foolhardy are concerned—venturing a recommendation or a piece of advice. Cognizance of reality is, at one and the same time, overall grasp, global perception, and the recognition of dimensions and factors that are partial, lasting or momentary, complementary or contradictory. There is as much need of one type of vision as of the other: the stereoscopic and the microscopic are equally necessary. There is also a constant risk of making do with the overall image while remaining blind to the intrinsic existence of its individual components, or else of giving pride of place to those components, or any particular one of them, to the detriment of their interplay. In which case, it may be tempting to isolate the action which may influence that factor as the only decisive action. If it is possible to identify, among the features of Mongol nomadism, ecological, technical, social, and historical factors (each of these domains being itself made up of a complex package of parameters and relations), the selection of just one of those factors as the sole or dominant criterion of interpretation or evaluation may have serious consequences. What is more, while a great many techniques, such as economic management models, are now able to act upon isolated factors and modify their parameters separately, any practical priority given to that factor in implementing a transformation strategy would cause serious imbalances. There are many instances in history of effects of this kind, including the contemporary illusion that settlement was of itself a harbinger of social progress. The same goes for the major environmental upheavals induced by heedless development strategies. The possibilities on offer nowadays clearly increase that danger.

I should like here to outline a model of the cohesive nature of nomadic pastoralism, to emphasize the presence of a logic which, far from denying the inherent reality of each partial phenomenon, more closely gauges its impact on all the other aspects or dimensions—both distinctive subjects of study (pertaining to the most varied natural and human sciences) and components of a whole possessing an existence and a history—able to be perceived in terms of a global identity. Approached from this angle, Mongol nomadic pastoralism offers the image of a culture and a history built up in a remarkably homogeneous setting over a long period (since the middle of the first millennium B.C.); in conditions, on bases, and in accordance with models quite different from the transformations of societies that are agrarian and urban-based but, ultimately, confronted with the same essential challenge of satisfying and assimilating the changing needs of a constantly evolving population.

One constant is of considerable significance here and that is that Central Asian nomadism and Mongol nomadism itself in due course, has had no other choice, like any other model of socio-economic activity and organization, but to optimize the relationship between the needs of society and whatever resources were at its disposal. In other words, since the final assessment can be expressed in terms of "adaptation" and "adaptability," success and failure are measured as the balance, whether credit or debit, between what something brings in and what it costs. The two notions being of course taken in a very broad sense, from the energy and food balance (does an act of food production provide more or fewer calories than it uses up?) to the values and criteria of acceptability that are built up throughout a society's history.

Ecological Conditions: Levels and Regimes

Pastoralism, from the growing priority given to the domestication of animals to the adoption of nomadic forms of activity and lifestyle, is a set of responses to that challenge, an appropriation and management of natural conditions and not a bid to evade them. In Mongol nomadism such management is confronted less with the rigour of absolute climatic levels (of aridity, cold, etc.) that often go to form the image than with the extreme irregularity both of physical regimes and of the ecological effects imposed by these, after all, classic features of continental climates.[1] This irregularity is no doubt the key to understanding entire segments of not only the economic, but also social and political, reality of Mongol nomadism. It helps dispel the illusion that one factor rather than another has a permanent decisive value and it needs to be well understood so as to ensure that nomadism is not measured by the criteria peculiar to the peasant societies of temperate zones.

Technical Constraints:
Extensiveness and Competitive Control of Resources

The ecologically optimum responses consist in a "dispersion pattern" associating non-specialization of the herd (each holding possessing animals of several species, even though disparities in the structure of the livestock denote the operation of firmly implanted cultural and social models) with the various reflections of an imperative need for extensiveness. Optimum adaptation would involve the nomadization of small population groups living off herds which were also of limited size. It is clear, and this has been constantly borne out up to the contemporary period, that the relation between the needs of the population and the resources deriving from nomadic pastoralism is permanently fragile and that available surpluses are usually modest, nearly always irregular, and unpredictable. In other words, overpopulation thresholds may be exceeded by populations or herds whose absolute numbers (or density) may on the face of it seem very modest.[2] It thus seems that present-day Mongolia, with a density of about one inhabitant per square kilometer, while there is nothing inviolable about it, does none the less convey the image of a very real threshold. Any departure from this configuration implies a deterioration which, if perpetuated, can only be fatal to the pastoral economy and society themselves. Population concentrations, herd concentrations, and prolonged occupation of the same site or grazing land are all factors in such deterioration and pressures to which the nomadic society is liable to succumb. Yet that society is neither subjected to the unyielding grip of an abstract doctrine nor faced with mere ecological constraints.

In view of these overpopulation thresholds and the abundance of favorable zones and sites (coupled with relief/grazing and water resources), it is possible to propose an optimum pattern: seasonal occupation by small population groups; living off modest-sized herds (livestock breeding in small family encampments or *ajil*); no large-scale livestock holdings; few or no population sectors not engaged in livestock breeding—the non-specialization of Mongol pastoralism being no doubt also attributable to this relative lack of division of labor. Under these optimum conditions of dispersion, however, the irregularity of resources becomes a significant factor. Competing pressures arise, necessitating the application of modes of regulation and prompting the formation and affirmation of bonds of fellowship and networks of alliances. Noteworthy in these processes is the direct and practical importance of communication and its implications for nomad culture.[3]

Both in their immediate social practice and in broader historical continuums, nomads must at times abandon their optimum dispersion in favor of multiple and often complex forms of assembly and grouping. It may be on account of techniques arising from the needs of pastoralism, such as sheep-shearing. It may also be on account of security and defense requirements engendered simultaneously by the optimum dispersion of nomadic pastoralism, the various competitive pressures it generates and the manifold relationships, networks, and strategies of alliance to counter them. A further factor may be the forms of urban development, in nomad territory having their origin in nomad history itself, forms of a far greater importance than sedentary populations are inclined to concede.[4] Being profoundly affected by the extreme irregularity of natural regimes; the availability, management, and control of resources can only be secured in the extremely shifting and unstable interplay that constitutes the establishment and maturation of power relations.

Here we have the beginnings of a possible settlement of the old debate on the priority of the dispersed/regrouped modes—the transition to nomadism comes about as a result of the dispersion of communities of farmers/stockbreeders, with the formation of *ajil*. Increasing competition for relatively scant and, above all, highly irregular resources gives rise to insecurity and produces not only multi-based groupings and self-defense positions, but also forums for establishing both social hierarchy (associated and usually intermingled consanguinity and neighborhood relations) and the strategies ultimately intended to permit a return to optimal, dispersed pastoralism as the only tangible means of ensuring the society's survival. The success of the concentration exercise is therefore crowned by its own negation (ephemeral and fragile nature of the hierarchies, necessity for the momentarily dominant groups to seek alternative bases of legitimacy—such as external prestige—in both the period formation and consolidation and when the bases of such legitimacy wane).

Such power relations cannot be maintained and perpetuated otherwise than in a profoundly contradictory mode: (1) aiming at the management of resources, they cannot but seek a return to nomadic society at its "optimum" state of dispersion; (2) in so doing, they undermine their own bases by restoring the free interplay of tensions, competing pressures, and alliances marked out to give rise to a new power relationship reflecting both the renewal of alliances and changes in material conditions.

On this basis stands the formation of the "empires of the steppes,"[5] the apparent suddenness and relative, near cyclical regularity of their emergence, their practically original divisions (particularly between an eastern wing and a western wing), and their usually limited life span. The same goes for the signs of revival at a very early stage, in empires in the making, of phenomena reflecting less a centralizing political will than the acknowledgement of relations peculiar to nomadic society. A striking example, and one that contrasts with the view of the Mongol Empire as springing solely from the authority of Genghis Khan, is provided by the detail of the formation of the ninety-five *mingtan*, less an administrative procedure than the lending of more official form to preestablished bonds (but also by the fact that the *Secret History of the Mongols* makes a point of supplying those particulars).[6] If the title of *mingtad-un nojan* is bestowed as a reward for services rendered and loyalty shown to Genghis Khan, the formation of the contingent was very much a matter of relations based on alliances and kinship peculiar to each nomadic group and not a mere distribution of persons. The circumscribed and often ephemeral sway of the political authorities also reveals one of their essential roles: their endeavor to perpetuate structures doomed by their very successes, successes which committed them, admittedly with varied strength and good fortune but with great regularity, to the path of continental conquests. From that point of view, the perception of a Central Asian area defined by its openness to nomadism—whether in terms of territories suited to pastoralism or the presence of ways and means of exchange to which the nomads had become accustomed in the course of more or less regular relations—certainly provides a more operational framework for analysis than the supposition of a Mongol will to "world domination" (a wholly European view supported by only a few observations, scarce in number and made long after the day of Genghis Khan) for identifying the deep-seated bond uniting, over various periods, the fate of many peripheral regions confronted with nomadic invasions. It is also this history, with its clashes and violence, whose essential motive force, however far it may have carried its often devastating effects, remains peculiar to nomadic pastoralism, that has ensured for the latter such a constant and, on the face of it, such a paradoxical role as a link, a channel of contact between the most diverse cultures of the huge Eurasian landmass. Both the nomadic cultures themselves and the sedentary cultures, which are more aware at such times of their neighbors and of themselves, are transformed by such changes.

Whether we look at the "barbarian" empires and dynasties that dominated northern China throughout most of its history[7] or at the invasions reaching western Eurasia, the nomad or nomad-inspired campaigns were first and foremost a response to one major circumstance: while the quest for ways of regulating access to resources made the formation of the nomad "empires" necessary, such regulation was quite incapable of modifying the actual level of those resources, or of freeing nomadic pastoralism from the irregular nature of its returns and from the overriding trait of all the wealth produced, specifically the highly perishable nature of the livestock. What is more, while the surpluses that could "pay for" empires were scant and irregular, the functioning and development, however modest, of such institutions as staging posts or the maintenance of permanent armed contingents and, *a fortiori*, the attempts such empires might make to maintain and consolidate their existence could not rest solely upon wealth derived from nomadic pastoralism. In these circumstances, it was essentially by resuming the patterns and channels of exchange, trade, and circulation in an already familiar area—by extending these patterns to partners who were themselves known—that conquests and also migratory movements, when such took place, for the benefit of the nomad empires and particularly their leaders, secured the vital resources that they sorely lacked themselves. The foregoing description applies, of course, to a highly developed and increasingly widespread form of nomadic pastoralism. To focus on that moment alone would adversely restrict the field of study. In other words, each episode—in this case, the Mongol conquests of the thirteenth century—must be situated in a succession of major stages, in the knowledge that the breaks between those stages are more likely to be the sometimes arbitrary, or even self-seeking, choices of later commentators than genuine frontiers, especially breaks experienced as such by their actors and their contemporaries. What simply looked like the intrusion of invaders from the East takes on another hue with the realization that, alongside other East-West movements (migrations of the Turkic peoples, in particular), and foreshadowing the last of them (the migration of the Kalmuks to the Volga in the first half of the seventeenth century), the Mongol conquests must also be inserted in a historical fabric just as open—for the whole of continental Eurasia—to West-East currents and impulses. This includes the spread of major forms of animal domestication (for example, horse-riding) as well as the spread of writing (for example, the encroachments of the Chinese graphic tradition are marginal in the Tangut, and partly Kitan, nomadic world to the extent that this point could contribute to the delimitation of Central Asia outlined above).

This is not the place for us to return to the "list" of those empires. It must simply be emphasized that the appearance of the Mongols is not, once more, to be seen in terms of a "sudden irruption." What is more, any attempt to draw a dividing line, in time and in space, between the internal workings of nomad society in the process of unification and its embarking upon the conquest of an established empire pertains, barring extreme precaution, to a doubtless rather vain formalism.

While the constitution and the evolution of networks and strategies of alliance were inseparable from the formation of nomadic empires, this dimension includes relations with partners outside the nomadic world proper. At the most elementary level, the notion of "partnership" put forward here quite simply does not imply that the partners were similar. What would seem startling between nomads and sedentary peoples comes as no surprise when both partners are in the latter category. The preferential relations maintained with a particular partner, wherever located, are a means of moving the balance of power in one's own favor. What the Mongols were concerned with, in their relations with China, were commercial exchanges (silk and cotton, cutlery, copper ware and arms traded, in particular, for horses)[8] and the securing of advantages, honorary titles, and recognition through marriage. The same is true, for example, at the very time of Mongol unification, with the marriage ties established between the Naimans and the Uighurs. This in due course proved to be one of the factors, or a pretext, precipitating the intervention of the Mongols in the oases of Central Asia, a conquest henceforth to be seen as a direct consequence of the unification conflicts.[9] More generally there should be no underestimating in the history of the Mongol conquests, the role of mechanical sequences, of automatic chains of events, and of the urge to flee from bad to worse. But would this vicious circle have had the same effect if the entire enterprise had not developed in accordance with a persistent logic and in an area only exceptionally a *terra incognita?* Characteristically, and Plan Carpin's testimony is essential here, the Mongols of the conquest experienced as an often terrifying leap into the unknown their incursions into areas outside of Central Asia such as their Indian campaign and their crossing of the Caucasus.[10]

There is, unquestionably, a link between conquest and migration, but it is one that conforms to a historical calendar that is in no way an abstract reflex. It is not nomadism that opened the door to Eurasian migrations—the Palaeolithic Age was already peopled by them—with the Neanderthals crossing into Asia and even more so with the spread of *homo sapiens*. Population movements did not come to an end when the nomads' role declined, even if the European settlement of Siberia was deeply beholden to the Turks and Mongols, who sold the landless peasants the livestock which they sorely lacked. The fact nonetheless remains that it was nomadic pastoralism that shaped the outlines and development of Central Asia for two millennia. In this sense, those stages which, even until recently, were tempting to look upon as the final stages of nomadic pastoralism, actually constitute a remarkable laboratory—almost still within our reach—of the specific forms which shaped the entire history of mankind in a vast region, on our doorstep. They make us realize that migration, whether several millennia ago or nowadays, is one of humanity's main forms of existence, and that it displays certain invariables which are disguised by its outward appearance. It consists both of rapid advances and leaps which easily match the adult life of the migrant, even over considerable distances, and, at the same time, a protracted period which does not imply a unilateral rejection of all links with the starting point. More than a mere displacement, a migration is effected by creating a zone which encompasses the new centers of habitation as well as transport and trade routes which continue to link them to their initial focal point and to be used, in all directions on, a long-term basis.

A Long History of Contemporary Cultures

One can hardly fail to be struck by the myriad contributions, exchanges, transfers, and influences which shaped the cultures in this context. Each people looked not only to the resources and images it had created in order to find, or at least search for, the answers to its own problems, but also to its neighbors. Something which hardly seems surprising any longer must here be assessed according to its scale and consistency over centuries.

The relationship between nomadic and sedentary peoples has tended to monopolize the debate. This is certainly understandable and we must hardly be surprised when the picture derived from this is often one of rivalry, of a "natural" hostility between them. But this picture is highly deceptive. So is the calm conviction of the sedentary cultures that they alone had something to offer. Much more than that, if viewed in the long term, this proximity, which is often many other things besides, must be seen as permeated by an essentially complementarity, by a multitude of interests which are shared, if not always common. Paradoxically, it is in this light that the brutalities and blows of history are most clearly explained.

Naturally, there were exchanges between nomads, and just as many, but whether the partners were nomads or sedentary people was not so much a choice, or indeed an expression of affinity or hostility as a consequence of varied and fluctuating needs. It would be rash to venture, in just a few lines, into the vast range of questions which arise from the links between nomadism and migrations, the creation of the pastoral zone and its nomadic development. As far as techniques and language are concerned, as on the level of symbolics, contacts between peoples of the steppe shaped all of them, and arguing over precedence is indeed futile here.[11]

This complementarity is presented in all areas: material, intellectual, and spiritual. A large number of techniques were passed to the nomads from the sedentary peoples. It would seem likely, in the very first place, that the spread of different breeds of domestic animal came about in this way, in particular the practices of harnessing and riding horses, which came from the most westerly regions of Central Eurasia (Northern Mesopotamia and the steppes of Southern Russia and of Ukraine).[12] Such exchanges were multifarious, including equipment and foodstuffs, but also extending to institutions. In the long term, they brought into play the most diverse relationships and propinquities, encouraging if not uniformity then, at least, the homogeneity shown by the "Sythian" steppe, from the Black Sea to the Altai, at the time of the formation and rapid spread of nomadic pastoralism (from the middle of the second millennium B.C.).[13] The most striking image of this homogeneity is provided by the wealth, but also the aesthetic and spiritual unity of the animal art of the steppes.[14]

With the formation and succession in the eastern part of Eurasia and the territory of what is now Mongolia of the great nomadic "empires" (initiated by the Hsiung-nu in the third century B.C.), the proximity of China (also in the making) altered the center of gravity of the exchanges between the nomadic cultures of the steppe and the "outside world" for many centuries. There is more to this shift than the work of chance. Northern China, nucleus of the Chinese entity, was formed in direct contact with the peoples of the steppe and often under their pressure (a considerable number of dynasties from the nomad world reigned in China as a result of conquest by "infiltration"). Its history is repeatedly marked by nomad encroachments, but the picture which emerges, while not obscuring the conflicts, is rather one of a symbolic process without which each would today be very different. In short, the "face" of China and the "face" of the steppe, as we know them and to which we attribute, along with the peoples concerned, an unquestionable identity, might hardly be recognizable if we stripped them of what the "Other" contributed to them.

From the time of the Hsiung-nu, the contribution of Han China was essential to the life of the steppe, and the objects from the "royal" tombs of Noin-Ula (first century B.C., northern Mongolia) are revealing. Moreover, they were found in association with other objects and pictures which obviously came from the most westerly regions of Central Eurasia. Textiles and clothes, metalware (copper and brass, cutlery, bronze mirrors), and probably certain foodstuffs too, albeit in limited quantity, but also building techniques (as indicated by the systems of underfloor heating reminiscent of the Chinese *khan* [caravanserai] discovered in the town of Ivolga in Ulan Ude, Buryatiya) were all prized and sought. These goods and this expertise were for the most part integrated into nomadic, and particularly Mongol, culture, and would not henceforth be lacking there. They were integrated through direct border trade, trade relations, gifts relating to diplomatic contacts, the gathering of spoils during military expeditions (often in response to a break in trade relations), or the multifarious expansions of China's zone of influence at the heart of Central Asia. Thus, even if some Chinese products only became popular in the steppe thanks to the continually greater advances of Chinese commerce linked to the political domination of the Ch'ing empire from the seventeenth and eighteenth centuries, they were taking their places on a market which had been long prepared to accept them.

While attention should be drawn to the difficulty of assessing the effects of these "imports" given our very fragmentary knowledge of the nomadic peoples' daily lives up to a very recent period, it can be said that silk, satin, and cotton (the latter less prestigious but equally present) were among the main products supplied by China to the nomads. Rice (often supplied in reponse to a food shortage among the nomads), tea, and other products became more widespread in the same way.[15]

But trade did not only flow in one direction. The nomads had at their disposal resources which were of interest to their neighbors, particularly furs. This, again, was an exchange with a long tradition. *The Secret History of the Mongols* gives the example of a merchant from the oases of Central Asia, Asan, who traveled as far as the River Argun, in the northeast of what is now Mongolia, to trade cattle for furs.[16] At other times, it was cattle that the nomads supplied to their neighbors. This was particularly the case when the Russian settlers, who were lacking in livestock, were moving into Siberia (this trading role being extended through control over the salt of the lakes, a strategic resource).

But the most decisive contribution of the nomadic peoples to the material culture of their neighbors was still in connection with the horse. Apart from technical improvements, where their inventiveness was unmistakeable (the rigid saddle and the stirrup), above all, the nomads supplied horses on a large scale. While Ancient China, with its limited horse-breeding abilities, hardly used horses except in conjunction with chariots, the Han and their successors equipped their cavalry with horses supplied by the nomads, through trade or tribute. There is both written and iconographic evidence (such as the famous bas reliefs in the tomb of the T'ang Emperor T'sai Tung 626-649) that this phenomenon persisted in Chinese history until the fall of the Ming dynasty. This change had far-reaching consequences not only in China's political history but also in its cultural history: it seems that China popularized the wearing of trousers at that time, a legacy linked to the importation of the Central Asian horse. Under the T'ang (618-907), in the field of arts the influence of the peoples of Central Asia was also appreciable; in particular, new musical instruments replaced the traditional ones. Thus, the contributions made by the nomads to the sedentary peoples were not insignificant.

It must be observed, and there is something symbolic in this, that once the musical instruments had become Chinese, these very same instruments were once more borne across the steppe where they established themselves again. There were many such comings and goings. One of the most fundamental and significant in world history, was undoubtedly the spread of the relay station. Attaining a remarkable degree of expansion, particularly under the T'ang, it seems likely that this institution, at least in rudimentary form, could have been introduced into China with, or at least have drawn inspiration from its most essential servant, the horse. In any case, in the thirteenth and fourteenth centuries the Mongol empire certainly based its own relay system on the Chinese post, even if the existence of a relay in the early years of Genghis Khan's campaigns would suggest that this was not only a question of a borrowing.[17]

This last example makes it possible to highlight the intermediary role played by the cultures and history of the nomads. To a great extent, it was more or less directly thanks to the Mongol post that the first European postal systems came into being. The effects were varied and manifold. Tea, for example, which had been brought from Southeast

Asia to China had, by the end of T'ang rule, changed from a medicinal stimulant into the popular drink that we know.[18] But it was in the company of the west Mongol khan Altan (Altyn Khan) in 1604 that the Russian envoy Vassiliy Tyumenets first became acquainted with this product, which was destined for such popularity in Eastern Europe, and took back samples.[19] It is this intermediary role which is again betokened in many linguistic conventions. Thus the name of the River Amur is known to us in its Mongol form *amur*, or "calm," which the guides of the Russian travelers called it, not in its Tungus autochthonous forms, which introduce the qualifier "black," still present in the river's Chinese name, Heilungkiang, "River of the Black Dragon."

It is once more this intermediary role that links the Central Asian nomads to the spread of Buddhism across the continent—in their own zone first of all. If the great expansion of that zone from east to west was quite obviously on a spectacular scale, it should not lead one to forget the abundance of contacts between north and south. Buddhism's journey to Central Asia undoubtedly took place in the steppe, the northern Wei dynasty (386-534), which was to introduce it into northern China, where it remained dominant, sometimes even intrusive, until the reaction and the T'ang persecutions in the period 841-845. But this is too wide-reaching a subject to be dealt with on a superficial level. At the most, I might suggest that the way in which Buddhism was introduced among the paths of the steppes seems to have affected both the successes it enjoyed and the resistance it provoked, but also its relationship with the great currents of Chinese thought, especially with Taoism. A whole host of questions remain unanswered about the development of an ideology and a culture which for many long years found common ground and a common language, but still remained alien to China. These questions remain to some extent those which originate in the history of nomads and sedentary peoples living in close proximity to one another.

Highlighting the importance of the borrowings and their reciprocity does not dispense with the need to observe that relations were often stormy, and sometimes even bloody. More than that, while basic affinities do emerge (thus, whilst not wishing to make too much of the image, I perceive in the cosmological conception of the Emperor of China as a pivot, major intermediary, and intercessor between Humanity and the Universe, something very close to a shamanistic role), some people have been stuck by the relatively few direct cultural influences—and not without reason.[20] Questions have really arisen as a result of the slight impact that Chinese culture seems to have had on its nomadic neighbors, indeed, the slight attraction it seems to have held for them. It must have been more important for the nomads to find a partner than a role model. At any rate, they both brought the cultures of the Mediterranean world and those of the furthest points of Asia into contact, from one edge of the continent to the other, without losing their identity in the process. In short, the nomads and nomadism were much more than a mere means or zone of transmission. It was their own history and their own culture which were for at least a millennium the active instruments of an unprecedented expansion of the planetary horizon.

These few remarks may have a common thread. I think, for my part, that I can discern in them the various forms, the countless stages through which, realization after realization, experience against experience, something was built in the history and consciousness of a people, something we call a tradition. Something which we could define quite simply, in other words, as the existence of that people in all its dimensions. Tradition is neither the statue of the Commander pointing an accusing finger at the present, nor a golden age to which we could return. It is more than ever, a dimension without which it would, every day, be more and more difficult for humanity to build a better future.

Notes

1. N. Sodnom, A.L. Yanshin et al., *BNMAU Undestnij Atlas* (National atlas of the Mongolian People's Republic) (Ulaanbaatar and Moskva, 1990), pp. 53-64.
2. C. Hell, P. Quere, "Étude du système d'élevage de Bannière d'Uzumunqui, Mongolie intérieure (Chine)" (Ph.D. diss., Institut National Agronomique, Paris-Grignon, 1992). The authors rightly lay emphasis on the bottlenecks and, in particular, on the slow reproduction of winter resources, but also on the outlay in labor terms that intensification would involve (pp. 53-54).
3. J. Legrand, "Vents d'herbe et de feutre," in *Dits et écrits de Mongolie* (Paris: Findakly, 1993).
4. X. Lxagvasüren, "Kharkhorum khotyg maltan shinzhilzh baygaa n'" (The excavations of the city of Qaraqorum), in *Dornodakhiny sudlakyn asuudal*, vol. 1, no. 16 (Ulaanbaatar, 1987): pp. 74-77; D. Maidar, *Mongolyn khot tosgony gurvan zurag* (Three maps of the cities and population centers of Mongolia) (Ulaanbaatar: ShUAKh [Shinzhlekh Ukhaany Akdemiin Khevlel], 1970); D. Maidar, *Mongolyn arkitektur be khot bayguulalt* (Mongol architecture and town planning) (Ulaanbaatar: UkhG [Ulsyn Khevleliin Gazar], 1972); Kh. Perlee, *Khayatan ulsyn khoër bêkhlêlt (khot)-iyn üldegdel (X-XI zuun)* (The ruins of two [10th-11th century] Kitan fortifications [cities]) (Ulaanbaatar: ShUKhKh [Shinzhlekh Ukhany Khevleliin Khoroo], 1957); and Kh. Perlee, *Mongol ard ulsyn êrt, dundad üeiyn khot suuriny tovchoon* (Cities in Mongolia in Antiquity and the Middle Ages) (Ulaanbaatar: UkhKhÊKh [Ulsyn Khevleliin Khoroony Erkhlekh Khoroo], 1961).
5. In the words of René Grousset, *L'Empire des steppes* (Paris: Payot, 1939).
6. *Secret History of the Mongols,* paras. 202-4.

7. See, in particular, F. Aubin and T.H. Hahn, "A Bibliography of European Non-English Works on Sung, Liao, Chin, Hsi-Hsia and Yuan," *Bulletin of Sung Yuan Studies,* vol. 21 (1989; published in 1991): pp. 115-48.

8. On a late but well-studied period, see H. Serruys, "The Tribute System and Diplomatic Missions (1400-1600)," *Sino-Mongol Relations During the Ming II,* (Mélanges chinois et bouddhiques), vol.14 (Brussels: Institut Belge des Hautes Etudes Chinoises, 1967).

9. J. Legrand, "Les Mongols en Asie centrale," *Autrement,* no. 64 (October, 1992), pp. 60-72.

10. Jean de Plan Carpin, *Histoire des Mongols* (Paris: Ed. Franciscaines, 1961), pp. 63-65.

11. J. Legrand, "Aux origines des Mongols, Formation ethnique, histoire et pastoralisme nomade," *Slovo,* Revue du CERES, Institut National des Langues et Civilisations, vol. 14 (1994), pp. 23-24.

12. On one of the first sites providing evidence of horse-breeding in the 4th and 3rd millennia B.C., see V.I. Bibkova, "Fauna Dereivki i eë osobennosti" (The Fauna of Dereikva and its Peculiarities), *Noveyshie otkrytiya sovetskikh arkeologov* (Recent Discoveries by Soviet Archaeologists) (Kiev, 1975), part 1.

13. S. Chard Chester, *Northeast Asia in Prehistory* (Madison and London: The University of Wisconsin Press, 1974), p. 153; and N. Sêr-Odzhav, *Mongolyn êrtnity tüükh* (Ancient History of Mongolia) (Ulaanbaatar: ShUAKh, 1977), pp. 79-93.

14. *Or des Scythes,* Grand Palais, Réunion des Musées Nationaux, 8 October-21 December 1975 (Paris, 1975).

15. H. Serruys, "The Tribute System and Diplomatic Missions."

16. *Secret History of the Mongols,* par. 182.

17. D. Gazagnadou, *La poste à relais, La diffusion d'une technique de pouvoir à travers l'Eurasie, Chine-Islam-Europe* (Paris: Kimé, 1994).

18. J.K. Fairbank, E.O. Reischauer, and A.M. Craig, *East Asia, Tradition and Transformation* (London: Allen & Unwin, 1973), p. 111.

19. M.I. Sladkovskiy, *Istoriya torgovo-êkonomicheskikh otnosheniy narodov Rossii s Kitaem (do 1917 g.)* (Moscow: Izd-vo Nauka, Glavnaya Redaktsiya Vostochnoy Literary, 1974), pp. 63-64.

20. C. Suzuki, "China's relations with Inner Asia: The Hsiung-nu, Tibet," in *The Chinese World Order, Traditional China's Foreign Relations,* 3d ed., edited by J.K. Fairbank (Cambridge, Mass., 1974), pp. 180-97.

Chapter 18

THE SPIRITUAL IDENTITY OF THE SILK ROADS
A Historical Overview of Buddhism and Islam

Amir H. Zekrgoo

The religious traditions of Buddhism and Islam emerged in two different eras and different geographical locations amongst peoples of different cultures, backgrounds, and history. Yet when we compare the socio-cultural aspects of the societies in which Buddhism and Islam were going to flourish, a number of outstanding similarities spring to mind.

Generally speaking, studying particular aspects of a society in which a new religion is being conceived can explain the social need for the emergence of a new spiritual system. When two societies share identical conditions and face similar social problems, we can expect to detect a strong analogy between ways of thinking that might emerge to solve these problems.

Pre-Buddhist Indian society and pre-Islamic Arab culture share many aspects among which the following three are prominent.

    a. Polytheism
    b. Worshipping Idols
    c. Distinctions Between Social Classes

Polytheism

India's long polytheistic tradition goes back to the Vedic Age. This tradition lived on as the dominant religious doctrine during the post-Vedic era when the Brahmanic religion was widely practiced. Though the Brahmanic view differed from the Vedic ones, there was still evidence of many pre-Vedic deities, mostly manifestations of natural forces, such as Indira (the thunder god), Surya (the sun god), Ushas (the dawn god), and others, present and in power in the post-Vedic Brahmanic era. Vishnu (the sustainer) was originally a Vedic god who successfully lived his celestial life and occupied the highest position among hundreds of Hindu deities.

People worshipped these gods and goddesses both out of fear of their anger and hope for their rewards. They feared them because their anger troubled their lives through natural disasters such as floods, drought, and disease, and they praised them devotedly because the same celestial creatures could grant them health, wealth, dignity, and prosperity. Worshippers prayed to the deities, sacrificed animals, presented offerings, and formulated a wide range of ceremonial acts around them.

The Buddha did not approve of such a system. He totally denied the existence of gods and became a serious threat to their Imperial throne in the realm of the heavens. He declared that religious ceremonies, sacrifices, and other rites were meaningless and that such acts would not do man any good.

Buddha's revolutionary ideas were offensive to the religious values of his time and the Brahmans took this offense quite seriously. But, as his teachings gave every individual an opportunity to elevate their social and religious status by devotion to truth and by doing good deeds, he was considered a savior and his ideas were welcomed by a wide range of people.

More than a thousand years after Buddha's death, in the Arabian peninsula far from the Buddha's region, a somewhat similar situation could be witnessed. Shortly before the advent of Islam, the Bedouin Arabs worshipped a variety of gods and goddesses. Islam's very first principle, "*Tawhid*," was in direct contradiction with their polytheism.

The word "*Tawhid*" is derived from the root "*ahad*" (one or oneness) and refers to God's unity. The God of the Quran is a transcendent infinitude over all other creatures, whose being is necessarily finite. Hence, God is one and no creature may share in His divinity. Belief in such a sharing is called "*Shirk*" and is condemned in the Quran as the most heinous and unforgivable sin. This new idea was disliked by some well-to-do people; but, just as adherents to Buddhism denied the existence of all gods, many people found the idea of *Tawhid* (unity) truer and more just, and therefore embraced the new religion.

Worshipping Idols

The second aspect common to pre-Buddhist and pre-Islamic society was the worshipping of idols. As mentioned above, the Buddha did not believe in gods. It was therefore natural that he did not approve of worshipping idols. The Buddha did not revolt against gods to occupy their position. He clearly declared that he was not a god, but a teacher and a guide to lead people towards salvation. He preached that worshipping idols is no solution for the pains and sufferings of life and that eternal bliss, enlightenment, and salvation may be achieved through one's effort in the context of the Eight-Fold Path.

Idols played a central role in the religious life and the social structure of the Arab nomads. The multitude of deities worshipped in the Hejaz were tribal deities. Each tribe had its own god or goddess, represented generally in the form of a baetyl or sacred stone. The nobility of nomadic life was linked with and depended on these idols.

Three tribal deities were prominent in Central Arabia. These goddesses were Uzza (عُزّی), Lat (لات), and Manat (مناّت) (Quran 53: 19-22). The last (Manat) was once stolen and taken to India. There a temple was built to accommodate the idol. The temple was then named Sumanat.[1]

Not only a religious act, idols played a key role in their trade and economic life as well. The Kaba in the city of Mecca was the house of the idols, and Mecca was the most popular trade center of the region. The fact is that the holy city of Mecca achieved renown through this famous sanctuary for idols. People of different tribes gathered in Mecca to pay homage to their idols. Merchants brought their goods and a great market was gradually established. Bearing in mind the socio-economic conditions of the Bedouin, it is easy to understand how much the idols meant to the conservative, wealthy merchants of Mecca. The monotheistic teachings of the Prophet Mohammad endangered the interests of this rich ruling class. To ease the situation, they agreed to worship Mohammad's God if the prophet accepted to praise theirs. What they wanted was a compromise from the side of the Prophet, but no compromise on the very basic principle of a divine religion was possible. The one God was the only truth and worshipping idols was nothing but ignorance: "Allah is the light of heaven and earth ... and who is cognizant of all things" (Quran, 24: 35). "Then we placed you on the path of Divine Rule to follow it" (Quran, 45: 18). "He indeed shall be successful who purifies himself, and invokes the name of his Lord and prays, Nay! You prefer the life of this world, while the hereafter is better and more lasting" (Quran 87: 14, 15, 16, 17).

Distinctions Between Social Classes

The caste system was among the social practices that the Brahmanic religion enforced. According to this way of thinking, people were divided into four classes depending on their family of origin. Sons of a Brahman or Kshatrya, regardless of their potential and talent, would end up having a respectable social and economic status; while a Sudra, no matter how bright and intelligent, was bound within the limits of his caste to do menial tasks throughout his life without any better future for himself or his son. Dasas (slaves) led an even worse life. They were considered untouchables, outside any caste—their position was such that it was assumed that they were the children of a lesser god.

The Buddha emerged in such a socio-religious context. He did not believe in distinctions separating humanity/nature, self/other, subject/object, and even Nirvana/Samsara. He taught that all men are equal and that high moral status can only be achieved through their efforts in living, earning, thinking, speaking, meditating, and doing right. Nirvana is achieved by penetrating and removing such distinctions. Nirvana entails a recognition of the inherent harmony and equality of all things.[2] This lofty notion of equality elevated Buddhism to the status of a civilizing religion and elicited widespread acceptance especially among the toiling masses.

Studying the social condition of Arabia at the time of the advent of Islam, evidence points to similar social injustice practiced among the tribes. It is said that the most valuable contribution of Islam to human society is its teaching of equality and brotherhood. This very quality in the course of time resulted in the elevation of Islam to the status of a cultural and a civilizing religion.

Out of all social phenomena recorded in the history of pre-Islamic Arabic, the two most outstanding are slavery and the killing of infant baby girls. These two are more than enough to explain how unjust and inhuman the living conditions were in those times. The Prophet Mohammad was the man who stood against the unfair rules of his time with the Islamic teachings of harmony, equality, and justice. He preached that there is no difference between a slave and a nobleman and that only *Taqwa* (virtue) makes one man better than another.

وجعلناكم شعوباً وقبائلاً لتعارفوا ان اكرمكم عند الله اتقيكم
انا خلقناكم من ذكر وانثى

O you people, we have created [all of] you from a male and a female, and we have made you into different nations and tribes [only] for the purpose of identification—otherwise the noblest of you in the sight of God is the one who is the most righteous (Quran 49: 13).

To wipe the shame of slavery and oppression off the face of human society, social legislation and doctrine were established. To seek salvation and forgiveness for their sins, people were asked to free slaves on freedom-purchasing contracts: "and if they (the slaves) are poor, you give them freedom from the wealth God has bestowed upon you" (Quran 24: 33).

This law was practically supported by a bold act from the prophet's side. He appointed Bilal, an African negro slave—the model of a good Muslim, a true believer, and his trusted follower—to prononce the first Azan[3] from the roof of Kaba. This was considered as the first official announcement of Islam after victory over the nonbelievers. The teachings of equality and care for the welfare of people were unequivocal and full of promise. That is why during a twelve-year struggle in Mecca (610-622 A.D.), the Prophet had gathered a devoted group of followers, largely among the poor but also among well-to-do merchants.

Man, in Islam, is God's representative on earth and duty of man is to establish heavenly laws on Earth "who, when we give them power on the earth, shall establish prayers and welfare of poor and shall command good and forbid evil" (Quran, 22: 40). Material wealth was only considered when it was directed towards the well-being of the poor. People are criticized for their persistent moral failures due to their narrow-mindedness, lack of vision, and weakness. The Quran describes all wrong done against an individual as a wrong against oneself (2: 231, 11: 101, 11: 118). Such pettiness is often represented in the Quran as greed, fraud, and holding back from giving to the poor: "If you were to possess all the treasures of the mercy of thy lord, you would still sit on them out of fear of spending (on the needy)" (Quran 17: 100). "It is Satan who whispers into people's ears that they would be impoverished by spending while God promises prosperity for such investment" (2: 268). Instead of establishing usurious accounts to exploit the poor, believers should establish credit with God (2: 245, 57: 11, 57: 18).

The structure of the Bedouin Arab society was male-oriented, and females were looked down upon as inferior creatures. Infant girls were defective, embarrassing components of families and signs of bad omen. Consequently, many baby girls were brutally slain or buried alive. Islam protested against such sinful inhuman acts by declaring the male and the female to be of the same origin and that only righteousness and virtue could make one a better human in the sight of God (49: 13). "They are lost indeed who kill their children foolishly without knowledge, and forbid what Allah has given to them, forging a lie against Allah: they have indeed gone astray, and they are not the followers of the right course" (6: 139). Prophet Mohammad himself had no son but a daughter—Fatimah is referred to in the Quran as Kauthar (كوثر), the heavenly fountain of unbounded grace and benefits (108:1).

These teachings of unity and righteousness overcame many social, political, and cultural obstacles and hastened the spread of Islam to the far-flung corners of India, North Africa, Spain, Sub-Saharan Africa,

Central Asia, China, South, Southeast Asia, and even Europe. Buddhism too, relying on a somewhat similar concept, conquered the spiritual realm of a large number of people in Central Asia, Southeast Asia, China, Tibet, the Southern Asian subcontinent, the Far Eastern countries, and parts of the western world.

The Silk Road and Its Spiritual Identity

East and West are not merely geographical, external identities. Every person in the essence of his or her being has an Eastern and a Western side and each side represents one major aspect of identity. The Eastern or the righthand dimension of human existence represents the concealed truth of the universe and is related to spiritual power. The Western side or the lefthand dimension of human existence, on the other hand, is the one that deals with the realm of unconcealed reality. It represents humanity's ability to control physical surroundings and to make the best use of them to live a comfortable life.

The Eastern world has been the cradle of the righthand dimension throughout history. Hinduism, for instance, is a religion that fully emphasizes the concealed dimension of existence. Anything which satisfies the materialistic aspirations or makes humanity dependent on this mortal life and its illusionary attractions is to be avoided as it is impermanent. True satisfaction and eternal bliss, according to this view, may not be achieved through the unconcealed tangible qualities of the material world. Hence, all efforts shall be directed towards a life away from matter. Moksha and earthly desires cannot unite—to have one, man is bound to leave the other.

Opposed to this is the western point of view, according to which humanity must develop its abilities in the realm of matter. Science, technology, and an analytical approach to the universe are the tools and means to reach the final goal. Spirituality and the realm of concealed truth may well exist, but a person who looks at his surroundings from the view point of the lefthand dimension of being certainly does not and will not attach much value to that side. To the Western mind, only those elements matter that can physically and directly affect life on Earth. Other dimensions that are beyond the reach of science or physical knowledge are therefore considered secondary as they do not play any significant role in the process of development. The ultimate goal according to western logic is development.

This dichotomy between Eastern and Western values raises the issue of the macrocosm and the microcosm. In the macrocosm, we find the sacred and the profane both present; in the microcosm too, as explained earlier, both Eastern and Western dimensions exist. Today, one of the most controversial debates amongst thinkers on our planet is the issue of the relationship between the eastern and the western world. People have recognized that they are not complete unless their two sides are united. Recall that these two sides, though manifested in two geographical locations, are essentially two states of being or two aspects of human existence.

Buddhism was among the very first of intellectual disciplines to make a serious attempt to give its purely Eastern base some Western touches. It was a step forward, and a sign pointing at a balanced life. Buddhist teaching combined philosophical and popular elements and from its early stages, the Buddhist community included both a significant monastic and a significant lay component.[4] This historical fact conveys an important message inherent in Buddhism. It declares that the philosophical/popular and monastic/lay dichotomies should be seen as complements rather than oppositions.

In the Islamic tradition, there is forceful eagerness for bringing together the lefthand and the righthand dimensions of human existence, the East side and the West side. Islam preaches that salvation lies neither in the East nor in the West, that only Siratul Mustaqeem—the right or straight path—leads to salvation and eternal life in heaven. In the opening chapter of the Quran, the Fatihah (opening), the idea of balance is expressed: "Keep us on the right path. The path of those upon whom thou bestowed favours. Not (the path) of those upon whom thy wrath is brought down, nor of those who go astray" (1: 5-7). "Allah is the light of the heavens and the earth ... neither eastern nor western (though both the east and west of the world receive brightness from His light). Allah guides to his light whom He pleases ... and Allah is cognizant of all beings" (24: 35).

In the Quranic verses and Ahadith (Traditions),[5] there are many phrases that appear contradictory at a first glance, as in the two following cases.

حب الدنيا رأس كل خطيئه

The love of worldly matters is the cause of all sins and errors.

من لا معاش له لا معادله

One who has no means of livelihood will have no resurrection.

The first tradition seems to encourage people to choose an ascetic life and to keep themselves away from any worldly means, in order to steer clear of sin and error. It can easily be assumed that such a phrase features among the guidelines of a monastic religion, but Muslims believe that " لا رهبانيت في الاسلام " (there is no monasticism in

Islam). The second tradition, on the other hand, is a clear approval of earning a livelihood, to the extent that resurrection in the world hereafter and meeting the Lord become dependent on being successful in worldly affairs. It sounds like a statement typical of a twentieth-century Western industrial society.

The answer to this enigma is the word "balance," inherent in most of the teachings of Islam. A good man is the one who earns his livelihood by hard work, while he is aware that everything he does could be viewed as negative or positive on the day of judgement. "So, he who has done an atom's weight of good shall see it. And he who has done an atom's weight of evil shall see it" (Quran 99: 7-8). So in the Siratul Mustaqeem (right path), man has to make the right choice. He should direct his worldly deeds towards a sacred destiny. He must sanctify matter through sacrifice. Among all God's creatures, it is only man who can select his state of existence, and this ability to choose makes him master of all creatures. That his existence should have two dimensions is most meaningful. Man makes history. In other words, history is the objectivization of man's spiritual journey in various stages of Being. By dwelling in two realms (i.e., the realm of the sacred and the realm of the profane), man is the *Majma-ul Bahrayn* (the confluence of two oceans) and his salvation depends on bringing the profane under the domain of the sacred. Man must sanctify his earthly dimension to reach unity with God and live in harmony with Nature.

In this cosmology, God is the ultimate truth and the totality of the universe: "He is the last and the first, and the manifest and the concealed" (57: 3). Hence, through only one side of his being, man can only achieve a portion of the ultimate truth, not the totality. People should relate both to physics and metaphysics in order to unite with Him. Nature is considered a sign of God and every atom in nature is believed to be alive and conscious. Man may commune with Nature through his consciousness and share its secrets. This whole idea is reflected in a masterly fashion in the words of Rumi:

باتو می‌گویند روز ان و شبان   جمله اعضای عالم در نهان

باشمانا محرمان ما خامشیم   ماسمیعیم و بصیریم و هُشیم

Every small bit of the world,
Tells you secretly, day and night.
We listen, we see, and we are conscious,
But, to you Na-Mahrams (strangers to the secret of existence) we are silent.

Obviously, reaching such an exalted state is not simple. It can be achieved only through sacrifice, or the selfgiving of a human being to the divinity: " موتوا قبل ان تموتوا ," i.e., let your ego die, before you enter the realm of death. It is the combination of invocation (Zikr) and meditation (Fikr) that makes such a frame of mind possible.

The Silk Road may be counted as the most important route in the history of mankind. Being the first route joining the Eastern and Western worlds, the Silk Road may be given a spiritual identity.

Along the Silk Roads, technology traveled, ideas were exchanged, and friendship and understanding between East and West were experienced for the first time on a large scale. Easterners were exposed to Western ideas and life-styles, and Westerners too, learned about Eastern culture and its spiritually-oriented cosmology. Buddhism as an Eastern religion received international attention through the Silk Roads.

Emperor Ashoka (c. 273-232 B.C.) of the Mauryan dynasty was the first powerful supporter of Buddhism. He devoted his life and his political skills to spreading the Dharma. He gave up conflict and bloodshed for nonviolence, but *ahimsa* did not make him feel weak as an emperor. Ashoka considered non-violence a more powerful weapon than arms. He won such victories beyond his own empire that he felt himself to be the ruler of a spiritual empire which embraced all humanity.[6]

The famous Ashokan pillars are among the very first outstanding Buddhist manifestation of art. Many of the pillars were produced according to highly sophisticated techniques imported from Persia. The Sarnath capital, being most famous of all, was adopted as India's national emblem. The pillars are of exceptional artistic and symbolic value, however, it was not until second and third century A.D. during the Kushan period that Buddhist art really flourished. At that time, Roman trade with Asia was almost at its peak. The great Silk Road spanning a quarter of the globe brought silk and spices to the western world, and objects of gold, glass, and other prized Roman creations were eagerly imported by the elite of the Orient. The Kushan dynasty reached the summit of its grandeur under King Kanishka (A.D. 78-144). This period also coincides with the fourth Buddhist council. Kanishka found himself maintaining control over a vital section of the rich network of trade crossing Asia. The emperor's personality was inclined to such interactions. Kanishka's coins vividly display his desire to live harmoniously with the various peoples and religions within his domain and beyond it. The elaborate pantheon struck on the face of his coins illustrates the various religions practiced beyond Gandhara in regions related through foreign trade: the deities of Persia, the gods of Rome, Alexandria, and the Hellenized Orient including Herakles, Helios, Serapis, and Victory, while Shiva and Skandakumara represented Brahmanic India.[7] One of these

Kushan coins shows a standing Buddha image with "Boddo" inscribed in Greek letters.

The process of cultural and technical exchange in the strategic location of the Silk Route, i.e., Gandhara, was not confined to the realm of coins. Ancient Gandhara, comprising modern north-west Pakistan and eastern Afghanistan, was the center of the great Kushan empire, of which Mathura and the upper Ganges-Jamuna Valley represented the outlying areas.[8] The Gandharan sculptures are the most fabulous examples of the East-West interaction along the Buddhist Routes. This very harmonious mixture of art upgraded the anthropomorphic dimension of Buddhist sculptures quite considerably. The evolving image of Buddha bears the traces of the artistic traditions of the Silk Road countries. The Gandharan solution was merely one of practical adoption and elaboration. A remarkable example of Gandharan sculpture is an excellent schist relief from the second century A.D. preserved in the Freer Gallery of Art, Washington, D.C. depicting the four major events of Buddha's life. In this beautiful relief, Persian, Indian, and Graeco-Roman styles, elements, and even costume designs were combined to create a sublime work of art.

The Silk Road was undoubtedly the junction of all the above-mentioned elements. The fact must not be overlooked, however, that the central pole drawing together the multiple components was Buddhism itself. In other words, it is the sublime content that makes possible the growth and exaltation of form.

Every piece of art comprises two basic components, form and content. Form is manifest while content is concealed. Content without form will have no opportunity to reveal itself, and form too, without a content, would be a mere façade. To achieve elevated artistic expression, both components should relate as it is the unity of the sublime (concealed) content and the mature form (manifest) which can create original valuable art.

Tawhid (unity) is the essential message. It is the very first principle of every divine religion. The Silk Road owes its importance and value to the unity it brought about. Today, UNESCO has taken an important step forward on the path to reviving the identity of this famous road. I hope that such studies and the meeting like the one we are having now, will serve the noble cause of declaring of the Silk Road's messages—the messages of knowledge and harmony, and the fine message of unity in diversity.

Notes

1. In Sultan Mahmood Ghaznavi's attack on India, the Sumanat temple was demolished and all its gold, jewelry, and valuable ornaments plundered by his army.
2. T.P. Kasulis, *Encyclopedia of Religion*, vol. 16 (1987), pp. 453-54.
3. "Azan" is a call for prayer and it comprises phrases stating that God is One and that the Prophet Mohammad is his messenger.
4. F.E. Reynolds and C. Hallisey, "Buddhism: An Overview," in *Encyclopedia of Religion*, vol. 2 (1987), pp. 334-51.
5. "Traditions" are sayings related to the Prophet Mohammad and his successors.
6. A.L. Basham, "Study of Ashokan Inscriptions," in *Encyclopedia of Religion*, vol. 1, (1987), pp. 460-68.
7. R.C. Craven, *Indian Art* (London, 1986), pp. 81-83.
8. D.L. Sneigrove, *The Image of Buddha* (UNESCO, 1978), p. 59.

APPENDIX

International Seminars and Colloquiums Held during the UNESCO Silk Roads Expeditions

Listed below, in chronological order, are the titles of the international seminars and colloquiums held during the land and sea route expeditions organized as part of the UNESCO Silk Roads Project.[1] Many of the papers presented at the expedition seminars have been published, or produced in book form, by local organizers for distribution to their national academic community. Whenever possible full references have been given.

Desert Route Expedition in China (20 July-3 August 1990)

"*Dunhuang and the Silk Roads,*" *Dunhuang, China, 1 August 1990.**

"Land Routes of the Silk Roads and the Cultural Exchanges between East and West before the 10th Century," Urumqi, China, 19-21 August 1990. Beijing: New World Press, 1996, 644 p. ISBN 7-80005-293-1. Texts in Chinese or English, with abstracts in English or Chinese as appropriate. (On sale: New World Press, 24 Baiwanzhuang Road, Beijing 100037, China.)

Maritime Route Expedition (23 October 1990-9 March 1991)

"Travel Literature or the Travels of Literature," Venice, Italy, 22-24 October 1990. A collection of papers presented at this seminar organized by Pen International and UNESCO has been published: "The Silk Road: A Symposium on Travel Literature." International PEN, vol. 41, no. 1 (London, 1991), pp. 42-70. (On sale: Pen International, 9/10 Charterhouse Buildings, London EC1M 7AT).

"Cultural and Commercial Exchanges between the Orient and the Greek World," Athens, 27 October 1990. Published under the above title by the national organizers: Centre for Neohellenic Research/ National Hellenic Research Foundation, Athens. 1991. 205 p. ISBN 960-7094-10-7. (On sale: Centre for Neohellenic Research/NHRF, 48 Vas. Constantinou Ave., 11635 Athens.)

"The Influence of the Silk Roads on Turkish Culture and Art," Kusadasi (Turkey), 29-31 October 1990. A collection of papers from the above seminar has been produced in the original languages (English, French and Turkish) under the title: *Ipek Yollari*. Ankara: Deniz Arastirma Konferanslari, Kültür Bakanligi, 1993. 128 p. ISBN 975-17-1371-4. (Requests for copies should be addressed to the publisher.)

"Cultural Relations between Egypt and Countries of the Silk Roads," Cairo, 4-5 November 1990. A collection of papers from the seminar have been produced in their original language (mainly Arabic with some in English) under the above title by the Faculty of Archaeology, Cairo University, 1990. (Requests for copies should be addressed to Cairo University.)

"The Significance of the Omani Maritime Heritage to the Silk Roads," Muscat, 20-21 November 1990. A collection of papers from the seminar has been produced in English by the Ministry of National Heritage and Culture, Sultanate of Oman, 1992. (Requests for copies should be addressed to the Ministry of National Heritage and Culture.)

"Al-Sind and Arab Seafaring: Culture, Commerce and Urbanization," Karachi, Pakistan, 29-30 November 1990.*

"Maritime Encounter of East and West during the 15th-16th Centuries A.D.," Goa, India, 6-7 December 1990.*

"Sri Lanka as the Mid-point in the East-West Silk Route and the Centre of Convergence of the Cross-Currents of Buddhist Philosophy," Colombo, 12-14 December 1990. To our knowledge the papers from this seminar have not been published. However, on the occasion of the seminar, the National Commission for UNESCO and the Central Cultural Fund, Colombo, published a preliminary work entitled *Sri Lanka and the Silk Road of the Sea* containing articles from thirty contributors, some of whom also presented a paper at the seminar. 1990. 291 pp. ISBN 955-9043-01-1. (Requests should be addressed to the National Commission for UNESCO, Ministry of Education and Cultural Affairs, Isurupaya, 3rd Floor, Battaramulla, Sri Lanka.)

"India and the Roman World between the First and Fourth Centuries A.D.," and "India's Cultural Relationship with East and Southeast Asia during the 4th to the 13th Century A.D.," Madras, (India), 20-21 December 1990.*

"Malaysian Maritime Traditions," Malacca, Malaysia, 4 January 1991.*

"Harbour Cities along the Silk Roads," Surabaya, Indonesia, 10-12 January 1991.*

"Ancient Trades and Cultural Contacts in Southeast Asia," Bangkok, 21-22 January 1991. Proceedings published by the Office of the National Culture Commission, Ratchadaphisek Road, Huay Khwang, Bangkok 10320. 1996. ISBN 974-8065-80-4.

"Effects and Influence of the Maritime Route on Brunei Cultures," Brunei, 29 January 1991.*

"Manila as an Entrepot in the Trans-Pacific Commerce," Manila, 5-6 Feburary 1991.*

"Guangzhou and the Maritime Silk Roads," Gangzhou, (Canton), China, 10 February 1991. On the occasion of the seminar, the texts (Chinese) and some abstracts (English) of the papers were produced in a preliminary form under the above title by Guangdong Science and Technology Press, Guangzhou, 1991. 200 pp.

"China and the Maritime Silk Route (Zhong guo vu Hai shang sizhou zhi lu)," Quanzhou, China, 17-20 February 1991. The papers presented at this seminar make up two volumes under the above title, published by Fujian People's Publishing House, Fuzhou, People's Republic of China. Vol. 1, 496 pp., ISBN 7-211-01586-1, was published in 1990 as a preliminary work on the occasion of the seminar, and vol. 2, 168 pp., ISBN 7-211-02315-5, followed in 1994. The texts are in Chinese and English, with abstracts in English or Chinese as appropriate. (On sale at Fujian People's Publishing House.)

"Korean Culture and the Silk Roads," Kyongju (Republic of Korea), 23-24 February 1991. The papers presented at this seminar have been produced in the original language (Korean or English) by the Korean National Commission for UNESCO, Seoul, 1991. (Requests should be addressed to the KNC, UNESCO House, C.P.O. Box 64, Seoul, Republic of Korea.)

"Hakata, Crossroads of the Silk Road, Ocean Routes and Continental Interchange," Hakata (Japan), 28 February 1991.*

"The Silk Roads and Japan. Part A: The Silk Roads and Shosoin; Part B: Ceramics Carried Along the Maritime Silk Roads," Nara (Japan), 6-8 March 1991.*

Steppe Route Expedition in Central Asia (19 April -17 June 1991)

"Importance of Caravanserais and Cities along the Northern Silk Route," Khiva, 2-3 May 1991.*

"Interaction between Nomadic and Sedentary Cultures on the Silk Road," Alma Ata, Kazakhstan, 15-16 June 1991. *

Nomads Route Expedition in Mongolia (10 July-5 August 1992)

"Nomads of Central Asia and the Silk Roads," Ulan Bator, 3-5 August 1992.*

Buddhist Route Expedition, Part I: Nepal (21-30 September 1995)

"Lumbini: Birth-Place of Lord Buddha," Lumbini (Nepal), 25 September 1995.*

"Buddhism in the Himalayas: Its Expansion and Present-Day Aspects," Kathmandu, 29 September 1995.*

* To our knowledge the papers from this seminar have not been published.

[1] A number of seminars organized as part of the Silk Roads Project, such as those relating to the International Research Programmes, are not included in this list.